A TIME TO SPEAK

BY THE SAME AUTHOR
Eight Hours from England
On Such a Night

ANTHONY QUAYLE

A TIME TO SPEAK

Preface by
DAME PEGGY ASHCROFT

BARRIE & JENKINS
LONDON

'Ithaka' from *Collected Poems* by C.P. Cavafy, translated by Edmund Keeley and Philip Sherrard, and edited by George Savidis, is printed by permission of the Estate of C.P. Cavafy.

First published in Great Britain in 1990 by Barrie & Jenkins Ltd
20 Vauxhall Bridge Road, London SW1V 2SA

British Library Cataloguing in Publication Data
Quayle, Anthony
A time to speak.
1. Acting. Biographies
I. Title
792.028092

ISBN 0–7126–3924–1

Typeset by Selectmove Ltd
Printed in Great Britain by
Clays, Bungay

FOR DOT
AND THE FAMILY

'Then said he, "I am going to my Father's and though with great difficulty I am got hither, yet now I do not repent me of all the trouble I have been at to arrive where I am."'

John Bunyan, *Pilgrim's Progress*

CONTENTS

Illustrations between pp. 118–119 and pp. 246–247
Map of Albania, drawn by Christopher Quayle, p. 266

PREFACE

'I f it be true that good wine needs no bush, 'tis true that a good play needs no epilogue'. Rosalind's argument could be extended, perhaps, to saying that a good book needs no preface.

Apart from wishing to pay tribute to an old friend, I am attempting to write one for a very specific reason: to prepare the reader for a shock which comes at the end of Chapter 20: only two chapters before the end of the book, but with forty years of Tony Quayle's life still to be covered. Having completed the twenty chapters and produced a wonderfully lucid portrait of his childhood, youth and apprentice years in the theatre, followed by a remarkable account of his war years, Tony was about to start on his post-war history. But, in August 1989, he was told he had between two to six months to live. With characteristic courage, resilience and tenacity, which were so much part of his nature, he took up the challenge, completing his account of his years as Director at the Stratford Memorial Theatre, 1948–56, which were to have such far-reaching results, his resignation after seven years 'hard', and his re-entry into his other vocation: that of actor rather than director.

He had little time to cover all his subsequent activities, but he manages to distil his beliefs and philosophy in his final chapters. It was his clear-sightedness, vision, and natural leadership that brought such success to his Stratford adventure. Besides his task of over-all directorship, he was also a member of the Company and was therefore in constant touch with his fellow actors. His enthusiasm and ebullience were infectious.

I have many special recollections of Tony's finest performances: his magnificent Henry VIII in Guthrie's production, Falstaff in *Henry IV*, and Aaron in Peter Brook's *Titus Andronicus* which towers above them all. He writes, 'it was the last play I ever acted at Stratford'. May I gently correct him? In 1977 we played together for the Royal Shakespeare Company at the Aldwych, in Arbuzov's *Old World*, which was dismissed by the critics but loved by our audiences. As Rodion Nikolayevich he was perfection and I have never enjoyed a happier partnership. Our last performance of it was actually at Stratford.

After Stratford, most memorable to me was his appearance in O'Neill's *Long Day's Journey into Night*. He and Gwen Ffrangcon-Davies were matchless, and I have never wanted to see the play again. Another lasting memory is his television performance in Don Taylor's *Testament of John*, with Jane Lapotaire and Rosalie Crutchley.

It was typical of him that he changed course once more and reverted to being creator, director, and sometimes actor, in his Compass Theatre Company, an idealistic venture, touring the provinces – great and small towns – initiating new audiences as well as young actors. And how right its title, 'Compass'. He was a man whose sense of proportion, of right and wrong, of the desirable as well as the attainable, was constant, and his complete lack of egotism was astonishing. He certainly steered his life with a good compass to guide him. He was a happy man, and those who were lucky enough to know him, knew that it was the life-long devotion between him and Dot that made him so. He enriched us all – and our theatre, which he never ceased to serve.

PEGGY ASHCROFT

PART 1

A Time
to be Born

CHAPTER 1

EVER SINCE I BECAME old enough to have a passport of my own, instead of travelling on my mother's like a kangaroo in its pouch, I have taken pleasure in completing Landing Cards. When I was young they gave me a sense of identity, a feeling of 'Look out. This is me. Here I come.' I am no longer so naive, but I still enjoy filling in the little white cards. As the plane begins its descent to New York, Cairo, Bombay, or God knows where, and the air hostess dredges up a last smile for her torpid charges, I meekly obey the instructions and press hard with my ballpoint. But, 'Oh, my masters,' I think to myself. 'Oh, my masters of Customs and Immigration, if you only knew the turbulence, the complexities that lie behind these bald statements of place and parentage, you would be astonished.'

Quayle is a Manx name. To my regret I have never lived in the Isle of Man, and all I know of my forefathers is that they were farmers, fishermen, harness-makers. I am not even sure exactly where they lived. Cholera decimated the island in the middle of the nineteenth century, tearing mortal gaps in the parish records as well as in the parishioners themselves. All the world knows that a Quayle has recently become Vice President of the United States, but before that historic event we Quayles had little claim to fame, or even notoriety, beyond a distant connection with Fletcher Christian of the *Bounty*. Did a Quayle seek the North-West Passage? Die fighting at Edgehill? Compose a string quartet? Not that I am aware: though uncommon, the name is relatively undistinguished. I am grateful for that: I have been free to follow my own course without incurring the disapproval of some illustrious ancestor.

3

The Isle of Man was for centuries a Viking stronghold, and those wild rovers left behind them something more basic than a few unusual names: they left their blood. Not that there was much of the Viking in either of my Quayle grandparents; those marauding genes had given them both a miss. They lived at 7 Scarisbrick New Road, Southport – a small red-brick box of primness and prudery on which the sun never seemed to shine. When I was little, I was thrown into a panic every time I had to step inside the house; it was joyless, sequestered, with an odour like that of an unventilated church – sanctity, tinged with stale biscuits. Every room was a declaration of hostility: the hard, anti-macassared chairs defied you to sit on them; the row of bobbles hanging from the funereal curtains were like a fringe of dead mice suspended by their tails. From the top of the narrow stairs, a stained-glass window, permanently closed, shed a lurid, semireligious light on the upper landing; this comprised two desolate bedrooms, an unwelcoming lavatory, and a bathroom reeking of gas and carbolic soap. It was a house of the dead.

My Grandfather Quayle – I called him 'Grandad' – was a neat, medium-sized man with a trim white beard. He had a collection of microscopes and was much given to the wearing of velvet smoking caps. Being a nonsmoker, these tassled articles of headgear had nothing to do with the enjoyment of tobacco; they were purely to keep his head warm. He was called Alfred; but if he had been baptized after the great warrior king, it was a sad misnomer. He could, when roused, as he sometimes was after a strong cup of afternoon tea, display a quaint, etymological humour; but never, in any imaginable circumstances, could he have been a scourge of the Danes.

His wife's name was Fanny. I called her 'Gran-Gran' and viewed her with deep misgiving. She wore long, stiff dresses of some unyielding material; her neck was fenced about with a lace choker, stiffened by whalebone; her hair, worn unfashionably short, was a cluster of fine white curls. These externals did not frighten me nearly so much as the smile she assumed when she saw me on her doorstep; this was enough to make me lose all self-control. It was a smile that did not light her eyes. It held no merriment; it was a grimace to cover her distaste for all kinds of crudeness – especially for the crudeness of little boys who have that moment, in fear and hostility, wet their pants.

But there they were: Dad's mother and father. From time to time I had to go and visit them. And I was expected to give them both a kiss.

The old Quayles were health faddists, and they brought up their son with a protectiveness that would have unmanned Leif Eriksson himself. Whatever audacity little Arthur might have inherited from his Viking

4

ancestors, his parents sucked out of him as neatly as a weasel sucks a pheasant's egg. On cold days he was not allowed to leave the house without a black pad – a 'comforter' – strapped over his mouth to protect him from germs and microbes; thus attired he would venture out into the choking respectability of Scarisbrick New Road. Past his small, muffled figure the ravening trams would clang their way till, on the outskirts of Southport, they ran out of tramlines and came to a halt amid flat potato fields. The driver would fish a cigarette stub from his pocket and have a quick drag before changing ends; the conductor would swing round the overhead arm to an accompaniment of sputtering blue sparks; then the tram would head back again to town.

And while their little Arthur braved the elements, Gran-Gran rustled about her household chores, and Grandad donned his smoking cap (for he too took sensible precautions to avoid a cold in the head) and withdrew to his study, surrounded by the microscopes through which he seldom peered but which fortified him in his opinion of himself as an amateur of science. And, just as a plant can sometimes manage to survive though almost deprived of sun and air, so my father grew to be a man – rather a sturdy man; and a lawyer – rather a skilful lawyer; and an alcoholic. Somehow he met my mother; somehow he proposed to her; and somehow he was accepted.

Behind that 'somehow' lies much sadness.

My other grandfather – John Overton, my mother's father – was a man of a different stamp. He was the son of an English doctor and a Miss Davies, whose family were hill farmers in South Wales. The old man spoke of his mother with great love, but he told me nothing of his father except that he drank and had abandoned his young family. Of the Davies's too I know little; they must have been reasonably prosperous because the day came when I inherited four silver forks and spoons from them. They were of a simple, lovely design, worn thin with use and engraved with a simple 'D'. They were stolen a few years ago by a thief in London – may a Welsh curse gripe him. Young John Overton was brought up on the Davies' farm, and one of his earliest recollections, he once told me, was of being frightened by *his* grandfather, an enormous man wearing a coat with many capes, who shouted at the farm children and cracked his long whip with such a noise that they ran squealing from him in fearful joy. This shouter, this whip-cracker, my grandfather's grandfather, was the coachman on the Cardiff Mail. I like to picture that scene: the big man, mud-spattered, wind-battered, laughing in the middle of the steaming yard, the whistle and crack of his whip, and the covey of children scattering and yelping with pretend fear.

Being the son of a doctor (albeit a drunken one) John Overton grew up with a bent for medicine and chemistry. In time, and with the help of his mother's savings which she bravely entrusted to him, he bought himself a junior partnership in the firm of R. Sumner and Company, a wholesale manufacturing druggist with premises at 40 Hanover Street, Liverpool. But old Sumner was a crook; he absconded to South America, taking all my grandfather's money, and was never heard of again. So young John Overton set to work to make something of the ruined business. He paid back all the money he had borrowed from his mother, and he prospered, making his pills and medicines down among the warehouses and cobbled streets of Liverpool. In due course he fell in love with, and married – in spite of violent opposition from her parents – the beautiful daughter of a certain Doctor Solomon, a Polish Jew who had come to England and set up in practice in Manchester. Of this love match there were born three children of which my mother, Esther, was the second. And she, as the fairy books say, 'was the apple of her father's eye'.

Better for her if she had not been; she might have had a happier life. Or again she might not: perhaps she might only have met a different set of misfortunes. Fruitless to speculate on what might have happened: hard enough to understand what did happen. For she went and married – of all unsuitable, illogical, downright impossible choices – my father.

My mother was born in 1885, a period when parental authority was all-powerful. Provincial, middle-class girls simply did not go off and get jobs as they do now. Women had no rights; they could not vote in parliamentary elections till 1918 and even then they had to be 'Married women, women householders, or women university graduates of thirty and over.' They could do nothing but live at home till they were married. If they did not get married, they just went on living at home – on and on – caring for their parents and declining into spinsterhood. Few had the courage or the money to break the pattern, go to university, get a job, lead an independent life. They were virtually bound in slavery – a comfortable sort of slavery, but one from which there was no escape. Esther, my mother, was sent to a 'Finishing School' in Switzerland where she learnt to ride a horse, speak French, cook well and sew beautifully. Since there were scant opportunities in Southport for the riding of horses or the speaking of French, those accomplishments were soon forgotten; but with her cooking and her needlework she helped to run the house – and she waited for a husband to come along.

What befell was told to me by mother, bit by bit, over several years. It is the story of my own genesis. If any movement in the dance had been different, then I would have been different: I would not have existed in my present form at all.

One day there arrived in Southport a handsome young man, a stranger from abroad; he was staying with friends over Christmas. The two fell in love. He proposed, and was accepted by my mother. But no less crucial was his acceptance by her father. The interview, she told me, was formal.

'May I ask, sir,' – my grandfather always addressed strangers as 'sir' – 'what is your trade or profession?'

'I am in banking,' the young man replied. And he named a famous Merchant Banker.

'Good. And your income?'

This too was satisfactory.

'I understand you are on leave?'

'That is so, sir.'

'And where do you intend to settle? Not too far from Southport, I trust.'

The moment of truth had arrived.

'I shall not be settling in England for several years, I'm afraid. I must return to my post in China. Peking, to be exact.'

My mother told me the gist of what was said, not the actual words; but it was easy enough to reconstruct the conversation. I knew the violence of Grandpa's rages, how red he went in the face, how blue his eyes could blaze.

'Did I hear you aright, sir? Did you say *China?*'

'But only for a few more years. And my prospects, as you see, are excellent.'

'Damn your prospects! Do you think you can take my girl off to live among a lot of heathen?'

'With respect, Mr Overton, the Buddhist religion — '

'And on the other side of the world?'

'Believe me, sir, with the new Trans-Siberian Railway, China is not that far off.'

'Too damn far for me. I might never see my girl again. No, sir. Out of the question.'

The young fellow begged my mother to run away with him, but she would not; she shrank from the hideous breach with her father that would follow an elopement. Sorrowfully the young man took himself back to China, and my mother, her eyes red with weeping, stayed behind in Southport.

But life at home was becoming intolerable for a young woman whose spirit matched her coppery-red hair. Mother and daughter could not rub along; the house was too small to hold two mistresses. Yet there was no escape except through a marriage of which her father would approve – and clearly he would approve of no one who planned to carry her off further than the next street.

'What happened then, Mum?'

'Then?' She gave a short laugh, full of regret and self-mockery. 'Oh – Arthur was what happened then. He lived in Southport. He seemed to be the solution.'

What she had just said and the tone in which she had said it were beyond my comprehension. 'Do you mean to say that you weren't in love with him?'

'Good God, no!'

'Then how could you bring yourself to marry him?'

She shook her head sadly. 'He was gentle. I knew he would be kind to me. I was absurdly innocent – almost as innocent as you are now. And no one told me he was drinking.'

'Drinking!'

'I found that out on our honeymoon. Honeymoon!' Again she laughed – not bitterly, but with an amused resignation.

Theirs could never have been a successful marriage; the very disparity of their natures forbade it. In whatever quality Arthur was weak, Esther was strong; where he was negative, she was positive; where he was ineffectual, she was assertive. Without intending him harm, indeed doing everything she could to support him, she crushed the poor man as comprehensively as a garden roller squashes a worm. They were doomed from the moment the confetti fell on their shoulders: doomed, not to any high drama, but to an empty, sterile life in which she grew increasingly to despise him and he grew utterly to despise himself. And at the root of it all was that generous-hearted but despotic man, John Overton. Did he ever look at his daughter's wasted life and accuse himself of wanton selfishness? I doubt it; he had only behaved in the manner of his time; with King Lear he could claim to have been 'so kind a father'. And yet I wonder: as the years passed he may have felt some qualms of conscience, for his loving generosity to my mother and myself was almost more than natural. But the harm was done: by the time he stepped into the vestry to sign the Marriage Certificate, his daughter's life was already headed for aridity and waste. Vital, impetuous, utterly feminine, she needed a mate of complementary strength and masculinity; such a man she would have loved and respected. Instead she married poor Arthur whom she could neither love nor respect, and who, after begetting me, never – as the saying goes – touched her again. Of course I cannot vouch for this last statement; I am only passing on what my mother told me. But I believe her.

That then was the couple who between them wrought my entry into the world and shaped me the way I am: both of them with virtues, but with their virtues conflicting so disastrously that my father drank himself to death and my mother was driven to seek what solace she could find in me, her only child. Oh, my poor father! I have so often thought of you – with more understanding, I believe, than when I was young. I hope that some of the compassion I now feel for you reaches your gentle, unassertive shade and is of comfort. Every morning you bicycled away to your office, hurrying to cover up the errors of yesterday's befuddlement; at the end of every day you pedalled home to face an evening of humiliation and self-reproach. Oh, my poor mother! Tied to a man for whom you could feel nothing but a sorrowful contempt, yet enduring the marriage for my sake. I can only thank you for all you gave me; thank you above all for the gift of life.

Enough. They are gone now, they and their fellow actors 'melted into air, into thin air'. And I, unconsciously, have been led in a circle to my own beginning, the elusive starting point I did not know where to find. It was in Llandudno! That was the spot chosen by the young couple for their honeymoon; that was where – after long delays caused by my father losing wallet, railway tickets and ready cash – they finally arrived. It was in Llandudno – that pleasant, modest, seaside town – that I was conceived.

Conception is the moment in the lives of every one of us that we hope was attended by rapture and harmony, not only because we wish retrospective joy to our parents, but because we instinctively believe that that moment of creation must have a profound bearing on our own natures, and therefore on the course of our lives. From what I know of the parties concerned, I have but slender confidence that much joy attended my own compounding. I doubt if it was interrupted in quite the same way as Tristram Shandy's, my father being punctilious in the winding-up of clocks and watches if in nothing else; but that it was a close-run, touch-and-go affair I have no doubt. Never mind: begotten I was – I am here to prove it – and, I think, in better shape than might have been expected from so fallible an occasion.

CHAPTER 2

M Y PARENTS HAD BOUGHT a bungalow on a new housing estate at Ainsdale, then a minor halt on the railway line between Southport and Liverpool. There, amid the sand dunes and marram grass of that flat coast, with much pain and difficulty to my mother, I was born on 7 September 1913. I do not know in what conjunction the stars were at my nativity, but I do know that I was born on the same day, even to its being a Sunday, as Queen Elizabeth. It is a tenuous bond with the Great Queen but I have always hoped that she may have inclined her head towards me, however slightly, from her remove of 380 years. It is no small matter to share a birthday with Gloriana.

There was nothing remarkable about my infancy; if there had been, my mother would certainly have told me. She so wanted to believe she had given birth to some sort of prodigy that if she had walked into the nursery and found me like the infant Hercules strangling a pair of serpents, it would have been only what she expected. But there were no such legends of my prowess; my early childhood was perfectly normal and, except for one thing, uneventful. But this one thing was so huge, so far-reaching, that it compensated (over-compensated, you might say) for the placidity of life in Ainsdale. Quite simply, the world blew up.

On 28 June 1914, when I was still less than a year old, a Serbian nationalist shot the Archduke Ferdinand of Austria in Sarajevo. He shot the Duchess too, but she, poor lady, is usually left out of the story. The European nations, like gamblers in a Western saloon, slammed down their cards, tipped over the table and reached for their guns. On 4 August while Britons downed their breakfasts and my father caught the train to Southport, the first shots were fired across the Belgian frontier. At

10

midnight Britain declared war on Germany, and the First World War was under way. By the time it came to an end four years later, the best blood of Europe had soaked away into the mud. The fanatic who fired those first pistolshots was more destructive than he probably intended: he killed not only the Archduke and his lady but 10,000,000 other men besides; and he split open the very foundations of Europe.

The murders in Sarajevo, however, did at least point up the prescience of old Bismarck who had once remarked, 'The next war will start with some damn fool thing in the Balkans.'

1915, which saw the collapse of the Russian armies under German attack, and the launch of the murderous Dardanelles campaign, found me crawling happily round on the carpet, playing with the clackety handles of the chest of drawers. I remember lying in my perambulator, breathing in the odd smell peculiar to all prams, smiling back at the mother who smiled down at me. Snug, cossetted and only two years old, I knew nothing of Neuve Chapelle, Loos or 2nd Ypres. Chlorine gas asphyxiated no one in Ainsdale, Lancs. For the Quayle family, 1915 marked their removal from the bungalow at Ainsdale to a small, pebble-dashed house at 5 York Road, Birkdale, the more fashionable end of Southport – or so it considered itself. My father had just been appointed Clerk to the Southport Magistrates, and found it inconvenient to live so far from the courts. The new job carried not only a slight financial improvement but also exemption from the Armed Forces. This must have come as a great relief to my father, for he was anything but a warlike man. If the Armed Forces had known the recruit they were being spared, it would doubtless have come as a relief to them too.

Now, instead of gulping his breakfast and running to catch the seven-forty from Ainsdale, my father could rise half an hour later, eat an unhurried meal, then don his bicycle clips and pedal off to work. Not that civilian life was without its hazards. Through the last years of the war, and long after, he carried a deep, livid scar that bisected his right eyebrow. Strangers would ask sympathetically how it had happened. Was it a war wound? Or was it a duelling scar, received at some German university? Heidelberg, perhaps? My father always disclaimed so romantic but unpatriotic an education, and would quickly change the subject.

In fact he had incurred the wound one night, bicycling home from an evening of quiet conviviality at the Rotary Club. He had been pedalling down a straight road when, suddenly and unaccountably, he had been pitched straight over the handlebars. Lying dazed in the road, he could not make out what had happened, or why his bike appeared still to be standing upright. Appeared? No, it was! Slowly, as his brain cleared and the blood dripped down his face, the cause of the accident became apparent: in a moment of aberration he had steered both wheels into a tramline. It was that inert but dangerous weapon, a tramline, that had brought him down and inflicted on him a gash requiring a dozen stitches.

The war to me meant soldiers – soldiers all the time and everywhere, with their khaki uniforms and their lumpy kitbags. In the streets there were soldiers; at home there were soldiers – uncles, friends, men on leave. They would play with me, show me where to place my toy artillery, how to build the parapet of a trench with my toy sandbags. After a few nights they would go away, back to France, or Mesopotamia, or wherever it was they had come from, and I would not see them again.

Then there were soldiers who were not in khaki, but who wore bright red ties and bright blue uniforms – very scratchy they were, too, when they brushed against your face. These were soldiers who had been wounded. My mother went to see them in hospital, and she took me with her. Some of them moved about on crutches; some were pushed in wheelchairs; some had bandages round their heads and sat quite still; some of them had lost an arm, or a leg; one man had been so badly blown up that he had no arms or legs at all. I could not think how he managed, but he was always cheerful. He laughed a lot.

Once I saw a great number of soldiers – a very great number – and they came right past our gate. I had just said, 'Hallo!' to the lamplighter; he came down our road each night, wheeling his bike and carrying a long pole with a flame that flickered at the end of it. He would push the pole up inside the street lamp and *plop*! the gas would come on, spreading a soft, yellowish pool of light. I used to run to the garden gate and stick my nose over it when I saw him coming. All I ever said to him was, 'Hallo!' and all he ever said to me was, 'Hallo, young man.' But it was a contact, a kind of conversation; I felt he was a friend.

One evening he had just gone on his way and I was still at the garden gate when I heard a drum beating in the distance: a single drum. *Tap – tap* – tappity – tappity – *tap*. It was coming nearer. Now I could hear the sound of men marching. Louder and louder, till the whole street began to shake under the tramping feet. Someone in the house opposite pulled the curtains back, and faces were pressed against the window. Then the soldiers started to come past, four abreast, line after line after line of them, so many that I thought there could not be any more. Yet still they came. I stood fascinated, in awe, peeking over the gate. Each man in all those ranks was different, yet they were all together, all steady, all keeping time to the solitary drum. They did not wave to me; they did not call out; they did not even turn their heads. It was as though they had made up their minds to something, and were going where they had a mind to go. I stood at the gate till they were all gone and I could no longer hear the tread of feet and the *tap-tap-tap* of the drum. Then I went back indoors, strangely disturbed.

The war meant other things besides soldiers; it meant songs – poignant, desperate songs. No radio then, no television, but the songs were in the air; they were hummed, they were whistled by errand boys on their bikes. Sometimes my mother would play the piano and sing them for me. Her favourite was 'There's a Long, Long Trail A-Winding', but she never got to the end of it. She would stop, draw in her breath, and say, 'No, I can't.' She was probably thinking of her younger brother, Reg, gassed at Ypres and now back at the Front. She adored Reg. Then she would cheer up and sing 'If You Were The Only Girl In The World', which I did not like at all. The one that made me cry was 'Keep The Home Fires Burning', though I did not understand the words or the pain that lay behind them. I understand now; and to this day, if I hear the song, I am overcome by a despairing sense of loss.

Death came and poked his nose into our house; not far – only the tip of his snout – but far enough for me to learn the smell of him and know his name.

I had a nanny: very young, very strict, and the first grown-up I ever saw cry. Nanny had a photo on her dressing table of someone who looked like a boy in uniform. I asked her once or twice who he was, but she never gave me a proper answer. So one day I asked my mother.

'Mummy. That photo on Nanny's dressing table. Is that her young man?'

'No, darling. It's her brother. But don't ask her about him.'

'Why not?'

She hesitated. 'Because he's dead.'

'Dead? What's that?'

'He was killed. In the war. He's gone away.'

'But he'll come back, won't he?'

'No, he won't come back. And it makes Nanny sad. So be a good boy and don't ask her about him.'

Dead? Killed? They were funny words. The grown-ups often used them. They had some odd meaning, and Mum had not explained it at all. Whatever could be stopping Nanny's brother from coming back? I had to find out. So one day, standing beside her while she brushed her hair, I picked up the photo and asked, in my most innocent voice, 'Is this your brother, Nanny?'

'Yes, darling. Put it down. There's a good boy.'

'Where is he, Nanny?'

There was no answer, so I went on, 'He's dead, isn't he?'

She stopped brushing her hair, and sat silent. At last she said, 'Yes.'

'I know that means he's gone away. But why doesn't he come back? Doesn't he want to?'

She lowered her head in silence; and, amazed, I saw that her eyes were full of tears. I had never seen such a thing, but I knew I was in the presence of something very powerful: like magic. I felt I ought not to look at her, yet I could not help staring.

At last, in a choked voice, she said, 'I can't talk about it. Don't ask. There's a good boy.'

So I did not. But I wondered. I wondered greatly.

A day of autumn sunshine came when everyone was laughing and crying at the same time. 'It's the Armistice, darling! The war is over! The Armistice has been signed!'

They all took me in their arms and kissed me, and hugged me, then kissed me all over again. I did not understand why they should be so excited and happy, though I pretended to. We went driving round the town in an open horse cab with our big Union Jack spread out over its folded hood. There were crowds everywhere, all shouting and singing and hugging each other. I tried to feel as excited as they did, and waved my little flag. But the crying and cheering made me tired and confused; all I wanted was to go home and get to bed.

Marshal Foch signed the Armistice in the railway carriage at Compiègne, and Germany's face was rubbed in the dirt. It went unnoticed in the euphoria of peace that the seeds of a second and even more terrible war were being sown: dragon's teeth, that in their season would turn into warplanes, and tanks, and pocket battleships.

In Britain, the first thought in every town and village was to raise a War Memorial. It took a bit of thought and money but, on the whole, the Glorious Dead were soon provided for; the problem of the Glorious Living was harder to solve. Some indeed returned to jobs that had been kept open for them; others were not so lucky. But, though peace took some getting used to, life went on; and I went on too, growing from a child into a boy – easy enough if you have a secure home and a loving mother.

E – it is time I began to call my mother by the initial she was always known by – was an unusual woman. She was not brilliant or beautiful, but she was an original; and, for better or worse, she moulded me into what I am. She was of medium height; her figure could only be called unathletic; her oval face was pleasing, but did not make heads turn in

14

the street. Her eyes could never have been likened to 'the fishpools in Heshbon', but they were observant eyes, full of feeling, quick to be amused. She had good hands too, strong, well-shaped, and at the same time feminine. But all those are externals and I never thought of them. She was simply my mother: a supporting, surrounding, loving presence – and fun. She had the ability to turn every trivial incident – catching a bus, scrambling an egg – into an adventure, a celebration of life. She was badly read and did little to remedy it, but she had a strong current of electricity flowing through her; this earth supply of energy was the source of her confidence, and she did her utmost to pass it on to me. It was not arrogance: she detested arrogance. What she tried to give me was a belief, not exactly in myself, but in my own buoyancy: a fundamental confidence that no matter what hit me I would not capsize; I would not sink.

When she found me out in some fault she never gave me a simple scolding. She would sit me down and make me listen to the reason for her rubuke. My crimes were varied, but they all evoked the same theme from her: the kind of man she wanted me to be.

One day we were out together in the back garden. I was on my way to the henhouse, holding a worm on my toy spade.

'What's that you've got, Bunt?' she called out. 'Bunt' was her name for me, an abbreviation of 'Bunting' – that coddled child of nursery rhyme whose father went a-hunting.

'It's a worm. I dug it up.' I held the horrible thing as far away from me as I could.

'Take it in your hand, then. It won't bite you. You look silly holding it on your spade.'

She knelt down beside me in the patch of kitchen garden. 'Don't tell me you're afraid of a worm.'

Indeed I was. The worm was huge, and acrobatic. 'I don't like it,' I said.

'Why not?'

'It's all wet and nasty.'

'Bunt, I do believe you're frightened of it.'

'No, I'm not.'

'Yes, you are. And you mustn't be frightened of anything. Not *anything*. What sort of man will you grow into if you're afraid of a worm?'

I steeled my mind to touch the creature, but it was no good; it revolted me.

Mum said, 'Bunt, the worst thing on earth to be is a coward. I don't like worms either. But look. I'm going to pick it up. And if I can make myself touch it, so can you.'

The worm writhed and tied itself in knots on the palm of her hand, but she made herself hold it for a long minute; then she put it down on the ground. 'Now, you,' she said.

There was no way out; I was shamed into picking up the horrid, pink creature. To my surprise it was not horrid at all: just a helpless, squirming piece of life. I felt quite sorry for it when I threw it into the hen run and the fowls ran clucking to tear it apart.

I must have been about six when I became enthralled by a tape measure. It was no ordinary measure, not one of those tangled objects that have to be fished out from the recesses of a work basket. I noticed the round, leather case in the window of our local ironmonger, and I gazed at it fascinated. What could it be? With an effort of courage I walked into the shop and asked.

'In the window, son? Where? Oh, you mean the tape measure? Here you are.' The shopkeeper put it casually on the counter, and turned away to serve a customer.

So that was what it was! – a tape measure! I could see now that the case was not made of real leather – but it was something very like it. And there was a brass handle, with a hinge so that it folded back on itself. It was a deeply satisfying, altogether manly piece of equipment.

The shopkeeper came back. 'Four and six,' he said. 'Not cheap – but it's a good article. The tape can't stretch – see? It's got wires running through it.'

I thanked him, and walked home in a state of exaltation. For the first time in my life I was in love. But what was I to do? I had only a shilling in my money box.

For the rest of that day, and to anyone who would listen, I talked of nothing but the tape measure. Next morning I dragged E to the ironmonger's. Perhaps, if I was extra good, she might buy it for me? Why not? I had seen her spend that much when she went to the fishmonger's, or the butcher's.

'There! There it is!' I cried. 'Look, Mum. D'you see what I mean?'

An outbreak of measles all over my face could not have been more evident than my lovesickness, but my mother did nothing either to encourage or to abate the fever.

'A tape measure,' she said. 'Yes, I do see. It's a very nice tape measure. What d'you want it for?'

Who at six can explain why he is in love? Who can explain it at any age? 'To measure things with,' was the best I could manage.

'Things? What things?'

'Just – things.'

She looked at me steadily. No smile at all. Neither for nor against. 'Yes,' she said, 'I do see it would come in very handy for measuring things. And it is extremely handsome. How much have you got in your money box?' I told her. 'Well then, you've got almost a quarter of the price. If you want it so badly, you should save up and buy it.'

That was that. I could never wheedle my way round her when she spoke in that tone.

I saved and saved; and every night I tipped my money out on the bed and counted it; and every day I walked past the shop to make sure my precious tape measure had not been sold. And then, just as I reached my target, just when I had accumulated the extra three shillings and sixpence, E was suddenly rushed to hospital for an operation.

What was I to do? I wanted to buy her some flowers, to help her get well and show how much I loved her. But if I bought only the smallest bunch of violets, even if they cost no more than sixpence, I would not have enough for the tape measure.

Inspiration came to me. Flowers were a silly idea; they would only die after a few days. No, I would not buy flowers; I would buy her a solid, wonderful present, a present that would last. I would buy her the tape measure! Then after a few days, when she saw how generous I had been, I would coax her into giving it back to me.

The first part of the plan worked well; I could see she was really touched by the gift. 'Oh, Bunt!' She raised herself on the pillows and hugged me. 'How absolutely dear of you! The tape measure you so wanted.'

'I thought it might be useful,' I said.

'Oh, indeed it will. I'll be able to measure all kinds of things with it. And I'll keep it always and always.'

I was happy to have pleased her, but I did not much like the sound of 'always and always'. Perhaps I had better make things clear at once.

'I'm glad you like it,' I said. 'I like it too.'

'I know you do, Bunt. That's what make it so special.'

'Yes, but – well, I do like it very much. And I was wondering – '

'What, darling?'

'I was wondering – of course only when you're better and don't really need it any more – if I could have it back again?'

She gave me a long, scrutinizing look, as though it were me she was dividing into feet and inches. 'No, Bunt,' she said. 'I'm not going to give it back.'

Total loss stared me in the face. 'Why not?'

'Because you have to learn that once you've given a present, you can't take it back. You just can't.'

I was in despair. 'But I want it very much.'

'I know you do. And because you want it so much I shall treasure it. You see, it's easy to give something you don't care about. What's hard is to give something you terribly want yourself. That's a gift that means a lot. So don't ask for it back. I shan't give it you.'

Then, seeing I was still disconsolate, she put an arm round me and drew me to her. 'Grow up, old Bunt. You've got to grow up into a man – a real man. You've got to. For my sake. Because – no, you won't understand this, but never mind – you are what my life is all about.'

She was right; I did not understand. Life was not *about* anything. It just *was*. We all just *were* – she, and Dad, and Kim the cocker spaniel. That is how it was and how it would go on being. What I did understand, and very clearly, was that my tape measure, my loved and longed-for tape measure, was lying on the coverlet of her bed and that she was not going to give it to me.

E steered her life by an emotional compass, not a rational one; but considering what a mixture of passionate blood ran in her veins her course was surprisingly steady. To me she gave endless support, but she was also quite capable of cutting me down to size. There was a day when I obstinately refused to follow her into some cafe in town; it was because of a new jacket I had been made to wear. In a frenzy of stubbornness I wedged myself in the doorway and refused to budge. My mother would have been justified in walking away and leaving me to yell my head off. But she did not; she was very calm, very reasonable. She said, 'Bunt, do stop making that horrible noise. Just tell me what's the matter.'

'I look silly. Everyone in there will laugh at me.'

'You really think so?'

'Yes, I do.'

'Very well. Answer me this.' She brought her face level with mine, and spaced her words out with deliberation. 'Who do you think is going to pay the smallest attention to you? Who will so much as look at such a very ordinary little boy?'

They were not the words of Pitt the Elder to his promising young son, but they were salutary: never forgotten.

CHAPTER 3

There was a young man who said 'Damn!'
I clearly perceive that I am
A creature that moves
In predestinate grooves —
Not a car, not a bus, but a tram.

I DO NOT KNOW WHICH disillusioned poet wrote those lines, but spiritually he was a true son of Southport: a *tram passant* should have been smack in the centre of the Municipal Coat of Arms. The men who lived in those well-built houses, all with sound guttering and privet hedges, earned their living for the most part in 'cotton' or the heavy engineering works of Manchester, Burnley and Wigan. The electric trains took them away on time in the morning and brought them home punctually in the evening. Every weekend they played golf. Their wives played golf too, unless it was raining too hard; then they played bridge. The housewives shopped, the golfers drove off from the first tee, the bridge players made their opening bids, all at predictable times. There was an ordered gentility about the place; even the sea appeared docile and obedient – perhaps because it had receded so far that it was seldom to be seen at all. But when it did come in – and at the top of spring tides it roared in like a conqueror – then Southport sprang its one unforgettable surprise: an event to rank in strangeness and beauty with the *aurora borealis*. When the water sucked at the barnacles and swooshed round the ironwork at the end of the pier; when the hat had been passed round a good many times; then, to the joy and astonishment of all present (myself included) a one-legged man wearing a red-and-white striped bathing costume would ride his bicycle full tilt off the high dive and plunge down sixty feet into the grey-green waters of the North Atlantic. 'Now beat that!' he seemed to cry, as he plummeted down and disappeared with an almighty splash.

We small covey of Quayles followed the pattern of all Southport families: every Sunday we had lunch with 'the old folk' – that is, with Grandpa and Aggie. They were hilarious meals. Grandpa sometimes became speechless with laughter, and Aggie, tears filling her eyes, would call from her end of the table, 'Oh, Jack! Do be careful! Look at him! He's gone red in the face. Esther, don't make your father laugh like that.'

Other parts of the weekly routine were less enjoyable: shopping with my mother was a penance. At intervals all the way down Lord Street were men who had been soldiers; they wore their medals pinned to their grubby raincoats, and they had cardboard placards hung round their necks saying which regiment they had been in, and what rank they had held, and in which battle they had been gassed or wounded. Some, thin-faced and motionless, stood in the trickling gutter selling matches; others had formed themselves into small brass bands, and paraded slowly up and down playing jaunty tunes. My mother would give me money to put in the box that one of them – the worst mutilated – held out and rattled. I did so as quickly as I could and then scuttled away; I was ashamed to meet their eyes.

I spent so many hours in shops that it put me off shopping for the rest of my life. Broadbent's, the drapers and haberdashers in Lord Street, was particularly detestable. It was airless, and full of pudgy female assistants, dressed in black; I felt stifled by them. The only thing to be said for Broadbent's was their communications system. The shop assistant would take the pound note, or whatever, from my mother and stuff it into a metal capsule which she then inserted in a tube. There would be a sucking sound, like a giant chameleon engorging a fly, and the capsule would vanish. Two minutes later there would come a faint whistle, a rush of air, and *fffflupp*! out would shoot the capsule, change exact and bill receipted. To see that happen was a wonder – almost worth being suffocated by femininity.

It is a strange journey to reach back seventy years into your memory: like going down into the Kingdom of Persephone and encountering the dead. I find myself standing on one bank of the dark river, while on the other is clustered a swarm of ghosts all waving and shouting to me; some I have cared for greatly; others I have hardly known at all. Their voices reach me across the black water like the insistent clamour of *paparazzi*, vying for my attention.

'Tony! Tony! Look this way, Tony! . . . Over here, Tony! Look over here! Remember me? Say something about me. Don't let me be forgotten. I was alive once, too. Call out my name up there in the sunlight. Say something about me . . . and me . . . and me . . .'

I hear their voices, but I have not the heart to tell them that there is no time to write about them all, and that no one would be interested if I did. They live for this moment in my memory, but soon they will be quite forgotten: just as I shall be forgotten when I join them on the far bank. I cannot tell them that; I can only hold out my hands in mute apology.

They seem to understand, for silently, sadly, they shuffle away.

One remains: an old woman with a worn face, rough hands and a weather-beaten hat from which escape a few straggles of grey hair. A light snowfall of chicken feathers clings to her sagging, brown jersey. She stands alone on the far bank, her head shaking slightly with the palsy of old age. I know her, yet I cannot place her. And she, seeing my doubt, looks at me with a wry, uncertain smile.

'You don't remember me? . . . All right, luv. Never mind.'

Suddenly, as in a dream, we are not separated by the river; she is standing right in front of me, her eyes blue-grey and sad as a gorilla's, lower jaw mumbling at her tongue. She reaches down into the pocket of her apron and pulls out a russet-brown apple. 'Here y'are, luv,' she whispers, her speech as honest as a lump of Lancashire cheese. Again she gives me that creased and crooked smile; then she turns and walks away.

And now, just as she is swallowed up by the river mist, just when it is too late to call out, I recognize her – the stooped back and the random feathers that fall gently from her arms. It is Mrs Flint, from the market; Mrs Flint, who had the vegetable and poultry stall; Mrs Flint, whose eyes would look so keenly into mine as if searching for the answer to some question.

Dear Mrs Flint, when I was seven you must have been seventy-seven. How can I repay you for your apple-kindness? What answer can I give to that odd, appraising look? I cannot restore you to your strong sons who flung about so lightly the big baskets of swedes, and turnips, and potatoes; I cannot bring you back to the flecked sunlight of the marketplace, the jingling cash register, the naked birds hanging in their long, plucked lines of death. I can only bear witness to your hard-fought passage through life; I can only testify that in my memory and esteem you stand beside any Captain or King that I have known.

Through those quiet years of growth my father was a gentle, amiable presence, little more. He would enjoy his breakfast, (sausages, well-daubed with mustard was his favourite dish), then – trouser-clipped and bowler-hatted – he would mount his three-speed bicycle and pedal off to the offices of Brown, Turner, Quayle, and Compton-Carr. I would not see him again till the evening unless my mother, as she sometimes did, took me to see him in his office. 'Go on,' she would say. 'You go in first. Give Daddy a surprise.'

'Why, look who's here!' he would call out, jovial but ill-at-ease. 'Hallo, old boy!' To my mother he would give a quick half smile and 'Hallo, E.'

They never called each other anything but their bare initials; and I, in my ignorance, took the restraint of their greeting to be the normal currency between man and wife.

'Hallo, A. I thought you might like to see Tony for a moment.' Then, seeing my father's hunted expression, 'But don't worry. We shan't stay.'

Dad's face, above his wing collar and blue bow tie, did often have an anxious look about it: probably, I thought, because his room was so dark, and he had to breathe in so much dust from all those files and leather-bound books. But his work too seemed to give him a lot of trouble; he was always losing some paper or other and having to send for Mr Briggs, his articled clerk.

'Mr Briggs, whatever can I have done with old Mr Johnson's will? It seems to have disappeared. I've searched everywhere.'

Mr Briggs was tall and cadaverous; he had thick spectacles and a prominent Adam's apple. This protuberance had a convulsive and separate life all of its own; it moved not only up and down, but also in and out. It was spellbinding – and repulsive.

'I'm sure it's quite safe, Mr Quayle. You took it away with you last night. Remember? I think you'll find it in your coat pocket.' Mr Briggs' tone was soothing, confidential.

'No, no. I wouldn't do that, I'm sure.' Dad was going through his pockets, pulling out his cheque book and all sorts of notes and envelopes. 'Good heavens, so I did. Here it is. Well – thank you, Mr Briggs.'

Another time it might be, 'Mr Briggs, have you found any precedent we could use in the Hetherington case? I'm rather concerned about it.'

Then Mr Briggs, all glinting spectacles and pumping Adam's apple, would lean over my father's shoulder and lay before him a sheaf of papers. 'Yes, indeed, Mr Quayle. I've turned up this case. *Musgrove* versus *The Crown 1901*. I think you might find it relevant. Perhaps you'd care to glance through these notes I've made?'

Mr Briggs was very useful to my father. Dad often said how grateful he was to him how he did not know where he would be without Mr Briggs. But children are aesthetic snobs, and Mr Briggs was very unattractive; I did not even like to touch his clammy hand.

I kept pretty busy on the whole; I helped Mum in the kitchen – shelling peas, or stirring things up in a pudding basin; I read books; I went for walks with Kim; I played in the garden – and not always alone. I had a friend, a pretty little girl called Cynthia, with innocent-wicked blue eyes and innocent-wicked blonde hair. Cynthia was rather more than a friend, and also rather less; in fact, considering that we were no more than five years old we had a surprisingly adult relationship. There was an undercurrent of challenge, almost hostility, between us, but there was also a strong sexual attraction; and in our infantile way we both knew it. We had no idea what sex was, or how the parts of the dual puzzle were meant to fit together, but I knew that Cynthia was in no way a boy; she was unmistakably a girl. We shared an intense interest in our mutual differences, and we made our researches with a not altogether childish innocence. We sensed, though we never exchanged a word about it, that these explorations should be a secret between us, not to told to any grown-up. Hand in hand, a diminutive Adam and Eve, we would make our way to the bottom of the garden where we were hidden from view. There was no serpent down there among the cabbages and Brussels sprouts, and we were too young for temptation to lead us into any evil; but the simple mysteries were revealed, appropriately enough, under an apple tree.

When I was six I became a Brownie. That is a bold statement, like claiming to have been a woman pirate or a *vivandière* in the French Foreign Legion, but it is true. A local lady decided to form a mixed pack of Wolf Cubs and Brownies with herself as Brown Owl. At her call a dozen small girls sprang forward but only one fellow – me. So a Brownie I perforce became, and found myself hopping round a canvas toadstool, singing Brownie songs and uttering Brownie cries. At least I came off better than Hercules: I hung on to my manly shirt and shorts; no one was going to get me into a skirt.

My days as a Brownie gave me an insight into female nature, but it was not an experience that I would recommend any boy to follow. My fellow Brownies looked like little girls, and while our fearless Leader was around they behaved like little girls; but the moment Brown Owl left the room, in that instant the Brownie gathering turned into a Saturnalia and those little girls, so sweet, so demure and gentle, were transformed into raging Bacchae. They never had time to tear me limb from limb; in the minute or two available to them they had to be content with pulling my hair but they did that with unimaginable ferocity. There was no way that I, a lone male, could retaliate or defend myself, and instinct warned me that if once I admitted how agonizing the ordeal was they would only pull the harder. So I pretended not to feel it though I often thought my entire scalp was coming off.

'Doesn't *that* hurt?' Diana Clegg would ask, giving my thick mop an extra-savage wrench.

'Not a bit.' There were tears in my eyes but I would pretend to laugh. 'Pull harder. I don't feel it at all.'

'You see?' Diana turned to her Brownie friends who ringed us round. 'I told you. He simply doesn't feel it. Come on, all of you. Pull.' And they pulled. They most certainly pulled.

I did not mind being an only child; it never occurred to me to feel lonely. Even when it rained and I had to stay indoors I was perfectly happy on my own. Books took the place of brothers and sisters. I loved books as greatly as I loathed the construction kits that bright little boys are given in the obvious hope that one day they will turn into bright little engineers. Not me. What was the point of fitting together all those depressing lengths of perforated metal, of fiddling with tiny nuts and bolts that were forever falling on the floor and getting lost, if the end product was nothing but a wobbly crane that could barely pick up an empty matchbox?

A model railway was a bit more fun, but its romance was short and circumscribed. I could make up adventures for it – send it to the North Pole or across the prairies of America – but wherever it went there was always the same delapidated bunch of toys waiting in ambush behind a book or a cushion – a few Red Indians with bent tomahawks, two knights in armour (one mounted, one on foot), some Red Cross nurses left over from the war and, on a ludicrously larger scale, an Arab riding a camel. Any fool could see the train was crossing no prairie; it was simply going round and round; and when Kim sniffed at it the stupid thing fell off its oval track, clockwork wheels spinning. My brain was numbed by these dead, mechanical playthings; somehow they made me feel trapped, defeated.

I never felt trapped or defeated by a teddy bear. Teddy had life; he accepted love, and gave it back again; he could respond; he held out limitless possibilities. And I never felt trapped by a book. Never.

Books had been read to me since I was tiny; they were my greatest joy – Edward Lear in particular. My favourite was 'The Dong with the Luminous Nose'; that shook me to the heart. I knew nothing of sorrow, yet I shared his grief; I knew nothing of loss, yet I knew with dreadful certainty that he would never find his Jumbly girl again – never, never, never, never, never. But more deeply moving than the Dong's sadness, more unbearable than his loneliness, was his crazy, steadfast resolve to seek his lost love for the rest of his life. The Dong could not, would not, see that he was beaten; he refused to admit defeat. And far from ending in misery and gloom the poem lifted itself up into a glory of gentle madness until, with the very last line, it burst out in triumph:

He goes! He goes! The Dong with the luminous nose!

I was too young to form the words properly, and in any case I was sobbing, but when my mother came to the end of the poem I would shout the last line in unison with her:

'A-goes! A-goes! A Dong – a – lumous nose!' Then I would make her read it to me all over again.

There were other books I could soon read for myself: Andrew Lang's *Fairy Stories*; Edmund Dulac's *Arabian Nights* – though I did not feel I had much in common with those turbaned Viziers, and Princess Baldroubadour's tapering fingers and almond eyes were a bit too Eastern for me. *The English Book of Fairy Stories*, with paintings by Arthur Rackham, appealed to me far more.

And there was that great woman Beatrix Potter, every one of whose characters have run, or flown, or hopped, or waddled with me through life. *The Tale of Pigling Bland* was published in the year that I was born, and that may account for the profound affection, the quite especial affinity I feel for him. As the whole world knows, Pigling Bland and his love Pig-wig are being chased by villainous men; their fate if caught is to be fattened and eaten. After desperate adventures, and in the nick of time, they manage to escape. Here are the last lines of the immortal story, redolent of the dales and becks of Cumberland:

They ran, and they ran, and they ran down the hill, and across a short cut on level green turf at the bottom, between pebble beds and rushes.

They came to the river, they came to the bridge – they crossed it hand in hand

Here you turned over the last page, and read,

then over the hills and far away she danced with Pigling Bland!

Over the hills and far away! But where was that? Where could I find those hills? How far was 'far away'? How could I get there? No one, not even my mother, could tell me. But there was such a place; I knew it; and I was going to find it. There had to be a place where two little pigs, one in a coat and waistcoat, the other wearing a blue dress and petticoats, danced and skipped while the sun set in the distance and a family of rabbits gazed in amazement.

If all the psychoanalysts in Europe were to lay themselves end to end, starting in Vienna and finishing in Hampstead, London NW3 (and there are quite enough of them to do so) I doubt if they would get nearer to the heart of me than *Pigling Bland* or 'The Dong with the Luminous Nose'.

25

I was six when I first went to school. Perhaps my mother noticed some unaccountable raw patches on my head after a vigorous Brownie session; perhaps she just thought it was time to push her lamb out into the world; anyway, off I went, satchel on my back. Every morning the undeviating tram carried me to 'Croxton' at the far end of town. Croxton was a Dame School run by two elderly maiden ladies, Miss Gertrude and Miss Leftwich; and for neither of them – simply because they were in the very mould of Gran-Gran – did I have any liking. Both wore their hair drawn up over a pad on the top of their heads; both were encased in whalebone up to their chins. Miss Gertrude's face was long and thin; her resigned expression spoke of spirituality and self-denial. Miss Leftwich's face was round and greasy; it spoke of spinsterhood and a mistaken diet. Miss Gertrude had iron-grey hair, while that of Miss Leftwich was a faded red; a few aberrant hairs, like outriders, sprouted here and there on the moist plain of her face.

I learned nothing at Croxton and it bequeathed me nothing except one friendship that has flowered late in my life and which I treasure. Another inmate of that modest establishment was a small boy called Laurence Evans; his mother and mine were friends, but did not see a great deal of each other since the Evanses had more money than we had, and people in Southport did not stray far outside their financial boundaries. The small Evans and I lost sight of each other after Croxton, but eventually we both found our separate ways into the theatre, I as an actor, he as an administrator. Now, both in our seventies, our paths have converged again and I am blessed in having Laurie as my friend and agent. Kind, humorous, wise, worldly and worldly-wise, he is literally my oldest friend. We seldom have time for more than a phone call, but our meetings, when we do achieve them, have a special piquancy; for however businesslike our discussions I know that we both can see the school cap of Croxton – blue with red blobs – perched on the other's balding crown.

On my first day at Croxton Miss Gertrude sat us down, quelled us into silence with a long stare, and said, 'Boys – I am now going to read to you. Listen carefully. Because when I have finished, you are going to learn this by heart.' She looked round again, daring us to stir or giggle. Then she opened a large book, sank her voice reverently, and intoned, '*In the beginning God created the Heaven and the earth*. That will do for a start. Now, after me, say it all together. *In the beginning* — '

I interrupted, 'Please, what is that book you're reading?'

I was not showing off or trying to be funny; I was truly interested. I could recite 'The Owl and the Pussycat' without a single mistake; I knew how King Arthur had drawn Excalibur from the stone; I could have told the class all about Mowgli and Baloo and Bagheera, but this sounded like no book that I had ever read or that had ever been read to me.

Miss Gertrude gave me a pale, blue glare. 'This, Tony, is the Book of God. This is the Holy Bible.'

I could tell I was being rebuked. But why?

'Oh,' I said. 'I've never heard of that book.'

'Indeed?' Miss Gertrude's voice curdled with genteel horror. 'Indeed?' she repeated, as though coming to a dark and regrettable conclusion. 'Well now, let us see. Are there any other little boys in this class who have never heard of the Holy Bible?'

Not a hand went up. They all sat transfixed, their eyes round as gobstoppers.

'So it seems you are alone. We shall have to put this to rights. Shall we not?'

'Yes, Miss Gertrude,' I said meekly. But inwardly I raged. I had been made to look a fool in front of all the other boys. 'The book of god': that was what Miss Gertrude had called it. An odd sort of title. Was the book *about* 'god' – whoever 'god' might be? Or had someone called 'god' written the book? I was going to get to the bottom of this 'god' business.

It did not take long. God, it appeared, was more like a sort of man than a sort of woman. Next, you must always use a capital letter for Him, even when He was only being a pronoun, because He was absolutely enormously powerful. So you had better be respectful. And at Croxton both Miss Gertrude and Miss Leftwich were very respectful indeed. At morning prayers they asked Him 'of His infinite goodness' to look kindly on us and our labours; then, before our midday meal, He was humbly requested 'of His infinite mercy' to bless the food we were about to eat. The food was not worth eating, let alone blessing; but when the last leathery prune had been stuffed down the last protesting gullet, He was gratefully thanked all over again. I thought all this asking and thanking was a bit over-submissive, but it seemed best to do what everyone else did so I bowed my head and mumbled away with the rest.

Within a week or two I had a pretty clear picture of God. He was very big, with long whiskers, and He was wrapped in a grey woolly dressing gown. He knew everything you did and everything you thought. He was kind and loving but He was also stern and revengeful, which was a bit confusing. But as He was so very far away and quite invisible there was no point in worrying about Him – certainly not for the present. What puzzled me far more than God were some of the words connected with Him – words like *Infinite* and *Eternal*. Those really were difficult.

One evening I was out in the garden with Dad, and he was explaining about the stars and constellations, and which of them was the Plough. I asked, 'What's out there beyond the stars?'

'Nothing.'

'There can't be nothing, Dad. There must be something.'

He shook his head. 'No. Infinity. That's all.'

There was that word again. 'What's Infinity?' I asked.

'Hard to explain, old Bunt. Just space. Space that goes on and on for ever.'

'But there must be *something* at the end of it all?'

'Not as far as we know. Just emptiness. On and on and on. Nothing.'

I looked up at the velvety sky, and all the stars, and the Milky Way, and I tried to think of emptiness going on and on for ever; but I could not imagine it. So I asked another question.

'Dad. Does God live up there?'

'No, Bunt. I don't think so.'

'Are you sure? Not above the sky? That's what it says in a hymn we sing at Croxton.'

This time he was more emphatic. 'No.'

'Then where does God live?'

He thought a bit; then he said, 'Everywhere. And that's as hard to understand as infinity, isn't it? Come on, let's go in. It's cold.'

I did not survive long at Croxton, or perhaps Croxton did not long survive with E. Whichever way it was, I left there and went away to boarding school. I was seven years old.

PART 2

A TIME TO WEEP,
AND A
TIME TO LAUGH . . .

CHAPTER 4

ABBERLEY IS IN THE MIDDLE of Worcestershire, close to the heart of England. There is a local legend that Henry IV pitched his Plantagenet tents on Abberley Hill, while Owen Glendower encamped his Welshmen a mile away on Woodbury, and that between them a ferocious battle was fought. It may well be so: the Welsh border is not far off – only two days' march. Legend, as Schliemann proved in far-off Troy, is often right, and the fields where we shrimps played football may once have soaked up the mingled blood of Welsh and English. What I do know is that to this day there are corners of that countryside so unchanged that they could be the very spot where Sir John Falstaff picked his ragged recruits and Master Justice Shallow offered him 'a last year's pippin of my own grafting'; there are the candle-snuffered oasthouses, and inns old enough to have been shaken by the midnight thunder of hooves as Falstaff and his crew galloped helter-skelter to young Hal's coronation at Westminster. And if it is objected that Shallow lived in Gloucestershire, I do not care; Shakespeare's geography was none too exact.

Abberley Hall is an imposing house with an Italianate, neo-Georgian look, built during the reign of Queen Victoria. It was bought in the 1880s by one John Joseph Jones, a gentleman from Oldham in Lancashire. Mr Jones must have had a desire to be noticed in life and remembered in death, for he erected in his grounds an enormous clock tower; it dominates the country for miles around, and speaks in the same commanding tones as that of Ozymandias, one-time king of kings: 'Look on my works, ye mighty, and despair.' Mr Jones' folly is in much better shape than that of Ozymandias, but the battle with time has scarcely been joined; we shall have to wait a couple of thousand years or so and then see who wins – Time or Mr Jones: I know which I am betting on. Already there is a falling off from the summer days when I first knew the clock tower, hung with all its pride of bells. Now half of them have been sold, and the poor thing can only sound the quarters, the halves, and the hours – glumly at that, as though it knew the glory had departed. But when I was a boy, when time did not exist and miracles were common, then it was a wondrous thing to hear the preliminary whirring of the massive, clockwork wheels and ratchets, to see the birds come tumbling out of the louvred, rook-infested tower, and to know that in half a minute the whole carillon of bells would break out into an elephantine, gloriously inappropriate rendering of 'The Bluebells of Scotland'.

Abberley, when I first went there with my trunk and wooden tuck box, both tenderly packed by E, was a difficult place to reach. No bus went past the gates and cars were rare. The school was deep in the country, a world away from Southport with its shops and pavements, its fairground and its golf links. To be sure I had been with my Welsh cousins to stay by the sea at Mumbles; I had been outside Southport as far as Parbold where the heavy barges slid along the canal, and sun-bonneted women at the tiller called out to the men and horses plodding the towpath. But I had never actually lived in the country. I knew the names of only two trees: the big one in the front garden, the one with the five-pointed leaves, was a sycamore; the prickly one in the back garden, with the red berries, was a holly. I was a complete town boy; I had never seen a tadpole swimming; never heard an owl hunting; the only fox I had ever met was in the illustrations of children's books.

We smallest boys were out for a walk one day with little Miss James when a red, bushy-tailed animal came trotting out of a wood. Someone called out, 'Look! There's a fox!'

I was not having any of that; I knew better. A fox walked on his hind legs; he wore a coat and breeches, and he carried a watch in his waistcoat pocket. I could produce Beatrix Potter as a witness. The argument became heated, then violent; blows were struck and noses bled before I was taken in hand by Miss James, and gently but forcibly made to understand my error.

Bit by bit I began to learn about the country, about the seasons, about birds and animals, about the people who lived close to them. I began dimly to comprehend that in all things there must be a balance: not least in myself.

I took with me to Abberley some extraordinary notions – the normal, everyday attire of foxes being only one of many. I was so excited to be at boarding school that my little brain was overheated. Much of this fever was due to the *Boy's Own Paper*, a journal to which I had just graduated after years of *The Rainbow* and *Tiger Tim's Weekly*. It was the raw meat of the *BOP* that had led me to think that Abberley would be nothing but a series of adventures. Every day I wondered when the boys in Form III, falsely accused of stealing school funds from the odious Maths master, would at last expose that sneaky character as a German spy. Another scene, so vivid in my imagination that I would look out from the dormitory window half-expecting it to happen, was that the school caught fire. A little girl was trapped on the roof; the inside of the house was an inferno, but as the flames licked upwards and the whole school held its breath, the Captain of the Football Team climbed up the ivy in a desperate bid to save the unhappy child. 'Hurrah!' we would all shout as the young hero, scorched but triumphant, clambered down again, cradling the precious infant in his arms.

Abberley was not in the least like that. Life was ordered, hard-working and regular. Accidents were rare; although one boy, sliding down the banisters, did overbalance and fall two flights, landing with a nasty thump on the stone floor at the bottom. He was taken away in an ambulance and not seen again – not referred to either: he was liked well enough, but it was generally thought he must have broken his neck, and we did not want to cause embarrassment to our teachers.

Apart from the restrained frenzy of Guy Fawkes' Night, Abberley followed the usual cycle of all preparatory schools. We had lessons on the usual required subjects; we played the usual robust games; we ate the usual indifferent food; we obeyed the usual strict discipline. Seen from outside, the school must have looked as calm and uneventful as a pond. Not a bit of it. We small water beetles, scooting about beneath the surface, led a vehement, combative, almost dangerous existence. My six years of pond life were crammed full with events – some pleasant, some painful, few of them calm. Put together they added up to one entire experience, and at the age when I was most impressionable, between seven and thirteen. Those years are so vivid to me that I can reach out and touch them. It is a commonplace that the old can remember their youth but not what was said half an hour ago. Well – maybe, but it is only partly true. I recall that time with such clarity because it was crucial.

Potters leave their thumbprints in the clay before it is fired. In the same way, though quite unconsciously, the men and women who taught me at Abberley left their imprints on me. It was through their eyes that I began to assess the world; their example, however casually they set it, has stayed with me all my life. Even their voices – and not all of them educated and scholarly – still hang in the air.

33

'Bugger you! You dirty great sod.'

Nevitt's voice was not scholarly at all. Nevitt was a small, superannuated groom, supposed to be giving me riding lessons but in fact wholly concentrated on a life-and-death struggle with his own mount, Punch – a mad, black, sixteen-hand stallion. Nevitt was at a disadvantage in the battle, for as well as his reins and his whip he was also holding a leading-rein at the other end of which was me and an equally frightened, fat pony.

E, always determined that I should master every manly pursuit, had seen 'Riding Lessons' in the School Prospectus and promptly put me down for them. Now, once a week, I was the terrified spectator of a fight to the death between a little, frail old man and this murderous brute of a horse. And murder it would have been if Punch could have got Nevitt off his back; his iron-shod hooves would soon have finished the job. And then what would become of me and the fat pony? I asked myself. The leading-rein was wrapped round Nevitt's wrist.

'Sod you!' Again Nevitt would bring his whip down across Punch's quarters, and the stallion would roll back its eyes and go into a frenzy of bucking and rearing, sparks flying up as he struck the flints.

The 'riding lesson' over, we would return to stables looking like the survivors of the Light Brigade – I quivering with fear, Punch covered in foam and lather, but Nevitt triumphant: once again the brute had failed to kick his brains out.

When the school holidays came I begged E to release me from riding lessons. Let me try again when I was eight, or even nine. Meanwhile, if Dad was prepared to pay for an 'extra', then please let it be something less terrifying. The piano, perhaps? She agreed. But though the piano never threatened to bite or kick me, I was not much of a hand at it and before long I gave that up too. Punch – poor, mad Punch – was shot. Nevitt, though less abruptly, was also translated to a better world. Wherever he is, I am sure he is getting a quieter ride than ever he did on Punch.

Here now is another voice – boyish, cheerful. 'Up you get, Tony! On your feet! You're no good lying there.' It is Gilbert Ashton, the Headmaster, refereeing a game of football. I had been knocked down and winded – genuinely hurt, but making the most of it too. He bent down to rub my aching stomach, and I could smell the comforting wool of his sweater.

'Poor old Tony. But up you get. You're no good on the ground.'

Few words: great wisdom.

So up I got and on I went. Because it was what Mr Ashton expected, and it was what Mr Ashton would do himself. That nimble, compact body might possibly be knocked down, but there was nothing – nothing short of death – that could keep him down. Death in fact had taken a pot shot at him four years earlier at Ypres, when Gilbert was twenty – and just missed. He absorbed a few shell splinters, but was not killed. He came out of the war with an MC and no thumb on his left hand; but that had not prevented him from gaining a Double-Blue at Cambridge and from playing cricket now for Worcestershire. He still had a lump of shrapnel embedded in the back of his hand; it moved up and down in a most distracting way when he sat beside me, helping me to solve one of those mind-numbing problems about the speed of locomotives.

Two trains are approaching one another – one at 54.3 mph, the other at 86.7 mph . . .

I would gaze at the question, my mind a blank.

'Come on, Tony.' He tapped me on the head with his little gold pencil. 'You can do it. Think.'

The trouble was that I did not want to think; I did not want to solve the problem; I just wished the wretched things would crash and have done with it.

'Think, Tony. *Think.*' And this time the blow from the little gold pencil was a bit harder.

Mr Greenwood, his friend and fellow Wykehamist, also played cricket for the county, but he was another character altogether. A tall, dark man with saturnine good looks, his renaissance face was marred – or was it made? – by a livid scar that covered one side of his face. No boy would have dared to ask him how he came by it, but it was assumed he must have been terribly burned in an air crash when he was in the Royal Flying Corps. Not so: the scar was a birth mark, and it made compelling a face already handsome. He was a stylish man, from his well-shaped, well-kept hands to his shirts, his walk, the way he played the piano. But this courteous poise was not the badge of impassivity; it was the leash to hold in check a complex and passionate nature. There was something unknown about him, something held in reserve, that made us all a good bit scared of Mr Greenwood.

He taught us English and Latin, and would gladly have taught us Greek if the curriculum had allowed it: he had a passion for Homer. As it was he had to make do with Virgil.

One term we had just started on the *Aeneid* when he said:

'Who can translate those words: *Tum pius Aeneas?*'

It seemed easy enough. Some boy said, 'Then pious Aeneas.'

'And what do you mean by "pious"?'

'It means "good". Or "religious". Or "holy".'

'Yes. That is what the word means to us British, today. But what did it mean to the Romans?'

None of us in the small, dusty classroom had the faintest idea.

'No? Then I'll try to explain. There were two qualities the Romans especially admired – *gravitas* and *pietas*. The first is easy. Come on, somebody. *Gravitas*?'

'Gravity, sir. Being serious.'

'That's right. Having a serious attitude to life. Now for *pietas*.' He paused, wondering no doubt how to explain an adult and complex idea to a class of little boys in short trousers. 'When you grow older, you will find that a man has many duties – a duty to his God, a duty to his country, to his community, his profession, his parents, his wife and children. A duty to himself.'

Leonard spoke as though his thoughts sprang directly from his own inner experience, which is what made him such a remarkable teacher, and why his words have stayed with me for sixty-five years. 'If you are lucky, very lucky, these different duties may march together in harmony. More often they are in conflict. They pull against one another. Then life becomes difficult. The ability to keep these conflicting duties in balance, in proportion, that was what the Romans meant by *pietas*. The adjective was *pius*. And to call a man "*Pius*" was the highest praise the Romans could give.'

Sixty-five years have passed since that Latin lesson, and there have been many architectural changes at Abberley since I was there, but I could find my way straight to the very room where Leonard spoke of *gravitas* and *pietas*.

I find I am slipping into the habit of calling these powerful men by their Christian names. That is because, as I grew older, we became good friends, and the fifteen-year gap between us meant little; but in those Abberley days it was nothing but 'Mr Ashton' and 'Mr Greenwood', and 'sir'.

One night, long after our light had been turned out, we were squeaking about in the darkness, pillows flying across the dormitory, when suddenly, shockingly, the door was thrown open. Eight small creatures dived for cover. Silhouetted in the bright doorway stood Mr Greenwood. He switched on the light, and we huddled guiltily under the bedclothes.

'What a noise! What a noise you're making in here!'

We lay still as young rabbits, surprised on open ground.

'Which of you was talking?' He did not sound angry; his voice was silky-quiet. 'No one? Really? A surprising amount of noise to come from no one.' He stooped and picked up a pillow from the floor. 'And whose might this be?'

'It's mine, sir.'

'Yours, Linton? I suppose it flew there, all on its own.'

'No, sir. I threw it.'

'And this pillow – ' He picked up another and searched for the name marked on the pillowslip. 'This seems to be Berry's. Did your pillow fly, Berry? Or did you throw yours too?'

'I threw it.'

'Did you now? Both in silence? Both without saying a word?'

'No, sir. I was talking,' said Linton.

A long, frightening pause. Then Berry said, 'I think I might have made a sound too. But only a very small one.'

It felt cowardly to leave them on their own, but really it was only fair: those two had started it, and they had been making by far the most noise. But would two confessions suffice? Would Mr Greenwood be appeased? Would he caution us and let it go at that?

Another long silence. Then the silky voice again.

'Extraordinary. Only Linton and Berry. And all that commotion.'

No, he was not going away. He was not finished yet. He stood quietly in the middle of the room as if prepared to stand there for ever. It was no good. One by one we owned up. Perhaps, if we confessed, he might yet spare us.

'I see. All of you were talking.' He looked round the dormitory while we lay with thumping hearts. 'You know, don't you, that there is a rule of No Talking After Lights Out? And you know that rules are meant to be obeyed?'

'Yes, sir,' we muttered.

'Very well. Put on your dressing gowns and follow me.'

Silent, terrified, nerving ourselves for the ordeal ahead, we shuffled along the empty corridors after the tall figure till we reached the door of his bedroom. Then,

'All right, MacSwiney. You first.' And the door closed on the hapless MacSwiney.

We, standing in our doleful line, could hear only too clearly through the closed door.

'Bend over the bed. Lift up your dressing gown.'

Then, unmistakable even to me who had never heard it before, came the swish and thud of a cane. *One.* It was an unnerving sound. How many strokes would it be? *Two.* Would there be another? Yes, here it came: *three.* Then Mr Greenwood's voice, 'Now, go back to bed.'

The door opened and out came MacSwiney. White-faced he scooted away without a word or a look back.

'Quayle. You next.'

I bent over the side of his bed and hoisted the skirt of my dressing gown. I could not believe that this was happening to me. But it was. Out of the corner of my eye I could see Mr Greenwood's legs and the end of the long cane. He was arranging his stance, measuring his swing like a man going to hit a golf ball. But it was not a golf ball he was going to hit: it was me. I was being whipped. Such a thing had never – the whistle of the cane cut across my thoughts and the pain bit into my buttocks. *One* . . . Grit your teeth. Don't make a squeak . . . *Two* . . . Oh Lord, there's another yet to come. Hang on . . . *Three*.

I could not look at Mr Greenwood; I did not want to see him standing like an executioner with the cane in his hand. I heard his voice.

'All right. Stand up. Go back to bed.'

I fled back to the dormitory, shocked and smarting. At least it was over; I was not still standing in line awaiting my turn.

When we were all back in bed there were soft whispers.

'Are you all right, Wootton?'

'Yes, thanks. Are you?'

'I'm all right. Goodnight.'

'Goodnight.'

Five minutes later we were asleep.

Next morning, as we dressed, we examined each other's stripes: three livid weals across each chubby bottom.

'Gosh! Look at Linton's! They're terrific.'

Linton ran his fingers gingerly over the welts. 'Are they standing up? It jolly well feels like it.'

'Beauties,' Berry assured him. 'Those will last for days.'

We were all rather proud of ourselves: we had come through an initiation ceremony and not cried out. My chief concern was to know how to address Mr Greenwood when I sat beside him at breakfast. What sort of cheery conversation did you make with a man who had recently subjected you and your friends to a sound thrashing? My social education had not prepared me for such a situation.

I need not have worried. Mr Greenwood just smiled at me pleasantly, and – would I pass the bread, please? And, did I think that Hendren would get his century at Lord's today? Clearly Mr Greenwood held nothing against us; and none of us held anything against him – except that I did think he had beaten us a good deal harder than he need have done. I still think so.

Third in the triumvirate of friends who ran the school was Michael Carr. When he was seventeen he had left Eton and been commissioned as an ensign in the Coldstream Guards. By the time he was nineteen he had gained the MC, been wounded, and taken prisoner. He had a rough time in the German prison camps, a combination of near-starvation and bitter cold that later caught up with him and led to an early death. But that was yet to come. When I first knew him he was all of twenty-three.

One evening, in the usual bathroom scramble, I was jostled by another boy and swore at him.

'Tony Quayle!' The voice came from behind me. It was 'Matey', the school matron, Scots and kindly, but a tigress for the proprieties. She grabbed me by the arms.

'That's a disgusting way for a boy to talk. Wicked. Go and report yourself to Mr Carr. He's on duty tonight.'

It was several terms since I had been beaten by Mr Greenwood, but the memory of pain clutched my stomach like an old familiar. I climbed the stairs to the upper corridor – the same corridor I had trodden before on my way to chastisement – and found Mr Carr walking towards me.

He stopped and looked down at me. 'Hallo. What are you doing up here?' He sounded very cheerful.

'Please, sir, Matey sent me to report myself to you.'

'Oh? What have you been doing?'

'I swore at Stewart, sir.'

The smile faded. The voice became judicial. 'What did you say to him?'

'I said "Damn you" to Jimmy Stewart.'

Mr Carr looked at me impassively for a long time. I could not read his mind, but this long silence could only portend the worst. At last, in a voice that was not like his usual one, he said, 'Did you now?'

With that, he turned his back and walked away from me. He walked to the very end of the long corridor; there he cleared his throat and did a bit of coughing. Then he turned and came back. There was no mistaking that he was in a rage; his face was flushed and his eyes were watery; when he spoke to me he kept his head averted as though I was something too unpleasant to look at. What he finally said was all the more surprising.

'You shouldn't swear. It's a bad habit. Go back to Matey – and tell her I sent you.'

Matey inflicted her own punishment on me; she made me wash my mouth out with carbolic soap. For her sake I carried on as though it was disgusting; I swished the froth round in my mouth, and went 'Ugh!' and pretended I was going to be sick; but really it was not too bad.

Compared with the punishment I expected at the hands of Mr Carr – punishment he had spared me for some mysterious reason – I found it positively delicious.

Mike Carr was non-conformist as well as merciful. He was the only one of the three friends to play rugby; every Saturday in the winter he would pull an old leather helmet over his spiky blonde hair, climb on his enormous Brough Superior motorbike, and thunder off to distant battles at Kidderminster, Oxford, or faraway Bristol. He had a quaint sense of humour; he made us laugh. It certainly hurt when he cuffed my head, but I was never afraid of him. Mr Ashton was sometimes preoccupied and impatient – and God knows he had reason to be, struggling to make a success of a small prep school; Mr Greenwood gave you the feeling that there was a dangerous animal inside him waiting to leap out; but with Mr Carr you felt you were on shared ground. His personality held an admission that he too was human and could make mistakes. It is not incidental that he was a fine painter.

Those were the three men, all very young, who had so much to do with my growing up. They were too young to be my fathers, too old to be my brothers, yet I had a family sense of belonging. I did not exactly love them: I was in too much awe of them; but I was proud to be connected with them. I saw them as heroes, men who had rowed with Jason and come back to Argos with the Golden Fleece. They were men whose approval I desired, but from whom it was prudent to keep a respectful distance.

I have left Miss James to the last, partly to get the male element out of the way, partly because her influence on me, though not the most profound, has been the most evident: she started the chain of events that ended in my becoming an actor. Miss James was as small and bright as a round little wren; she took us tiddlers for walks; she taught us the names of wild flowers, and encouraged us to press them and take them home all properly labelled at the end of term to show our parents; on Sundays she invited us in twos and threes to her tiny sitting room to have tea with her, or to roast chestnuts in the fire; she instructed the youngest of us in the thorny mysteries of elementary Maths. It must have been during her equally elementary English lessons that she noticed I had an aptitude for reciting poetry, because she got me to learn an A. A. Milne poem and deliver it at a school concert. School concerts took place in the front hall, on the 'private side' of the house, where the Ashtons lived. The staff sat on chairs, the boys squatted on the floor, and an assortment of large stuffed animals – only their heads, to be precise – looked on from the walls. These were a legacy from John Joseph Jones and now immovable, the mid-Victorian decor of the front hall and its adjacent rooms having been 'listed'. Nothing daunted by the glassy stares of a moose, a couple of stags, a buffalo and a hippopotamus, I launched out into my first-ever performance:

A bear, however hard he tries
Grows tubby without exercise —

To my surprise everyone laughed; they went on laughing to the end; and when it was over Miss James was delighted. I was pleased of course — it was fun to make people laugh — but I did not take it as a compliment; I was only doing something that came naturally. It was not difficult to understand silly old Pooh and make fun of him; it was not difficult to feel the beat of the verse. I could do that as easily as Billy Permewan could solve equations; it was no special credit to either of us.

When I came back to Abberley for my second term (I was eight by now) Miss James told me she had me down for a part in the School Play at Christmas time. It was going to be *The Three Bears*, and Clive MacSwiney and I would be imps. 'Imps Attendant on the Ogre' was our full title. They were not large parts — in fact they did not speak a word between them — but, she assured us, they had a very important dance to perform, and this dance was going to need a lot of practice through the coming winter term. Practise we did — in cold, empty classrooms before breakfast; and winter it certainly was. It grew colder and colder until, on the great night itself, all Worcestershire lay buried under snow.

The School Play was presented once a year in a loft over the stable yard, at one end of which was a stage. Behind this stage — I doubt if it was more than twelve feet wide — were a couple of rooms, each the size of an American walk-in closet, and each containing a fireplace so diminutive that it might have come out of a doll's house; they were the rooms where the stablelads must have slept in the old horse-drawn days.

Here I came that night, to one of these cells, the fire burning to keep out the bitter cold, to don my costume and have my face painted. Miss James had just helped me into my imp's outfit when there was a serious production crisis; one of the leading actors had got his head stuck inside Mother Bear's mask and was in danger of asphyxiation. Miss James wrapped me in a blanket, told me to stay still and keep warm, and rushed off in the manner of all true impresarios. During the minute or two that I was left alone in front of the fire, a small but unforgettable experience came my way.

It had to do with being eight years old and dressed as an imp — the possibility that, if I stayed quiet inside myself and thought hard enough,

41

I might actually become an imp; it had to do with the miniature fire glowing red behind its bars while the snow fell outside; it had to do with the bareness of the room and with the rich smell of horses and hay that came up through the floorboards; it had to do with the sounds of the animals stirring about below, blowing softly down their nostrils. For a timeless moment I slipped through the chink between imagination and reality.

Alexander the Great once paid a momentous visit to the oracle of Ammon in the oasis of Siwah. Why he made that harsh journey to a remote spot on the borders between Egypt and Libya, and what befell him there, has always been a mystery; but it affected the whole of his short life. The holiest shrine at Siwah, says Robin Lane Fox, was 'a small room about ten foot wide and twenty foot long'; there Alexander put his questions to the god and received his answer. The cell where I glimpsed some kind of truth was little more than half the size of Ammon's shrine and doubtless quite as bare, but that is where some god or other spoke to me. I could not hear what he said; I did not even know I was being addressed. I had to wait several years before that became clear.

The door opened, and Miss James came bustling back with last-minute admonitions. 'Remember, Tony, you count two beats and step off on the third.'

'What about Mother Bear?' I asked. 'Is Heathcote all right?'

She seemed to have forgotten that crisis. 'Oh, he's all right,' she said, laughing. 'Don't worry. He'll live.'

So he did, for another twenty years; then his bomber was shot down in a daylight attack on Brest, and Gilbert Heathcote was never heard of again. Goodbye, Mother Bear. Good hunting.

The dance did not go well: partly my fault, partly an error in costume design. E and Clive MacSwiney's mother had been asked to make costumes for their respective offspring; beyond the suggestion that red would be an appropriate colour there were no other stipulations. Considering that E lived in Lancashire while Clive's mother lived in County Monaghan, the two ladies had done pretty well. Our costumes were of different reds – but what of that? Our headdresses too were different: E had drawn her inspiration from England, from the Lincoln Imp. I had a button-up headpiece and two horns stuffed with cotton wool; the whole contraption was held by strong fastenings under the chin. Clive's mother, coming of an Irish tradition, had provided her son with a conical hat that perched precariously on his head and was something between a dunce's cap and the headgear worn since time immemorial by the Little

42

People. It was a fine hat, a handsome hat; *but it had no fastenings under the chin.*

The moment arrived when the Ogre laid violent hands on the Old Woman gathering firewood. Growling horribly, he uttered the awesome lines,

> *Fetch out the thumbscrews and the rack,*
> *And have all ready by the time I'm back.*

Then, still growling, he stalked off the stage to mixed booing and applause. As the clapping died, Miss James struck a resounding chord on the old upright piano and called out,

' – and ONE . . . and TWO . . . and –' at which point we imps went into our *pas de deux.*

We skipped and hopped most devilishly round the stage while Miss James thumped out the beat. Then, at bar ten, came the great Diagonal Movement, a sort of gallop, in which we moved crabwise across the stage, waving our arms up and down, meeting and passing each other in the centre. It may not sound much, but it was a hazardous piece of choreography. We accomplished the first crossing without mishap, but, as we passed one another for the second time, we collided. Clive's leprechaun hat went askew like a drunken man's at closing time; he put up a hand to straighten it – and knocked it to the ground. This was something for which we were totally unprepared. We stopped in mid-gallop, paralysed.

Loud and clear, I said, 'Oh, heck!'

The audience gave a roar of laughter; Miss James pounded the piano and shouted to us to pick up the steps; but we were done for. We made a simultaneous dive for Clive's hat, collided again, then fled incontinent.

'Oh, heck!' Those were the first words I spoke on any stage. At least they got a laugh.

My ignorance of the Bible was soon made good at Abberley; even Miss Gertrude would have been satisfied. Every week we had lessons in the Old Testament from Mr Ashton, and in the New Testament from the vicar, Mr Cathcart Davies. We had prayers every day before breakfast, and we walked across the fields to the village church every Sunday morning. During the summer we walked back there again in the evening too – if it was not pouring with rain; if it was, we knelt down and prayed in the dining hall. I had not been inside a church since I had been taken there to be christened, so I was intrigued to be let in on this great and grown-up mystery. I was puzzled, too, because no matter how many hours we spent in Scripture lessons or at church no one could explain to me quite what the mystery was.

I did not let it bother me too much; children – boys at any rate – are adept at protecting themselves from insoluble puzzles; they live simply and happily by instinct; they do little thinking beyond how to kick a ball, or conjugate a French verb, or avoid being beaten. Very sensibly they inhabit only the ground floor, as it were, of thought; there are rooms upstairs, but they are all empty; and the entrance to the building is well guarded against the intrusion of such perplexing and dangerous things as Ideas. Occasionally, though, an Idea does find its way in through the front door: either it strays in by mistake, or it has been given a deliberate push by some grown-up. When that happens, and the child becomes aware that an Idea is on the loose in his snug little home, he keeps perfectly calm and deals with it in one of two ways. The first way is to kick the intruder up into the topmost attic of his mind and there leave it to fend for itself; the chances are it will soon die of neglect. The second way is more complicated, and only used when grown-up interest is perceived to be involved: then the Idea is escorted courteously upstairs and shown into one of the spare bedrooms. From then on it has the freedom of the house, and roams at will. It is sometimes heard muttering in its room, sometimes singing in its bath; occasionally it affords a glimpse of itself at the far end of some corridor of the mind. As the years pass, the uninvited but by now familiar Idea grows more confident; it comes downstairs and frequents the living room; it sits quite at ease and chats across the kitchen table. Eventually it turns into an old friend whose existence in the house has never been accounted for, whose credentials are still dubious, but who has now become an integral part of oneself.

That is how I coped with the Idea of Religion; and that is how Religion coped with me.

Coping was a long process, and there were preliminaries to be cleared up. First, it was important to understand that the Holy Bible was not one book: it was two books, called the Old Testament and the New Testament. They were quite separate; they dealt with entirely different periods of history, but when they were bound together they were called the Holy Bible. Second, this enormous book was not written by a single author – like Rudyard Kipling for example, or Stanley Weyman. It was not written by God either, though Miss Gertrude had called it 'The Word of God' (well, she was a batty old girl, and she could have made a mistake). No, it had been written by a lot of different people – though not by women, it seemed: only by men. Women came into the stories sometimes, and they certainly livened things up when they did, but they had done none of the writing. Third: when all these different books had been written (by whoever it was that wrote them) then they had all been translated into a different language, and then into another, and another, until at last the whole book had been turned into English, and ordinary people like us could read it. That was roughly the same time as Queen Elizabeth and the Spanish Armada.

There was something else you had to understand. You occasionally saw another big book lying about, called *Shakespeare*. It was about the same thickness and weight as the Holy Bible. So you might think that *Shakespeare* had also been written by a lot of different people and then translated into English. But you would be wrong: *Shakespeare* had been written by just one man – called Shakespeare – and he had written it straight down in English. That too was about the time of Queen Elizabeth and the Spanish Armada. It was a busy time, that.

I enjoyed Old Testament lessons so long as they kept off Exodus and Deuteronomy. I knew the Children of Israel were meant to be the heroes of the whole story, but I just could not take to them. Term after term I trudged with them through the Sinai desert, and I learnt by heart the names of all their confounded tribes. But they were such a pushy lot; and when they were not pushing they were whinging; and they were always carving up the Hittites, and the Jebusites, and the Hivites, and the Amorites, and anyone else who stood in their way. I could not think why God had chosen them; they were a bore.

But the books of Samuel, Judges, Joshua – ah, that was the stuff! Tales filled with the thunder of iron chariots, the braying of trumpets. Jael welcoming Sisera as a guest, then driving a tent peg smack through his temples when he slept. The triumphant song of Deborah the prophetess after the bloody victory at Migiddo.

The stars in their courses fought against Sisera . . . At her feet he bowed, he fell, he lay down; at her feet he bowed, he fell: where he bowed, there he fell down dead.

The stories were exciting for their own sake, but even more thrilling was the language – the changing rhythm and cadence of the words. King David's lament for his son struck my ears like the voice of Grief itself.

O my son Absalom, my son, my son Absalom! Would God I had died for thee. O Absalom, my son, my son!

I could see David lurching down the long corridors of his palace, none daring to come near him; I could hear his sobs going further and further into the distance.

Scripture lessons were not always solemn; a few Old Testament characters could always be counted on for a laugh. There was Og, the king of Bashan – though the only funny thing about Og was his name; there was Agag who 'walked delicately' and came to a very nasty end. And there was always the chance that some boy might dare to be a bit provocative and liven things up.

'Please, sir, there's a word in verse eight I don't understand.'

'Yes, Priday? What word?'

'*Appurtenances*, sir. It's talking about things you mustn't eat – about rams, sir. And it says in verse eight, " – *his legs and the appurtenances thereof*". What's an *appurtenance*, sir? We don't eat *appurtenances*, do we, sir? Not here in England?'

But you had to be careful with Mr Ashton; if he thought you were fooling, or if you caught him in the wrong mood, you could be in serious trouble.

The New Testament did not feel as if it had anything to do with the Old; I could not think why they were bound together in the same book. I asked Miss James, but she only said, 'I expect it's easier to publish the Bible that way. Perhaps they sell more copies.'

Sell more copies? What was she talking about? If this book was 'The Word of God', if it was all that holy, then how could *selling* come into it? But clearly Miss James did not want to go any further into the matter. Never mind; forget it; kick the question upstairs into the attic; one day it would find an answer.

Meanwhile, it was good to walk out into the air and sunshine of Galilee, and escape from those remorseless old men of the Old Testament – all begetting, or prophesying, or avenging; all offering up lumps of charred meat for Jehovah to sniff at. The people round Jesus had such friendly, familiar names – Mary, Martha, Simon, Peter, John: the story became almost English. Except that all the time I had a feeling that what really happened must have been quite un-English, and we were being taught a sugary version of it – like the coloured postcard called 'The Good Shepherd': Jesus with a sickly smile and a lamb tucked under His arm. Why, for example, at that Feast of the Passover, had Jesus walked right into Jerusalem and into the hands of his enemies? Why ask to be caught and killed in that appalling way? He must have known what was going to happen. He did know: He said so. Then why do it?

46

But when I asked Mr Cathcart Davies to explain (and being a clergyman, he ought to know if anyone did) he only smiled gently down at me and said, 'Jesus sacrificed himself to atone for all our sins.'

What sort of an answer was that? What sins? I had not committed any sins. I had just been a bit naughty at times. And how could Jesus be punished in advance for what we did thousands of years later? It made no sense.

Going to church did not provide any answers either; it only added to the questions. Mum had sent me off to Abberley with a prayer book, and here I found that Jesus had somehow become drawn into a mysterious threesome, called the Trinity. Jesus was definitely one of three, and I was very glad of that because He was the only one I could begin to understand. Of the other two, one of them was God – who had changed quite a bit since the Old Testament. He was now called 'The Father' and was supposed to love us all; but He showed jolly few signs of doing so. He had given up thundering, and He did not speak out of burning bushes any more; in fact, He seemed to have lost interest in what was going on down here. Finally, there was a Holy Ghost, who sometimes turned into a dove and flew down through gaps in the sky. This last was more bewildering than two trains heading for collision at X miles per hour. This was near to lunacy.

And why did our teachers, who had been their normal, cheerful selves all the way across the fields, become different people when they stepped inside the church? They all put on holy expressions – especially Mr Greenwood. He sat in the front pew, and his dark, branded face glowed with fervour. He sang very loudly too – and very well. The only one who stayed unchanged and quite himself was Mr Carr. But if you wanted to see Mr Carr you had to turn your head round and pretend you were looking for something at the back of the church, because that was where he always hid himself: at the very back. And he did not sing loudly at all.

We had to learn the Creed by heart, and I was delighted with myself because I could rattle it off pat. But before long I began to have difficulties with the Creed. Here it came now: first the leathery wheeze of the bellows, then a chord from the organ giving the vicar his note. At that point the village choirboys had to stop pulling faces at us little toffs, get up from their knees and turn towards the altar.

I believe – Mr Cathcart Davies had a perfectly ordinary voice when he talked to you in class, but his singing voice was plummy and hollow; it was hard not to laugh.

I believe in God the Father Almighty. I glanced towards Mr Greenwood; he was looking especially mysterious and devout.

47

On the third day He rose again from the dead. I was saying it because it was expected of me, but did I really believe it? Did Mr Greenwood really believe it?

He sitteth on the right hand of God. But if God was a spirit and must be worshipped in spirit – and that was what we had been reading in St John – then how could He have a right hand? And where was He sitting? Out there beyond the stars, in all that space? Dad had been quite positive that God was not out there. Yet here were Mr Greenwood and Mr Ashton, only a few feet from me, saying it with all their hearts.

I believe in the resurrection of the body. No, it was no good. When little Miss James died she could not be resurrected looking like she did now. The moths would have had her clothes for a start. And she would be all eaten by maggots like the dead sparrow I had found in our garden at home. But there she stood, saying the words and looking as though she meant every one of them. It was beyond me. I could not possibly say to her, 'Please Miss James, do you really mean what you say in the Creed?' It would be like asking Mr Ashton if he really loved Mrs Ashton? Of course he loved her, or he would not be married to her. Of course he meant the Creed, or he would not be saying it – or rather singing it on one wobbly note. I would ask Mum when I saw her – though that would not be much help; I doubted if she even knew the Creed.

It was a relief to get out of morning church and be walking back through the fields, skirting the cowpats. Everyone seemed much happier, teachers as well as boys; we had become ourselves again.

'Miss James. Please, Miss James. Do you know what's for lunch today?'

I was always glad to emerge from Morning Service, but I really looked forward to Evensong. The church door stood open, and from the trees and fields there drifted in a rich mingling of sounds and smells: the lush, evening scent of grasses and wild flowers; the domestic sounds of small birds settling down to sleep. The long, hot day was done, and all life accepted its inevitable close. Even the humans showed no strain, assumed no other-worldly expressions, no holy, hollow voices. The world was disappearing into shadow, and all that was left was cupped within the soft light of the church. The church itself was wrapped around by all the leaves and lanes of Worcestershire, and Worcestershire was wrapped around by all of England. Into this sheltering bowl there dropped the *Nunc Dimittis*, so serene and simple that it reached out beyond the grey stone walls, beyond the dusky churchyard where a blackbird sang; it reached out all the way to my mother in the distant north and told me how far from her I was.

Lord, now lettest Thou thy servant depart in peace – I could get so far, and then a deep emotion, a compound both of happiness and sorrow, welled up in me and stopped my voice. It was more than simple grief at being parted from my mother, though that was part of it; it was sorrow, sorrow so poignant that it was close to joy, for the beauty, the exact rightness, of this passing moment.

All term long I lived happily enough inside the days and hours, but as half term approached I grew more and more restive until a day came when I was almost numb with anticipation.

'Tony, don't wool-gather. I know it is Saturday, and I know your mother is coming to see you today. But it is only ten thirty and you are still in school. So come along. The Future Indicative of "to love".'

Amabo . . . amabis . . . amabit . . . Oh God, please make the time go quickly.

He never did, though; I think He dragged it out longer. But at last, at last, the interminable morning was over and I raced on skidding feet to fling open the green baize door that separated the two worlds of Abberley – the stone-flagged, carbolic-swilled corridors where we boys hooted and clattered – and the carpeted decorum of the 'private side'. The baize door swung joyously on its two-way hinges as I rushed through, and there – though heaven knows by what means she had travelled, for we had no car there she would unfailingly be, to hug me and carry me off with laughter to the pub in the village where she stayed.

Saturday afternoon was bliss, for we held eternity in our hands. True, I had to be back in school by six, but I could fall asleep knowing that Mum was close and Sunday was yet to come. Half of eternity remained unspent.

But Sunday was a swindle. We were never excused church, and we did not get back from that till long past midday. So half of eternity, when you came to live it, was not more than the time it took to eat lunch. Around three the direful shadow would begin to fall, the tortured knowledge that time had almost run out. I tried to be brave, but it was beyond me. I grew quieter and quieter; I yawned more and more. At last I burst into great sobs.

'Oh Mum, Mum. Don't go. I don't want you to go.' I buried my face against her.

'Don't, my darling. Please don't. I don't want to leave you either. But you know I must.'

The storm would go on all afternoon till we were both exhausted. Then she would take me back to school, blow my nose for the last time, for the last time tell me to be brave, then leave me clutching my sodden handkerchief and watching the tail light of the hire car vanish down the drive. Perhaps a miracle would happen. Perhaps the car would stop and bring her back. But no, God was never in the mood for miracles. The sound of the engine died away, and she was gone; irrevocably gone. There was nothing for it but to walk back through the silent 'private side', past the indifferent eyes of the stuffed hippo, the stags and the buffalo, and rejoin the human herd. I pushed through the baize door; it swung as easily one way as the other, making no comment on my changed fortune. I was late for supper, but that was good; the boys would be too busy jabbering and stuffing themselves to notice me and my red eyes.

'Sorry I'm late, Miss James.'

'That's all right, Tony.' She gave me a shrewd glance, but was too wise to offer sympathy. 'Hungry?'

'Not very, thank you.'

'Oh, I should eat something if I were you. There's some spaghetti left. A bit cold, but it's very good.'

It was stone cold, but it wasn't as foul as it looked; and with each soggy mouthful a kind of optimism returned. There would be a letter from Mum in a few days: that was something to look forward to. By next morning I was myself again, cheerful, full of spirits, enjoying all that could be enjoyed and putting up with all that could not.

I doubt if E recovered so quickly from such an emotional battering. It was a long time before I understood what it must have cost her to send me away from her for three quarters of every year, and for more than ten years. I had no concept then of how barren her life was with me away. But she was a woman of determination. She had made up her mind to give this son of hers the best education she could, and nothing would deflect her.

'Bunt,' she would say. 'Understand this. You can have anything in this world that you want. Anything. But you cannot control the price you must pay.'

Both she and I paid a stiff price for my early years at Abberley. Neither of us regretted it, then or after. But we paid all right; and much as it cost me, I am sure it cost her more.

CHAPTER 5

IN THE SCHOOL HOLIDAYS I CAME home to Southport (or more properly, Birkdale) and got on with the cheerful business of being an upward-growing, outward-looking, inevitably juvenile, town mouse; and a very happy little creature I was. I had a mother who was both loving and fun to be with, a father who may not have counted for much but who was endlessly kind, and a darling grandmother who took me to the movies – the silent movies: 'talkies' were not yet invented.

Aggie was addicted to the flicks, and I was her ever-ready accomplice. What a beauty she must have been when she was a girl and ran off with Grandpa. She was still enchanting in her old age, but brainy she was not. She looked at the pictures in the newspaper, but she never read the text; I suspect she was not very good at reading. She bluffed her way along under an endearing pretence of vagueness; she would point to the paper with an arthritic finger and say, 'What's all that about, Tony? I can't see. I've left my silly specs somewhere.' Not that she had much interest in the so-called realities of daily life; what she loved was a good laugh and a good cry. So once a week we two would sneak off to one of the picture houses, hold hands, suck peppermints, and watch the stars: Greta Garbo, Charlie Chaplin, Tom Mix, George Arliss. My brain was jerked from place to place, from century to century: from the Barbary Coast to the Frozen Yukon, from the Wild West to Paris and the French Revolution. What heroisms. What villainies. What duellings and rescuings. I was almost concussed. When *Orphans of the Storm* was over and we stood on the pavement outside the Picture Drome, Aggie fumbling for her brolly, and the lights from the shop windows dazzling across the wet streets, I could not make out where

51

I was. What had happened to the mob? The tumbrils? Where was the bloodstained guillotine?

'Aggie. Which way do we go?'

'You silly boy.' Her voice was always very gentle, very loving. 'You know the way. Right for the Promenade – left for Lord Street and the trams.' She slipped my hand under her arm and we headed for the trams.

It was not Chimborazo or Cotopaxi who had stolen my soul away, but the Gish Sisters. So had Douglas Fairbanks, slicing his way from top to bottom of the enemy's mainsail; so had Milton Sills, stripped naked and shackled to a galley slave's bench; so had Ramon Novarro and Francis X. Bushman, lashing their chariot teams round the Roman stadium; so had Buster Keaton in every mortal thing he did, but most especially in *The General*.

What flicks they were in those days. Not only did they flicker, but they whirred. The pianist was usually thumping away too loud for you to hear the film running over the sprockets; but when the love scenes came and the piano went soft and mushy, then the projectionist came into his own. Every time Rudolph Valentino narrowed his eyes and the heroine shrank from him in mingled love and loathing, then, just as surely as the next caption would be '*I Love You!*' and the one after would be '*No, No!*', so without fail would be heard the whirring, chirring rattle of the projector.

Sometimes the machine broke down. When that happened the whole audience, Aggie and me included, would groan loudly; then, as the lights came on, we would all laugh and applaud ourselves for being such audacious wags. After a few minutes the lights would be turned out again to renewed cheers and whistles. The whirring started up once more, a few feet of film jerked onto the screen – only to suffer a further collapse. Louder groans from the audience: more ribald cheering. No one ever made a fuss or complained about breakdowns; they were accepted as part of the entertainment. You paid your money, you came out of the cold and rain, and whichever way things went you had a good time.

Quite different – oh, altogether different – was the theatre. The Southport Opera House was the social centre of the town: the spiritual centre too, I dare say, in so far as Southport had such a thing. The theatre was knocked down decades ago to make way for an office block, but in the twenties it was a good touring date and almost every company played there either before or after London. Mum enjoyed the theatre, but with Dad it was a consuming passion; he had been a dedicated amateur before his marriage, and sometimes he would act out for me the plays he had performed in his bachelor days; plays like Galsworthy's *Strife*, and *Loyalties*.

Dad had his own small bedroom, and that was where he gave these recitals. Shut away in private, living in his imagination, he became another man – vigorous, assured. He had seen Henry Irving several times and he knew by heart whole passages from *The Bells*. To me, his rapt audience of one, he gave such performances of the guilty murderer, Matthias, that I was transported. Before my eyes Dad had become another being. And somewhere in my mind there must have dawned a faint perception that the world we know is only the outer wrapping of a world we do not know at all, and that a man is neither singular, nor even plural: he is legion.

As yet I had never seen a play acted. I had been an imp; I had experienced, in the groom's room above the stable, an odd sense of entering a different layer of reality; but I had never been inside a proper theatre.

'Oh, Dad,' I begged. 'Do please take me. I do so want to go.'

'Very well. But we've got to find the right play for you.' He picked up the local paper from his bedside. 'This week – Tallulah Bankhead. That's a bit grown-up for you.'

'Oh why, Dad? I go to the movies all the time with Aggie.'

'I know. But the theatre's not like the movies.'

'You mean – love scenes? I don't mind. I saw Rudolph Valentino in *The Sheik*. It was just plain dull.'

'No, I don't only mean love scenes.' He stopped, searching for words. 'I mean that the theatre is a kind of grown-up game. Sometimes simple. Sometimes rather complicated . . . Like a lot of things in life.'

'But you can explain it to me, can't you? Oh, please, please take me.'

'All right.' He shook out the paper. 'Here we are. The very thing. Two weeks from now. *Sherlock Holmes*!'

'Sherlock Holmes?'

'Yes.'

'You mean *the* Sherlock Holmes?'

'That's right.'

'He's coming to Southport? Really and truly? You mean it?'

He hesitated. 'Well, yes – in a way. Good – then I'll get seats and we'll all three go – you, and Mum, and me.'

We went. We walked up the steps of the theatre and into the foyer. There were crowds of people all round us, and, 'Hallo Esther,' they said, and, 'Hallo Arthur.'

'Hallo!' said Mum and Dad.

'I see you've brought your little boy with you. Or should I say "your big boy"?' They smiled at me in the sickly way that grown-ups do, and there was nothing for it but to smile back.

What was the matter with them? This was no time for making rotten jokes. Did they not understand that any moment they would be inside 221B Baker Street, in the very presence of Sherlock Holmes? They would hear him play his violin, smell the tobacco burning in his meerschaum pipe. They were about to witness his mortal fight with the archenemy, Professor Moriarty.

Mum said, 'Don't get so excited, Bunt. You'd better go and have a last widdle. Dad'll take you. Look — there's the Gents.'

At last, frozen with tension, I saw for the first time the house lights go out and the curtain rise. But what was that curious, spicey smell that seemed to be wafting out from the stage? It could not be glue.

'Dad. Dad.' I whispered. 'What's that funny smell?'

He leant towards me and whispered, 'Make-up.'

'What?'

'Paint. Powder. Sh!' He lifted his finger to stop more questions, and turned back towards the stage.

When the curtain fell on the first act, Mum said, 'Well, darling, which do you like better? The theatre or the movies?'

'Oh, the theatre.' The depth of my fervour must have surprised them. 'Really? Why?'

'Because . . . because . . .' I could not explain; I had not got the words. I could only say, 'Because it's happening. The actors are really there. You could reach out and touch them. And — and you can even smell them.'

Which was not altogether such a bad answer.

Liverpool in the twenties. A misty, murky metropolis of the north. Ferryboats hooted and churned their way through the Mersey fog. Great locomotives, hot and hissing from the London or Glasgow run, threaded their way over the points to their arrival platforms. Electric trains vibrated and hummed, carrying in and out of the city tens of thousands of men — solid men of substance, men who had started at the bottom and fought for their brass, and now, as King Cotton began to totter, were fighting to keep it. Women in clogs and shawls bawled the evening papers. Wizened, underfed boys with shaven heads and bare feet scratched and scrabbled to open the doors of cabs and earn themselves a penny. And down by the docks the gentle shire horses dripped moisture from their curled moustaches, threw their giant strength against the harness and pulled the massive, rumbling drays over the cobblestones.

In the middle of this raw capital were the premises of R. Sumner and Co., Wholesale Manufacturing Druggists – the life's work of my grandfather, John Overton; and every school holidays E went there to visit her father, taking me along with her. E loved her father dearly, but I suspect it was not only filial affection that drew her to Liverpool; it was pragmatism. She wanted to remind her father that he had as yet only one grandchild – and this was he.

When you pushed open the swing door of Sumner's you left behind the rattle and rumble of Liverpool and stepped into a scene written by Charles Dickens. You found yourself in an entrance hall lined with cases of surgical instruments, alluringly – if gruesomely – displayed to catch the eye of visiting doctors. A glass partition separated this hall from the main office where, perched on stools, the ledger clerks worked at their high desks; and there, raised on a shallow step that enabled him to see all that went on, my grandfather presided over his small kingdom.

Always close at hand was his devoted secretary, Miss Bolton. With her thin face, her intelligent smile, her boundless loyalty, she had been his secretary and confidante from the beginning. It was she who, when my name began to appear in the newspapers, in no matter how modest a capacity, would cut out the paragraph and place it proudly on my grandfather's desk. Then, when he had absorbed the news that his grandson would be appearing in an insignificant part in some wholly unimportant London production, she would remove the slip of newsprint and paste it in an enormous book. Miss Bolton must have had great confidence in her own longevity as well as in my future, for the book she had chosen for these records was a full-size ledger. Alas, I was slow to furnish her with material, and she had only filled a page and a half of the great tome before she died.

When E and I had talked to Miss Bolton and all the clerks – not one of them could be missed out – Grandpa would take us on a grand tour of the warehouses. He called every man who worked for him by his first name, but he introduced them with courteous formality by their surnames. 'My darling girl, you remember Mr Arkwright? He's been with us – how long is it, Frank? Thirty-two years?'

And Frank Arkwright, beaming, would reply, 'Almost thirty-four, Mr John.'

Grandpa would lay an affectionate hand on his arm, make an enquiry about some linctus, or the pills that were churning round in a metal vat, and then on we would go from one intriguing medicinal smell to another.

Grandpa was an assured man, not easily frightened, but there was one room on the first floor past which he skedaddled as quickly and quietly as he could. The door had a panel of frosted glass on which was printed

Mr PERCY OVERTON
(West African Drug Company)

This was the office of my Uncle Percy, E's older brother, a co-director of Sumner's and a creature of uncertain temper; he had recently pulled an electric fire from its socket and flung it at his father's head. With such missiles flying through the air, it was understandable that the old man should walk softly past Percy's door; but it was not altogether out of fear that he did so: it was shame for his own son as a human being. We were tiptoeing through the danger zone on one occasion, half-laughing, half-fearful, when the door opened and out came my uncle – bulky, waistcoated, aggressive: a pig in a business suit.

'Good heavens!' he exclaimed. 'It's Esther.' His voice was hoarse and thick, as though it had been strained through suet. 'What brings you to Sumner's?'

The Overtons were a vehement family, every one of them, and E's loathing for her elder brother was as extreme as her love for her younger brother, Reg. Caught out now like a naughty child she pretended nonchalance.

'Oh, Tony and I just dropped in to see Father. We're in Liverpool for the day.'

Uncle Percy's small eyes flicked from me to his father, then back to his sister. 'I see.' His voice was hurt and accusatory. 'Well – I wish you had let me know, Esther. I don't see you all that often. Or the boy,' he added, as an afterthought.

Father, son and daughter stood locked in silence while I stared down at my feet, awkward and out of place. Uncle Percy shifted his weight and moved his neck about; he seemed to be trying to express some painful emotion. At last he made a small, strangled noise, turned back into his office and slammed the glass door.

My uncle Percy looked like a pig and behaved like a pig, but in his defence it must be said that he was a passionate pig; and much as I disliked him I came to think that any man who had been at the Front and fought through the whole of the 1914–18 war was entitled to be a bit mad. You might wish to exterminate him, but you had no right to condemn him.

When I was older and felt more deserving of an answer, I asked my grandfather straight out, 'Grandpa, when did you take Uncle Percy into Sumner's? When he came out of the army?'

He nodded. 'Yes.'

'Why did you make him a director?'

'Because he is my son.'

'But why make him equal to yourself?'

Grandpa sighed heavily and regarded me with the sad, quizzical look of a man trying to explain the inexplicable to the uncomprehending.

'Because —' he began, then paused. 'Because —' and again he paused, rubbing his eyes with thumb and middle finger. 'Because all men make mistakes. Even your grandfather.'

Grandpa never stayed in Liverpool; he took the electric train back every evening to Southport. Mum and I always travelled with him after one of our visits, and he would pay the extra for us to ride First Class instead of our normal Third. The atmosphere of the First Class Smoker was rich, and dark, and fruity. The upholstery, the inlaid woodwork, had been pickled in years of expensive pipe tobacco; the carriage reeked of unassailable security. I enjoyed it as a rule; but one winter night, as I sat in the warmth, wiping the condensation from the window to see where we had stopped — was it Ormskirk or Formby? — I took no pleasure in my surroundings: I was troubled by the small, shrivelled boys at Lime Street Station who had been running barefoot in the snow and slush.

'Why didn't they have any socks or boots?' I asked Grandpa.

He looked uncomfortable. 'There are differences between people's lives,' he said. 'It takes a long time to put things right.'

I said, 'But it isn't fair. It seems all wrong.'

He looked at me steadily. 'Yes. It is wrong. There are many things that are wrong. But no one can put them all to rights in one lifetime. You have to do what you can.'

I could not let it drop. 'So — the woman you bought the evening paper from — the one in a man's cap —'

'What about her?'

'Was that why you gave her half a crown?'

He stared at me without expression. 'Did I?'

'Grandpa! You know you did. I saw you.'

'You're a nosey little boy, aren't you?' He looked so stern that I thought I had better change the subject.

'Grandpa, are you a commuter?'

This question only put him in a worse mood. He gathered his anger round him in black thunderclouds. 'A "commuter"? Am I a "commuter"? What exactly do you mean by that word?'

I wished I had never asked the silly question. It was only to get myself out of a fix, and now I was in worse trouble than before.

I said lamely, 'I think it means someone who goes to work by train every day and comes back again at night.'

'You think, do you?' His tone was withering. 'You *think*. Then, young man, I shall give you something to think about. To "commute" means to change one thing into another. It is a transitive verb. Do they teach you at school what a transitive verb is?'

'Yes, Grandpa.' I knew this anger was all because of the boys with no shoes, but I was quite frightened by him.

'Good. At Sumner's we "commute" one substance into another by various chemical means. The sentence passed on a criminal may be "commuted". But don't tell me that by sitting in a train every day and going to Liverpool I am a "commuter"!'

'No, Grandpa. I'm sorry, Grandpa.'

He calmed down a bit and relit his pipe. Through the dense blue smoke he asked, 'You know what language we speak here in these islands?'

'English.'

'Quite right. English. It's a good language. A great language. Learn to speak it properly. Don't play ducks and drakes with it.'

Grandpa knew nothing about the arts — and was not interested. He read a lot of history, he had a decent twenty-five handicap at golf, and he had a chef's dexterity with a carving knife. He was always trying to pass his skill on to me.

'Come on, boy. You must learn to carve. You don't want to grow up a fool, do you? Now, put the fork in there . . . No, no. What d'you think you're carving? This isn't a leg. It's a shoulder. They're different things, aren't they?'

'Yes, Grandpa.'

'I should think so. You'll be married one day, and you don't want to make that sort of mistake with your wife.'

The small ribaldry would set him off laughing, while from the other end of the table Aggie would rebuke him gently.

'Oh, Jack. Don't say such things to the boy. Tony, don't listen to your grandfather. He's incorrigible.'

By this time though he'd have worked himself into one of his choking fits; and now a look of awful solemnity would pass over his face as though he were in the very presence of death. He would fasten his eyes on each of us in turn – whether imploring help or stamping our faces on his mind before he died I never knew, because the choking passed, death drew back a pace or two, and the old man would laugh again with the wholehearted abandon of a child.

I came home from Abberley at the end of one term to be told that Kim had died.

Kim? Dead? It was not possible. Yes, it was a fact. And he had been buried in the front garden.

'Where?'

Dad said, 'In the corner under the laurel bush. I thought he'd like to be near the house.' He must have seen my distress because he went on, 'He didn't have any pain. He just went to sleep. He was getting on, you know. And dogs don't live as long as we do.'

Kim *dead*? It was awful. Kim had been as much a part of my life as I had been, and for just as long. I had taken him for granted, but only in the same way that I took myself for granted. And now my smelly, neglected old friend had gone without saying goodbye; he had gone without a sound. I had said nothing to him either, neglectful to the last. He had simply vanished, like the conjuror's white rabbit, while I was not looking. But this was not a children's party; there was no conjuror to tap three times with his magic wand, draw the silk handkerchief back and produce Kim from a top hat. Not that any hat would have been large enough; Kim was so big and fat you could not have hidden him in a wheelbarrow. No, he had gone for good. All that was left of him was his lead, still hanging from its peg in the hall.

I went out into the front garden and crouched under the laurel bush, weeping. There was nothing I could say or do to bring him back. I could only pat the black earth that covered him and say his name again and again. 'Kim . . . Kim . . . Kim.'

I mourned him bitterly, but only for a couple of days. Then I burnt his lead on a funeral pyre in the back garden and felt much better about it all. I intended to make a cross and set it up under the laurel bush, but I never got round to it.

My secure little world was shaken by another tremor: E told me that we would soon be leaving our house in York Road and moving to a flat. I could not believe it.

'Leave *home*? But why?'

'Never mind why, darling. It's all to do with money.'

'You mean bills? We can't pay the bills?'

'No, it's not that.' She hesitated. 'There's been a bit of a muddle at the office, you see – and Dad has to find some money. So as to put things right.'

'Oh, Lord. P'raps I ought to leave Abberley?'

'No.' Her reply was positive. 'You're not going to do that. But we can't afford to go on living in a house this size.'

'It's a very small house,' I protested.

'Yes, I know. But if we sell it, then Dad will have some money. Now don't bother him with questions. He's got a lot on his mind.'

Whatever was on Dad's mind must have been serious, because he lost his appetite – could not even eat his sausages for breakfast. He did not look at all well, either. I told him I was very sorry he had all these problems.

'Oh, it'll be all right in the end,' he said. 'Thanks to Mr Briggs. I don't know where I'd be without him.'

He talked a lot about Mr Briggs – what a dependable, loyal friend he had been. Dad was so grateful that I felt I ought to try and like Mr Briggs a bit more; but I could not. There was something creepy about him; and it was not just his clammy hands and the convulsive Adam's apple.

Dad bought me an air gun – probably to console me for leaving York Road. It came in a cardboard box with a number of printed targets and several boxes of lead slugs. It was called 'The Daisy' – perhaps to reassure the parents of young marksmen that no serious harm could come from a weapon so pacifically named. It did not give me the same delight that the tape measure had done a few years back, but it had a wooden stock that was very satisfying to handle. I pinned one target after another to the door of the tool shed in the back garden and plugged away at them till the door must have sagged under the weight of lead.

It was good fun for a few days; then it began to pall. What was the point of all that loading and aiming and firing when there was no one to share it with, no one to see if I had done well or badly? Dad had gone to the office and Mum was always busy in the kitchen. Not that I was much of a shot; at a distance of twelve strides I never hit the bull's-eye, and there were times when I missed the target altogether. I could blame that on a cross wind or some defect of The Daisy's sights, but in my heart I knew the fault was my own.

Well – there was one way to put that right: close the range. I moved in from twelve paces to six – and still missed. From six I closed to three – and fairly pulverized the target. I felt sick with self-disgust; I knew perfectly well that I was cheating, that my score was a miserable lie, but I did so desperately want to prove my prowess. When the target was more holes than cardboard I pulled it off the door of the shed and ran indoors to show it to Mum.

'Look, Mum! Look what I scored! With only ten shots!'

But E was too busy to pay much attention; she was weighing flour in the kitchen scales and beating up some eggs. 'Oh, very good. Well done, Bunt. Now out you go and shoot some more. I'm busy making a cake for your birthday.'

Back in the garden I stalked moodily up and down the weedy path between the potatoes and the sprouting cabbages. It was a waste of time shooting at silly cardboard targets. No one understood how hard it was to score a bull's-eye. I felt aggrieved, hard and ruthless. I tucked the gun under my arm like a white hunter prowling the African *veldt*. I would show them. I would bring back something for the pot; rhino, wildebeest, warthog – it was all the same to me.

The neighbour's ginger cat leapt lightly down from the partition fence. I raised The Daisy to my shoulder and took aim – not *at* the cat but a couple of feet behind it. God forbid I should hit the beast. Yes, but what if I shot it by accident? The rifle's sights were not properly aligned. They could not be; I had just proved it. The surest way to hit the cat might be to try and miss it. That would be appalling. I could picture the poor thing stretched out like a tiger-skin rug: or worse – wounded, in agony. I lowered the gun, and the ginger cat continued to pick its way delicately between the cabbage stalks, all unknowing that for a moment a deadly marksman had held it in his sights.

A blackbird flew chattering away. That was it. I would shoot a bird. I had not the smallest wish to shoot one; I would have been horrified if I had; but since there was not a chance of doing so I felt safe to blaze away at each and every little bird that sped across our garden or wheeled high in the air. And all the time there came the steady, monotonous whirr of our neighbour's mowing machine as he pushed it up and down, up and down his patch of lawn. I sent lead pellets flying in all directions, but thank God not a bird did I hit. I was grateful for that, and yet there was growing in me a resolve that I must hit *something*. It had become a matter of pride.

My hunter's mind was whipping itself into a frenzy when I noticed something moving on the flat stone where the gravelly path joined our plot of grass. A snail. Neck out, horns up, he was confidently oozing forward. I watched his progress with pity – and with an icy resolve.

A snail might not be the most challenging of targets, but at least it was moving; it had a sporting chance. I lay down on the ground a few paces off where I could see my quarry through the blades of grass, took careful aim – and missed.

The lead pellet must have whistled past the snail's nose, for he drew in his horns and sat still.

Now what? I got up and stood over the animal, looking down on him. I glanced towards the kitchen. Through the open window I could see Mum busy by the oven; she was not looking my way. Very well; there was only one thing to be done, and I nerved myself to do it. It was wrong, dreadful, obscene, worse than anything in the Old Testament; but I would do it. I loaded the air gun, put the muzzle against the snail's shell, and pulled the trigger.

I did not know what would happen. Of course the snail would die – it could not choose otherwise – but I had braced myself to endure something appalling, apocalyptic: a total eclipse perhaps, and a Great Voice speaking to me out of the darkness. Or maybe – worst punishment of all – Mum calling from the kitchen, 'Tony! I saw you! You cruel, disgusting boy!'

But nothing like that happened. Nothing happened at all. The sun continued to shine on the row of back gardens; the tits and blackbirds fluttered about; the mowing machine next door churned steadily on. God was silent. And the snail, apart from a neat hole in its roof and a certain amount of frothing, looked none the worse for wear; but I could imagine the pain and panic dismay it must be feeling. I put my foot on the poor beast to end its suffering. One sharp crunch – then a splodgy mess on the slab of York stone.

To shoot a sitting snail at point blank range must be the ultimate in depravity. But I did it; I confess my guilt; it has long been a burden to me. Even now I know that I am lightening the story, trying to make it sound funny; but I am only half succeeding. In truth it is not a very funny story at all.

I was nine when we left York Road and moved to the flat. It was only round the corner, but the move made me feel odd for a while – like being someone else. When I came home now in the school holidays I shared a bedroom with Dad; I enjoyed getting to know him better, though he did have some funny ways. I threw a paper dart one day that landed on top of the wardrobe, and when I climbed on a chair to retrieve it I found lots and lots of empty whisky bottles lying on their sides – fifteen, twenty of them. What on earth were they doing up there? Why store a lot of useless old bottles? And of all places on top of a wardrobe? I was just going to call Mum and tell her what I had found; then I stopped. No one could have put those bottles up there except Dad; he must be hiding them for some private reason of his own. In that case I would not give away his secret. I climbed down off the chair and said nothing about the bottles, either to Mum or to him.

We lived in the flat for only a couple of years; then Dad said we could not afford that either, so we moved to a 'Residential Hotel' – a whole series of them in fact. There was not a tinned sardine to choose between the Hesketh Park Hydro, the Windsor, the Clairemont and the Avondale; they all smelled of dust and dishwater; they all employed dubious headwaiters with crumpled shirtfronts and gravy-stained clothes; they all gave shelter to a flock of interchangeable old people, so shrunken with age that when I glanced into the 'Residents' Lounge' their heads did not appear above the backs of the armchairs.

I disliked the hotels one and all, but I became good friends with the page boy at the Avondale. Alf was no bigger than me though he was eighteen; his hair grew in a cow's lick and he smelled of metal polish; he showed me how to play snooker, and he could whip a lighted cigarette into his mouth with a flick of his tongue. The cigarette would vanish into his mouth, but no smoke came out of his nose. He stood staring at me with a look of injured innocence; then he opened his mouth, emitted a billow of smoke, gave another flick of his tongue – and there would be the lighted cigarette again between his lips.

'Good heavens!' I said. 'How did you do that?'

'Dead easy.' Alf's tone was lofty. 'Me Dad taught me how. He learned it in the Army. Wasn't your Dad in the Army?'

Alf assumed that all Dads served in the Army, and the first humane principle every father taught his son was how to conceal a lighted cigarette in his mouth.

'Er – no. Actually he wasn't.'

I hoped my hesitation would imply that the Army might have been fine for Alf's Dad, but my father had been in something far more dangerous, far more secret. But Alf was not impressed; he looked at me with condescension.

'Well,' he said. 'You've got a few things to learn, haven't you?'

Winter holidays in Southport were bleak. There were occasional days when the light was clear and the air crackled; then you could just make out Blackpool Tower across the shallow waters to the north. Mostly it rained, and when it was not raining the grey clouds were like a giant's long johns thrown over the dustbin of the earth. The light faded in the early afternoon, and the air struck chill; then folk made up their fires with big lumps of coal and shovelled half a bucket of slack on top so that black smoke poured from all the chimneys. Southport was a pleasant, kindly town, full of generous-hearted people; beautiful it was not. But that did not matter to me; I enjoyed everything, even the bleakness. Why not? I was alive. And I was blessed with a mother who had an amused, challenging attitude to every day, every hour; she dared the separate minutes to be dull, and she dared me to accept them dully.

'Look, look!' she would say, glancing over my shoulder at the playing cards spread before me on the carpet. 'You can put the red Jack on the black Queen.'

'Oh, so I can,' I said. I was never much good at cards, not even at Patience.

'That's right. And now what?'

'I don't know,' I said. 'What?'

'Oh, come on, Bunt. I'm not going to do it for you. Look. Just look.'

And of course there was the move staring me in the face. 'Ooooh – I see.'

'Ooooh,' she mocked. 'Yes – that's right. And now the six on the seven, which leaves a space – and my goodness you're going out. Well done.'

E could make an adventure out of a game of Patience, but she was never one for the cold and wet; so on winter days I went for long walks by myself. The glass shelters along the promenade stood empty; swirls of sand and old toffee papers piled up in the corners; on the artificial lake the wind sliced the tops off the waves and whipped the spray against the stacks of upturned rowing boats; at the far end of the pier, with only the gulls to keep them wild company, two workmen laboured to replace some rotten planks. I took a joy in these solitary walks, and sometimes I would be rewarded by a glimpse of the shrimping carts coming back from work. First I would hear the muffled voices of the men calling to one another in the mist; then the rhythmic beat of hooves splashing through the shallows; then up the big horses would come, sea water pouring from their flanks, and the oil-skinned men swaying high above them as the wheels came free from the suck of the sand.

A cart reined in beside me one day. 'Hey. Youngster. D'you want a ride?'

The face looking down on me was so powerful, so gnawed by wind and weather, that I could not speak. I was looking at a being from another world – Poseidon himself, or one of his sons, risen from the salty depths.

'I said, d'you want a ride?'

'Oh,' I managed. 'Well – thank you very much.'

'Put your foot on the hub, and I'll give you a pull.'

He reached down a wet, leathery hand and with one heave lifted me into the cart. I stood beside him, clinging to the side, while the mass of grey-brown shrimps slithered about at our feet. He shook the reins, the horse leaned into the harness, and we rolled up the cobbled ramp onto the deserted promenade, and turned north.

Abruptly he asked, 'What's your name, lad?'

'Quayle,' I said. 'Tony Quayle.' My voice, my very name, sounded ludicrous, effete. It did not seem to offend him.

'Quayle? Oh, ay? Mine's Smith.'

Conversation lapsed. The sea god clicked his tongue at the steaming horse, and I tried not to stand on the shrimps and squash them.

At last I ventured, 'Mr Smith – '

'Sorry?' I was not sure what he had said.

'Me name is Smudger.'

'Smudger?' Again I was ashamed of my inadequate, genteel accent.

'Ay, that's me name.' He spoke slowly, with long pauses for cogitation between each sentence. 'Me son's a Smudger too. And so's me feyther. And his feyther before him. Smudgers, every one of us. Me and my family's been shrimpin' here for more than two hundred years.'

'Really? That's a long time.'

'Ay. It is that. And all of us have been Smudgers.'

By now we were almost outside the Avondale Hotel. 'Mr Smith – ' I ventured. I could not possibly address this Triton as 'Smudger'. 'Could I get down here, please?'

'Get down? Why?'

I glanced at the hotel. I must not sound apologetic; I must not be disloyal. 'Because I live here', I said.

He reined in and gave me a hand down.

'Thank you,' I said. 'Thank you very much.'

'Live here, do you?' He turned his impassive, mediaeval face, and I saw him taking in the ugly, red-brick front of the hotel, the net-curtained windows, the name board from which the gold lettering was flaking. Then he looked down at me again, and there was something of Alf's pitying expression in his eyes.

'Well, lad – take care of thysen.'

He gave the reins a shake, and rumbled off without looking back, the huge shrimp net sticking out over the tailboard.

CHAPTER 6

EVERY AUGUST E WOULD ARRANGE some great adventure; it might last for only two weeks, but she saw to it that we always went somewhere different. She was like a bear, nudging her cub to venture further afield and learn the land that was his inheritance. One summer we stayed with our cousins, the Harraps, in Merthyr Tydfil, and I met scores of other Welsh cousins – Davies's and Pearces. I felt great pride to have even one-eighth kinship with such a people as the Welsh – people who could sing as they did, cut coal as they did, tame the roaring blast furnaces and make them to pour out rivers of molten steel.

Another time we went to Cornwall. I swam in Sennen Cove, ate Cornish pasties, caught mackerel and learnt to row a heavy boat using both oars. I was taken to see a great ruined castle, Tintagel.

'King Arthur's Tintagel? Where he was born?' I was incredulous; I had not known that it was a real place.

'That's it.'

I gazed at the crumbling shell and told myself that where I stood, on this very cliff top, Arthur himself had stood – and Guinevere, and Lancelot, and Gawain, and Mordred. They were not just a legend; they had been real people; they had lived, and lived here in this very place, this southernmost rocky tip of England. So they were part of me too. And I was part of them. Indeed and indeed.

There was a summer when we stayed at an inn on Ullswater and I walked up the winding pass to Martindale, a valley of scattered sheep farms with a beck running through it. On either side the fells rose in bare, impartial dignity. 'We have nothing to do with you transients,' they said. 'We have seen the centuries pass, and we shall still be here, enduring, when you and your kind are vanished and forgotten.'

Along the crest of the eastern ridge ran the High Street, the Roman road that had once linked the XXth Legion at Chester with the soldiers who manned the furthest outposts of the Empire: the men on Hadrian's Wall.

There was a tiny church in Martindale, beautiful in its simplicity and possessing two treasures: a stone pedestal brought down from the Roman road and now consecrated as a Christian font, and an ancient yew tree from which the men of Martindale had cut their bows 500 years ago. If I put out my hand I was touching the stone that Roman soldiers had leant their backs against; if I fingered the leathery fronds of the yew I was at only one remove from the bowmen who, outnumbered and weak with dysentery, had stood against the mounted chivalry of France at Agincourt, and cut them down. The past felt very close in Martindale; you could feel it, almost hear it breathe.

Of all E's summer achievements nothing equalled the great fishing holiday in Scotland; advance news of it came in one of her letters to Abberley.

'Bunt,' she wrote. 'We are going next hols to Scotland – a little place called Tyndrum, near the borders of Perthshire and Argyll. There's a great friend coming too. His name is Kingsley Lewis. He is a doctor and lives in South Wales. He is going to teach you how to fish for trout. I hope you're excited!'

I was beside myself. I had been brought up on *Kidnapped* and *Catriona*; I knew all about Bonnie Prince Charlie and the brutal massacre of the Highlanders at Culloden. Scotland, to my mind, was the most romantic country in the whole world. And now I was going there!

'Mr Ashton, sir – ' I was eleven now, and had moved up the school till I sat at his table for meals. 'Please, sir – '

'Yes, Tony. What is it?'

I had got his attention at last. It had taken long enough: all through the boiled cod and carrots, all through the sago pudding.

'I've just had a letter from home, sir. We're going to Scotland next hols.'

'Are you? Good.' He smiled and turned away, his eye weighing up the chattering boys, sorting them out into balanced teams for the afternoon's cricket.

'Could you tell me, sir – do they all wear kilts in Scotland?'

'What's that? Kilts?' He was jotting down the teams now on the back of an old envelope; he held the envelope in his thumbless hand and his little gold pencil in the other. 'Oh, yes. I dare say.'

He was not listening to me! All he could think of was cricket. Cricket! And I was going to Scotland!

'And bagpipes, sir?' I must engage him somehow. 'Do they play bagpipes a lot?'

'Bagpipes?' Mr Ashton brought his attention back from the boys at the far end of the dining hall. For the first time he seemed to take in what I was saying. 'Bagpipes?' he repeated, in bewilderment. 'What on earth are you talking about? Look – shut up for a minute, will you? Can't you see I'm busy?'

I shut up. But for the rest of term my thoughts were not in Abberley, not in England; they had flown ahead to hills purple with heather, where the pipes skirled and clansmen leapt from crag to crag, brandishing their claymores on the rugged, untamed borders of Perthshire and Argyll.

As it turned out, there were a few hazards before ever I reached Scotland. I came home ('home' was now the Windsor; we had left the Avondale) to find that Mum and Dad had given me a fabulous pre-birthday present: a trout rod, a reel, and a box of flies. I spun the reel; I opened the metal box and gazed at the feathery, barbed jewels; I pulled the sections of the rod out of their case and fitted them together.

Dad said, 'Oh, I wouldn't do that in the bedroom, old chap.'

'Why not?' He was always so stupidly over-anxious. 'Look, Dad! See how it bends!'

'Because there's no room in here. And – steady on – mind out! You'll break the lampshade.'

'Don't worry. I'll take care. Look, Dad! Just see how whippy it is.'

Pang! I hit the contraption that dangled from the ceiling; the light bulb exploded and the glass bowl flew into smithereens.

Dad forgave me at once (I sometimes wished he would not be quite so forgiving) but I felt very chastened; and it took ages to pick the glass splinters out of the carpet and blankets.

I had a more serious setback over Stirling. There was a famous railway poster at that time entitled 'STIRLING. GATEWAY TO THE NORTH.' It was the painting of a knight in chain mail, carrying the banner of Saint George, and just about to ride his horse under a massive portcullis. At that very moment he had turned his head as though to answer some question that had been thrown at him. His expression was not arrogant; it was not humble either; it was challenging. And through some trick of the painter he seemed to be looking straight at me, as though it was I who had asked the question. I was fascinated by this poster. What was it he had been asked? It might have been important. On the other hand, it could have been quite trivial. *Who are you?* – something like that.

I longed to know, and I was convinced that if I kept my eyes skinned as we passed through Stirling I would see that horseman. I might only catch a glimpse of him, but at the very least I would see the battlements and the portcullis under which he had just ridden.

And now – catastrophe! – here was Dad telling me that we would travel north by the night train. I was dismayed.

'Will it be dark, then, when we go through Stirling?'

'Stirling? Oh, yes. The middle of the night. You'll be fast asleep.'

'Then you must wake me up. Promise, Dad. Promise to wake me up when we get there.'

'All right, old chap. But what's so special about Stirling?'

I could not tell him; it was too complicated. I knew that Crusaders had disappeared long ago; I had never met, never would meet, a knight in chain mail with a banner in his hand and a big red cross on his chest, riding his charger into the Town Hall. I knew I lived in a world of trams, and steam-engines, and newspapers, and golf-pro's; but for me they were shadows compared with that Crusader; he was more alive than they could ever be. He would always be there, riding into the castle, and he would find some way of showing himself to me. At the same time, balanced against this conviction, was a painful suspicion that my vision might be nothing but a dream, an illusion, that I might be hankering after the impossible. If so, then I wanted to face my absurdity alone, not have it pointed out to me by grown-ups.

In the railway carriage I rolled my raincoat into a bundle to make a pillow, and over it I spread a flag I had somehow got hold of. The Lion of Scotland, rampant, black on a yellow ground. A proud flag, but an extremely scratchy one. Mum pointed out the handicap.

'Yes, darling. It's very handsome. And if you sleep with your face on it you'll have no skin left by morning.'

'No, it's what I want, Mum. If not, I won't lie down at all. I just won't.'

'All right. But don't blame me when you wake up with a sore face. Now, go to sleep – there's a good boy.'

'I'll try to, Mum. But I'll never be able to. I'm too excited.'

But of course I did; and of course they never woke me at Stirling. When I opened my eyes we were in Scotland, and the proud flag was lying where I had thrown it in my sleep – on the floor.

As for the horseman, though I said goodbye to him as a reality, he endures in my mind more substantial than any dream. I can see him this minute, turning in his saddle to look at me; and I am aware that for years I have been in error. He has turned, not to make reply, but to demand an answer of me. And now that it confronts me in my old age I find the question anything but trivial.

You . . . Yes, you standing there . . . Who are you?

It will not suffice to serve up a jest in reply. The question bites deep. Somehow it must be answered.

We spent three weeks in Scotland, and in all that time I never saw a kilt, never heard the pipes, never saw a clansman brandishing a claymore; but the mountains and lochs were all I had dreamed of, and the hotel was a fishing inn where the day's catches were laid out on the flagstones in the hall. Tyndrum itself was a village where you could at a pinch hire a horse and cart, but not a motorcar; there was not a petrol pump within miles. The village slept peacefully, not dreaming of what it was destined to become – a thriving, driving, gobble-and-go, road junction.

Dr Lewis – Kingsley, as I soon called him – had arrived from South Wales before us. He was a big man in his early forties, clean-shaven, with thick, greying hair plastered down in the fashion of those days. I took to him at once, without reserve. He was a quiet man, but quietly he made things happen. He was not like Dad, who was never too sure of himself. He was not like the masters at Abberley; perhaps, being a doctor, he knew less about books than they did and more about living and dying.

Dad did not fish – did not want to fish; he went for enormous walks every day carrying maps and a compass. Kingsley, Mum and I went fishing for trout on one of the lochs around Tyndrum – Tulla, Dochart, or little Lochan na Bi. Kingsley taught me the names of the flies, how to tie them to the cast, how to tie the cast to the line; he taught me to watch for a fish to rise, then drop the cast right in the centre of the spreading ripples. He was so patient and cheerful, even when the midges were biting us alive, that I never thought how bored he must be with lochs and how he must be longing for his salmon rod and the fast-flowing Orchy. He did get one day's salmon-fishing, but that was all.

There were two brothers staying at the hotel whom I regarded with awe and admiration. The Vernons had an enormous Hispano Suiza, and they had come to shoot stags. Their open touring car, bright yellow, was the most beautiful and powerful that I had seen, and to go deer-stalking seemed to me a most heroic sport. They had no luck for a few days, but every evening they came back from the hills looking leaner and tougher, more and more tanned, with bright handkerchiefs knotted round their necks.

One evening, just before dinner, I heard the unmistakable thunder of the Hispano pulling up outside the hotel. I rushed out to look, and saw, roped down across the back seat, a large antlered body. The great spread of horns had twelve points.

'Kingsley!' I yelled. 'Come and look. The Vernons have got a "Royal".'

The Vernons were climbing out of the front seat, collecting their guns and gear; guests were strolling out of the hotel, drinks in hand, to congratulate them. I walked to the back of the car and looked again at the stag. His body sagged down on the leather cushions, but his neck was twisted upwards, and his great antlers projected far beyond the width of the car. His tongue lolled from the side of his mouth and there was a trickle of congealed blood dangling from it. I felt a savage shock of revulsion. Why should this wonderful animal, all covered with fur, be so violently brought low? An hour or two ago the mountains and the sky had belonged to him, and now he was roped down in ignominious death whilst we naked, pink monkeys crowded round his corpse and poked at his antlers with our puny fingers. It was indecent, revolting. And the Vernons, so pleased with themselves, were no better than me when I had shot the snail. At least I had had the grace to be ashamed.

It was no use Mum explaining to me that a certain number of stags had to be shot each year, or the herds would grow too big.

'Then do it quietly,' I said. 'Don't make such a fuss. There's nothing brave or clever about it.'

From then on I did not admire the Vernons at all, and I avoided looking at the Hispano Suiza.

Kingsley had an infectious cheerfulness that thawed all reserve. There were several children staying at the hotel and he soon had us playing stump cricket in the evenings; the grown-ups stood by and watched, indulgent but aloof. But the games were so uproarious that before long everyone wanted to join in, women as well as men. Then it was discovered that Kingsley could play the piano, so every night he was made to sit down and perform. He could play anything, from Bach to jazz, and every night I fell asleep to the sound of the piano down below. The hotel fused into a single family, all revolving round this quiet, amused man.

'Mum – where does Kingsley live?' I was sitting on her bed while she brushed her hair.

'I told you, darling. In South Wales. He's a doctor in Pontypridd. You like him, don't you?'

'Yes, I do. How did you and Dad get to know him?'

'He was a friend of your Uncle Reg when Reg was training to be a doctor in London. That's how I first met him.'

'But that's years ago, Mum.'

71

'Only three. And last year – you'd gone back to school – he came to stay with us for the Grand National. That was when we planned this holiday.' She began to powder her face, and her eyes met mine in the mirror. 'Bunt – '

'Yes?'

'Kingsley says you can come and stay with him in your next school hols. Would you like that?'

'Rath*er*!'

'Good. Then we'll fix it up.'

Even Dad seemed happy on that holiday, though I did not see a great deal of him. He enjoyed his huge walks over the moors and came back cheerfully tired in the evenings. He did not seem to mind being on his own, and his normally pale face became quite brown. But he found crises difficult to cope with.

I was sick one night and could not get to the basin in time. Dad made a brave attempt to clean me up, but he soon had to shoot out of the room, retching. It was Kingsley who dealt with the mess – and did not make me feel guilty in the process.

'Poor old chap. Never mind. It happens to the best of us. Now, I've got a spare bed in my room. Why don't you hop into that?'

No fuss, no retching, and the beastly puddle of sick mopped up in a moment.

The glorious holiday ended. Kingsley took the train to Pontypridd; Mum, Dad and I returned to Southport; and in due course I went back to Abberley.

The term was only a few weeks old when I got a letter from Kingsley. There was such a din going on in the classroom that I took the letter into the lavatory and read it in cubicled peace. I read it several times, and it made such an impression on me that now, after more than sixty years, I can vouch not only for the gist of the letter but for some of his actual words and phrases.

He started by saying that I might think it odd, his writing to me in this way, but there were a few things he wanted to say that I might find worth listening to.

'Whatever you are doing,' he went on, 'do it flat out. Go for it. You may not succeed – but that doesn't matter. What matters is that you've tried. Never mind if you get hurt. So tackle hard—and if you get hurt you can be proud of it. The same with cricket. You may not be able to bowl or bat well [I could do neither] but anyone has it in him to be a good fielder. So don't funk a ball that is coming at you fast.

[How did he know that I did?] Get your hands to it. It may hurt like blazes, but you'll be glad you stopped it. Much better than pretending you couldn't reach it.'

And he finished, 'I'm looking forward to seeing you here in your next holidays.

Good luck, and love –

KINGSLEY '

I was astonished. No one had ever written or talked to me like that before, certainly not dear old Dad.

I tried to do what Kingsley had said – and it worked. The harder you went at it, the more energy you had; it surged up in you like a demon. Sure, if you tackled really hard you might hurt yourself a bit; but you hurt the other fellow a hell of a lot more. It was a good feeling, exciting, to find this power inside yourself. I got my First XV 'Colours' that term. I wrote to Kingsley to tell him that it was all thanks to him – and that I was counting off the days till I came to visit him in Pontypridd.

The visit was a total failure.

Kingsley lived with his widowed father in a small, bare house that reminded me unpleasantly of the old Quayles and 7 Scarisbrick New Road. The old man had practised medicine himself but was now retired, leaving the practice to Kingsley. He was a querulous old tyrant, always finding fault with his son, endlessly fiddling with the wireless set, a shawl wrapped round his shoulders.

'Kingsley. Kingsley.'

'Yes, Father. What is it?' Kingsley sounded so resigned, so lacking in spirit, so unlike himself.

'This damn wireless set won't work.'

Kingsley drew a deep breath. 'It was working when I went on my rounds this morning.'

'Well, it isn't working now. Listen.' The old devil spun the knobs wantonly; tormented howls came from the set.

Kingsley heaved his tired body from the armchair and examined the thing.

'You've been fiddling with the cat's whisker, Father.'

'I haven't touched it, I tell you. I think it's a valve gone. You promised to get me a new one, but you never did.' The old man pulled his shawl round his neck, and his head stuck out like a petulant tortoise.

Kingsley made no reply, but patiently adjusted the set till, in a minute or two, it worked perfectly.

73

I could not make out what had happened to him. This defeated resignation was not like him. Outwardly he looked the same, but inwardly he was changed – diminished in some way. He had no real solicitude for his father, yet he appeared almost subservient to the old brute, as though he had lost the energy to fight back. The amusement had gone from his eyes, leaving them always sombre. I could appreciate that to live in a gloomy, cold house with a foul-tempered old father would be enough to drive anyone batty – but that was not enough to account for the transformation. Where was the Kingsley whom I had seen waist-deep in the Orchy, his hat stuck with salmon flies? What had happened to the man who told me to get my hand to a hard-driven ball and not to mind if it hurt? I could not understand.

Every day he took me with him on his rounds. Up and down the Rhondda Valley we went, as far as Treorchy and beyond. He had a two-seater Morris, and the radiator cap was a temperature gauge that I had brought him as a present from E. As we drove up and down the steep hills I kept up a ceaseless chattering about the wretched thing.

'Look, Kingsley, look. It's almost boiling.'

'Yes.' That was all he would say – and not always that; sometimes he just grunted.

I must have driven him mad, but I only chattered in order to break the long, unaccountable silences that oppressed me and filled me with unease.

The weather was bitterly cold; a powdering of snow lay over the valleys; outside rows and rows of identical cottages the coal miners squatted on their hunkers. This was the time of the Great Depression; the pits were idle, the winding-gear motionless, the men on the dole.

Kingsley disappeared into one cottage after another, leaving me to sit in the car and keep warm. Sometimes he would be away only a few minutes; other times he would be gone for almost an hour. I could only sit in wretched isolation, ashamed to be so plump and prosperous, so warmly coated, in the midst of such poverty and courage. These were my own people; Grandpa's mother was a Davies – Welsh of the Welsh; yet I could not get out of the car and speak to them. I looked wrong; I spoke wrong; and I was far too young. I could do nothing but sit there and wait for Kingsley.

When at last he emerged from a particularly long visit, I asked, 'Who was that you were seeing?'

He answered shortly, 'Mrs Griffiths.'

'What's wrong with her?'

'Arthritis. And starvation.'

'What can you do to help her?'

'Nothing. She's old. She'll die soon.' He lit a cigarette and opened the window to toss the match out.

We were just passing a group of miners at a corner, some standing, some squatting, their thin mufflers folded across their chests. I said, 'It's terrible – such hopelessness. Can't they go somewhere else? Do something else?'

I had asked in innocence, almost in desperation. Kingsley replied with such harshness that I felt as though he had struck me. 'Where else can they go? What else can they do? They are coal miners.'

For the rest of his rounds that day we hardly spoke. In the evening, Kingsley sat in silence while his father, wrapped in his shawl, snuffled and sniffed and played with the knobs of the wireless.

I was thankful to climb into the train and go home.

'Did you have a good time, darling?' It was E's first question when she met me at the station.

One of the troubles with being young is that you are so desperately anxious to tell your elders what they want to hear that you are led into lying. I said, 'Oh, yes. It was lovely.' Then a nagging honesty forced me to add, 'It was a bit awful too.'

E laughed. 'How could it be both awful and lovely?'

I said, 'Well, it was Kingsley.'

'Kingsley? Why? What about him?'

'He was – I don't know – miserable somehow. And his father is just horrible to him.'

We jiggled along in the taxi, and she turned away from me to look out of the window. We were not going to the Windsor; we had moved now to the Hesketh Park Hotel.

I went on, 'Kingsley really needs cheering up. He's not like he was – not at all. D'you think we might go to Scotland again next year?'

There was no answer for a while. Mum was busy blowing her nose and searching in her bag for money. Then she said, in an offhand way, 'I don't know. We'll see.'

Summer came, and we did not go to Scotland. Mum explained the reasons. 'It's terribly expensive. And Dad can't come. He's got some big problems in the office. He has to stay here in Southport and work. So it would be an awful waste of money – just you and me going.'

'But what about Kingsley? Can't he come?'

'No. I think he wants to go fishing by himself. Somewhere in Wales.'

I was crestfallen. I felt guilty too. 'Is it my fault?' I asked.

'You old idiot! How could it be your fault?'

'Because it must be such a bore, teaching me to fish. And I know I talked a terrible lot when I was staying with him.'

Mum laughed. 'No, it's nothing to do with you. It's just that it's important for men to be on their own sometimes. Don't be sad, Bunt. I know what we'll do.' She looked at me, her eyes full of fun. 'You and I will have a marvellous time together. We'll go and stay with the Pughs in Cumberland. We'll be "paying guests" – because the Pughs don't have much money. And they'd love to have us.'

'Will I be able to fish?'

She made a little noise to signify that fishing did not matter one way or the other. 'No – I doubt if you will. But there'll be plenty of other things to do. There are lakes, and mountains – '

'And moors? And heather?'

'I'm not too sure about the heather,' she admitted. 'But there are lots of moors. Remember Ullswater? And Martindale? Well then, cheer up. You and I can manage without trout-fishing, for heaven's sake. And we'll show Dr Kingsley Lewis that we can manage without him either.' And she pulled such a funny, clown-like face that it made me laugh in spite of my dumps. 'That's better. Cumberland – here we come. Think of it, Bunt. It's where Beatrix Potter lives. Where Mrs Tiggy-winkle does the laundry.'

What a zest for life she had. In good times or in bad she lived every minute up to the hilt, and she led me to do the same.

We had a happy holiday. The Pughs were a pair of loveable eccentrics: Kenneth, monosyllabic and gentle, wearing plus fours and thick-lensed glasses; Madge, with tangerine hair that was going dangerously thin, but indomitably ruling her own and every other roost. They drove us everywhere in their little two-seater, Mum and I huddled together in the dicky-seat, cowering from the Cumbrian rain under an old tarpaulin. We went to the Sheepdog Trials at Patterdale, and I backed the winner of the Hound Trail. The bookie paid me with a massive silver piece, a 'crown'. I meant to keep it all my life in memory of the foxhound who had run so bravely; but it lay in a drawer for a year or two, and then I lost it. A pity: I have never seen another five-shilling piece.

One day I followed Kenneth's directions and crossed a moor of squelching moss to find the ruins of a Roman fort. Desolate and remote, it lay close to a black tarn among a few rowan trees and wind-bent bushes. It was a small place; it could not have held more than twenty men – thirty at most, and they must have been damnably lonely up there. Were they local men, I wondered? From Spain? From Gaul? From Rome itself? Had I perhaps any of their invader blood in my own veins to mingle with the

Viking, the Anglo-Saxon, the Celt and the Jew? I picked my way back over the mossy tussocks and marvelled at how powerfully attached I was to this land and people. Britain did not belong to me, not one square foot of it, but by strong ties of blood I belonged to Britain, to the men and women who had gone before and made me.

The Pughs lived in a pink-washed little house set in an orchard of fruit trees. It had been built in the eighteenth century as a farm, and it had the simplicity of a child's drawing. The sitting room was on the upper floor and ran the whole width of the house; it was a sunny room that smelt deliciously of beeswax. On the walls hung eight or ten Chinese paintings, some inheritance of Kenneth's. They were of exquisite draughtsmanship and painted in the most delicate pinks, and greens, and blues. They were however all variations on a revolting theme – the torture and execution of criminals. Each frame contained a dozen or so of these miniatures – men suspended by their pigtails; men with their limbs clamped in heavy, wooden blocks; men having their heads cut off, the blood spurting from their severed necks. From a distance they looked pretty and elegant, but when I looked at them closely, as I was frequently drawn to do in spite of myself, they were so gruesome that I felt sick. It was in this drawing room, when we were alone one day, that E laid down her sewing and turned to look at me.

'Bunt,' she said, 'I have something important to tell you.'

I knew what she was going to say before she uttered the words.

'Dad and I are separating.'

Of course they were. What else could they do? But I sat quiet and said nothing.

She told me the whole miserable story of their marriage and the emptiness of their life together; how, after my birth, they had never lived together as man and wife. My father had been drinking secretly long before they were married; his parents knew, but had not warned her. She had done her utmost to back him up in his work and give him a background, but the last few years had been disastrous. He had somehow lost a large sum of money belonging to a client, and had made this good only by selling our house in York Road. Since then there had been worse bungling; he had made so many mistakes that his senior partners had at last decided that they must be rid of him; it would all be handled discreetly, but go he must. He himself was now in a state of maudlin collapse, largely brought on by alcohol, and he had been warned by his doctor that he must immediately stop all work. After he had recovered from his collapse he might be able to resume his post as Magistrates' Clerk, since the duties were not onerous, but that depended on whether or not Mr Briggs would see him through this period of nervous breakdown. In short, he could no longer support either E or myself; we must fend for ourselves.

'So what will happen?' I was not in the least dismayed; I was exhilarated, rather. This cloud, never spoken of but always present, had been hanging over us for years; now Mum and I could adventure out together. Where we went did not matter; anywhere, everywhere, would be fun with her.

She told me that Grandpa had undertaken to pay for the rest of my schooling, and that she had decided to move to London and look for a job.

'But Mum, you're not trained. What work could you do?'

'Good God. I'm not helpless. I can sew. And I'm a damn good cook.'

Her domestic skills, real though they were, sounded so inadequate that it made us both laugh. Then she became serious again. 'There's something else I have to tell you. And this is more difficult.' She turned her head away slightly.

Again I knew what she was about to say. I had never consciously thought of it, but I must have had an awareness of the situation, for I felt no shock when she said, 'Kingsley and I have been lovers.'

They had met – she had told me this before – through her brother Reg; their love for one another had been immediate, but their lives were set so far apart that they had been able to meet but little. It was a hopeless love; it had no future. All this while her head had been turned away; now she looked straight at me.

'Can you understand, Bunt? Do you blame me?'

Blame her? Never. She was my mother. Nothing that she did could be wrong. Besides, without any knowledge of such matters, I had an innocent understanding.

'Why don't you marry Kingsley now?' I asked.

She gave a wry smile. 'He wants me to. But there's a problem.'

'What problem? If you and Dad are separating – it's simple.'

'The problem is you, my darling.'

'Me?' I was aghast.

'Yes, you. Oh, you're too young to be burdened with all this.'

'No, I'm not. I understand. But how can I be a problem? I'm very fond of Kingsley. I really love him.'

She gave a deep sigh. 'Divorce is a damnable business. Married people can agree to separate, but they can't get divorced by agreement. That is the law. In order to be divorced, one of the two has to be what is called "the guilty party". As a lawyer, Dad could never be that. He could never work in Southport again. It would finish him. So he will never give me grounds for divorcing him.'

'Then let him divorce you – because of Kingsley.' I spoke as though I were Solomon himself.

'That is what Kingsley wants. But I told you – there's a problem. If I go off with Kingsley, then in the eyes of the law I shall be "the guilty party". The court will give you into Arthur's custody. You would have to go and live with him. And I couldn't allow that. I couldn't leave you to be brought up by Arthur. You know as well as I do that he isn't fit to bring up a . . . a spider.'

The word burst out of her with such unexpected vehemence that it made us laugh again. It was typical of my poor father that he could be the cause of such exasperation and at the same time give so much amusement. It was typical of E too that in her unhappy situation she could find something to laugh at – even at herself.

My mind was suddenly filled with the picture of Kingsley as I had last seen him – all day caring for his patients in their stoic hopelessness; at night coping with his fractious, demanding old father. And there I had been, the obstacle in the way of all his happiness, bouncing up and down in his car, asking fatuous questions. I marvelled he had not struck me.

'Poor Kingsley,' I said. 'What will he do?'

E's laughter faded. 'I don't know. I've brought him a lot of unhappiness. I've told him that I can't marry him. I love him – but my first duty is to you. You didn't ask to come into this world. I'm not going to leave you now.'

'Poor Kingsley,' I said again.

'Oh well. He must find someone else to marry. And he will. He'll make such a wonderful father.' Then she added, more to herself than me, 'And husband.'

We sat in silence for a while. I wished I could help her, but I did not know what comfort I could give. At length she spoke again.

'So I have an idea,' and her eyes travelled unseemingly over the Chinese tortures, 'that Kingsley may not want to see me any more.'

My parents were never divorced; they just separated. E went to London in search of a job. Dad fell into invalidism and retirement; I saw him only half a dozen times more in my life. Mr Briggs, he of the mobile Adam's apple, replaced Dad as a partner in the law firm; it did not surprise me.

Kingsley behaved more drastically. He got into a hot bath, cut his arteries with a razor, and bled to death. He was a quiet man, but one of irreversible decisions.

It had always been assumed that I would one day go to Winchester, an assumption made by E in the first place because that was what she had made up her mind to, and next by me because I had no reason to doubt what she said. At the time I did not know, could not have understood, the full extent of my mother's hopes for me; maturity led me to understand that they were high fantastical. She looked at her chubby-faced boy and saw him as he would be in early middle age – amusing, distinguished, a little grey at the temples, with an enchanting wife and a cluster of adorable children. This admired and influential son of hers would have received several decorations for gallantry – perhaps not a Victoria Cross (that would be aiming a bit too high even for E) but certainly the DSO and at least two MCs. He would be a prominent member of the Bar, hotly tipped as a coming Lord Chancellor.

'I think Grandpa wants me to go into Sumner's,' I had said to her one day.

'Yes.' She put down her sewing and lit a cigarette. 'I dare say he does. But I think the Bar is where you'll finish up. You'll make a splendid barrister. And I shall be so proud of you.'

In her mind there was only one school possible as the springboard for her great design. I do not know why she was so taken with Winchester; none of her family had been there, and she herself had never seen the place, but Winchester was her fixed goal. I think that from the moment she had known she was pregnant her mind was made up on three counts: her child would be a boy, he would be called John Anthony, and he would go to Winchester.

I went along readily enough with her ideas; at twelve-pushing-thirteen you cannot see far ahead, and you do not want to, either. I was a bit uneasy though about the 'Bar'; I had only the haziest notion of what it was, but it sounded rather an airless, indoor profession where men in black, striped trousers and scratchy wigs faced one another across a wooden barrier, a sort of telegraph pole laid on its side; they took it in turns to make crafty speeches and outwit one another. I doubted I would ever have the brains or the stomach for the 'Bar'. But I kept quiet; there would be time enough to argue that out when I left Winchester. Meantime, I looked forward to walking under the same arches, strolling through the same cloisters, as Mr Greenwood and Mr Ashton had done. Something of their spirit, I felt sure, would be handed down to me.

One evening during my last year at Abberley I was in the changing room, scraping the caked mud from my football boots, when Jimmy Stewart came looking for me.

'Mr Ashton wants to see you in his study.'

'Me?'

'Yes, you. So hurry.'

Oh Lord, what had I done wrong? It had to be something serious. But what? I rinsed my hands under the tap (cold water: there was no hot), wiped off the rest of the mud on the sodden roller towel, and ran up the stone stairs towards the 'private side'.

'Ge-dunk-Ge-donk'went the green baize doors, impervious to the feelings of all who pushed through them. Apprehension, guilt, misery, joy – it was all the same to them.

The big front hall was empty, but Mr Ashton was just coming out of his study.

'Ah, Tony – there you are. Good. I wanted to see you.'

I followed him a few steps till we stood in front of the empty marble fireplace, the head of the stuffed hippopotamus protruding from the wall above our heads. He was not in a fury; that was a relief. In fact, he was smiling in his friendliest way.

'I want to have a chat with you about Winchester.'

My entrails froze, and I had the feeling that the earth had shaken slightly.

I said, as nonchalantly as I could, 'Oh yes, sir?'

'Mr Greenwood and I have been talking about your chances of getting in.'

This time there was no mistaking it; the ground under my feet had trembled. Yet nothing had fallen over. The potted palms were still in place; the hippopotamus and the water buffalo went on staring into eternity, and Mr Ashton continued to smile, his thumbless hand resting on the mantelpiece. *Chances?* What was he talking about? I was going to Winchester. It was all settled – had been settled ever since I could remember — just as surely as the sun would rise tomorrow and the next day would be Friday.

'Come as a bit of a blow, has it?' His head was tipped a little to one side in sympathy and concern.

'Yes, it has, rather.'

'The trouble is that Winchester has such a long waiting list that your only hope would be a scholarship. And – frankly — we don't think you'd have much chance of that.'

I wished he would not be so kind. I wished I was not going to cry.

'I never thought I would get a scholarship, sir. I know I couldn't.'

His smile was so regretful and so amused that I had to smile too; and that brought the tears closer.

'Your Maths would have let you down for a start, wouldn't they?'

I nodded. O God, what a fool I had been. The hours that Mr Ashton had spent trying to make me understand Maths. He had cuffed me, mocked me, explained patiently to me – all to no purpose. My mind rejected the entire subject. I was a duffer; that was all there was to it. Of course Winchester would not accept me. What school would?

'Mind you,' Mr Ashton went on, always with that affectionate smile, 'if your father was at Winchester that could make a difference. But I don't think he was, was he?'

He knew jolly well Dad had not been to Winchester. Dad had been to the Southport Grammar School. So why ask?

'No, sir. He wasn't.' A sort of gulping sound broke from me; it was a sob.

I could not adjust my mind to it. Year after year I had been climbing up a flight of stone steps; at the top was the arched doorway into Winchester. And now that I was called on to push the door open I could not do it; I was not strong enough. And it was all my own fault. I looked up at the hippopotamus, but his unchanging eyes offered no solace; he had long forgotten all suffering. I glanced at Mr Ashton's hand, the familiar piece of shrapnel embedded between the tendons; that at least was comforting in an altered world.

'So what will happen?' I asked.

He answered lightly. 'You must work hard and get into Rugby. You're down for Rugby, you know. If you put your mind to it I'm sure you'll pass in very well. And a jolly good school it is. So cheer up.'

'Cheer up'? How could I be cheerful when I had just tripped over my own shoelaces and fallen flat? How could I be cheerful at the prospect of going to Rugby – always supposing I got in? *Rugby!* The very word had a thumping sound; it conjured up a beefy, bashing sort of school. How could I be cheerful when I had to tell my mother that I had destroyed all her dreams? The tears were pouring down my face; I knew it, but there was nowhere to hide.

Mr Ashton laid a hand on my heaving shoulder. 'Don't take it so hard. Listen to me. Listen.'

I listened, wetly.

'I'm going to tell you something – and I mean it. I promise you – promise – that in the long run it doesn't matter a hoot which school we go to. Each of us has to find his own way in life. Schools are not that important.'

He did his best to console me, but I was inconsolable. At last he hit on something that cut through my sodden wrappings of woe.

'Don't think, Tony, that all my family went to Winchester.'

'They didn't?'

'No, indeed. Two of my uncles went to Rugby. They both played cricket for the school.'

That was something to cling to – a slender link with the wonderful family of Ashtons.

'I'll tell you something else,' he went on. 'Rugby is the only cricket team – not just in the country, but in the world – that doesn't wear white shirts.'

'No? What do they wear?'

'They wear blue shirts.'

'Blue?'

'Pale blue.'

Five minutes later Mr Ashton gave me a final pat and sent me back through the green baize doors, a happy boy. Rugby sounded a fine school, an altogether different sort of school. Everybody went to Winchester, but I was going to Rugby.

CHAPTER 7

'QUAYLE – YOU NASTY, DIRTY, MINDLESS YOUNG WORM –
stand up on the bench.'

The Reverend E.F. Waddy had a tuberous face; it bore a resemblance, especially when adorned with its mortarboard, to an elongated potato; his accent was unblemished New South Wales. In his youth Mr Waddy had played cricket for Australia, and his aim with a piece of chalk was deadly. He was no intellectual, but he was a great disciplinarian; which was probably why he was saddled with teaching Mathematics to us new boys in the bottom form at Rugby. It was his task to clear away the fog that surrounded Logarithms, Sines and Cosines, and reveal them to us in all their shimmering beauty. For me the fog remained impenetrable: hence my present elevation to the bench. I knew from experience that there would follow a period of target practice with pieces of chalk, and that before the lesson ended I would be sure to hear,

'Quayle – you nasty, dirty, mindless young worm – stand on the top of the desk.'

Up I would have to climb; and there, balanced unsteadily on the sloping surface, I would stay for the rest of the lesson.

I did not mind the ritual mockery; I did not mind being treated as a fool; as far as Maths were concerned, I was one. I accepted the role and played it without difficulty. Mr Waddy felt no more malice towards me than he did to all boys – possibly less, for I was his jester; I kept the class amused and made his lessons come alive.

In the holidays after I had left Abberley, benevolent elders had assumed a roguish expression and said to me, 'So, Tony, you're off to Rugby. You must be looking forward to that.'

84

I had answered, 'Oh, I am. Rath*er*.'

It was the answer that was expected of me – and it happened to be true. I knew I had reached the top of my little prep-school beanstalk, and I was impatient to start climbing the next – the one that would take me up into giant land, into the unknown clouds of manhood. I could not imagine what Rugby would be like, so I tried to prepare myself by reading *Tom Brown's Schooldays*; it was so tedious that I soon gave up.

A few months later the same elders asked, with the same conspiratorial cheerfulness, 'How's Rugby? Enjoying it?'

And I replied, with feigned enthusiasm, 'Oh yes, thank you. It's great.'

It was not 'great' at all: it was ugly, cold, challenging, impersonal and unexpected. But since I discovered in myself an equal and unexpected store of resilience, the scales were kept reasonably balanced between the grisly and the acceptable. After Rugby, I told myself, life could only improve; and in that faith I just got on with it.

All the same, standing up aloft in Mr Waddy's classroom, looking down on the scuffed heads of my fellows – some busy writing, some chewing their pencils in perplexity – I did feel a certain weariness of spirit. How many years of this Caliban existence must I endure before I was free, before I could start living? Through the window I could see one side of New Quad and a wall of the Chapel. The whole group of buildings was designed in the Italianate-Victorian style; it reeked of Victorian attitudes and morality; it was impossible for us boys, locked in its classrooms, to escape its Victorian influence. *Fear God* was the message it proclaimed. *Be a stalwart fellow. Do your duty and accept the inevitable without flinching.* It proclaimed nothing of the subtle, mysterious, mind-boggling, once-and-for-all adventure of actually being alive.

I could see, too, the patch of grass in the middle of the Quad where the beaks ('beaks' we called them – not 'masters') congregated between classes. It was empty now, but soon there would be twenty of them out there, hobbing and nobbing together; they were like a flock of crows in their black gowns and mortarboards. Burst a paper bag and you would see the whole lot take to the air, cawing and flapping.

Oh God, how much longer would I have to stand up here? How much longer would this boring lesson go on? How much longer must I go on being a boy? I shut my eyes and made the wish that of late had sprung more and more often to my mind. It was an unusual wish, occasioned by a Southport acquaintance – one Basil Himbury who had lived, together with his parents, at our last dismal hotel. Basil was twenty-one and something between a 'bounder' and a 'rotter'. Of this dubious character – not yet in trouble with the police, but heading that way – I was deeply envious. He had no apparent means of support, but was never short of cash; he was a devilish snooker player; he had nicotine-stained fingers, a Ronald Colman moustache, and a beat-up old Alvis with a strap round its bonnet. What most aroused my envy was his flaunted intimacy with a girl called Dulcie – the sexiest, dishiest manicurist you ever saw. For months now, whenever I saw the new moon or took the first bite of the first cherry, I had made the same wish.

'I wish I was twenty-one and had a sports Alvis.'

Being only thirteen I felt the gods might think me a bit presumptuous to ask for what I really wanted, but I was confident that if the first two wishes were granted, the third would quickly follow of itself.

A piece of chalk stung my ear. I ducked, turned to face the thrower, and caught the next piece full in the face.

'Yes, Quayle. Pay attention. You won't find the answer outside the window.'

From my perch I replied meekly, 'No, sir.'

'Now then – let's see if any of you boys are awake. Quick – before I can count three. Who was the last wicketkeeper to score a century in first-class cricket? One . . . two . . . three. I knew it. You're all asleep. No, I'm not going to tell you. Find out for yourselves before next lesson. Oh, get down Quayle. I'm sick of seeing you up there. Now here's your prep for tonight. A cricket ball leaves a bowler's hand at 83.7 miles per hour. It travels twenty yards, losing speed at the rate of fourteen feet per second per second . . . '

But long before he had reached the end of the problem my mind was stampeding away. 'I can't do it. I don't want to do it. What is more, I bloody won't do it.'

I appreciated how lucky I was to go to a Public School; I was grateful to Grandpa for stepping in and paying my school fees; but for all that, I could never develop any affection for Rugby. I got on well with boys and masters; I was not bullied; I was not punished more than I deserved, and I was not a failure. But from the day I arrived, with my old Abberley trunk and tuck box, I looked forward to the day when I should leave.

The House to which I had been assigned was a fairly recent red-brick building. It is now called Tudor House, though there is nothing Tudor about it save its emblem of a rose. Two tiled corridors, one above the other, gave access to the studies – a euphemism for four rows of hutches. A few senior boys had studies to themselves; others had to share. These double studies were, to say the least, cramped; if a pair of calves had been confined in one of them the offending farmer would have been taken to court by the RSPCA.

There was another imbalance in the design of the House; while the dining hall was big enough to accommodate the seventy-odd inmates at one sitting, the same could not be said of the lavatory: it was brutally short of seating accommodation. The 'Topos' as it was called (Greek=the 'Place') had no doors to any of its eight cubicles; under relaxed conditions – on a summer's evening, say, with the light fading and the birds twittering outside – this lack of privacy made for a cogenial, club-like atmosphere; but under pressure, after breakfast for example, the 'Topos' was a scene of desperation.

'You finished soon, Hawksworth? I'm in trouble.'

Hawksworth, senior and serene, trousers round his ankles and a book of Advanced Trigonometry open on his knees, looks up.

'Yes – just finishing. But Thompson's bagged it. He's next.'

In the adjoining cubicle Pringle, a very new boy, is bent almost double and bright red in the face.

'Oh, for God's sake Pringle, do get a move on. You're taking for ever.'

But Pringle, new boy though he is and devoid of all privileges, cannot be hurried, cannot be dragged from his throne. The 'Topos' is the only place in the House, in the whole School, where the new boy has his own unassailable rights: as long as he wants to go on sitting there he is protected by mediaeval Rights of Sanctuary.

Backhouse was the boy with whom I seemed destined to share a study till death did us part. We had been paired together in our first term, and so we stayed together, a grouchy old married couple, mutually resentful but unwilling to hurt each other's feelings by separation. Backhouse was a tall, moon-faced boy with no objectionable habits; his only fault – and it drove me to exasperation – was a supine acceptance of everything. He had no fight in him; he was like a decent, biddable sheep. He and I were fellow prisoners in a long-drawn-out misfortune; and it speaks well of our charity to one another that we rubbed along without worse conflict, for there are few creatures so inwardly tormented, so outwardly unappetizing, so limited in conversation, so totally unattractive, as boys between the ages of thirteen and seventeen.

Backhouse and I sometimes walked down to the railway bridge on Sunday afternoons to see The Flying Scot come hurtling through, scooping up water as she went. She was an awesome sight, thundering over the points at full speed, her whistle shrieking, a wall of spray rising high on either side of her. For a full ten seconds her transit ripped like a meteor through the lassitude of the Sunday afternoon; then she was gone, racing south towards London. There was a pause, during which you found you had been holding your breath; then the signals clicked back into place – and waves of boredom came washing in again. There was nothing to look at now; only a few shunting engines and the big electrical works half a mile up the line. We turned away from the gleaming rails and meandered back through empty Sunday streets.

Our Housemaster was a Mr Whitworth – a soldierly man with a bristling moustache and halitosis that stunned at ten paces. When I arrived back at Rugby for my second term I was summoned to his study. I faced him across his desk, standing as far back as I decently could.

'Now Quayle – I've a serious question for you. Do you want to put your name down for Confirmation?'

I was taken by surprise. Confirmation? I had never given it a thought; and now that it was thrust at me I felt no urgent or overpowering need of it. I had never sorted out my feelings about the Creed, even though I mumbled my way through it every Sunday, but I knew darn well that I was in no position to take over the vows made on my behalf by my godfathers and godmothers. Come to think of it, I only had one of each – beloved Aunty Sis who lived in Merthyr and would not care one way or the other, and Quentin Slater who had given me a gold sovereign when I was a baby, and then died of syphilis during the war. He would not care much either.

My instinct was to say, 'No thank you, sir. I'd sooner give it a miss, if you don't mind.' But I did not have the courage: he so obviously *would* mind; and by tomorrow he would have passed the word round all his reverend colleagues that this new boy, Quayle, was a dangerous influence, a rebel, a dissenter. I was thrown into dithering confusion.

Mr Whitworth had not been a major in the war for nothing; he spotted the weakness of my defences and went straight in to the attack.

'Do it. Get it over with,' he advised, exuding soldierly confidence and a sulphurous waft of dragon's breath. It enveloped me so densely that I had to clap a handkerchief over my nose and mouth. I tried to back away, but found I was already in the fireplace. I looked round to see if there was an open window towards which I could work my way; both windows were tight shut.

Mr Whitworth misinterpreted my frantic search for air. 'It's no good, Quayle. This is a question you can't duck.' Through his avuncular tone I could now hear the ring of iron. 'Most boys are confirmed, y'know.'

I wanted to protest. 'I am not "most boys". I am *me*.' But you cannot talk like that to a Housemaster. You cannot talk at all when you are being stifled by a deadly miasma. I drew in a quick breath through my home-made gas mask and gasped out, 'Yes, sir.'

One bushy eyebrow shot up; he gave an indulgent but ironic smile. 'What do you mean by "Yes, sir?" Yes, you know that most boys are confirmed? Or, yes, you want to be confirmed yourself?'

I did not know what I meant. I only knew that I must escape, at once, from his indescribably baleful breath.

'Yes, sir,' I said. 'Both, sir. Thank you, sir.' And, choking into my handkerchief, I bolted.

'Take care of that cough,' he called after me.

Back in the noisome, badger-like side of the house, amid familiar sounds and smells – the communal lavatory, the scuffling of small boys in corridors, the shouts of a sixth-former yelling for a fag – I felt ashamed of myself. I should have shown some spirit; I should have stood up for my disbeliefs, my uncertainties. But I had collapsed at the first threat of public opinion, at 'Most boys are, y'know'. It was too late now to recant; soon I would be having to swear that I truly believed the Nicene Creed when I did not believe in half of it; it even seemed contrary to what Jesus had said. And it was no use making a joke of it and saying I had only given in because of Mr Whitworth's breath. True, it was horrendous, asphyxiating; but a lion's breath must have smelt a lot worse to Christians in the amphitheatre. If I had had any courage I should have been able to hold out against mere human halitosis.

I had to face it; cowardice had led me into this Confirmation business, just as cowardice had led me into the Boxing Competition. It was Dickson who had trapped me into that. Dickson was very senior in the House, and Captain of School Boxing. He had stopped me one day in the echoing, tiled corridor.

'Can I have a word with you, Quayle?'

Good heavens, he knew my name.

'Why don't you go in for the Boxing Tournament?'

Dickson had pinned up a sheet on the House notice board a couple of days before, asking for volunteers, but no one had signed it.

'I can't box,' I said. 'I've never boxed.'

Dickson smiled. 'Time you learnt, then.' He was a quiet, self-assured boy: more of a man really. 'You're new here, and it's important to make a good impression right off. Do something for the House. Everyone will think so well of you if you go in for the boxing.'

I knew damn well I did not want to go in for the beastly boxing, but I also knew I was caught.

'Really, I don't know how.' It was the last feeble struggle of the gaffed fish before it is landed.

'Don't worry,' said Dickson. 'I'll show you myself. Good. Then that's settled. I'll put your name down.'

So all that winter term I was 'prepared' for two events – Confirmation and the Boxing Tournament. They were markedly dissimilar, and I did not look forward to either of them.

Once a week I had to race through my prep, then walk over to the school gym. Dickson's tuition was rudimentary.

'Lead with your left and keep your guard up,' were the only instructions he gave me – followed by a few taps on the nose to show me how feeble my guard was. I did some desultory skipping; occasionally I punched the heavy bag and felt almost like a real fighter, but the ominous news that at ten and a half stone I would be in the Light Heavyweight class quickly reminded me that I was nothing but a sham.

Confirmation Class called for less exertion; it meant no more than having tea once a week with Mr Sugden, our House Tutor. Mr Sugden was a civilized man, tall and bony, with close-cropped grey hair and a ruddy complexion that in cold weather turned bright blue. He was a mighty walker and could often be seen striding through the wintry blasts with no more protection than a walking stick and a pair of knitted gloves. His eager nose was held at an upward tilt, and his mouth was habitually open as though it were a door from which laughter could burst out; his laughter, like his walking, verged on the manic.

There were three of us from Tudor House undergoing 'Preparation for Confirmation' – Maclean Jack, Backhouse and myself – and to each of us Mr Sugden gave a copy of Robert Bridges' anthology, *The Spirit of Man*. Sometimes we read extracts aloud and Mr Sugden made literary jokes about them; sometimes he drifted off into observations on Jane Austen, or the influence of H.G. Wells on today's society. Always there were gales of laughter, but of our impending embracement of the Christian Faith – not a word. This was disconcerting, because the more I understood (or thought I understood) the teachings of Jesus, the less I could understand the pronouncements of the Church. I had never asked E about such things; she would have looked puzzled, lit a cigarette, and said,

'Bunt, I can show you how to make a decent omelette, but don't ask me anything about religion. I don't know.'

I had never been able to ask them at Abberley: they would have been horrified.

But Mr Sugden was an intelligent man, a scholar, and I really needed to ask him what he made, for example, of the Old Testament? Did he really think we were created by God – hey, presto – as it said in Genesis? Did the Church really think so? If it did not – and surely no one could maintain that belief after Mr Darwin had spoken – then why did we go on having the story of the Creation drummed into us as though it proceeded from the very mouth of God? And while we were talking of God, why was God 'He' and not 'She'? Who said so? Only a tribe of male chauvinist nomads a very long time ago. Remarkable folk no doubt and fine poets, but of a monstrous arrogance: people who dared to believe that they were created in God's image, and that He had given them *dominion over the fish of the sea, and over the fowl of the air; and over the cattle, and over all the earth, and over every creeping thing that creepeth upon the earth*. It was pretty clear to me that if we continued in this way, exercising our 'dominion' over the elephants, and the hippopotamuses, and the polar bears, and the elks, and the otters, and every furry feathery creature that stirred, then we images of God were soon going to find ourselves in extreme loneliness on this earth of His creation. And serve us bloody well right for swallowing whole the Book of Genesis.

But never once did Mr Sugden give me an opening. He talked, he laughed at his own jokes – and then the session was over. There was never a chance to pin him.

'Don't you find that odd?' I asked Backhouse one night; we were walking back to the House through the lamplit streets.

'Oh, I don't know,' he said.

It was a typical Backhouse reply. He always 'didn't know'. He just slopped along with his well-bred moon face, accepting everything.

'Well, I think it's damned odd,' I persisted. 'He laughs a lot, but he's never discussed anything. I believe he funks it. Doesn't know what to say. So he's skated over the whole business. And now there's only one more Confirmation Class to go.'

'Perhaps he's saving it all till then,' Backhouse suggested, but without enthusiasm.

The last class came, and Mr Sugden's jokes abounded till suddenly he looked at his watch:

'My goodness. That's all, boys. I have to go out to dinner. Off you go.'

We were bundled out into the dark street, each of us clutching his *Spirit of Man*, but not one crumb the wiser about the beliefs we were about to affirm. Confirmation was only two days off; the Bishop of Coventry himself was coming to conduct the service. Well – there was nothing for it but to go through with this 'Laying-on of Hands', dubious ritual though it sounded. But somewhere deep down inside me, as deep as the

500 Fathom Line, a large bubble was forming – a bubble not exactly of mutiny, not even of rejection, but of questioning, a most persistent questioning. Meanwhile, there was an interview to be faced next morning with the 'Bodger'.

How did the Headmaster of Rugby, over generations, come to be called the 'Bodger'? I never found out; but irreverence is the surest way to rob an ogre of his terror. Dr Vaughan, the Bodger of my day, was far from being an ogre, but he was a figure of enormous authority. 'The last of the great Victorian Headmasters' was a massive man; he had a shaggy mane of hair and a moustache that sprouted from beneath an heroically broken nose. He was renowned for a singular mannerism: where ordinary men slip a hesitant 'mmm . . . er . . . ' into their speech when lost for a word, the Bodger would declaim 'Aaaaaah'. There were no half measures either; he said it very loud, and he was capable of holding the sound almost indefinitely. One boy, a keen Bodger-watcher and owner of a stopwatch, always timed him when he addressed the assembled school in the Speech Room. The record for an unbroken 'Aaaaaah', he maintained, was 12.5 seconds.

I had no reason to be fearful, but it took courage to knock on the great man's door at the appointed hour.

'Come in.'

The Bodger sat at his desk, an old lion at his ease, barricaded behind a stack of papers.

'Now, you are – aaaaaah – ' and his eye ran down the list in his hand; ' – Aaaaaah – Quayle. Yes?' He smiled, and the rugged face lit up.

'Yes, sir.'

He sat back, large and expansive in his leather chair, spreading wide his arms.

'Well now, is there anything you want to ask me before you are confirmed? Anything at all?'

He could not have been more friendly, more generous, if he had been the Spirit of Christmas Present; but I was in such awe of him, so conscious of his vast seniority, that I could only answer, 'No, thank you, sir.'

'You're sure? Quite sure?'

'Yes, thank you, sir.'

He sat for a while smiling at me, waiting for me to find my tongue, but as I remained silent he said at last, 'Very well. Then that's that.' He sounded almost disappointed. 'Will you please send in whoever's next.'

As I crossed the carpet, the questioning bubble within me quietly detached itself from the bottom of my consciousness and began to float upwards. I turned with my hand on the door handle and, to my astonishment, heard myself say, 'There is one thing, sir.'

'Good. Let's hear it.'

'Well, sir,' – and it was not I who spoke; it was someone who spoke through me – 'I know that tomorrow I have to take a solemn oath – an oath to be a good Christian.'

'Indeed.' The shaggy head nodded. 'A most solemn oath.'

'Well, sir,' – the bubble had reached the surface and now became speech – 'I know there are lots of religions in the world. There are millions of Buddhists, and Moslems, and Hindus, and – all sorts of things. And all those people believe that theirs is the one true religion. So how can I swear to be a Christian all my life when I know nothing at all about all those other religions?'

The Bodger looked at me steadily for a long time. Then he gave vent to a sound of inordinate length:

'Aaaaaaaaaaaaaaaaaaaaah – '

The sound stopped. He shuffled the papers on his desk; discovered his fountain pen under a pile of them; pulled its cap off; put it back again; looked across the room to me, then looked away again. I stood waiting in fear. What in heaven's name had possessed me to ask such a question?

His answer came at last, and slowly. 'I can only tell you that different people have evolved the religion that best suits them. It has to do with their history, their climate. The faith you are now promising to embrace is the one that best suits us. It is the faith of your father, of your father's father, and of his father before him. You had better take it on trust that it is best for you too.'

He was sidestepping, and he jolly well knew it. What was more, I had a strong feeling that he knew I knew it. That glint in his eyes – was it suppressed amusement at our mutual predicament? He gave a shrug. 'We have to take some things on trust, Quayle. Life's too short to do otherwise.'

I waited for him to say more, but he did not look as though he were going to. I could see, too, that this was not the moment for further questions when there were half a dozen boys outside his door all waiting to be seen. So I said, 'Thank you, sir,' and cleared off.

I liked Dr Vaughan, liked him very much; he had not avoided my question in the fast-talking way Mr Sugden had done, but he had not given me a proper answer either; he had been wise, but evasive. It was no good telling me about religions that 'best suit' people. That was like saying that it suits Eskimos to wear different clothes from Arabs. Yes, of course different customs suited different peoples. But *Religion*? Ah, no.

That had to be absolute, or it was nothing. You could not half-believe in a whole religion, or wholly believe in half a religion. What sort of belief was that? That was not religion; it was expediency.

All this I thought, but I am not of the stuff from which martyrs are made; I took the easy option and went through with my Confirmation.

The Bishop of Coventry had a thin, ascetic face and a mellifluous voice. His white lawn sleeves ended at his wrists in little frills, and from them his hands emerged as delicate as lamb cutlets. All through the service I longed to believe wholeheartedly in what I was saying, but I could not; and I felt I was a traitor. Who to? To God? Whoever, whatever, God might be. To Jesus? To myself? I did not know; but a traitor to someone, something, for sure.

I knelt at the Bishop's feet when my turn came; I felt his hand on my head, and inside me I shouted, loud enough for God to hear, 'No! Don't lay your frilly hand *on*! Take your frilly hand *off*!' Now surely God must send a sign of His displeasure? An electric shock? A rumble of thunder? No – nothing happened at all. I walked back to my place in the nave, and the service droned on.

The Bodger was just to my left, sitting on his red cushion under a carved oak canopy. He looked full of a deep and unshakable confidence: I wished that I could feel the same.

The Boxing Tournament was a less episcopal 'laying-on of hands'. I was drawn to fight Williams, the School Fly Half, four years older than me and with no frills whatever round his wrists. I tried to follow Dickson's advice – lead with my left and keep my guard up – but Williams never gave me time; he came storming in with both hands. He did not knock me out, but that was what it felt like.

Maclean Jack came along to be my second, and after the fight we walked back to the House under the dark, dripping elms.

'You did bloody well,' he assured me. 'Bloody well.'

I shook my head. 'What about the second round?'

'When he had you in the corner? Yes – nasty. He gave you a bit of a dusting then.'

'I couldn't get out of the blasted corner,' I said. 'In the end I had to cover up and run.'

'Run?' Maclean was indignant in my defence. 'Balls! You didn't run. You took "evasive action". Unorthodox. Admirable.'

'And cowardly,' I said.

'Oh, shut up.' He looked at his watch. 'Twenty minutes to closing time. Come on. We'll go to the Stodge Shop and I'll stand you a Malted Milk Shake.'

Confirmation and boxing were not the only tribulations. During my first two terms at Rugby, before I learnt how to keep out of trouble, I was thrashed with a dismal regularity. Beatings were handed out for every sort of footling offence: for not being in bed when the lights were switched off by Ernest, the House 'butler'; for not having both feet inside the door of the dining hall when Ernest stopped ringing the bell for early morning roll call. Beatings were administered with the heel of a shoe and carried out by the Sixth-Former in charge of the dormitory. When the day was over and the House was plunged in darkness the Head of the Dormitory would light his candle (these men of power were permitted to work late if they so wished) and pronounce the long-awaited words of doom.

'All right, Quayle. Out of bed.'

A hiding is not the worst of punishments; all the same it is lonely to walk the length of a cold, dark dormitory and submit to being thrashed by a beefy young man wielding a heavy shoe. You cannot fight back, and you cannot escape; you are trapped by generations of custom; you can only submit – which may be good for the soul, but is only painful to the body.

'Bend over.' The execution block is a chest of drawers in the middle of the room.

You do as you're told, bracing yourself to receive the first blow. But it doesn't come; there's a delay. Now what? A reprieve? Don't fool yourself: it's the candle that needs trimming. That done, another freezing minute passes while the position of the light is carefully readjusted.

At last, three thudding strokes delivered with exactitude, each landing on precisely the same spot. Then the aching limp back to bed.

Not a sound in the dark room; only the metallic creak of bedsprings as you climb in; no word of sympathy from the other denizens of the silent dormitory; talking is forbidden after 'Lights Out'. Besides, each of them is busy offering up his own heartfelt prayer to the Throne of the Heavenly Grace: 'Oh God, I do thank You that it was Quayle tonight and not me.'

The day arrived when I was put in charge of a dormitory myself and, inevitably, it fell to me one night to deal out punishment. I got as far as arming myself with a shoe and ordering the poor wretch to bend over. (Child, I think, was his name.) I had always thought the custom barbarous, but now, in the light of the candle, I saw it as plain ludicrous; I dropped the shoe on the floor.

'Oh, go back to bed,' I said. 'I'm not going to beat you.'

In the shadows I could feel the dormitory holding its breath. Nothing like this had happened in living memory. I had broken every rule, every time-hallowed custom. Well – good; it was time a few hallowed customs were got rid of.

'And while I'm at it,' I said, 'I may as well tell you that I'm never going to beat one of you. Never.'

An even longer silence. Then a stirring of bedclothes, a squeaking of bedsprings, a muffled, muttering noise.

'Shut up!' I said. 'Shut up all of you. I've told you, there'll be no beatings in this dorm – not while I'm in charge of it. But don't you take advantage of it. This is going to be the best-behaved dormitory in the House. So don't you bloody dare let me down.'

And they did not – not by a whisker.

The terms passed; I moved slowly up the school, never brilliant, but above average. I played rugger for the House and had my collarbone broken at the bottom of a scrum. I got out of cricket – which was easy, since no one wanted me. Instead I went for enormous bike rides through Warwickshire. Some masters were encouraging; others were not. Mr Jennings made me really believe I had it in me to write; so of course while I was in his form I wrote better and better. When I moved up, Mr Smith gave me to know that my essays and poems were worthless; so that was what they became. The beaks were distant creatures; some of the younger ones seemed willing to break through the barrier of caps and gowns and treat us as fellow humans, even friends. One of them was a bit over-friendly, almost flirtatious. I did not know then what his manner betokened, but I found it rather embarrassing. A few years later he became Headmaster of a famous school (a 'Bodgeress', perhaps). For the most part the beaks went their magisterial ways, leaving us in no doubt that they saw us as smelly, hostile, potentially dangerous beasts who had to be licked into shape in order to pass University Exams. Between 'us' and 'them' there was an undefined but warlike frontier that did no good at all and may have contributed to my one serious 'crime'.

My form master at the time of the offence was a Mr Harrison, an elderly man of gentle demeanour who wore cravats and high, starched collars; he was charming and delightful but lacking in authority. In addition to Mr Harrison and myself there were two other characters in this sorry little tale – a tall, gangling boy called d'Aeth who sat beside me at the very back of the classroom, and a dashing, outrageous youth named McColl. McColl was a provocative sort of boy and a natty dresser; his white starched collar would have graced a member of Lloyds; his black jacket was always brushed, his trousers pressed, his shoes polished. He was small, good-looking, cheeky and bone idle.

During the end-of-term exams d'Aeth and I evolved an excellent system of helping one another. I was good at Latin and English but hopeless at Maths; his skills were the other way round. So while Mr Harrison read his book and nodded off, lulled by the steady scratching of fountain pens, d'Aeth and I exchanged questions and answers on little scraps of paper that we slid between us along the bench. We did not think of it as cheating; we were doing nobody any harm; on the contrary, we were brave fighters in the never-ending war between boys and beaks. At the end of each exam – and there were several exams during a day – d'Aeth and I simply scrumpled up our incriminating correspondence and chucked it into the wastepaper box together with all the other scraps of rough paper. It was a big box, as big as a tea chest, and it did not need emptying all day long.

Fools. Fools. But no one had warned us. It took another fifteen years and the Second World War to teach me the most elementary rule for all clandestine operations: *Incriminating documents must be immediately destroyed, if necessary by swallowing them*. I would gladly have eaten the entire contents of the wastepaper box rather than endure what followed.

The last exam, on the last day of exams, was the English paper. It was divided into three sections – A, B and C, the last being an essay on one of half a dozen given poets.

'All right. Time's up.' Mr Harrison rose to his gentle, scholarly feet and gave his gown a twitch. 'Now I want you to put your papers in three piles on my desk. The As here. The Bs here. And the Cs there at the end. Otherwise I shall get into such a muddle.'

For once there had been no correspondence between d'Aeth and me; our consciences were spotless. We deposited our offerings as instructed, then went back to our seats while Mr Harrison checked through each pile.

'McColl,' he called out.

'Yes, sir?' McColl stood up.

'I don't seem to have your Section C.'

McColl's place was at the front of the class. While Mr Harrison rummaged anew, McColl turned round to all of us behind him and pulled a face of mock horror. There was some suppressed laughter, but Mr Harrison seemed not to hear it; perhaps, like the Speaker in the House of Commons, he chose not to. McColl uncrossed his eyes and faced the front again.

'Oh, it's there all right, sir.' Very brisk he was, very confident.

Mr Harrison clicked his tongue. 'Well, I can't find it.'

'But it's there, sir. I've just put it there.'

'Who did you choose for your essay?'

McColl's answer came pat. 'Shelley, sir.'

'Shelley?' Mr Harrison bowed his head anew over the piles of foolscap. 'Oh dear, this is most distressing.'

'It is for me, sir. I wrote three whole pages on him.'

Another ripple of suppressed laughter swept over the class. McColl would have been hard put to it to write three lines on Shelley, let alone three pages; he would have known more about the day's runners at Lingfield.

McColl sensed that he had his audience with him and took end-of-term audacity a step further. 'Do you think perhaps you might have lost it, sir?' His tone was hilariously deferential. 'I jolly well know I wrote it. But maybe you threw it away – oh, by mistake, of course.'

Mr Harrison reflected. 'Yes, I am absent-minded. Though I doubt if I could be as stupid as that. All right, you boys. I won't keep you. Off you go.'

There was a clatter of books and desk tops as the class headed for the door, chattering and grinning covertly at one another. Over the racket came Mr Harrison's raised voice. 'No – not you, McColl. You stay behind. You and I are going to find your essay if we have to search through the whole wastepaper box.'

The wastepaper box. My heart dropped into the abyss; fear clutched my bowels. D'Aeth, beside me, had turned the colour of cheese. We stood petrified in the middle of the classroom while the others shoved past us. There, not six feet away, was the box that held the deadly evidence of a day's collusion; and McColl and Mr Harrison were settling down before our eyes to comb through it.

D'Aeth whispered, 'We must stop them.'

'How?'

'I don't know.'

'Neither do I. Better keep moving.'

We stood together on the pavement outside, sick and nerveless, while cars honked and boys jostled in the narrow street. For a moment I thought of pretending to be mad. Overwork. A nervous breakdown. I would rush back, yelling, and set fire to the wastepaper box. Set fire to the classroom. Burn down the whole building. It was no good; I had no matches.

'Perhaps,' d'Aeth ventured '– perhaps he won't find our notes.'

'He can't miss them. The last exam was Stinks. Remember?'

'Oh God.' He was thinking of the formula he had pushed towards me.

'And before that was History – The Treaty of Utrecht.'

I thought d'Aeth was going to be sick, or faint, or die. I thought I was too. He looked absurd with his face ashen and his cap askew. I am sure I looked no better.

'What the hell can we do?'

'Nothing. Just pray.'

We headed back to our different Houses, and the earth sounded hollow under my tread.

The afternoon passed, and the evening too. No summons to appear before Mr Harrison: no call to the Housemaster's study. Perhaps we had got away with it? I clutched at the hope, knowing it was impossible.

Next morning, being the last day of term, the school assembled in the Speech Room instead of the usual morning service in Chapel; prayers were followed by the Headmaster's address. Leonine and benevolent – but dangerous, Dr Vaughan spoke of the successes and failures in the past term, revealed such administrative changes as were fitting for the school to know, and bade farewell to those who were leaving. Then he fell silent. Not a sound came from him: not the vestige of an 'Aaaaaaaah'. In the interminable silence my heart began to thump. 'Oh, God,' I thought, 'here it comes.' I looked around hoping to see d'Aeth, but I had no idea where he was sitting in the crowded hall.

At last Dr Vaughan broke the silence.

'I am sorry to say that the end of term has been marred by the action of two boys who have been caught cheating. I will not name them. They know who I am referring to. Cheating in exams is an odious practice, and these two boys are flagrantly guilty. They will stay behind in their respective Houses when the rest of the School breaks up. They will not be allowed to go home till their punishment has been decided on.'

School broke up with the usual jubilation; buses and taxis came to carry boys and their trunks off to the station. I was left alone in the empty, echoing House to ponder my crime and await my punishment. Word came that my Housemaster wished to see me. Mr Whitworth had gone to take over a Headmastership and breathe his effluvium over other boys; another now sat in his place – grey-haired, solemn, terse.

'I have heard from the Headmaster. He has decided on your punishment.' He paused.

Well – what was it to be? A beating, for sure. That meant six with the cane. The Bodger never gave less than six.

'First you will go to Mr Harrison – here's his address – and you will apologize to him. Then you will come back here and write out a thousand times, "I must not cheat in exams". You understand?'

'Yes, sir.' 1,000 lines sounded a lot. I had never heard of such a punishment. But at least I was not getting six with the cane.

'That will take you several hours, so I will phone your mother and tell her. She might be coming to meet you.'

'Might be coming'? Of course she would be coming. Even now it might be too late to stop her; she would be just about leaving her little hotel bedroom in Lancaster Gate. What was I to say to her? How could I tell her what I had done? I took the telephone that was held out to me; I could hear E's voice, but I could not speak.

'Hallo? . . . Bunt? What's happened? Are you in trouble?'

'Yes. I'm sorry, Mum. I'm afraid I've let you down.'

A pause; then her voice again. 'That's all right, darling. Just come home as soon as you can. And try to let me know what train you'll be on. I'll be there to meet you.'

I went to Mr Harrison's little house and apologized. He accepted my contrition with dignity, inclining his head above the blue, polka-dot cravat. I expected him to excoriate me, but he did not; he looked at me with a grave amusement, and – 'Oh, Quayle,' was all the reproach he made.

Back at the House, alone in the empty, panelled dining hall, I settled down to write 1,000 lines. By the time I had covered seventeen or eighteen sides of foolscap with the same unchanging admonition I would have taken the beating with relief. Hours passed. Nausea gripped me and my writing became illegible. A couple of times the Housemaster came through to see how I was doing. Around four in the afternoon he came again.

'How many have you done?'

'I don't know, sir. I've lost count. Eight hundred – I think.'

He looked at his watch. 'Are you packed?'

'Oh yes, sir.'

'Well – I think you've done enough. There's a train to London at five. You'll catch it if you hurry. I'll phone your mother.'

I flew, like a swallow that has been left behind in the great migration. And there waiting to meet me on Euston station was E. I dropped my bags and put my arms round her.

'Oh Mum, I am sorry. I am terribly sorry. Forgive me.'

She laughed. 'Idiot, of course I forgive you. But what a damn fool thing to do. And more fool to be caught.'

She looked so out of place – my mother, my own particular friend – under this impersonal, echoing roof of glass. There was such a public blur of noise, such a collective smell of fish and soot, of pigeon shit and engine oil – I did not know what to say to her.

'You've shrunk,' I said. 'You look smaller.'

'No. You've grown. What are you now? Six foot?'

'Almost.'

She took my hand. 'Come on. You've wasted ten whole hours already. Let's not waste any more.'

And off we went, spinning into the hols.

E had somehow got herself employed by a small wholesaler of women's clothes behind Regent Street – a dreary nine-to-six job, but it paid a wage. She had settled, pigeon-like, on the top floor of a seedy hotel in Lancaster Gate: hot in summer, cold in winter, but high enough above the traffic in Bayswater Road to hold a conversation without actually shouting. When I came on my school holidays she usually contrived to get me a room on the same floor. They were good holidays; looking back on them I can recognize real happiness. Happiness was to have escaped from the kind but muffling embrace of a provincial town and to be launched into one of the world's great capitals; happiness was to be so short of cash that every halfpenny had to be counted – yet not so poor that poverty could reach out and maul you; happiness was to be young, and full of expectation and crassly ignorant.

E was working all day, but she bought me a *Pocket Atlas of Central London* (falling apart now, but I still use it) and pushed me off to find the 'Places of Interest' listed at the back. I put on a disillusioned expression and strode purposefully about. I was only fourteen and did not have a purpose in the world; but that was how Londoners looked, and I wanted to be taken for a Londoner. I walked till I was exhausted, then rode the wild bus tops. The upper decks of London buses were open in those days, and in bad weather I had them to myself: a lone mariner on my rain-lashed bridge. All London was mine to explore: Smithfield, where the bloodstained butchers swapped bawdry and laughed amid the carcasses; the City, whose bobbing bowler hats and sombre suits filled me with alarm; the Great Abbey itself where, beneath his simple covering, the Unknown Soldier slept oblivious of his honour.

And just as all London lay before me, so did the whole of my life – though I seldom paused to consider that; life was to be lived, not thought about. Sometimes I did wonder why I was 'me' and not someone else. Why had I not been born an Indian, perhaps? Or a girl? Or a dog? Why 'me'? As a line of questioning it did not lead far because I was undoubtedly who I was – and very happy to be so. Everything ahead was unknown – so it was bound to be exciting. And it would go on, and on, and on – for ever. Life Everlasting – what else?

This was the late twenties. London then had a different face, a different atmosphere: less brash, less pushing, less cosmopolitan. Social differences were more clearly marked, but the strands of society were closer knit. London was a mighty capital; but it was the capital of an offshore island, isolated from every other country in the world, accessible only from the sea. As a result you seldom heard a foreign accent in the streets, let alone a different language; you hardly ever saw a black face, or a brown. Britain was inescapably for the British.

There were architectural differences too, and not just the obvious ones of high-rise buildings. Covent Garden had not become a prettified Tourist Attraction; it was a hard-living, hard-driving market, boisterous with shouts and wheels, pungent with onions, bananas, flower blossoms and squashed oranges. Boswell would have found it little changed since he went whoring there 150 years ago. Soho was another area that had not been raped and ruined; the 'developer' had not yet attacked the jumbled elegance of centuries; the pornographer had not smeared degradation on the streets. To the west, Park Lane was shady and quiet; it contained only the mansions of the vastly rich: nothing so vulgar as an hotel or a motorcar showroom would have been tolerated. There were sounds as well as sights that lived on from the past: in the quiet streets of Chelsea and South Kensington vendors sang the same cries that Hogarth must have heard: 'Chairs to Mend', 'Lavender – Sweet Lavender'. Sunday afternoons brought the tinkling bell of the muffin man, his tray of muffins and crumpets balanced on his head. Clothes and customs lingered on too: women rode side-saddle in Rotten Row, and men raised their hats when they passed the Cenotaph.

London was not a solemn place; it had a flippant, raffish side. Music halls were packed; the Big Bands – Jack Hylton, Jack Payne – were pulling them in. It was less opulent than New York, but part of it belonged in the same world as Scott Fitzgerald. Around the 'fast set' there was more than a whiff of drugs. Noel Coward dazzled and darling'd the West End; Gordon Selfridge was delighted to pose for the photographers – not with one of his racehorses, but with his latest twofold acquisition: the Dolly Sisters.

'Old fool,' was E's comment, flicking the pages of her *Daily Telegraph*. 'All that white hair. What does he think he's doing?'

I had a rough idea of what Mr Selfridge was doing, and I envied him. Not that I envied him either of the Dolly Sisters – God forbid – but because I longed to know a real, live girl, a girl I could talk to and touch. The idea of a girl was very much in my mind – scarcely out of it, in fact: not all girls; not any girl; but one particular, altogether wonderful girl who I was sure must exist somewhere. It was the start of the quest for love.

I had met one girl in London – Nancy, the model at the place where E worked; she was far beyond my reach, but she touched my heart. Nancy was tall and delicately thin, almost emaciated. She had the finest of ash-blonde hair, hanging down almost to her shoulders, forlorn and appealing, like Veronica Lake. I made one or two visits to the showroom and then, rather to E's surprise, made what she thought was a quixotic offer.

'All those dress boxes you send off. How do you get them to the Post Office?'

'We pay a man to take them to the Post Office.'

'Couldn't I do it?'

'You? You don't want to do that.'

'Sure. Be glad to.'

The going rate was half a crown – and very welcome. But what inspired me was not the chronic shortage of cash, not the wish to be of help: it was the hope of seeing Nancy. Sometimes when she was busy, I would miss her; then all my parcel-carrying was wasted. If my luck held I might catch a glimpse of thin, bare arms and silken legs before the curtain was whisked across her cubicle. But Nancy, I was sure, must be all of twenty-five, and I did not know how to speak to her.

E refused to understand my hesitancy. 'Oh, don't be a fool. Just ask her. Take her to the movies. Take her ice-skating.'

'I couldn't.'

'Why not?'

'She'd be bored. She'd never come.'

'How d'you know till you ask her? Go on. She won't bite.'

I did ask her, and she did not bite; she accepted straight off. 'Oh, thank you very much,' she said in her thin little London voice. 'I'd love to.'

So on her next afternoon off we two went slithering round the Hammersmith Ice Rink with a hundred other novices, while the desperadoes cut in and out at breakneck speed. Skating was better than going to the movies; it cost no more, and it gave me an excuse to hold Nancy's hand. She needed propping up too; she was an even worse skater than I was – always falling down.

'No, reelly – I'm not hurt.' It was enchanting, the way she said 'reelly'; it went with her cheekbones, pink with rouge, her small powdered nose. And she made no fuss at all about the really beastly cough she had. We wobbled round the rink for a couple of hours while the 'Skaters' Waltz' blared and the wild boys sped past us backwards, or came to a dramatic halt in a spray of ice. Then the party was over and it was time to go. We walked to the Hammersmith Underground and, for want of any better suggestion, went our separate ways home. It was a sad anticlimax.

E had not returned from work when I got back to Lancaster Gate, so I started to prepare our evening meal. Cooking was forbidden in the bedrooms, but E kept a small saucepan hidden under her bed, and in this you could eventually boil water on top of the shilling-in-the-slot gas fire. Then you could heat up something that was not too smelly: baked beans, or spaghetti – that sort of thing.

The water was boiling when E came in; she sat down on her bed, tired from climbing the stairs.

'Give me a drink – there's a darling.'

I poured into her toothglass a stiff slug of the Empire Sherry she kept in her wardrobe. She eyed the can that was bumping gently up and down in the boiling water. 'What's that?'

'Spaghetti.'

'Aha . . . Well – enjoy yourselves?'

'Yes, it was fun. But Nancy grazed her knee. Did for her stockings too.'

'Poor love.' E was very fond of Nancy. 'I'll buy her another pair.'

'And that's an awful cough she's got.'

E made no comment; I thought she had not heard. 'I'm famished,' she said. 'Surely that spaghetti's ready. How long have you had it on?'

I began to pour off the boiling water into the handbasin. 'Can't she take something for it?' I asked through the steam.

E took a moment to answer; then she said quietly, 'Not much she can do. She's got TB.'

'TB!' I had got the tin-opener poised in my hand. 'Oh, no.'

'Oh, yes.'

'But that's awful. Can't – can't something be done?' It was not a real question: just a bleat.

E never bleated; she took realities head-on. 'Done?' she repeated. 'What, for example? Go to Switzerland? A sanatorium? Who's to pay? You? Me? No – she's been in and out of hospitals for years. There's nothing more to be done. Nancy's a working girl. She has to earn her living – if living is the right word.' She gave her head a toss, dismissing a subject she found painful. 'Come on, let's get that tin open. And mind the stuff doesn't squirt all over the ceiling.'

Nancy and I went skating several times, but our friendship did not develop; it was doomed to begin and end on ice. She, for all her looks, was reticent, modest; I was painfully aware of my lack of years, certain that any girl who looked as stunning as she did must have a whole regiment of admirers, all handsome and stalwart, all fighting to love and protect her. Perhaps I was wrong; perhaps she was lonely, even frightened; perhaps she would not have minded if I had taken the first tentative step. Who knows? I have left it too late to ask – sixty years too late. And I doubt if Nancy is still around to answer the question.

Nancy was a powerful attraction, but I was discovering that there was another just as strong – the theatre. Plays absorbed and fascinated me. Plays were a revelation of mankind; and there was nothing on the face of earth so heroic, so monstrous, so open, so devious, as Man – as *us*. No subject was half so important, half so worth studying; yet it was not taught at school, not recognized as a means of entry to a university. But here in London, night after night – or as often as we could scratch together the money – was the greatest university in the world: the English theatre. I was at the age when childish assumptions are dropping away, discredited. I was beginning to realize that under the plus fours that bestrode the golf courses, under the bowler hats that bobbed along Throgmorton Street, under all this decorous uniformity, there seethed and boiled some weird fantasies. People were not what they seemed. To expose what they truly were, and what they might be if they stretched out far enough, that was the business of the theatre. Some part of theatre was 'Show-Biz' – a rightful and important part; it had to do with the skill and charm of the Astaires, with that sensational girl second from the left in the chorus line. But at bottom, theatre was about the inner workings of all us short-lived, self-regarding, miraculous monkeys.

I could not have explained any of that; I did not have the words or the authority. Then one day I came across Alexander Pope – his *Essay on Man*:

> *Know then thyself, presume not God to scan,*
> *The proper study of mankind is man.*

There – 200 years ago Pope had said it:

> *Created half to rise, and half to fall,*
> *Great lord of all things, yet a prey to all:*
> *Sole judge of truth, in endless error hurled;*
> *The glory, jest, and riddle of the world!*

E and I did not feel much like the lords of anything; but once a week – twice if we were in funds – we paid our shilling and climbed up to the gallery to see Gladys Cooper, Edith Evans, Cedric Hardwicke,

Gwen Ffrangcon-Davies, or Charles Laughton. They were all there, all acting in London, all embodying in their different ways this *glory, jest, and riddle of the world*.

Rugby was flat and sterile after holidays in London: an imprisonment of the mind as well as of the body. I went back to the same cold dormitory, ducked under the same icy shower, squeezed myself into the same ill-smelling hutch with Backhouse. Nothing changed – not the conversation, not the outlook, not the boys, not the masters, and certainly not Backhouse; he simply became more regressive.

'What's that?' he asked. I was pinning up a photo I had torn from a magazine.

'It's a play I saw in London.'

'Oh.'

'*Dear Brutus*. By Barrie.'

'Oh.' A long pause, then, 'Funny title.'

'Not very,' I said. 'It's a quotation from Shakespeare.'

'Oh – Shakespeare.'

I pointed to the photo. 'That's Gerald du Maurier.'

He nodded. At least he did not ask, 'Who's he?'

'And that's Mary Casson. Sybil Thorndike's daughter.'

The shadow of something like an emotion crossed his normally blank face. What was it? Alarm? Disapproval?

'Thorndike? That's odd. Why is her daughter called Casson?'

I started to explain, but stopped. He was being obtuse on purpose. I was not going to tell Backhouse, of all people, how far my thoughts had gone towards the theatre. I was scared to admit, even to myself, how fast my hopes were hardening into resolve.

Rugby did little to foster my passion for the theatre. We had been studying *Richard II* for the best part of a year, and a touring company – led by quite a famous actor – was engaged to perform the play in the Speech Room, no doubt to help us pass our exams. I was full of expectancy; I felt a personal bond with the actors; I longed for them to succeed. 600 boys, crammed almost to nausea with *Richard II*, were not likely to be an easy audience: they would stand up and cheer if the actors were good; they would make their disapproval equally clear if the actors were bad.

The visitors were not merely bad; they were so exquisitely dreadful that I wished to God they had stayed away. The rot started early on with King Richard himself; alone and unaided he was beginning to get some big laughs; given a few more minutes and he would have had the audience in stitches. But suddenly, to everyone's delight – for it was as unexpected and dramatic as an outsider coming up on the rails – King Richard was overtaken, outclassed, by Sir Thomas Mowbray, Earl of Norfolk.

Sir Thomas must have weighed 400 pounds on the hoof; further, he was encased in full armour – helmet, gorget, breastplate, greaves and gauntlets. Banished by the king, Sir Thomas delivered his final couplet with sonorous dignity.

> *Farewell, my Liege, now no way can I stray,*
> *Save back to England, all the world's my way.*

Sir Thomas did not stray very far. He turned and clanked into the wings; a moment later there was a thunderous crash, a yell of agony, and a stream of obscenities that reached every furthest corner of the Speech Room. The Earl of Norfolk had fallen clean off the stage; and, from the muffled heavings and cursings that reached our ears, it was proving a major problem to put him together again.

600 schoolboys – and, be it said, their masters too – laughed till they cried, howled till they broke into cheers. And I, who should have stood shoulder to shoulder with the actors against this rabble, I who dreamed one day of becoming an actor, laughed and cheered with the rest. But in my heart I was ashamed; I knew how it felt to be a traitor.

Abberley had ill-prepared me for a conventional public school like Rugby; it had led me to expect too much. Abberley had been hard-working and disciplined, but it had also been liberal-minded and loving: Rugby was neither. Perhaps that is the right preparation for entering a world that is markedly short of love and liberality; after all, boys – like piglets – have to be weaned. Perhaps I was unlucky in not meeting one teacher of inspiration; there were a few who taught their own subjects with great skill, but I never came across a single one who could throw open a window on life. My years at Rugby were, I think, the most frustrating I have known; they were passed in a sort of marking time, a lifting up of my feet and a putting of them down again. I was always listening for the command to step forward into life, but no command came.

It was not all the fault of the school; it was as much my fault for being adolescent. All schoolboys are the same – unnaturally confined and sexually segregated. They are, I think, not a little mad. What else can they be? Their bodies are at the peak of sexual activity, yet the billions of spermatozoa that they are producing have absolutely nowhere to go. Correction: there is somewhere for them to go – dismally uncreative, but a sort of a kind of a somewhere. Yet I must declare that in all my time at Rugby I never came across homosexuality; it must have been around, but I never met it.

Who was around, and whom I often met, was the Headmaster – sometimes aloof and magisterial in cap and gown, sometimes smiling and human in a crumpled suit and homburg hat. He always stopped and peered at me as if trying to recall my name. I am certain he remembered perfectly well the name of the boy who had once asked him an awkward question before Confirmation – the same boy he had decided not to thrash for cheating in exams; this scrutiny was all part of his role as 'Bodger'.

'Aaaaaaaaaaaah –' he would say at last, '– the Partridge.' Always the same joke; he never tired of it.

I gained from Rugby an odd ragbag of knowledge; I became an expert on The War of the Spanish Succession, but I knew nothing of contemporary Germany or the barbarities that Graziani was inflicting on Tripolitania. I am grateful to the school, though; it held a steady middle course, it was not snobbish, and inadvertently it drummed into me some basic laws of the jungle:

1. Always remember that, at one and the same time,
   you are both a somebody and a nobody.
2. Large communities have to insist on conformity:
   be skilful in concealing your non-conformity.
3. Adversity is our common lot; get used to it.
4. Friends are a joy and comfort, but few can
   be trusted beyond the limit of their own
   interests.
5. Keep your distance from predators more powerful than yourself.

Abundantly counteracting these cynicisms was a stone tablet set in the wall of the Headmaster's garden at the end of the Close:

THIS STONE COMMEMORATES THE EXPLOIT OF WILLIAM WEBB ELLIS
WHO WITH A FINE DISREGARD FOR THE RULES OF FOOTBALL
AS PLAYED IN HIS TIME
FIRST TOOK THE BALL IN HIS ARMS AND RAN WITH IT
THUS ORIGINATING THE DISTINCTIVE FEATURE OF
THE RUGBY GAME

I walked past this tablet several times a day, and every time it spoke to me in a small persistent voice.

'Promise me,' Mr Greenwood had said, 'that when you get to Rugby you will study Greek. You will never have the joy of understanding the ancient Greeks unless you can read their language.'

Leonard Greenwood had a passion for the Greeks, and he would talk to us for hours about their lives, their politics, their wars, their architecture, their poetry. He told us how they believed there was a living spirit in all things – in stones, in trees, in rivers. He talked of Homer and the Trojan War, of how the Greeks had rejoiced in sunlight, in living; how they had seen Religion, Theatre and the Games as being interwoven, all part of a celebration of life.

The day I arrived in Rugby I put my name down to learn Greek – and encountered a teacher of a very different kind. Mr G.A.F.M. Chatwin was a clergyman in the Church of England; he was short, elderly, rotund; his face was a ferocious pink, his eyes an even fiercer blue, and the bald dome of his head rose from a surrounding thicket of the very whitest hair.

It would be absurd and wrongful to hold any of those items against Mr Chatwin, but there is one charge that he shall not escape and for which there is no pardon. By some process of mental aridity he had achieved the impossible: he managed and without effort to make the Greeks dull. Mr Chatwin was the author of the required Grammar that we studied, and while he force-fed us with its dusty crumbs he avoided saying one word about the inspired people who had laid the foundations of our civilization. What had become of those splendidly ambiguous gods and goddesses? The naked nymphs and dryads? Where were Socrates and Plato? Where was Alexander the Great?

It took me twenty minutes to realize that if I stayed under Mr Chatwin's tuition, I was going to be put off the ancient Greeks for the rest of my life and I did not want that to happen. I endured his parsings and declensions till the end of term and then went over to the Modern Side. There was both gain and loss in that; for while I enjoyed Modern Languages and was reasonably good at them, I was thrown heavily into Chemistry and Physics – subjects for which I had no aptitude at all.

A much better experience was the Officers' Training Corps (OTC). I thoroughly enjoyed that, not through any militaristic tendency, but because it was like being back at Abberley in the Boy Scouts. 'D' Company had simply replaced the Peewit Patrol. Maclean Jack, a first-class drummer, kept urging me to join the band.

'I know they're looking for someone to play the big drum. You could do that.'

'But I can't read music,' I protested.

'Oh piddle! Just keep in time and thump the thing. You'll get a leopardskin to wear too.'

I could not resist the leopardskin – but I was too late: Oliver Chesterton had got to the big drum before me. I had to be content with the cymbals – and no leopardskin.

The OTC was like a holiday, especially on Field Days. We put on a brave display as we marched through the town on our way to the railway station, buttons shining, caps straight, puttees neatly wound. Field Days meant freedom from lessons, an escape into the country, and a licence to unravel long streamers of lavatory paper from the train windows as we returned, tired, blistered, but endlessly exuberant.

One hot Field Day, our platoon was lying – midge-infested – in a ditch. We had done well; we had not caught sight of the 'enemy' all day long, and except for one occasion when an umpire had yelled that we were under mortar fire and ordered us to scatter, we had avoided any undue exertion. We were munching the remains of our limited rations, giving a desultory twirl to a large wooden rattle, to show anyone interested that we were in possession of a machine gun, when there was the thudding of hooves and a sweating umpire came galloping up: the same man who, an hour back, had made us scatter to avoid mortar fire.

'Who the hell are you?' he shouted. 'What in God's name d'you think you're doing here?'

We scrambled to our feet, doing up our buttons. Coghlan, our corporal, seventeen years old and needing to shave twice a week, saluted smartly.

'Number Three Platoon, "D" Company. Giving covering fire, sir!' He saluted again.

'Are you indeed?' The horseman was small and ratty. He wore an array of 1914–18 medal ribbons. 'And who, pray, are you covering?'

Coghlan had no idea, but he was inventive. '"A" Company, sir,' he replied without hesitation. '"A" Company is now attacking that rise to our left. The one with the haystack on it.'

The field of stubble to our left was devoid of 'A' Company – devoid of anyone else for that matter – but Coghlan was composed; like all of us he had sized the man up. For all his aggression he could do us no great harm; he was not one of our beaks. He might have fought in the last war; he might have a horse to gallop about on today; but none of that mattered: his power over us reached no further than the here and now. He was to be confronted – if possible, put in his place.

'Show me your map, corporal.' The umpire dismounted.

110

Coghlan removed his cap — the normal receptacle for important documents. He searched inside it, then turned to Lance Corporal Gosling.

'The map, Gozzle. I gave it to you.'

Gosling, fair-haired, overweight, a classical scholar and deeply out of love with the whole proceedings, rummaged in his pack among the stale crusts and bits of melting chocolate.

'It must have fallen out,' he apologized. 'That ploughed field. Remember? When we came under fire and had to run.' Gosling shot a baleful glance at the umpire; he had not enjoyed the sprint.

'So you have no map? Oh, very good! Congratulations.' The umpire's words were curdled with sarcasm. We stared back with the owlish innocence acquired only through years of schooling. 'Allow me to inform you that "A" Company is *not* attacking that rise to your left.'

We all peered solemnly over the hedge at the deserted field. There was not a living thing in the vicinity of the haystack save a few crows pecking about in the stubble.

'Well? What do you think has happened to "A" Company? Have you any suggestions?'

'Only one, sir.'

'I shall be fascinated to hear it.'

Coghlan looked the umpire steadily in the eye. With manliness, but at the same time with compassion, he said, 'As you know, sir, we ran into mortar fire, and that delayed us. I'm afraid we've arrived too late. "A" Company must be all wiped out.'

The umpire was not a man to hang about when he was licked; he started to remount. With one foot in the stirrup he said, acidly, '"A" Company, you will be relieved to know, are alive and well. They and the rest of your contingent are waiting to entrain over there.' He pointed with his riding crop to a church spire just discernible in the hazy distance. 'At this moment they are stuffing themselves with tea and sausages.' He swung himself into the saddle and the horse began to move off. 'You'd better hurry,' he called out, throwing a malevolent grin over his shoulder. 'You won't find many sausages left.'

He was right: every sausage had been eaten; only the tantalizing smell lingered in the still, evening air. The platoon had to board the train hungry and thirsty, but we accounted the sausages well lost: we had fought a battle with a powerful enemy — and we had seen him off.

We tumbled out of the train at Rugby under the hostile eye of the stationmaster, turned our backs on the indecorously festooned carriages, and started to tramp back up the hill to school. At the start of the day we had marched down bravely behind the band, rifles at the 'slope', arms swinging level with the shoulder; we came back through the dusky streets, rifles slung over our shoulders, in good spirits but bedraggled. From time to time we broke into song, too weary to be boisterous, but in a mood of happy melancholy. Sometimes we whistled; 'John Brown's Body' was a favourite. When we had whistled our way through the verse we always sang the chorus – the bit that goes 'Glory, Glory, Hallelujah!' The words that we sang, *fortissimo*, were not the orthodox ones; they were the full, resplendent names of my recent mentor in Greek Grammar, Mr G.A.F.M. Chatwin. It was a sonorous roll call of names out of all proportion to such a small, round man:

> 'Greville Augustus Francis Mason Chatwin,
> Greville Augustus Francis Mason Chatwin,
> Greville Augustus Francis Mason Chatwin,
> Chat-Chat-Chat-Chat-Win.'

What the words lost in repetition they made up for in insolence. I delighted in them, for I felt I was exacting a modest revenge: not for the gods – they were big enough to take care of themselves – but for those heroic shades who were so insultingly overlooked by the Reverend G.A.F.M. Chatwin. My revenge was for Achilles; it was for Hector, Prince of Troy.

At last it is, 'Dis – miss . . . Fall out.'

So to the Armoury; clean and oil your rifle before handing it in.

'My rifle doesn't need cleaning, Sarn't Major. It's not dirty. I haven't fired it. Not one single blank.'

'Lemme see.' Sergeant Major Sherwood squints down the barrel. 'Not dirty?' he barks, and his top set of teeth shoot out of his mouth. He catches them deftly and pushes them back in again. 'Not dirty? It's bloody filthy. Where've you been pokin' it, eh? No, don't tell me. I'd be disgusted.'

Back to the House; clean your boots, brush the dried mud off your puttees and roll them up tight; fold your uniform and stow it away on the rack till the next Field Day, or the next Parade. It is good fun, this playing at soldiers and waving rattles, but a silly old waste of time. Who does anyone think we are going to fight, anyway?

As if in answer, Whittall, sitting on his bed reading a days-old newspaper calls out, 'Hey, listen to this.' He puts on a posh army accent and reads aloud, 'The Army is not likely to be used for a big war for many years to come.'

'Who says so?'

Whittall refers back to the paper, and intones, 'The Chief of the Imperial General Staff. Field Marshal Montgomery-Massingberd.'

'Good old Messybum! Always did talk through his arse.' The witticism comes from Brymer, and the dormitory laughs.

'Messybum!' calls Thompson, mouth full of toothpaste. 'Advance three paces. About turn. Bend over – and be recognized.' Gales of laughter.

But I'm in bed. I'm falling asleep. No, I mustn't – not yet. I haven't done my prep for tomorrow's Chemistry class, and I can't remember the formula for Hydrogen Peroxide. What the devil is it? H_2O_2? Or is it KO_2? No, that's some other foul stuff. Oh, to hell with Hydrogen Peroxide. To hell with old Birdmess . . . and Umpires . . . and Covering Fire . . . Pity we missed the sausages, though. I'd have liked a sausage . . . No, it must be H_2O_2 . . . Don't worry. Go to sleep. Only three more days and E will be here . . . Sleep.

And three days later there she was. She came every term without fail, staying in the cheapest of lodgings for the briefest of weekends, transforming each dingy bedroom with her presence. She brought laughter, and a sense of belonging, and a heavenly smell of scent. Above all, she brought love. My heart must have been growing armour of a kind, for when she caught the train back to London I no longer felt the stabbing grief of Abberley days. Now the parting only numbed me; I fell into a pit of depression, but I found the way to drag myself out of it – mug after mug of hot, malted milk shakes.

Parents were important status symbols in our tribal society – especially mothers. A boy might be a despised nonentity, but if he could produce a beautiful mother his prestige would soar. ('I say – did you see Clarke's mother yesterday? Woof! Wasn't she something?') Fathers counted for less, but scored well if they were men of prowess. To have a father in the RAF was very big, especially if he had had something to do with winning the Schneider Trophy. But any sort of brilliance would do: Ormerod's father was bald and his ears stuck out, but rumour had it that he was a tremendous scientist, just going to split the atom or something; so even Ormerod was treated with respect. Top scorers in the Fathers' Handicap were the Kaulback brothers. No one knew what their father did, but he looked like a Norse warrior, like Beowulf, with his broken nose, his one arm, and his thick grey hair. He would come roaring up to Old Quad in an enormous open Lagonda, tipping out his two Herculean sons as if they were hunting dogs; then he would give a wave of his arm, a shout that could have been heard above the crash of breakers, and off he would thunder, leaving us beholders in admiring wonder.

Dad came to see me one weekend; he turned up wearing spats and a bowler. If he had come dressed in a fisherman's jersey, in muddy corduroys, in overalls, he would have been respected. But spats and a bowler were shaming. Few saw him, luckily, and those that did were kind enough not to hold it against me. Cruel? Yes, but boys are cruel; the life they lead is cruel; the situation was cruel. I loved him in a quiet way. I had known him all my life, and he had always been kind and good to me; but he had never been much of a father, and now he had opted out altogether. So why on earth come here to Rugby? And why wear spats and a bowler? He embarrassed me, and at the same time he tore at my heart. What was I to make of him? I was no Merlin; I had no insight into the complexities of every living creature, least of all my own unhappy, over-sensitive father.

We had breakfast together on the Sunday morning, and we both tried to be chatty.

'I see you still like sausages,' I said; and he laughed, unconvincingly.

Later, we were walking round the Close together when he asked, 'How long before you leave here?'

'Oh – another couple of terms, I suppose.'

'And then?'

I shrugged. 'Grandpa wants me to go into Sumner's.'

'Do you?'

'Not really. What I want –' I broke off.

'Yes?'

I had told no one what was in my heart; it would have sounded absurd, too hard to achieve. But I needed to speak my dream aloud; and no one would understand it better than this dear, hopeless old father of mine – looking so out of place in his bowler hat.

'What I really want is to go on the stage.' He stopped dead. 'Do you think it's a silly idea?'

He shook his head regretfully. 'No, I don't. I wanted to be an actor. Wanted it above anything. But I knew I hadn't the strength of purpose. I had a bit of talent – yes, I know I had that. But not the character, not the tenacity. It's a hard life, an actor's. But if that's what you want – good luck.'

I was grateful to him for saying that, but it was our only moment of true contact; for the rest of the day we just made derelict conversation – which was all we had done for years. He withdrew into false cheeriness, and with each minute I felt that my own inner current was carrying me further and further away from him and all he represented. When he boarded his train for Southport I felt nothing but relief. I was done with Southport and its

114

golf clubs; done with Liverpool and its solid worth; done with bowler hats and respectability. I had the whole adventure of my life ahead of me; what it might be I had no idea, but it would be revealed if I stood alone and lived it.

All this I knew; but I was hemmed in by dependence on Grandpa, who longed for me to go into Sumner's and was staying alive in order to hold open the door for me. I could not even be sure of E's support for my eccentric dream; she had given up her hopes of my becoming a barrister, but the conventional side of her nature wanted to see her Bunt with his feet set on the path to security.

Wait – that was all I could do – wait and see what would happen.

I discovered that there was some kind of 'acting school' in London; I found the address and wrote for a prospectus. It duly arrived – an outlandish incongruity in the surroundings of Tudor House, Rugby. I hid the document away, and read it over and over to myself in secret; it might have been a communication between Catesby and Guy Fawkes. I muttered the magic words as I walked between classes – 'Royal Academy of Dramatic Art'. They were an incantation that had the power to lead me into a world quite beyond my present reach: a world where imagination, and language, and human lives were all fused – a mysterious, unknown world. I had only eagerness for that: I could talk with confidence into the unknown; it was the known that daunted me.

Meantime, all that stood between me and a life dedicated to the manufacture of pills seemed to be my own school reports. Each holiday started with my sitting in E's attic bedroom while she read them aloud.

'*Science . . . Quayle is not unintelligent.*' She looked up, Empire sherry in hand. 'What's the matter with that? It's very good.'

'Read on. You'll see.'

She pushed her glasses up her nose and turned back to the report. '*But he seems unable to grasp the simplest principles*. Yes – well, I do see.'

'I'm just no good at it,' I said.

She took another sip of sherry, and ploughed on. '*Chemistry*,' she read out, then stopped.

'Is that the one that says, *Tries, but is baffled*?'

She nodded.

'So I am,' I said. 'It's true. But look at these other subjects. Look, Mum. I was top in English. Third in History. Above middle in French and German.'

She put a hand on my arm. 'I know, darling. Don't get upset. I know there are things you're good at. But if these two are what you're bad at, what sort of a life are you going to have at Sumner's?'

'I don't know,' I answered. 'It's a problem.'

It was my Uncle Percy who solved the problem, and in an unexpected way. Out of the blue he called us up and invited us to have dinner with him. I had not seen him for years, and he had slid away into the mists of my mind, like an ogre once encountered in a fairy tale. And now here was the ogre, speaking on the telephone in his odd, hoarse voice and giving me the address of a restaurant in Church Street, Kensington.

E was greatly intrigued. 'Well, I'll be damned!' she said. 'Now what does my dear brother want?'

'Perhaps he just wants to be friendly,' I offered.

'Percy? Friendly? Not on your life. No, he wants something – it must be something to do with Sumner's. Perhaps he wants you in the firm quickly. Perhaps he's dying.'

She was so hopeful that it made me laugh. 'Why should he be dying?'

'Cancer. Didn't I tell you? He had one of his eyes removed a few months ago.'

'How awful. Which eye?'

'Oh, I don't know. The right one, I think. No, maybe it was the left. I can't remember. What difference does it make?'

Her callousness was shocking: funny, too. I was beginning to understand the extremes of my mother's nature. To those she cared for – dustman or duke – she gave friendship as generous as the sun; to anyone who affronted or offended her she could be as cold, as indifferent, as the permafrost.

The family reunion was not festive. Percy was much as I remembered him, only more so: pallid, porcine, self-esteeming. E and her brother sat side by side, linked by their genes and profound mutual dislike; I faced them across the narrow table. Most of the time I kept my gaze on the plate before me – not that the food was deserving of interest, but because I could not look my uncle in the eye: I did not know which eye to look in. Both of his little eyes had expression of a sort, but each eye had a different sort of expression.

All through the indifferent meal, brother and sister cut and slashed at one another in a series of cavalry skirmishes. Other patrons doubtless took the stain on our tablecloth to be beetroot juice. I knew better: it was freshly spilt blood. Yet, for all the hostility, neither side was willing to make an outright declaration of war, though once it came very close. The conversation had turned to Grandpa.

'Do tell me how Father is.' E was trying to be conciliatory at that stage. 'I worry a lot about him.'

Her love and concern inflamed my uncle; he turned on her like an infuriated boar, shaking, barely in control; and it came to me in a moment of insight that the man was insanely jealous of the love between E and her father; that he had been jealous since he was a tiny boy; and – ironically – that this jealousy might well be the source of all his energy.

'Father?' He gave an ugly laugh. 'The kindest thing to say about our august father is that he is getting old.'

He was not placed, as I was, to notice the two red spots that flared up in his sister's cheeks, but he must have known that his whip had stung her.

I thought she would get up and leave the table; instead, she replied with steely gentleness, 'Not getting old, Percy. He is old. Almost eighty.'

'Exactly. And still trying to run Sumner's. But he's incapable. Senile.'

E looked away from him, and I heard her draw in her breath. But she turned and smiled at her brother. 'Then isn't he lucky that he has you, Percy, to help him? Poor old man, where would he be without your wonderful loyalty?'

That was the moment when I thought a declaration of open war was inevitable. But, as though by tacit agreement, both sides galloped off and took up their positions on less exposed ground. In the ensuing silence the dessert trolley was trundled up.

'Now then, Esther – what about a pudding?' Percy waved an expansive hand towards the transparent jellies, the opaque and hazardous custards.

E studied the things for an insultingly long time. At last, in a tone devoid of expression, she said, 'No, thank you, Percy.'

'Really? Then what about the boy?'

'No, thank you, Uncle Percy.'

'Goodness, what are boys coming to?' He cleared his throat portentously. 'In that case we had better discuss the matter before us – the reason for this meeting.' He turned his head, and for a moment both his eyes looked at me at once; one of them appeared friendly, the other hostile. 'As you will know, Esther – since I am sure that there are none of Sumner's secrets hidden from you – Father wants this boy of yours to come into the firm. Well – I have no objection to that.'

No objection? He had no objection to me? Well, I had a very large objection to *him*. This rude, flabby, insufferable man – disloyal to his father, insulting to his sister, patronizing to me – I despised him. Yet the code of behaviour in which I had been schooled made me sit silent. He went on.

'But I must make it clear to you, Esther, that I could not contemplate a directorship for the boy for many years to come.'

117

It was not what he said that was so deeply offensive; it was his manner of saying it. I had not been 'talked across' in this way since I was a small boy; and I was not a boy any more. I was seventeen years old, and a man. I was a House Prefect and a full corporal in the OTC; I had a 'Cap' for rugger; I was six foot tall and I weighed eleven and a half stone. It would have given me no trouble, only pleasure, to have twisted my Uncle Percy's fat nose and thrown him into the street. But I said nothing, and the thick voice went on.

'One other point, Esther. Before I could even begin to consider him for a directorship, it will be essential for the boy to have two degrees. One in Science – one in Chemistry.'

Oh, Joy . . . Oh, Salvation . . . Oh, Hallelujah! . . . Had I heard right? Could I believe what he had said? His words had sounded in my ears like the voice of Deliverance, like the sound of the polar ice cracking under the advance of spring. I sat there in silence, but inwardly shouting for joy. At that very moment, in that dingy restaurant with its blood-stained tablecloth, my life had been changed. A degree in Science? A degree in Chemistry? Not if I studied for the rest of my life could I get one of them, let alone both. Glory be to God, I was saved. My pig-faced uncle had discharged a heavenly purpose. By making conditional the one condition I could never fulfil he had set me free. Without meaning to, he had released me from a load of obligation. Now I could follow my own left-handed adventure, not take the right-hand course expected of me by my grandfather.

All unknowing that he had sent my spirit flying up into the stars, Percy paid the bill, called for his bowler hat and umbrella, and led the way out into Church Street, where he hailed a cab. 'Can I give you a lift, Esther?' It was not a pressing invitation.

'We'll walk, thanks.' Her voice sounded shaky.

'As you please. Goodnight.' He drove off.

E stood on the pavement, biting her lip. There were tears in her eyes.

'Mum . . . Mum . . . What's the matter? Don't cry.'

'Forgive me, Bunt.' She found her handkerchief and gave her nose a blow. 'Please forgive me.'

'Whatever for?'

'Because I've messed up your life tonight. That's what I've done.'

'No, you haven't.'

'Yes, I have. He's such a beast – such a bully – that brother of mine. He hasn't changed. He was just the same when he was little. But I shouldn't have lost my temper. Now he'll never let you into Sumner's. Tonight was a catastrophe.'

118

Above: 'E'; my mother, Esther Quayle.
(*Dorothy Wilding*)

Above right: my father, Arthur Quayle.

Below: Two years old.

Right: At Abberley *c.* 1922

Far left: With *The Meanest Man On Earth*, 1932

Left: With Lilian Braithwaite in *Elizabeth, la Femme sans Homme*, London 1938.

Bottom left: As Rutland in *Richard of Bordeaux* with Peggy Ashcroft and John Gielgud, London 1932. (*Houston Rogers*)

Right: 'Mason-Mac'.

Below: 'Mason-Mac' and his staff at Gibraltar, 1942. From l to r: Sqdn. Ldr. Ken Gatward, Major AQ, Major Shepard-Capurro, Lt. Gen. Mason-Macfarlane, Comm. Brown, Capt. David Woodford.

Above: With Noël Coward and John
Perry, Gibraltar 1942.

Left: As Noah in André Obey's *Noah*
(aged 28), Gibraltar 1940.

Right: In Albania.

Above: As Enobarbus in *Antony and Cleopatra* with Godfrey Tearle and Edith Evans, London 1946. (*Houston Rogers*)

Left: As Othello, Stratford, 1954. (*Angus McBean*)

Right: As Iago, London 1947. (*John Vickers*)

Overleaf: Dot as Lady Windermere, London 1946 (*Costume and photo: Cecil Beaton*)

She was adult, childish, serious, comical – all at once. I put my arm round her shoulders.

'Precious Mum, you were wonderful. And tonight was the best thing that has ever happened. I don't want to go into Sumner's.'

She pulled away from me, suddenly angry. Physically, my darling mother was not built for speed, but emotionally she could turn on a dime. 'Don't want to?' she repeated. 'Don't *want?*'

'No. And now I don't have to.'

'Indeed? Well – that's big talk I must say.' She was full of confusion and distress. 'Perhaps you'd tell me what you think you'll do if you don't.'

'All right,' I said. 'I'll tell you exactly what I'll do if I don't. Come on – let's walk.'

We went up to Southport to tell Grandpa what had happened and what I now planned to do. Both he and Aggie had aged since I last saw them; Aggie was frail, Grandpa shrunken and spent. In the rage of his youth he had forged a wheel and tied himself to it; now the wheel was carrying him along and he could no longer control it. He sat in his big armchair by the fire, lighting and relighting his pipe, and there was not much I could say to relieve his distress.

'An actor . . .' He kept repeating the words. If I had told him I wanted to be a deep-sea diver he could not have been more bewildered.

He had taken the news of Uncle Percy philosophically. 'I understand, my boy. There is nothing we can do. Percy will make your life hell. And I won't be around to give you any protection.' It was this 'actor' business that he could not understand. 'Why not go to university? Take a degree. I'll find the money.'

'No, really Grandpa. You are very generous. But no.'

'Why not?'

'Because I'd be wasting your money. Because I'm not academic at all. Because I want to get on with acting – and living.'

He gave a great sigh. 'Very well. Try to get into this "Royal Academy" place. Then at the end of a year we'll look at the situation again.'

There was a small happening during my last term at Rugby that has stuck in my mind: a miniature revelation. Many men have had moments of revelation, some of a supreme and violent kind. Zacharias held talk with the angel Gabriel: an experience that – understandably – left him speechless; Saul of Tarsus had a revelation that flung him to the ground and temporarily blinded him. My own experience can hardly be compared with theirs; but trivial and transient as it was, it has stayed in my memory for sixty years, so it may be worth recording.

Morning school was over; it was raining, and I was walking through the Close, when there came over me a most unusual sense of being in harmony – I can think of no other way to put it – with everything about me. Perhaps what I felt was no more than self-congratulation on having found a way to 'disregard the rules'; perhaps it was because my shoes had come back from the cobbler resoled, and for the first time in weeks I could walk in the rain without getting wet feet. But I think it was more than an attack of mere smugness: it was a sense that, for a moment, I was filling adequately the space in life allotted to me, and that I was in tune with everything: with earth, sea, sky, with birds and fishes, with elephants and whales – with the majestic, magnanimous old Bodger.

In honesty I must confess that this vivid sensation of being at one with the universe lasted no longer than the few minutes it took me to arrive back at the House.

CHAPTER 8

I WAS EIGHTEEN WHEN I WENT TO RADA – almost twenty-six when the Second World War broke out: eight jagged years of adolescence and infatuation, often painful to live through. But I must try to describe them because they are the link between boy and man, and because some people came into my life at that time who became lasting friends and had a profound influence on me.

I am only capable of telling this story in chronological order, but life itself is not orderly. I know the clock goes *tick-tock*, and I know that Shakespeare lived from 1564 till 1616; I know there is order in the majestic, incomprehensible movement of the universe; order in the seasons who tread sisterly on one another's heels; but there is no such order in man's short life. The telephone numbers, the daily appointments, the trivial events of a lifetime can all be comprised in a neat row of pocket diaries gathering dust on the shelf; but the yearnings, the instincts, the dark winds that shake and drive us before them, they admit of no order. They are like the great Atlantic storms in their furious power; but, unlike the storms, their season cannot be predicted; they come howling and raging when they are least expected.

> *To every thing there is a season, and a time to every purpose under the heaven:*
> *A time to be born, and a time to die;*
> *A time to plant, and a time to pluck up that which is planted;*
> *A time to kill, and a time to heal;*
> *A time to break down, and a time to build up;*
> *A time to weep, and a time to laugh;*

A time to mourn, and a time to dance;
A time to cast away stones, and a time to gather stones together;
A time to embrace, and a time to refrain from embracing;
A time to get, and a time to lose;
A time to keep and a time to cast away;
A time to rend, and a time to sew;
A time to keep silence, and a time to speak;
A time to love, and a time to hate;
A time of war, and a time of peace.

That is life as I have met it: passionate, unpredictable, haphazard – often confusing. There is unmistakably a time to be born and a time to die; it would take great obtuseness to miss either of them. It is the intermediate times that are sometimes hard to identify: they overlap; they get jumbled up; they even contradict one another.

But Ecclesiastes is the work of a mighty poet, one who can spread his wings and soar above the absurdities of clocks and calendars. I have to tread a more mundane path – the one marked 'What happened next'.

What happened next was that I left Rugby and was accepted by the Royal Academy of Dramatic Art. With Caliban, I could leap and cry aloud, *'Freedome, high-day, high-day, freedome.'* From now on everything, good or bad, would depend on me alone: not on the wishes – or even the generosity – of others.

Before the RADA term started, E flew her perch in Lancaster Gate and moved, with Grandpa's help, to 59B Linden Gardens. It was a flat on the first floor and quite inelegant; but glory be, it was a real home after years of hotel bells and hotel smells. I had a bedroom with a real London view of drainpipes and a blank wall; there was a living room with a real fireplace, a kitchen with a real gas cooker; and from Southport came a furniture van with a crew of sturdy, bald-headed men who marched up the stairs carrying real friends, old friends I had not seen for years – pictures, tables, chairs, the grandfather clock.

E was as happy as any woman can be who is driven to pour her love into a boy who was, after all, only a son. The years of boarding school were over; she had me back home with her at last. I was beside myself to have been accepted by RADA. I had no idea what 'acting' involved, but I knew I had found my way to the bottom of the beanstalk; I could touch the stem, look up and see it disappearing into the clouds. Life was miraculous . . . I was grown-up . . . I took to smoking cigarettes – three a day if I felt like it.

The term started and I went prancing off to RADA in a fever of excitement. The fever swept me along for weeks; but before the end of my first term, as the novelty of being a young dog of a drama student began to wear off, I found myself sniffing the air of the Academy with a cautious mistrust – as though it were milk that might be on the turn. I was not being critical; I would not have presumed criticism; but there was something in the atmosphere that made me doubt I would complete the whole three-year course – something negative, faintly backward-looking, almost incestuous. It emanated from the busts and portraits of past actors that adorned the hall. 'Poor infants,' they seemed to say, 'you will never be as witty, as brilliant, as famous as we were.' It emanated from the Principal, Kenneth Barnes; he was a caring man, but had been in charge of the school for so many years that he had by now acquired Limpet's Rights – and something of a limpet's outlook. It emanated from our teachers – dutiful, good people, but, with two exceptions, dispiriting. The exceptions were Dorothy Green and Alice Gachet.

The very names of those two women are scarcely remembered today; they have gone below to join all the other ghosts that throng the further bank of the Styx. But I am still here for a while longer in the sunlight; I remember them, and I speak their names with love and gratitude.

I was still at school when I went for the first time to the Old Vic. Like most boys I had been made to learn a few passages from Shakespeare: I knew, *Once more unto the breach, dear friends, once more*; I could recite – rather inappropriately on account of my size – *Where the bee sucks there suck I; in a cowslip's bell I lie.* But the only time I had seen a Shakespeare play through from beginning to end was the catastrophic *Richard II* at Rugby. So I went to the Old Vic, not exactly under protest, but in no way expecting to be struck by lightning; and I was – twice over – first by the writing, then by the acting. The play was *The Tempest*, with John Gielgud and Ralph Richardson; and playing Juno was an actress with a personality as ardent as a ship's prow – Dorothy Green. I went again to the Vic, this time to see *Much Ado About Nothing*, and there was this actress playing Beatrice; I went to see *King Lear* and there she was again, a deadly-smiling Goneril. Those productions, threadbare as they were, imprinted on me for life; they were my first, unforgettable glimpse of the High Himalaya. Till then I had only known that I wanted to be some sort – any sort – of an actor; now I knew exactly what sort of an actor I had to be or count myself a failure. I had got to try and follow in the giant footsteps of Gielgud and Richardson – and Dorothy Green. And now here she was, directing us students in *The Winter's Tale*.

As Autolycus I was seriously bad; the part was beyond me. I danced madly round with Mopsa and Dorcas; I sang, '*Will you buy any tape or lace for your cape?*' enthusiastically but off-key; I brimmed over with vitality; and all the time I knew I was dreadful. But 'Greenie', from her generous heart, gave out nothing but encouragement. She was my first contact with the living stage, a working actress who called me by my name – 'Tony'. It was enough to show me that the door into the theatre was not nailed shut; it could be opened. I did not have to stay always on the outside, looking in. She, as much as anyone I have known, took me by the hand and pulled me in.

God knows what the poor woman must have suffered at our beginners' hands, but she never even winced; she merely smiled and lit another cigarette. The worse we acted, the more she smoked. She could easily get through a packet of twenty in an hour's rehearsal, then gratefully cadge another ten from the students. Cigarettes and students – they were a bad combination, and they did for her in the end: lung cancer.

Alice Gachet was more than a good teacher, more than a great teacher: she was a teacher of genius. She was an archetypal French peasant – indomitable – with a shrewd, sensitive face. She would waddle into the classroom on painful feet, give us all an amused, sardonic '*Alors, mes enfants*' – and with her presence breathe vitality and fun into the flattest, most unprofitable day. She was encouraging to those who used their brains, intolerant of all who wasted her time. I learned from her that there is a natural, changing rhythm and colour in dialogue, just as there is in the weather; that a pause can be as long and as interesting as the thought that sustains it; above all, that acting and living are the intertwined stems of the same plant. These things she taught by being what she was rather than by what she said. She was a great woman: a great ambassadress of France.

RADA had little or no artistic policy, no discernible outlook on the profession that it served. But then, with the exception of the great Repertories like Birmingham and Liverpool, there was little policy or artistic outlook in the nation's theatre as a whole. The English Theatre was a moderately lively, wholly commercial, game of catch-as-catch-can. In London, the Old Vic had begun to make itself felt, but it was spider-poor and as yet hardly fashionable. At Stratford the theatre had been burnt down and was in the pangs of rebuilding. In the West End, plays were mostly about charming, middle-class matters – infidelities and the like; they appealed to charming, middle-class audiences and called for charming, middle-class performers. The Royal Academy of Dramatic Art, for all the grandiosity of its name, was simply a purveyor of talent to this commercial marketplace; it nodded towards the classics but its main purpose was to promote the young actors and actresses most likely to succeed on

Shaftesbury Avenue. It encouraged 'The Cult of Personality' before the phrase was coined; it bestowed prizes of Gold, Silver and Bronze as though acting were some sort of Olympic Games. That Drama was a great art, a Mystery – that it was possible for acting to be not just a profession but a calling – such ideas were never discussed.

This was not the atmosphere I had looked forward to. The competition for parts that would stand out in the Public Show was ferocious. I found it disappointing, but I accepted it – just as I accepted the fact that girls outnumbered the men by a good ten to one; in time I realized that this was a simple matter of market forces. RADA was in perpetual financial difficulties. Bernard Shaw was still very much alive; he had not yet endowed RADA with a third of his estate; *Pygmalion* had not been turned into *My Fair Lady* and brought the royalties rolling in. Kenneth Barnes was doing the only thing he could – finance the training of the talented few by accepting the fees of the untalented many. (On which side of that dividing line, I wondered, did I come down? Could my prompt admission have been influenced more by Grandpa's cheque than my own small gift? It was an uncomfortable thought and I quickly put it from me.) Middle-class girls in those days were more addicted to the stage than to ponies, and middle-class parents found it cheaper to send their daughters to RADA than to a Finishing School in Switzerland. So – short, tall, fat, slim, smart, dowdy, modest, brazen, with red-lacquered fingernails or with bitten stubs, with a tiny talent or with none at all, they swarmed everywhere – filling in time, waiting for a husband, or a lover, or *anorexia nervosa*, to come and point the way their lives were meant to go.

The inevitable happened: I fell in love. No, that expression is both conventional and inadequate. I did nothing so passive as to fall; I hurled myself into love like a madman leaping from a plane without a parachute. Her name was Hermione, and it suited her, for there was something cool and Greek about her whole appearance. She was a lovely girl with soft, brown hair and a way of looking quizzically out at life from inside herself. She gave me no encouragement, which only made my infatuation the greater.

Hermione was the daughter of Nicholas Hannen, a distinguished actor always known as 'Beau' – because that is exactly what he was, from his gentlemanly features to his beautifully polished shoes. Her stepmother was Athene Seyler, a fine actress and a woman of wit and wisdom. She also had a brother, Peter, several years older than herself, and they all lived together in a little, crooked house: 79 Chelsea Manor Street, to be precise. Beau and Athene accepted me with great kindness, but as the months of courtship turned into years I saw them looking at me with increasing bewilderment; and God knows I must have been bewildering. For my part, I regarded them with reverence. I knew myself to be so juvenile, such an outsider in this London world of theatre, while they belonged to the innermost ring of insiders. They moved with no apparent difficulty from one West End production to the next; their friends were novelists and playwrights like Hugh Walpole; they had supper with 'Sybil and Lewis' – the Cassons; they talked of spending Sunday with 'Marie and Willie' – and they meant Marie Tempest and her husband.

I seldom met Peter; when I did he was friendly but guarded, as any twenty-three-year-old will be with a boy who is in thrall to his sister. I hung back a bit too. I was envious of Peter; partly because he was already an up-and-coming young actor at the Old Vic, partly for the reason that I had once been envious of Basil Himbury with his Sports Alvis – and all that went with it. Peter was genuinely handsome, cultured, poised, intelligent; he was no cheap seducer with a lounge-lizard moustache, steering a billiard cue between nicotine-stained fingers. No, perhaps not, but he damn well did have a car, a beguiling little Austin Seven, and he also had what went with it – the most desirable, sought-after young actress on the London stage: Diana Wynyard. While here was I, eighteen, penniless, a paltry drama student, making no headway at all with his sister.

I was not envious for long. One day at the Academy Hermione mentioned that Peter was not well, and was having to miss a few performances at the Old Vic. She did not know what was wrong with him, but she thought it was something to do with his kidneys. There was nothing to worry about; Beau and Athene were Christian Scientists and had called in their practitioner to 'work' for him.

Ten days later when I asked after Peter she told me that the practitioner was working away, but so far without result. Just as a precaution, her brother was being moved to the Homeopathic Hospital, and more practitioners were being set to work. Peter's response was to grow progressively worse. I went to visit him in hospital, and even to me it was apparent that he was dying. At last the Hannens were left with no place to hide; they came into the open and admitted that, in this one case, Christian Science did not appear to be effective. With great reluctance they called in more orthodox practitioners.

> *Physicians of the utmost fame*
> *Were called at once, but when they came*
> *They murmured, as they took their fees,*
> *'There is no cure for this disease.'*

126

Nephritis in those days was a killer; proper nursing from the start might have saved him, but by now it was too late. Peter was brought back home; he died in Hermione's bedroom, in her bed. Then what remained of all that promise, youth, looks, intelligence, was put in a coffin, screwed down, and with some hazardous manoeuvring on the narrow staircase, carried feet first into Manor Street and driven away.

Hermione forgave her father; she accounted him weak, but she loved him. Her stepmother, the dominant spirit of the two, she held responsible for Peter's death. Outwardly she showed no more than a coolness towards Athene, but inwardly the grudge lived on for years and bore bitter fruit. To add to her distress she was told by the doctors that she was herself liable to contract Bright's disease, that her hold on life was precarious, and that a pregnancy would be fatal. Already introverted, over-conscious of mortality, she now became more so. I saw her, white-faced, endure these miseries, but I could not help; she was not interested in what I had to offer.

To go moping after a moon goddess – a moon goddess made doubly appealing by her griefs – might easily have become a full-time occupation if I had not been so eager to press on and make my way in the world. I had got to earn my living; I had got to stop being a drag on E and Grandpa. It was a waste of time to doddle on in the false security of RADA; there were other students, full of talent and far senior to me, who would surely be groomed for those Gold and Silver Medals, then launched with flags and fanfares down the slipway of a Public Show. I might hang around for another two years and at the end come away from RADA with nothing but a useless Diploma.

I nosed about and discovered that at Kew Bridge there was a small theatre called the 'Q' where a Mr and Mrs Jack De Leon ran weekly repertory. As soon as the term ended I found my way there to look for a job.

The 'Q' was small, with no balcony; it looked as though it had sat down and squeezed itself in beside a big, boisterous pub. There were posters outside displaying the week's 'attraction': *Many Waters*, starring Louise Hampton. I pushed open the door to the draughty foyer and assumed an air of confidence.

'Could I see either Mr or Mrs De Leon?' I asked at the box office.

A female – frizzy-haired, hostile – answered through the grille. 'Got an appointment?'

'Not exactly an appointment.'

'Then you'll have to wait. Mr De Leon's in London. Mrs De Leon may be in later.'

I waited. One hour. Two hours. Mist seeped in from the river; there was a smell of escaping gas. For lunch I went and had a sandwich and a glass of beer at the pub next door. Then I came back and waited some more. Business was slow at the box office, and it was very cold. I tracked down the smell of gas; it came from a number of antique radiators that were around the place – but unlit. From time to time I walked over to the frizzy-haired lady and asked brightly, 'Any news of Mrs De Leon?'

The answer was always the same. 'No. No news.'

In the late afternoon a man in shirtsleeves and shabby green trousers wandered through, putting a match to the row of gas jets under each radiator. The place smelt as if it were about to explode, but it grew perceptibly warmer and for that I was thankful. It was shortly before the audience started to come in for the evening performance that the man, now fully uniformed but looking even shabbier, came up and gave me a long, flat look.

'You bin 'ere a long time,' he said. It was a statement of fact, not calling for an answer. 'Waitin' to see someone?'

'Mrs De Leon.'

'What for?'

I did not think there was much to be gained by telling him, so I said, 'I just want to see her. That's all.'

He gave me a suspicious look and went away. Soon he was back. 'This way.' He jerked his head, and I followed him down a corridor to the open door of a small, untidy office.

Mrs De Leon – I took it to be her – was standing bundled up in an overcoat behind a desk piled with scripts and papers. She was short, with lively brown eyes.

'Yes?' Her manner was distinctly aggressive.

I had been waiting so long that now I hardly knew what to say. 'I just wondered – ' I began. But she cut in on me.

'Listen to me, young man. I've got your bill here – and it's disgraceful. I've paid a deposit, and you'll get no more out of me till the end of the week. You should never have hired out a sofa in that condition. You must have known the leg was broken. Barely glued together. Miss Hampton might have broken her neck.'

'I'm sorry,' I managed to get in. 'I'm not here about a sofa.'

'No? Then what are you here about?'

'A job.'

'A job! Not a hope. We're full up. What are you? Carpenter? Electrician?'

'I'm an actor,' I said. 'At least, I'm a student.'

Mrs De Leon gazed at me in astonishment; then her face broke into a most engaging and unexpected smile. 'Oh, heavens – and I thought you were from the furniture company. I've been dodging you all day. Well, now you're here, let's have a look at you.' She gave me the long, appraising look of a farmer buying an animal at auction. 'Student, eh? . . . RADA?'

'Yes.'

'Hmmmm.'

'You don't approve?'

'Oh, RADA's all right. Don't start talking posh, that's all.'

'I'll try not to.'

'How old are you?'

Should I lie? Should I tell the truth? I plumped for the truth. 'Eighteen,' I said, and immediately regretted it.

'Eighteen!' She made the word sound repugnant. 'Hopeless. Much too young.'

'But I can look older – much older. With a white beard I can look seventy . . . eighty. I've just been doing a scene from *Heartbreak House* . . .'

She was not listening. 'Turn sideways . . . Yes – a moustache might help. Have you got a suit?'

I did not have a suit, but to possess one was clearly of great importance. I repeated her words, hoping to sound ambiguous. 'A suit?'

'Yes. A lounge suit – single-breasted, double-breasted – it doesn't matter which. But Henry must wear a suit. Wouldn't be right without a suit.'

'Henry?' Her mind worked so fast that I could not follow her.

'The juvenile in *The Ghost Train*. Don't you know *The Ghost Train*?'

'I'm afraid not.'

'Pity. Good play. Good part. But you're too young. Although – ' She broke off and surveyed me once more. 'You say you have a suit? What sort of a suit is it?'

This time I did not hesitate. 'A sort of a blue suit,' I lied.

'Blue, eh? Should really be a tweed suit, but blue will have to do. All right – you've got yourself a job. Here's the script.' She picked one off the pile on her desk. 'Give Brenda your name and address. She's the one in the next room behind a typewriter. Give her your phone too, if you have one. Rehearsals start next Monday. Ten sharp. Here.'

'Thank you,' I stammered. 'Thank you very much.'

I was almost out of the door when she called to me. 'We haven't talked about money. You know – pay.'

'Oh, no. Nor we have.'

She drove straight on. 'That's because there isn't any. Right? You're lucky to have a chance like this. Look at all the famous people playing here – Louise Hampton this week, Nancy Price the next. Experience – that's your pay. Nothing like experience. It's gold. All right?'

'Yes,' I said. 'Oh yes. Quite all right.'

An hour later I burst in on E. 'Mum . . . Mum . . . I've got a job.'

'Bunt – you haven't.'

'Yes, I have. It doesn't pay anything and I've got to buy a suit. But I'm going to act at the "Q".'

It was the first time, paid or unpaid, that I had appeared professionally on the stage: the first time I could truthfully say, 'I am an Actor.' It was the first time I had opened a dressing-room door holding in my mind a whole new world waiting for creation, and found myself looking at the debris left by the last occupant – empty beer bottles, decaying sandwich crusts, soiled rags, lumps of filthy cotton wool. It was the first time I had hopefully laid out the tools of my trade – greasepaint, spirit gum, crepe hair, (I had been told that at all costs I must make Henry look older) – and then faced my own inadequate features in the mirror. It was the first time I had heard through the curtain the hum and chatter of an audience coming in to take their seats, the unexplained guffaws from remote parts of the house, the snatches of half-audible conversation from the front stalls.

The performance was a triumph – thanks entirely to Jack De Leon. The manager of the 'Q' was a dark-eyed Sephardi who looked less like a theatre owner than a mysterious physician at the Court of Queen Elizabeth I. But Jack was a shrewd man; he knew that with *The Ghost Train* the text was immaterial, the acting irrelevant; all that mattered was the train itself. Backstage he had mustered and drilled a whole orchestra of stagehands armed with cannonballs, drums, tanks of galvanized iron, huge cylinders of compressed air. Like a Toscanini he held his men in check till the great moment arrived, then brought them in, section by section, till they built to a deafening climax. First came a long, mournful whistle from the far-off train; again it came – but closer, louder; and now could be heard the rumble and thunder of the approaching wheels, the roar of the engine. The audience sat mesmerized. They *knew* that what they heard was impossible – and yet they heard it. Louder and louder grew the noise till every member of the audience willingly, ecstatically, suspended all disbelief. Clutching their companions' hands, spilling their chocolates all over the floor, they not only heard but saw – thay actually saw – a thirty-ton locomotive, firebox glowing, lights blazing, whistle shrieking, thunder across the stage before their very eyes.

E came to the opening night and was as proud as if she had been sitting at the Haymarket or the Old Vic itself. We rode home to Notting Hill Gate, changing buses as we went. She was full of praise and reassurance.

'Yes, of course I could hear you. Every single word. And the suit looks fine.' It had been run up by a cheap tailor who owed E a favour.

'And the moustache?'

She had said nothing about that, and the thing had given me a lot of trouble. It is not at all easy to make your own moustache out of crepe hair. The first three or four that I had stuck on had been lopsided; I had ripped them off one after the other – ripped off a considerable amount of skin too. Even when I had completed the final version, spirit gum all over my fingers and some of it up my nose, I was not too happy with the result; it was almost half an inch thick. I was so determined it should be seen that now I had some difficulty in speaking; my upper lip could hardly move.

'The moustache? Oh, it suits you,' E assured me. 'It really does. But – turn your head this way a second. Ouch! Your poor lip does look a mess. Do you really have to stick the thing on every night?'

'Absolutely. Henry's older than me. Years older.'

'Couldn't you – couldn't you just paint it on?'

'Good heavens, no. The audience must be able to see it when it's in profile. Could you see it? Honestly – could you see it when I was standing sideways?'

'Darling, of course I could. It's very noticeable. No one could possibly miss it whichever way you stand.' All the time she was anxiously examining my lip. 'Oh dear – I do hope that doesn't get any worse. It looks to me as if it might turn septic. I'll give you some stuff to put on it when we get home.'

My blue suit must have passed muster, and my RADA accent been kept under control, for the De Leons were very good to me and gave me a whole string of parts. I stayed three terms at RADA, and between each of them I went and acted at Kew. The theatre became a home to me; I never earned any money but, as Beattie De Leon had said, I was paid in the pure gold of experience. I worked shoulder to shoulder with real actors and actresses. Not all were brilliant; not all could be bothered with me; but some of them took the trouble to make me understand a few basic lessons that can only be learnt in front of an audience – when to move and when to keep still; how to listen as well as how to speak; how to deliver a line so that it 'feeds' a laugh; how to apply the pressure that keeps a play moving forward.

I landed another job during the summer vacation from RADA; it had no significance beyond earning me a welcome fiver, but it gives a picture of an epoch that has vanished, and it throws some light on my naïveté – a naïveté that the young of today would hardly believe.

Gerald Cooper was a wealthy man and a pianist of note, but he was afflicted with an unfortunate craving to perform on the stage; above all, he longed to act Malvolio. Since he would never be offered the part in the professional theatre, he decided – for this was before the days of Equity – to stage his own production. He accordingly presented *Twelfth Night* for a week at the Croydon Repertory Theatre, directing the play himself and starring as Malvolio. It was not the salary that attracted me – though who was I to turn down the chance of earning a fiver? – and it was not that I thought I would learn much by playing Orsino in this curious setup. What drew me was that, when our week at Croydon was done, we were to cross over to the Isle of Wight and give an open-air performance in the grounds of Admiral Lord Jellicoe's house. I was not sure how far the Isle of Wight lay from England and how close to France, but it was an island, and to get there involved a sea crossing; it would be almost like going abroad.

I had only once been out of Britain; that was when I was thirteen, and Grandpa had taken Mum and me to the north coast of Brittany. We stayed at a small hotel that might have been the model for *Monsieur Hulot's Holiday*, and I fell in love with an English girl called Edna. She was my age, her hair was bobbed, and she wore a blue, one-piece bathing costume. I knew she liked me too. But we were both far too self-conscious to make a display of ourselves in front of our families, so we devised a secret way of making contact: we swam towards each other under water and held hands for as long as we could before we were driven, gasping, to the surface. It was not very satisfying, but it was thrillingly romantic.

Now I was eighteen, grown-up, a young actor, sniffing the air for adventure; and here was the chance to travel abroad – well, almost abroad. I leapt at it.

We crossed over to the Isle of Wight in a full gale. At the Jellicoes' house, great trees were bending before the storm and deck chairs were flying through the air; but, we were told, there would be no alteration to the plans: the performance was to go ahead. Lady Jellicoe, organizer of the Garden Fête, was a commanding lady, tall and ample. Her consort, the Admiral, was tiny. I wondered how so small a man could have commanded so vast a fleet at the Battle of Jutland? Twenty-four battleships, three battle cruisers, and Lord knows how many cruiser and destroyer squadrons? He would have been hard put to it to see over the top of his own bridge.

The audience – villagers and assorted local worthies – were seated in orderly ranks across the tennis court. They were arranged in order of precedence; the grandees in front were provided with deck chairs, while lesser folk perched behind them on wooden benches. In the centre of the front row, enthroned on a well-upholstered chair, sat an elderly, minor member of the Royal Family – Princess Beatrice, I think. She was quite venerable, and was sensibly clad in an equally venerable, somewhat moth-eaten, fur coat.

We actors performed our rites on a raised bank that ran the length of one side of the tennis court. Immediately behind us, and towering over our heads, rose an enormous copper beech. The play began.

'*If music be the food of love*,' I bellowed, striving to make myself heard above the tumult of the leaves.

But the wind snatched sweet Master Shakespeare's words from my mouth and flung them out to sea, while overhead the branches of the great tree swayed and crashed as the gale tore at them. Throughout the whole deafening ordeal that followed, an ordeal for audience and actors alike, Lady Jellicoe kept unflinching station beside her guest of honour – ready, no doubt, to fall on top of the Royal Person and hold her down should she threaten to be blown away. Meanwhile the Admiral could be seen busying himself round the perimeter of the tennis court, carrying rugs, blankets, and other comforts to his shivering guests.

The final line was spoken, the audience thankfully dispersed, and we mummers were paraded in the hall of the Jellicoes' house to be presented to the Princess. We stood in an awkward circle round a large refectory table while the Princess trotted round saying alternately, 'Most enjoyable,' and, 'Quite delightful,' and sometimes just nodding civilly.

The presentations over – they did not take long since no one knew our names – a silence fell. The Princess looked as though she had shot her bolt; the Jellicoes smiled wanly but said nothing; my fellow actors were equally at a loss. In truth, there was nothing constructive or cheerful to be said; it had been a terrible occasion. At the same time I was acutely aware that someone (it did not matter who) should speak up and say something (it did not matter what) to break the encircling silence. All right, I thought, if no one else will, then I must; it is my duty. I drew in my breath to speak.

At that moment I happened to notice that Lord Jellicoe was looking straight at me. To be sure, he was on the far side of the hall and the refectory table was between us, but there was no mistaking his look of interest and anticipation – of gratitude too, maybe. Raising my voice, I called across the room, 'Were you able to hear all right, sir?'

But even as I spoke the Admiral turned to look in another direction; clearly, he had been distracted. Someone touched his arm and drew his attention back to me; once again he looked across and gave me a friendly, expectant smile. No one else spoke. Feeling increasingly foolish, I repeated my enquiry, this time a little louder.

'You were rather towards the back, sir. Could you hear all right from there?'

For a long time he appeared to be giving serious consideration to this idiotic question. Everyone else in the hall, like a bunch of half-drowned men praying to be saved, hung on his reply. At last he came to a decision; on small, neat feet, the hero of Jutland trotted round the room till he stood in front of me. Then he looked up, put his hand to his ear, and said, 'Would you mind repeating that? I'm rather deaf.'

At the end of a year the De Leons tried out a new play and gave me the leading part – a young Cornish fisherman falsely accused of murder. I was exultant: the play would transfer to the West End, run for as long as *Yellow Sands*, and be my first step on a path of limitless glory. My opinion of the play was not shared by the few third-string critics who came to see it; they dismissed it as piffle. I read their reviews in my ramshackle dressing room, and a dank, depressing wind whistled round my ears. But in the middle of the week I got an enigmatic note. 'Come and see me,' it read; it was signed 'Lee Ephraim'.

Lee Ephraim was a big producer of musical comedies. His hits at Drury Lane included *Rose Marie* and *The Desert Song*. This cryptic message could mean only one thing: Lee Ephraim was preparing a new musical with a Cornish setting, and in me he had spotted the very man he was looking for. I found it surprising, for I had never thought I had the voice or special talent to appear in a musical, but if the great Lee Ephraim thought otherwise who was I to question his judgment? Next day, shoes polished, bushy hair plastered down, I sat in his Regent Street office.

Mr Ephraim was not what I had expected. He was a benign, twinkling, grey little man – a New Yorker with the strangled voice of the Lower East Side.

He said, 'I saw your show Monday. It's got no future. But I liked your performance.'

'Oh. Thank you. I'm glad.'

'Yes – I liked it very much.'

Hope rose high into the sky as I waited for the proposal that would change my life.

'Unfortunately . . .' He broke off, leaving the ominous word hanging in midair. 'Unfortunately I'm not putting anything on at present. So I have nothing very interesting to offer you.'

Hope came plummeting down.

'But I have a suggestion to make.' Mr Ephraim was still smiling at me, twinkling and avuncular. 'I have an interest in a Jewish comedian – Naylor Grimson. Maybe you've heard of him?'

'No,' I ventured, 'I don't think I have.' A Jewish comedian? What on earth was he talking about?

'No? He's a fine artist. I present him in a sketch. Very funny. *The Meanest Man On Earth* – that's what it's called. Now, there's the part of a young fellow in it. The "Stooge" – or the "Straight Man". Doesn't matter what you call him. That's what he is. Would that interest you?'

'A sketch?' I faltered. 'I'm afraid I don't follow you. Where is it performed?'

'On the Music Halls. All over the country. You've heard of Moss Empires?'

Who had not? The Holborn Empire, the Chiswick Empire – every Empire in the land.

'Well, there you are. I'll pay you ten pounds a week. What d'you say?'

I could say nothing. I was poleaxed. Ten pounds a week. It was a fortune.

But Mr Ephraim misunderstood my dazed expression; he began to back-pedal: 'I'm afraid the part doesn't carry more than that. There's a girl to pay too – Lennie Deane. You know her? No? Never mind. I expect you want to finish your course at RADA. And this will be a long tour. Well – nice to have met you.' He rose.

What was happening? The job was sliding away between my outstretched hands.

'No,' I said. 'No, no. I don't mind leaving RADA one bit. I would very much like to do this tour with Mr – er . . .'

'Grimson.'

'Of course. Yes – Grimson. I'd be thrilled. Thank you. Thank you.'

My fairy godfather beamed at me: we might have concluded a deal for Drury Lane. 'Then that's that. You open two weeks Monday at the Empire, Leeds.'

That is how, just one year after leaving Rugby, I came to go on the 'Halls', on the great Moss Empire Circuit.

My departure from RADA was abrupt. The authorities made a few token protests but no one seriously objected, and before I left I was able to take part in Gachet's production of *Saint Joan*. I was glad: we had been rehearsing it for weeks and it would be my last contact with what might be called 'real' theatre before I took my flying leap into vaudeville.

135

We were halfway through the performance, not doing badly but far from making theatre history, when word got around that Tyrone Guthrie was in front. A rumour that the Lord of Hosts Himself had dropped in on our student show could not have caused more of a stir. Tyrone Guthrie, still a very young director but already hailed as a prodigy, had recently brought his company from Cambridge to the Westminster Theatre and was now busy giving London an iconoclastic shake-up. Rumour proved to be true; at curtain fall Gachet emerged from the wings, proud of her pupils and flushed with praise, telling us to wait on stage as Mr Guthrie wanted to say how much he had enjoyed the performance.

I had no idea what manner of man this Guthrie was or even what he looked like, but I assumed he would fit into the normal pattern of human appearance and that, as with other men, his opinions and personality would be politely shielded behind a few civilized ambiguities. I got a shock: Tyrone Guthrie was about as ambiguous as a sword thrust through the ribs.

Tony – he was never called anything else – was exceedingly tall: six foot seven I would have thought – but perhaps he was only six foot five; hair cut very short; a clipped, military moustache; front teeth sloping slightly backwards; a sharp nose and grey-blue eyes that held the discomforting stare of a bird of prey. He carried himself upright and with fluid ease, but his clothes showed a lack of concern for any conventions; at the same time he made no parade of being unconventional either. He was what he was, with the minimum of fuss. The whole long creature was dressed in grey flannel trousers, a tweed jacket, a shirt without a collar, a long blue scarf wound round his neck, and sandals. In contrast with the formidable military appearance was a most un-military, almost auntie-ish manner of speech that gave quirkiness to his personality and a wicked edge to his humour. Tony's brilliance sprang from an array of contradictions in his nature, but through all the years I knew him he remained steadfast in his no-nonsense attitude to life, in his scorn of luxury, in his loyalty to his friends, and in his enjoyment of a dram of whisky. It could be either Scotch or Irish: the nationality of the *cratur* was immaterial.

I am running on, describing what I only later came to know and understand, but something of this essential quality – a quality both provocative and reassuring – radiated from the man that afternoon at the Academy. He gave encouragement without flattery; he made us laugh at ourselves as well as at Bernard Shaw. As he left the stage he tapped my arm and said quietly, 'Come and see me at the Westminster.'

I did so; and he spoke to me not as an eminent man twelve years my senior, but as an equal and a fellow worker. It was a new experience, and it caused me to re-evaluate myself. He told me to get in touch with him again in the spring when the music-hall tour brought me back to London for a few weeks.

I walked away from the Westminster Theatre in a state of elation. I was not at all sure how to define a 'great man', but I could have sworn that for the first time in my life I had met one.

CHAPTER 9

ON A BITTER SUNDAY EVENING in January 1932 I stood hesitant outside a small terraced house in Acker Street, Leeds. I hesitated because of all the wretched little houses in this forlorn little street this was undoubtedly the most forlorn and wretched; and because behind the front door lay the digs I had booked for the week.

Naylor Grimson himself had given me the address, picking it out of the grubby diary he kept in an inner pocket. 'I've never stayed there myself, Tony. But it's a well-spoken-of address. Must be, or I wouldn't have it in my little book, would I?' He had looked at me under puffy eyelids, smiling like a travesty of Mephistopheles – a Mephistopheles with a pendulous stomach and a nose that was the ultimate caricature of all Jewish noses. 'Go on, Tony. Try it. Send her two pounds deposit. Mind you register the letter. Then she can't deny getting it, can she?' He had looked at me slyly, and winked.

Now here I was, loath to knock at the door but unable to run away. I had parted with my two pounds and had no idea where else in the whole of Leeds – and on a Sunday night – I might find digs I could afford. There was nothing else for it: I was trapped. I knocked on the door.

The sound reverberated as though through an empty coffin. There was no reply: only a faint scratching noise from within, a noise like fairy knitting needles being scraped along the floor; then a light scampering sound; then silence. I knocked again.

A woman's shrill voice rose from some cavernous region and emerged into Acker Street through the broken flap of the letter box. 'Who is it?'

I was not sure how to answer that question. I thought of shouting, 'My name is Quayle,' but refrained; it seemed an idiotic statement to be bawling through a letter box. To call out, 'I'm the lodger,' would be equally fatuous – an invitation to ribaldry. In this street of semi-poverty I shrank from making any noise at all: I had the wrong accent. I put my mouth to the letter box and called into the echoing darkness, 'It's me.'

As identification it was tenuous, but it worked. There was a shuffling of slippers, a sliding of bolts, then the door was opened by a tired-faced woman. Past her shoulder I could see a dark, narrow hall, lino-covered, and in the background the shirt-sleeved figure of a man.

'I booked a room,' I offered. 'I sent a deposit.'

'Oh, it's you, is it? Come in. You're the Ground Floor Back.' She closed the front door, then led the way to the back of the house. The man stood watching; like the woman he looked ill and seedy.

It was a small room into which she showed me, with a minimum of furniture – a bed, a horsehair settee, and a shilling-in-the-slot gas fire. The floor was covered with the same brownish, mottled linoleum as the hall. Through the dirty window I could see a vista of rotting fences, weeds, dustbins, and sagging bicycle sheds.

'You'll be nice and comfortable here,' the woman said.

I wanted to say, 'No, I shall not be comfortable here or uncomfortable either. Keep my two pounds. I'm off.' But I could not say it. It was not only the loss of two pounds that stopped me, grievous though that would have been; it was not only that I shrank from hurting the poor woman's feelings; it was an inner conscience that spoke in my ear. 'So you wanted to get on with life, did you? All right – try this for a start.'

'Thank you,' I said. 'I shall be fine.'

A scrabbling sound – the sound I had heard through the letter box – made me glance towards the open door. Some kind of small animal had crossed the shaft of watery light and vanished into the murk of the hall. I looked questioningly at the landlady. She looked straight back at me. We stood in a constrained silence.

At length I asked, 'What was that?'

There was another long pause before she replied, 'What was what?'

'That. Out in the hall. And there's another one. Look!'

She looked. Then she turned back to me, her face blank. 'It's nothing.'

This was developing into a battle of wits; it was liable to go on for ever. 'It can't be *nothing*,' I said. 'It must be *something*.'

She shrugged. 'Just one of the rabbits.'

'Rabbits?'

'Yes, rabbits.' She must have decided that attack was the best form of defence, for she continued sarcastically, 'They won't bite, y'know. There's no call to be afraid.'

'I'm not afraid.'

'Oh – good. I thought you were. There's half a dozen of them. They've got the run of the house.'

Having established ascendancy over the Ground Floor Back, she left the room, but before quite closing the door, she fired a parting shot. 'We think the world of our rabbits. So watch out you don't tread on them on the stairs – that's all.'

The house in Acker Street gave shelter to a wide variety of life. The basement was headquarters for the landlady, her consort, and the rabbits. From that underground bunker they made frequent sorties, dropping their pellets (I speak, of course, of the rabbits) without fear or favour from top to bottom of the house. Sometimes I would wake in the night to hear their tiny sentry claws scratching at the linoleum outside my door. Upstairs was the one and only lavatory; it was called 'the bathroom', but the bath was so begrimed and filthy that no one valuing their skin would have dared climb into it. In the only other upstairs room a game of poker went on all day, every day, and all night too. The door was open that first evening, a thick haze of cigarette smoke drifting out onto the landing. I looked in, and through the fog made out half a dozen men huddled round a table, the light pulled down low over their heads. I suppose some of the players may have changed as the week passed, but I never saw any of them come or go, and they were still at it when I left the following Sunday morning.

Sandwiched in between these upper and nether regions were two chorus girls from a touring revue in the Ground Floor Front, and myself in the Ground Floor Back.

My room at the back was bleak, but no bleaker than all the dormitories I had slept in for years. The electric light was a bit of a nuisance; a naked bulb dangled from the ceiling, and the only way to turn it on or off was by a switch near the door. This meant finding my way back to bed in the dark, usually stubbing my toes on the horsehair settee. But this was nothing – a mere inconvenience – compared with an onslaught of fleas. At least, I took them to be fleas, and plural they had to be; no one flea could have inflicted on me such a number of embossed and livid welts. I could not find the brutes either – and I was an experienced flea-hunter. By the Wednesday morning I was in such a mess that I decided to seek help from the girls next door; they had invited me to supper that night and I was sure they would have good advice to give.

We were not playing at the same theatre, the girls and I. *The Meanest Man On Earth* was part of the Variety Show at the Empire, with Jack Hylton's Band topping the bill; Babs and Doreen were dancers in a touring revue at the Grand. Babs was blonde, mid-twenties, ripe as a nectarine; Doreen was a bony sixteen with dark, frizzy hair, and eyes that were just the least bit too close together. They were merry little mice, and so breathtakingly silly that I did not know how to talk to them. But then I was such a sheltered little prig, so ignorant of their world — or of any other world for that matter — that they cannot have known how to talk to me either. Rugby provided sound training for many professions — for the Law, the Army, the Church, the Indian Civil Service. Rugby's influence had stood many a young fellow in good stead when he had to face his country's foes — be they Afghans, Fuzzy-Wuzzies, or the Kaiser's 'Huns'. Rugby stood me in no kind of stead whatever when I found myself at close quarters with a couple of chorus girls — especially when the younger of the two was looking at me with predatory, close-set eyes. It was that hungry, speculative glint that got me out of bed each morning when only the rabbits were stirring, and drove me to walk all day on Ilkley Moor till darkness fell and it was time to catch the bus back to Leeds. But a giggling, formal invitation could not be refused — and tonight, they told me, I would meet Jimmy, comedian of the touring revue, lover and protector of the luscious Babs.

Jimmy turned out to be a small, sad-faced man, old enough to be Babs' father. He had rubbery features which he twisted into a series of grimaces to illustrate whatever he was saying. He never gave his face a rest; it was continually being called on to give yet another comic performance. I was disconcerted at the start; I could not make out the man behind his gallery of funny masks. But after a while I realized that all this squinting and winking and pulling of faces was nothing but a facade; behind it there hid two people — both called Jimmy: one was a comic who had never made it to the top, and knew that now he never would; the other was a rather vain, and deeply jealous man.

Jimmy was quick to make clear to me his proprietory rights in Babs. 'Look at her, Tony. Isn't she lovely?' He gave a caveman growl. 'Look at that hair. That's real, natural blonde, Tony. You don't mind if I call you Tony?'

'Of course not. It's my name.'

'And look at those boobs.' He gave one of them a squeeze, as if he were testing melons from a barrow in Berwick Market. 'They're natural too, I can tell you.' He buried his face between the twin promontories and gave them a nuzzle.

Babs made no objection; she stood smiling patiently, like a cut-price earth goddess. 'Oh, give over Jimmy,' she said. 'You're awful.'

He straightened up, and his face turned into a portrait of misery. 'I tell you, Tony, I'm havin' the most awful bloody week. You know what? I've got the missus here.' He groaned and gave me one of his contorted winks. 'Come up from Penge, she has. D'you know Penge?'

I had to admit that I did not.

'Well, she has. All the way from bloody Penge. So I'm havin' to be good, aren't I? No time for a romp with this lovely girl.' He fondled her bottom, and she let out a squeak.

Doreen had been busy round the table. 'Oh, shut up, Jimmy,' she called. 'Leave her alone and come and eat your supper. Here, Tony — you come and sit here.' She gave me a honey-sweet smile and patted the chair next to her.

'What's this you've bought?' Jimmy threw up his hands in mock-amazement. 'My God — tinned salmon? Who's this in aid of? Tony, I tell you Doreen here must really fancy you. I'm never given tinned salmon.'

'And you know why.' Doreen was quite trenchant. 'He's got this dreadful ulcer,' she explained to me.

'Yes — duodenal.' Jimmy sounded like a mourner at his own graveside. 'Can't eat nothin' solid.'

'Then finish your milk, and stop pawin' Babs about. You'll put Tony off his food.'

'Listen, young lady — ' Jimmy wagged his finger at Doreen to show he was joking, but there was an ugly note of jealousy in his voice. 'Just because you're sharin' a bed with Babs this week doesn't mean you own her.'

I glanced round the room. Indeed, there was just the one double bed. Babs caught my look.

'Well, it's cold weather, isn't it?' she said, with a flirtatious toss of her head. 'And I don't like sleepin' alone. So . . .' She thumped the upturned bottle of salad cream, and the yellow liquid glugged out on her plate. 'While Jimmy's got his wife around, Doreen and I save money and cuddle up together. What's wrong in that?'

'Don't you try cuddlin' up with no one else — that's all.' Jimmy leant forward with such vehemence that he knocked the bottle of salad cream off the table. It was a timely diversion; there had been an ugly note in the air. We were busy cleaning up the mess when Doreen noticed the red lumps on my neck.

'Hey!' she cried. 'What's happened to you? You got mumps, or what?'

I assured her that I was not infectious, and unbuttoned my shirt to show them the bites.

'Now, those are real beauties.' Jimmy was really impressed. 'I've never seen anything like that. Have you ever seen anything like that, girls?'

The girls had not.

'They're all over me,' I said. 'These Yorkshire fleas are in a class of their own.'

'Fleas? Those aren't fleas.'

'No? What are they then?'

Jimmy delivered his diagnosis with a slow, gruesome relish. 'You, my boy, are the victim of an attack by bugs.'

'Bugs!'

'Haven't you met bedbugs before?'

'Never.'

'At least you know what they look like?'

'No, I don't.'

He sighed, raising his eyebrows in pitying contempt for all such greenhorns as me. 'Well – they've got red, horny backs. And they're about so big.' He held out his hand and measured off the little fingernail.

As big as *that*? I thought he must be joking, and glanced at the girls; they both stared back at me, solemn and serious-eyed.

'Where do they come from?' I asked. 'Where do they live?'

'Inside the bed.'

'But I've hunted. I've had all the sheets off. All the blankets. Nothing there.'

'Of course not. They're too cunning for that. They live in the ticking. Right inside the mattress. They wouldn't think of coming out till the bed is nice and warm.'

I must have looked dismayed, for he put his hand on my arm, friendly and reassuring, like an old 'sweat' talking to a young recruit.

'Don't you worry, Tony boy. I'll tell you what you have to do. You turn off the light, and you lie there in the dark till the bed is really warm. You must lie still, though. Don't frighten them – they scare dead easy. And don't fall asleep – or they'll have you all over again.'

I hung on his instructions. 'I see. Then what?'

'Ah, now comes the tricky bit. You must have a shoe handy – or a slipper. Right? Then, all of a sudden, you throw back the clothes, turn on your bedside light – and there they'll be, crawlin' about in the bed. Then you bash them with your slipper. Mind, they'll make a mess of the sheets because they'll be full of your blood. But don't you mind that. Just lay into them.'

I said, 'But there's no bedside light.'

'There isn't?'

'No. The switch is over by the door.'

143

'Oh, well – that's a problem.' He was put out for a moment; then he brightened up. 'All right. The next best thing – not perfect, I admit, but it'll have to do – is buy yourself a candle. An ordinary candle. And have a box of matches handy. Then carry out the same instructions – only this time you've first got to light the candle. And be damn quick about it or those bugs will have run back into the mattress.'

'Suppose I miss them? Then what?'

Jimmy spread out his hands in a gesture of philosophic resignation. 'Then you begin all over again, Tony boy. Startin' from the top.'

I followed his instructions to the letter. Not only was there no bedside light, there was no bedside table either; so I set the candle on the floor, turned off the switch by the door, climbed back into bed in the dark, and waited for the bed to warm up. It took a long time; the room was damnably cold; water would have frozen in a tooth glass if I had had a tooth glass. Apart from spasms of shivering I did not stir. Quarter of an hour passed; then I thought I felt a slight tickling sensation. I could not be sure, but something seemed to be creeping slowly across my stomach. I stuck it out for another ten minutes; then in one movement I rolled out of bed, lit the candle and flung back the bedclothes. Nothing. No red, horny backs running for cover; no bloodstains; no footprints. I tore off my pyjamas, turned them inside out and searched the seams; I stripped the sheets and blankets off the bed; I tugged the pillow out of its case. Nothing.

I repeated the process – not once, but again and again. I experimented with different techniques: I tried lighting the candle and then throwing back the covers; I tried throwing back the covers and then slamming out wildly in the dark. All methods were equally futile; the bugs had their own alarm system.

Around two in the morning I admitted defeat. The sheets and blankets had slid off the bed and were covered with candle wax; a flaring match had stuck to my finger and burnt a hole in it; stumbling about in the dark, cursing the pain, I had stubbed my toes once again on the leg of the settee and tipped the entire contents of my suitcase over the floor. I was licked. I wrapped myself in a tangle of blankets, and left the bedbugs to get on with it: they did.

I awoke with the unlovely dawn to find my bites redoubled and a freezing fog drifting across the back yards. That meant no escape to the moors; the buses would not be running. I stepped into the hall; the sound of snoring came from the Ground Floor Front. I climbed up to the bathroom and stumbled over two rabbits coupling on the stairs; the air stank of cigarette smoke from the poker school.

I knew it: I had been had for a sucker. Jimmy – damn his solicitude – had not just pulled my leg; he had amputated it. All right, I was fair game, as green as a stick of unripe rhubarb, but he need not have carried his joke to quite such lengths. And those two snoring girls, why could they not have had the heart to warn me? Leeds had become a sour dose of medicine; I wanted to be finished with the place. But Leeds was not quite finished with me; it still had a few items to add to my education.

I sat by my gas fire all day, feeding it from a dwindling store of shillings and dabbing antiseptic on my sores. I was relieved that neither of my neighbours came near me. In the early afternoon I heard voices through the thin partition wall; one of them was Babs', the other was a man's – presumably Jimmy's. I paid no attention for several minutes; then the voices moved closer to the dividing wall, and it became clearly audible that the gentleman caller was being entertained to tea. Further, this was none of your *thé ordinaire*: this was *thé complet*.

Where could Doreen have got to, I wondered? Surely she could not be next door with this performance going on? At last embarrassment drove me out; I pulled on my overcoat, and started to leave the house. I had barely stepped into the hall when there came a violent knocking at the front door, and a voice – unmistakably Jimmy's – started yelling through the letter box. I stood rooted to the brown lino. If it was Jimmy outside in the street – and it certainly was – then who was the gent in the Ground Floor Front? And what would happen next?

Doreen happened next. She erupted, screaming, up the stairs from the basement. (So that was where she had been banished.) 'Go away, Jimmy. Get away. Babs can't see you. She's sick. Go and fetch a doctor. She might be dying.' Screaming all the time like the heroine of a melodrama, she threw her weight against the front door and slid home the bolts.

At the same time the bedroom door opened and out came a young man, smirking mightily, but in considerable disarray. I knew him. He was a stocky, fulvous young man who played the saxophone in Jack Hylton's Band and did a 'spot' every evening in a comic straw hat. He was clearly seeking a way of escape; so, while Jimmy banged at the door and Doreen kept up her screaming, I pulled him into my room, heaved up the bottom half of the window, and pushed him out still doing up his buttons. He turned for a moment to grin his thanks, then disappeared into the fog, picking his tomcat way between the dustbins on black, pointy shoes.

I felt I had gone some of the way to level the score with Jimmy, and I stood by ready to be of help in the scene of violence that was bound to follow – the choking, the stabbing, the battering to death. But no – within minutes Jimmy was being made to grovel for having bundled his wife off

145

back to Penge without giving Babs notice. How dared he treat her like that? Who did he think he was – Clark Gable? Now he could damn well go and find something at the chemist to cure her agonizing headache. He crept humbly away, and later that night was admitted back to Acker Street to share with his Babs the pleasures of her now trebly-frequented bed.

This change in Babs' arrangements gave Doreen a problem – and, I suppose, an opportunity. She came knocking on my door that night to explain that, because of Jimmy's return, she had nowhere to sleep. Could I perhaps take her in? Her demureness outdid the Gish Sisters, but the look in her close-set little eyes was that of a hungry ocelot.

I invited her in – young ladies cannot be left standing in their pyjamas in a cold, rabbit-infested hall – but I was in a predicament. For years I had been thinking of girls, dreaming of girls, longing for girls; and now here was a girl actually proposing to spend the night with me. The quandary was that she was in no way the girl of my imagining; I was not in the least attracted to her; I did not even like her. I could not very well tell her that; and I was too shy, too lacking in confidence, to give downright sensuality a chance to break down the barriers. So, I think, was she. I suspect she was as much a virgin as I was – both of us eager to explore the other side of the frontier, but too inexperienced, too fearful of rebuff, to make the first advances. Doreen climbed into bed; I wrapped myself in my overcoat, switched off the light, and lay down on the horsehair settee.

Why, I wondered, did she not invite me to join her? I half hoped she would, half feared she might. After a long time her voice came out of the darkness.

'Aren't you cold, lying there under the window?'

'Yes, I am a bit cold.'

'Why don't you come over here?'

I padded across the room in the dark and felt for the bed. She seemed to have moved over towards the wall so as to make room for me, but she gave no indication that I would be actually welcome under the bedclothes. Not being bold enough to take this drastic step without further encouragement I lay down on top of them, confused, confounded, and three parts frozen. Doreen made no further gesture; she lay still and silent. After some minutes I climbed off the bed and went back to the settee. And that was that.

Leeds had one final lesson to teach me – professional, not personal. Our sketch immediately preceded Jack Hylton's Band. The audience on Saturday night were restless; they wanted the Band – the thumping beat, the serried ranks of saxophones, the massed trombones, the trumpets, the clarinets, the percussion. That was what they had paid good money for – not for a string of Jewish jokes. We were no more than halfway through when the commotion blew up like a tropical storm. First they started to rustle, then to whistle, then to clap. I could not make out what was happening; it was as unexpected as an earthquake, and almost as alarming. Naylor, in mid-sentence and under his breath, hissed at me,

'It's the bird! Cut to cue and scram!'

A moment later we were standing in the wings, Naylor shaking with fright and wiping the sweat from his face, while the theatre reverberated and shook to its foundations with the cannonade of Jack Hylton and His Boys. They had stepped straight into the breach.

Of all my novice's lessons in Leeds that was the clearest, the most unequivocal: *If they give you the bird, get off the stage – and quick!*

The Meanest Man On Earth concerned a Jewish tailor (Naylor Grimson), his daughter (Lennie Deane) and a young fellow who comes courting the daughter and has a pair of trousers flung at his head. That is all I can remember; it was nothing to be proud of, but it was not totally shaming. The joy of it was that it brought me into the company of the last kings and queens of the Music Hall before they were blown to oblivion by a deadly combination – bombs and the Movies. At the time I did not appreciate my luck, but for six months I was in daily contact with a species as rare and fascinating as the ridge-back gorilla, and already on its way to extinction. Now all of them are gone and their like will not be seen again, for the conditions that nourished them have vanished. Harry Champion, Flanagan and Allen, Will Fyffe, Jasper Maskelyne, Nellie Wallace – those are just some of the artists I was on the stage with. I put them in alphabetical order because, wherever they are – even in the Kingdom of Persephone – billing is bound to be a sore point with them. There were others just as wonderful and only slightly less famous – Coram and Jerry, the Rego Twins, Billy Danvers, Ted Ray, and a whole cavalcade of strong men, vocalists, adagio dancers, tightrope walkers, trampolinists, jugglers, comics and clowns. There was Sid Moorhouse, billed as 'Nature's Nobleman', a performer of sensational coarseness but one who nightly roused his audience to cheers with his last, ghastly ballad:

> *O, she may have been somebody's mother,*
> *Flung aside like a poor broken toy;*
> *But even if she isn't somebody's mother*
> *Remember you're somebody's boy.*

And there was Prince Sun Yat Sen, 'The Great Chinese Illusionist'. He was not a prince and he did not have a drop of Chinese blood in him, but when we arrived in Bristol we found that he was top of the bill, while Max Miller – a rising star, but not yet fully arrived – was second. This meant that 'The Cheeky Chappie' wound up the first half of the programme while the Prince ended the second. In fact there was no other way to arrange things: in performing his last trick, the Prince sloshed such quantities of water all over the place that the only act capable of following him would have been a troupe of performing ducks. The Prince toured a lavish production, with 'willow pattern' scenery, a number of pretty girls and half a dozen midgets – all of them dressed in Chinese costumes. The girls and the midgets were put to many uses; they brought mysterious pieces of magical equipment onto the stage and they dragged them off again; they were sliced in half with razor-sharp swords, stuffed into canisters of tea, shot from a cannon's mouth, and variously made to disappear – or reappear, as the case might be.

The Prince's make-up was simple but effective; he shaved the top of his head, grew his own pigtail, and elongated his eyes with narrow strips of sticking plaster. He wore a superb mandarin costume, in whose wide sleeves he always kept his hands concealed except when making magic passes. These passes were clearly of the Chinese School; they were not basically different from the more conventional European variety, but far more dignified, more inscrutable. At all times he was absolutely silent – and for good reason: he had a full-blown Cockney accent. Any needful communication with the audience was made by his son, who acted throughout as the Prince's assistant; he too was kitted out as a mandarin – but a mandarin of an unmistakably lower grade than his father.

The climax of the act was the Great Water Trick. At a signal from the Prince, and to the accompaniment of gongs, bells, and a long-drawn-out chord of Chinese-type music from the orchestra, water came spouting from every imaginable, and unimaginable, place on the stage. It spurted from the curved points of the pagodas, from the top of the Prince's mandarin hat, from his very fingers; it shot up like a geyser from the blade of the sword carried by his son. At this aquatic display, as though transported with amazement and delight, the entire company – girls, midgets and all – rushed on, waving their arms, shouting and gesticulating. The curtain fell on this frenzied scene, to rise a moment later and reveal the Prince, austere and alone in the centre of the stage, bowing with his usual inscrutable dignity. For this solo call to be effective it was needful to clear the stage quickly and take the curtain up again before the audience got tired of clapping and started to make for the exits.

On the Monday night I stood in the wings watching the performance. The final trick arrived; water cascaded; girls and midgets rushed on, waving their arms and yelling; down came the curtain. Prince Sun Yat Sen moved centre-stage and signalled the stage manager to take it up again. But one unhappy midget was trapped on stage; he had slipped in the water, fallen, and become panic-stricken. Now he was scuttling about, emitting cries of alarm in his native tongue (most of them came from Czechoslovakia) and seeking a way off into the wings.

The Prince eyed him balefully; the applause was dying; his curtain call was being ruined. He aimed a savage kick at the disoriented midget and muttered the only words that had passed his lips that night.

'Fuck off, you little sausage.'

I never met the Prince again, never heard what became of him. But fifty years later I was in Los Angeles, finishing off an American TV series, and one evening I visited 'The Castle of Mysteries' to watch some of the most elegant sleights of hand I have ever seen. At one point I wandered off in search of food and found myself in a room decorated from floor to ceiling with the fading playbills of past master illusionists. It occurred to me that one of the Prince's posters might well be among them; he could have left England around the time of the war and settled in the United States. I searched the walls, found no relic of 'The Great Chinese Illusionist'. Then it struck me that there was one place I had not looked – immediately above my head. I turned, and there he was! Prince Sun Yat Sen himself. I bowed my head to his inscrutable shade, and I bowed even more deeply to the ghost of that nameless, unsung, bewildered midget.

Up and down the land we went, always changing trains at Crewe. Crewe Junction on a Sunday was the meeting place for half the touring companies in the kingdom. While the trains hissed and shunted, and carriages slammed against their buffers, little flocks of chorus girls would scamper away between the crates of fish and the hampers of racing pigeons; up the stairs they ran and across the bridge to hug and kiss their transient friends on other platforms – the sisters, lovers, friends or sweethearts who were in other shows and whom they might not have seen for months. They were snatched encounters, never longer than for a few minutes; then the guard's whistle would sound from Platform 6, or the green flag be spotted across the track on Platform 3, and back the girls would scurry on their high heels, all laughter and merriment – even when the mascara was running down their cheeks.

To stand on Crewe Station was like being in Looking Glass Land; the scene was always changing – one moment hectic, the next tranquil; reality dissolved and re-formed in clouds of steam. The Great and the Famous had to change trains there too: I saw Arthur Askey once, and thought what a cheerful, friendly little cove he looked; another time I passed Jack Buchanan stalking moodily along the platform, camelhair coat thrown over his shoulders, speaking to no one. I could hardly believe that I was close enough to touch him. And once – but in the distance – I saw Gracie Fields. I goggled at all these people of renown – but with a sort of double vision. I had the feeling that I was almost part of their world, but not quite; as though I had somehow got stranded with a foot and a leg either side of the Looking Glass.

In Birmingham I became friends with an American tightrope walker called Jansen; Bob was a great performer on the wire, and a pretty good female impersonator too. His wife, Georgie, was a knockout beauty. She did little but come on in a series of stunning little costumes and hand up to Bob the coloured balls he juggled with, the parasol that added to his femininity. I used to watch the act every night from the wings; I am not sure which was the main attraction – Bob's back somersault on the slack wire or Georgie's long legs in their fishnet stockings; both were worth watching. The Jansens were a surprisingly serious-minded couple; among other things, they were curious to know the difference between a British 'public' school and an American one. So one day I took them over to Rugby.

It was term time, February, and the streets were full of boys and masters moving between classes; no one recognized me or paid me the slightest attention. Again, as at Crewe, I had a sense of being in Looking Glass Land. Bud Flanagan, Chesney Allen, Jack Hylton and his rutting bandboys, were on one side of the mirror; Rugby was on the other. In a year I had greatly changed; Rugby had remained unaltered. I felt off-balance; and, as though to confirm my sense of being in a slightly unpleasant dream, I saw walking towards us – Mr Walker.

Mr Walker had taught me Latin, off and on, for years; he was a dry, exacting, little man. I had forgotten all about him; and suddenly there he was, the same as ever: capped, gowned, his eyes red-rimmed, the personification of smugness. As I watched him approach, so neat, so trim, his mortarboard set so correctly on his head, there rose up in me an urge to strike a blow for all of us boys who, term after term, had endured his caustic pedantry. I was free now, free and flying, and I longed to make some gesture of liberty – let off a firecracker under his nose, do something, anything, to shake his buttoned-up, overweening self-esteem.

By now he was abreast of us. 'Good morning, sir,' I said.

His eyes gave a flick of semi-recognition and he paused, trying to place me.

'It's Quayle,' I said. 'I left school a year ago.'

'Ah, yes – Quayle.' His voice was dry as salted hake. 'And where have you sprung from?'

'From Birmingham.'

'University?'

'No, sir. Music Hall.'

Mr Walker looked a trifle scared, like a man who finds himself at night in unknown, hostile country.

'These are my friends,' I went on. 'Georgie and Bob Jansen from the United States. Bob is a famous tightrope artist.'

There may have been some unorthodox professions that Mr Walker could have faced with composure; 'tightrope artist' was not one of them. If I had said that Bob was a fishmonger, a French-polisher, a taxidermist, a specialist in sewage-disposal, he might have managed some kind of civil retort; but 'tightrope artist' was a blow to the heart. He muttered something under his breath and gathered his gown round him as though to avoid contamination.

He made me angry. Who was Mr Walker to look down on my profession? By what right did he treat my friends with disdain? What, for heaven's sake, did he weigh in the scales against people like Bob and Georgie? Anger gave me inspiration.

'Bob is more than a tightrope artist,' I said. 'He is a wonderful female impersonator.'

I do not know what raw nerve I touched, what childhood terror I uncovered, but Mr Walker's reaction was extreme; he reared back as though I had slipped a live rat down his trousers; for a moment he stood transfixed, staring at the three of us, then he turned and ran – literally ran – towards the safety of the school buildings.

I think the Jansens enjoyed their visit to Rugby; I know I did.

It was at Nottingham – odd that I should so exactly recall where it was, but I do – that I ran into Sid Moorhouse one Monday morning at the stage door. He would lie in wait there for newly arrived chorus girls, and chat them up when they came to collect their mail. Sid did not do too badly with the girls either, though why, and how was a mystery to me; he had a singularly unattractive face – a fundamentally rude face – in fact, less of a face than a bottom. He was leaning against the wall when I came in, scanning the racing pages of the evening paper.

'Hallo, boy,' he said. 'What d'you know?'

He always asked me that, and I was always nonplussed. Being a question, it demanded an answer. But what? I had no idea. I muttered something about the weather, and got away. But I took it as a small defeat; try as I might, I knew that I did not really fit into this world of vaudeville: I looked wrong; I sounded wrong; I could not even cope with the most ordinary backstage remark.

'You do make a fuss,' said Lennie Deane when I asked her advice that night. '"What d'you know?" is just a greeting. Like saying "Hallo". It doesn't mean anything. It's just "What d'you know?"'

'But it's a question. How can I answer it?'

'Oh, heavens, there are lots of things you could say.'

'Go on. Tell me.'

'Well, for example – "Not much for my age".' And she gave me a less than friendly look from under her red eyelashes.

Her little dagger struck home. She was right: I did not know much for my age. In fact, I did not add up to anything in any direction. What made me think I could become an actor? How was I to interest managements when I could not even interest Hermione Hannen? What had I done? What had I achieved? Nothing but a six-month tour of *The Meanest Man On Earth*; it was pathetic. Perhaps I had made a mistake? Perhaps I should give it all up? Do something challenging, but less infinitely complicated – like swim the Channel. Why not? I was a good swimmer – a very good swimmer. With training I could do it. Then I would have achieved something – and that would make Hermione see what a wonderful fellow I was and fall in love with me. And if she did not fall in love with me after I had swum the Channel – well then, I would learn to play the guitar and wander off, alone, all over Europe and have strange, lonely adventures.

No – that was all self-dramatizing nonsense. I knew the goal at which I had aimed myself; it lay in the Waterloo Road, at the Old Vic. But God help me, in a few months I would be nineteen. My life was slipping by. I wrote a letter to Harcourt Williams, the Director of the Old Vic, asking for an audition; for good measure I wrote another to Lilian Baylis herself. Then I wrote follow-up letters to them both, in case the first had gone astray. There was no reply.

For the last weeks of the sketch we had bookings all over London: New Cross, Chiswick, Finsbury Park, Shepherd's Bush – even a week of glory at the Holborn Empire. I was sad we had not made it to the Palladium, but I told myself that the Holborn Empire was almost as good. Will Fyffe was there singing 'I Belong to Glasgow', and 'I'm the Guard upon the Train that Runs from Inverness to Wick'. I reverenced him, and one night made bold to tell him so. He seemed delighted – which surprised me. He was successful, world famous; he must surely have known how good he was. Why should he be so pleased to hear my youthful appreciation? But he was; he even invited me to his dressing room and gave me a dram of whisky.

Bud Flanagan and Chesney Allen were on the bill that week too; they were riding a monster tidal wave of success, driving themselves to play three, sometimes four, engagements a night. They were old friends by now, and if I had to pick a song to conjure up that period of my life, it would be 'Underneath the Arches'; and the image would be Bud's chalk-white face, his broken-brimmed hat, his enveloping racoon coat.

There was still no reply from the Old Vic; it was very depressing. E suggested I go and see Tyrone Guthrie. 'After all, he told you to.'

'He may not have meant it. I don't want to bother him.'

'You're a fool,' she said. 'Diffidence won't get you anywhere.'

At last, on a sunny day in June, I went.

I have met a lot of great leaders – Churchill, Eisenhower, de Gaulle; others less famous, but quite as remarkable – 'Tubby' Linton VC, the submariner; Ken Gatward, who finished the war commanding a Canadian Striker Wing. They were different kinds of men, and their attributes of leadership were as different as their stations and their characters; but they all shared one essential quality – confidence in themselves. Being human they were all a prey to self-criticism, and doubt, and fear; but at bottom they all knew who they were; they knew what they were doing and why they were doing it; and they were all happy to serve a cause they knew to be greater than themselves. Tony Guthrie had this quality of leadership, and his own confidence was the cause of confidence in others.

I need not have worried about bothering him; he seemed genuinely pleased to see me. I do not know if he lifted me up to his level or he came down to mine, but once again he made me feel like an equal. He laughed a lot at my music-hall tales, but regretted he had no job at present to offer me; however, he promised to write to his old theatre at Cambridge, and try to get me in there.

Judy, his wife, turned up while we were talking. She too was very tall, with a quiet beauty of bone, and so like Tony that they might have been brother and sister. She wore a faded cotton dress and a straw hat with cherries round it – a hat so old and sunburnt that it must have belonged to her when she was a schoolgirl. They gave me a lift in their small, open car, and we went through Hyde Park, Judy driving, Tony singing Bach. The sun shone down through the chestnut leaves; I could hardly believe that such wonderful people existed. It was a day of great happiness.

Tony's arm stretched a long way; within days the Festival Theatre, Cambridge were on the phone offering me the part of Hector in *Troilus and Cressida*. The excitement in Linden Gardens would have set fire to a snowman.

'Of course. I'd be thrilled. When do you want me?'

'Rehearsals start on Monday.'

'This coming Monday? Oh, but I can't. It's the last week of my tour.'

'Oh . . . Oh, dear . . . That's awkward. Hold on.' The unknown speaker in Cambridge put a hand over the phone and conferred; in Linden Gardens I prayed I had not lost the job.

'Very well,' said the voice. 'Monday week. But be sure to come word perfect.'

We were playing down at the Elephant and Castle that last week. One night Chesney Allen drifted into my dressing room. 'I hear your sketch is coming to an end,' he said. 'Too bad. But now's your chance, Tony.'

'How d'you mean?'

'Now's the time to find yourself a real good comic. Your old Naylor Grimson — well he's not the greatest, is he? No — don't you say a word. You've got to be loyal. But I'm telling you — find someone better. You owe it to yourself.'

I had never talked to anyone on the halls about my real ambitions; they would have thought me mad — or, at the least, too big for my boots. But I could not keep the truth from Ches after what he had just said; I told him I was off to Cambridge to start rehearsals.

'Rehearsals? What for?'

'A play — a play by Shakespeare.'

He was taken aback. 'Oh — really? Well — if that's what you want, I'm very pleased for you.'

The call boy knocked on the door. 'Mr Allen? On stage please, Mr Allen. This is your five-minute call.'

Twenty minutes later Ches was back again. He must have been thinking of what I had told him all the while he was on stage.

'Tony, I must talk to you seriously,' he said. 'And you mustn't be offended.'

'Of course not. Sit down.'

'I'm taking a liberty, I know, but — if I may say so — you remind me of what I used to be a few years back. I was stuck with a comic who was only half good. It was before I had the luck to meet Bud. All I thought of then was to be a proper actor — to go "legit". I was crazy for the "legit". So, believe me, I understand just how you feel. But Tony,' — and he looked at me with great earnestness — 'don't do it. It's a mug's game. There's no money in it. Nothing but heartbreak. Take my advice. Do what I did. Find yourself a good comic and stick to him.'

I did not take his advice, but Chesney's words have always lurked in my mind, not far below the surface. There have been times when they have risen up, mocking and sardonic, and stuck their tongues out at me.

Troilus and Cressida was my Shakespearean baptism – a baptism by total immersion. I became so involved in the rehearsing and opening of the play that I had almost forgotten my importunate pleas to the Old Vic when, out of the blue, E phoned to say that I had been summoned at short notice to appear there and give an audition.

I was thrown into agitation; I had never given an audition. What should I perform? I knew my own speeches from *Troilus*, but they did not seem colourful enough for an audition. *Hamlet* then: why not? *How all occasions do inform against me*: that would be perfect. I knew it, anyway; now I settled down to study it. But, with only one day left, a doubt entered my mind: to walk onto the stage of the Old Vic, of all theatres, and deliver a soliloquy from *Hamlet* might appear dreadfully presumptuous. No, *Hamlet* was a rotten idea. What then? From school I could remember *Once more unto the breach, dear friends*; but again, it was too arrogant. *Where the bee sucks, there suck I* would be plain ludicrous. Then, suddenly, I had an inspiration: the Bastard in *King John* – the speech where he thanks his mother for providing him with such a father as Richard Coeur de Lion. It was amusing, ironic, and it had a ring to it as well. I might just be able to learn it in time.

All the night before, and all the way up in the train, I kept running through the speech; by the time I reached London I was dead sure, word perfect.

I saw the theatre when I was still a couple of hundred yards away; it stood on the corner of the grimy, barrow-raucous street – a princess disguised as a goose girl. At the sight, my small store of confidence dissolved and trickled away into the gutter of the Waterloo Road. I had to force myself to walk on.

'What did y'say yer name was?' The doorman glared at me from inside his cubbyhole. 'Quinn?'

'No, not Quinn. Quayle. Q-U-A-Y-L-E.'

He started to run a yellow fingernail down a long list of names, reading them aloud as he went. I looked about me: stone floor, stone stairs, bare walls; cold and ugly as a prison. But this was no prison; this was the Old Vic, the greatest theatre in the land. Through this stage door had walked Sybil Thorndike, and Edith Evans, and John Gielgud, and Ralph Richardson, and God knows how many other great actors. I was filled with reverence, weighed down by a sense of my own inadequacy. I was an impostor. I must run away – get back to Cambridge and hide.

'Aha – I've got you now. "Q" – that's what you're under. Letter "Q".' The doorman was triumphant. 'Right, son. Up them stairs. Turn left through that door – and it'll bring you onto the stage.'

I had lost even the will to escape. I did as I was told, pulled back the heavy door and walked through into the darkened wings of the stage. There was an odd, but not unpleasant, smell: paint, size, wood shavings, mice, cake crumbs, and layer upon layer of aromatic dust. I could make out ten or twelve young men sitting or standing about. From the stage, which was masked by hangings, I could hear a voice declaiming,

> *'How all occasions do inform against me*
> *And spur my dull revenge!'*

Thank God I had decided against *Hamlet*. The speaker droned on for a few more lines, then appeared to have been arrested in mid-flow, for he came stalking off the stage looking very put out. Another young man was summoned to take his place. I heard him start.

'I should like to do Hamlet's Advice to the Players.' A pause. Then, 'Speak the speech I pway you, as I pwonounced it to you, twippingly on the tongue . . .'

Poor fellow, he was fighting a losing battle against his 'r's. But I could not worry about him; I closed my eyes and concentrated on my party piece.

> *Now by this light, were I to get again,*
> *Madam I would not wish a better father . . .*

Yes, that flowed through my mind, but what came next? I could not remember. There was a fair-sized clump of lines, and then,

> *With all my heart I thank thee for my father.*

I could say the first two lines and the last one – but what the hell were all the others in between? My mind was a shimmering blank.

'Quayle? Which of you is Quayle?'

I rose nervously to my feet, and a stage manager propelled me onto the stage.

I came out of darkness into stabbing light: spotlights from above, footlights from below, all shone in my eyes. In front of me was a black void – and silence.

I cleared my throat. 'This is from *King John*, Act One, Scene One. The Bastard is talking to his mother.'

I could hear whisperings from out in front. Was I meant to start, or should I wait for them to finish? I wished I could remember the third line. I wished I had turned back when I was in the Waterloo Road.

A man's impatient voice shouted, 'On you go. On you go.'

I drew a deep breath, and started.

> *'Now by this light, were I to get again,*
> *Madam I would not wish a better father.'*

Then I stopped. Not only could I not remember the lines, I could not remember who I was, or where I was, or why I was standing all alone in this hideous limbo. Why was I pretending to be somebody else? And who cared, anyway?

From the darkness in front, the same impatient voice called out, '*Some sins do bear their privilege on earth.* Go on. Pick it up.'

Whoever my prompter was, he evidently knew the play by heart. Perhaps it was Harcourt Williams himself? Haltingly I repeated the line he had thrown to me. Then I dried up again.

'You don't know the speech very well, do you?'

Screening my eyes against the lights I could make out a man's face down in the stalls near the orchestra rail; he had ruffled hair and a generally harassed look about him.

'I'm afraid I don't. I learnt it in a hurry.'

'Is there something you *do* know? Something you can be sure of?'

In my misery – Saint Sebastian with three arrows already sticking out of me – I never thought of *Troilus and Cressida*. Hector, the one part I knew backwards, did not occur to me. Instead, my mind went spinning away into the past, and with disbelief I heard myself say, 'Yes. I know Autolycus.'

'Good. Then let's have some Autolycus.'

Autolycus? What possessed me? I did not remember it at all. I had not looked at *The Winter's Tale* since RADA, and a sorry mess I had made of it then. But now there was no way to go but forward. And I had no one to blame but myself.

I tried to recall the dance – that awful dance – with Mopsa and Dorcas. I began to jump about the stage like a lunatic. With manic vitality I sang,

> *'Will you buy any Tape, or Lace for your Cape?*
> *My dainty duck, my dear-a?'*

There I stopped: not because I had forgotten the words of the song, but because I had reached the limits of self-inflicted pain.

'This is dreadful,' I said. 'If you don't mind, I would rather not do any more.'

From the front, and for an appreciable time, there came no sound at all – only what I took to be an astounded silence. Then there were whisperings; then a woman's voice – an unrefined, workaday voice – called out, 'All right, dear. Come down and have a word before you go.' As I slunk through the pass door I heard the next contestant being ushered onto the stage.

A stout, shortish person came forward to meet me. Lilian Baylis. I knew it was she; I had seen her photo many times. She looked like a Mrs Tiggy-winkle, but urban and harder, with a mouth that was twisted sideways.

'You chose a difficult speech, dear,' she said. 'You need to be older – have more authority – before you can tackle a speech like that. Never mind. Come back another year and try again.'

Harcourt Williams did not have time even to speak to me; he was already focused on my successor. As I made my retreat I could hear a monotonous voice intoning,

> *'Oh what a rogue and peasant slave am I . . .'*

For all my smarting wounds I could not but smile. Mr Harcourt Williams was having enough badly-cooked *Hamlet* served up to him to put him off the play for ever.

Three days later, a Senior Member of the *Troilus* company, a smug sort of fellow and greatly in love with himself, let it be known that Harcourt Williams would be in front that night. It was pretty well concluded, said the Senior Member, that he would be joining the Old Vic Company in the autumn; it was now only a question of which parts he should play. It was obviously desirable that Williams should see him play this important role.

It was gall and wormwood to listen to him; but I could only try to conceal my envy, and act Hector with the energy born of despair.

At curtain fall I was summoned to the manager's office. There sat Harcourt Williams, ruffled and crumpled as when I had seen him a few days before, but now surprisingly friendly.

'Well done,' he said. 'A fine performance. How would you feel like joining the company at the Old Vic?'

I told him I would feel very good indeed about it – in fact, I would feel overjoyed.

'You would? Well then – there's nothing much more to say, is there?' He had a countryman's face, brown and lined; he might have been a harassed beekeeper. 'We can settle all the details – parts, salary, all that sort of stuff – when you come back to London.'

'But Mr Williams,' I said. 'What has made you change your mind in so short a time?'

'What d'you mean?'

'I auditioned for you at the Vic three days ago.'

'Really? Did you?' He looked amazed.

'It was a disaster. You couldn't have forgotten. I was too bad to forget.'

'What an extraordinary thing. I don't remember you at all. As far as I knew, tonight was the first time I'd ever seen or heard of you.' He gave a cheerful laugh. 'There you are – that shows how much auditions are worth.'

Two weeks later, *Troilus* now over, I turned up again at the Old Vic – but in a different frame of mind.

Miss Baylis's office was a shabby little room at the back of the Old Vic. The windows were begrimed; her desk, an ugly roll-top, was cluttered with papers; from the adjoining room, which was little more than a cupboard, came the roar of a primus stove and the smell of some unidentifiable food being prepared by her secretary. It was hard to believe that this dumpy little woman could be the heroine of such legendary achievements: that she had founded the Old Vic Company and steered it through more than fifteen years of continuous battle; that she had rebuilt Sadler's Wells; that she had opened it as a home for Opera, and – of all impossible dreams come true – for English Ballet. But one minute in her presence was enough to explain how this dowdy, podgy-faced lady could breathe courage into the most timid Board of Governors; how she could wear down, subjugate, and finally bring to heel all the Commissioners of the London County Council together with the entire Ministry of Works. She was an Irresistible Force.

'There, dear.' She handed me some scribbles on a slip of paper. 'Those are the parts that dear Billy Williams wants you to play.' The words came sideways out of her twisted mouth. Had she suffered a stroke, I wondered?

The parts were, to say the least, disappointing.

'They're not very great, are they?'

'No, dear. They're not great. But they're all that's left. Do your best, and you'll make something of them.' She dismissed the parts as though they were irrelevant. 'Now – salary. I can't pay much. We're very poor here. I'll give you three pounds a week.'

The figure took me by surprise. I had not expected much, but I had never thought it could be as little as three pounds. Five was what I had hoped for, and I would gladly have settled for a pound less. But three . . . Should I accept it while it was still on offer? Or should I put up a fight? I decided to fight. The first move was not to speak: keep quiet and look worried.

'You don't say anything. What's the matter? Don't you want the job?' Her eyes, like a poker player's, gave nothing away.

'Oh, I want it, Miss Baylis. Indeed I do. It's just that I don't think – I really don't think – I can manage to live on only three pounds a week. Could you possibly stretch it to three pounds ten?'

There was a long silence. Miss Baylis sat motionless at her desk; I stood waiting. From the cupboard kitchen came the now unmistakable smell of oxtail soup. Had I overreached myself? If so, I must find a way – and quickly – to back-pedal. On the other hand, if I could keep up this silence for a while longer I might yet win.

At length Miss Baylis gave a great sigh – something close to a groan. She lifted her face and looked up towards God.

'Very well,' she said. 'Three pounds ten shillings.' The vestige of a smile appeared in her eyes. 'But you're costing me a lot. Make sure you're worth the extra.'

So it was concluded that I should go to the Old Vic that autumn. The Senior Member, who had all unwittingly given me my second chance, was not even asked.

CHAPTER 10

WHEN I WAS YOUNG I NEVER paused to wonder if there might be some pattern in my life, some discernible influence. It would have been pleasant to believe, as Moses did, that every step of my way was watched over by the Lord; but it would have been presumptuous to think that the Almighty took such a personal interest in me. Nor have I ever noticed Him striking those who do not listen to His words 'with a fever, and with an inflammation, and with an extreme burning'. I know several people, conspicuously inattentive to His voice, who have all salted away fortunes in Swiss bank accounts, and with the utmost coolness. It was not until the war, and then only dimly, that I became aware how often decisions seemed to have been made for me and that some giant hand would bar me from one road and propel me irresistibly down another. I suppose the signs of intervention were always there, but I could not see them – was not even looking for them. Now that I am old I can make out some of the currents that carried me along; I do perceive the start of some sort of pattern.

It was Tony Guthrie who steered me to Cambridge; it was at Cambridge that I met a fellow actor who gave me an introduction to John Gielgud; and, for the next seven years, right up to the outbreak of the war, any work of consequence that I did and almost every constructive idea that I had on the theatre was due to those two men. To both I owe an immense debt of gratitude; both were just starting to exert their great influence in the theatre; both leant down and, in the most practical of ways – by giving me work – helped me to scramble up the prickly stem of the beanstalk; both became my great friends; and neither of them particularly liked the other.

In that summer of 1932 John Gielgud tried out, on two successive Sunday nights, his production of *Richard of Bordeaux* in which he gave me the small part of Rutland. At the same time Tony Guthrie asked me to play the King of Navarre in *Love's Labour's Lost* at the Westminster. The two engagements fitted together like pieces of a jigsaw puzzle, and both would be over before the season started at the Old Vic. Of the *Richard* rehearsals I remember how struck I was by John's elegant clothes – his suede shoes, his beautifully cut suits, his immaculate shirts, the long gold key chain that went around his waist before diving into a trouser pocket; I had never seen the like. I remember how courteous he was to the older and very distinguished members of his cast – and well he may have been: though God-like to me in his eminence, he was only twenty-eight. I recall next to nothing of Rutland, there being next to nothing to recall; but I do remember that our pointed mediaeval shoes were made for us by an unusual man with a bald head and a bushy red beard, who went on to become the foremost theatrical photographer of his time – Angus McBean. Mostly I remember how impressed I was to meet Gwen Ffrangcon-Davies and actually make an entrance with her: to be more accurate she made the entrance and I followed after. The last time I had seen her was as Elizabeth Barrett Browning in *The Barretts of Wimpole Street*; then I had been dazzled by her performance, and now she was standing beside me in the wings waiting for her cue, her hand giving convulsive little clutches at my sleeve. When the cue came she gave a high musical laugh, tinkled at me, '*Oh Rutland – you foolish boy*' and stepped onto the stage.

Richard of Bordeaux was a triumph for John G. He had been a prince of the theatre and enjoyed princely success for a long time; now he moved into absolute dominance. In addition to directing the play and giving a magnetic performance in the leading part, he had pulled off a brilliant managerial coup. In Gordon Daviot he had found a new playwright who could write dialogue that spoke to the twentieth century without betraying the fourteenth; in Motley he had discovered a young innovative design team whose work was as fresh as a spring breeze, and he had shown that romantic costume drama could once again be brought to life in the West End – and made to pay. *Richard* stayed on at the New and ran for over a year. I did not stay with it; I went to the Westminster and then to the Old Vic.

Tony's production of *Love's Labour's Lost* was far less ambitious than *Richard of Bordeaux*; it had great charm but no aspiration to the making of theatre history. For me it marked the time when the Guthries started to invite me to their home in Lincoln's Inn and took me fully into their friendship. 23 Old Buildings was their address; their phone number – it springs to my mind from decades past – was HOLborn 6029. I remember everything about them with such affection and the homely talisman of their phone number brings tears to my eyes.

Tony and Judy had what can only be called an 'abode' at the very top of an ancient building redolent of the law and of the Inns of Court. 'Chambers' would be too grand a name; it could not really be called a 'flat' either – the word conjures up central heating and wall-to-wall carpeting, and the Guthries boasted only one rug in the whole place. It would be inexact too because there was another storey: an attic with a hazardously sloping floor; it contained a bath at one end and a bed at the other, both firmly wedged to prevent either of them taking off across the incline with a startled occupant. No, it was an abode: a small, square area divided into four small, square rooms – like a tennis court or a slice of Battenburg cake. To visit the Guthries you had to climb several flights of wooden stairs, on each landing passing a heavy, black-painted, wooden door. These doors – silently inviting litigants to enter, and emitting from their inner regions a faint aroma of Torts and Actions for Damages – could not have changed from the days of Mr Pickwick and Sergeant Buzfuz. At night the atmosphere was different: the doors were shut, the 'Barristers at Law' all gone, the wooden staircase silent and ghost-ridden. Only the Guthries still roosted high up under the roof, hospitable and lively, their front door always open. Arrived at the top landing you called out – then walked on in.

The 'hall' was more or less a junk room where suitcases were piled, galoshes and raincoats could be discarded. A miscellany of cardboard boxes lay about, sometimes containing, sometimes spilling, books, cat food, play scripts and the morning's groceries. As a rule Myrtle, the grey Tabby, would be lying in one of the boxes giving nourishment to the latest of her innumerable litters of kittens. Myrtle, much to the Guthries' delight, usually chose the chest of drawers in their bedroom for her *accouchements*. In due course she would pick up her kittens one at a time in her mouth and carry them out to the hall; the drawer in the bedroom was her chosen maternity ward, but the hall was the place to bring up her kittens and instruct them in basic hygiene. Myrtle's move completed, Tony could put his socks and shirts back in the drawer – but only till he received notice that the next litter was imminent.

From the hall you walked through into the kitchen; it contained nothing so modern and costly as a refrigerator, but running the length of the kitchen table was an overhead 'clothes rack' operated by pulleys, and hanging from this contraption there was always a friendly display of Guthrie laundry. There was an old gas cooker on which Judy would whip up savoury little meals – sardines on toast, Welsh Rarebit, and every sort of risotto. She would stand over her frying pan, hot-faced but queenly, a cigarette stuck in her mouth and the smoke of it drifting up into her nose and into her eyes while she listened to the talk that was going on in the living room, and shouted occasional contributions through the open door.

The living room was small, it held a gas fire, an upright piano, a couple of wobbly tables, and a sufficiency of busted chairs. It was simple but not squalid: a room where thoughts and ideas could inhabit and breed without formality or prejudice. The Guthries were a lively-minded pair, fond of argument and full of laughter, but I never heard Tony or Judy discuss politics or give tongue to gossip; they were not interested in what party was in power or who was in bed with whom – except when it affected a play that Tony was casting and then he could become very interested indeed. They lived on little money, so whisky was a rarity; when there was a bottle in the house, they were generous with it, but as a rule they offered you tea.

That leaves only the bedroom, and about that there is little to say: the small space was entirely filled by an ancient brass bedstead; there was no room for any other furniture save a wooden chest where a spare blanket was stowed, and Myrtle's chest of drawers.

From that time on the Guthries became more than friends to me; they became, I suppose, my adopted family.

Before the Old Vic season started, the Hannens set off on a year's tour of Australia, taking Hermione with them. In truth, I was glad when she went. To be so green-sickly in love with love was to be loaded with penitential chains; it was a blessed relief when they were lifted off, even though I knew they would feel doubly heavy when they were loaded on again. Perhaps, perhaps, a year would cure me of my infection; I wished it would – but I doubted it.

The 1932 season at the Old Vic was not an illustrious one, though there were some fine actors in the company. As well as Peggy Ashcroft, there were Malcolm Keen, Roger Livesey, Alastair Sim, Bill Fox, Marius Goring and George Devine. We turned out bad work for many reasons – the chief one being that dear Billy Williams (he was never called 'Harcourt', always 'Billy') was as stale as an old crust. He was also strapped in a financial straitjacket. The permanent designer at the Vic, Paul Smythe, once told me that his entire budget for mounting a production was twenty-eight pounds; he had to mend and make do with stuff that had been venerable in the days of Benson. Old scenery and old costumes that should have been burnt long ago were still being trotted out; inevitably a few old ideas were being trotted out too.

Presiding over the wardrobe was a remarkable character – Orlando Whitehead, the walking image of Mr Pickwick, but sharp as the acid drops he was always sucking. Orlando had a hard job; he was responsible not only for the company at the Vic but also for the newly opened opera company at Sadler's Wells – and he was without assistance. We young actors must have driven him mad; the moment we learned what parts we were allotted in the next production we would rush to the wardrobe and scramble for the few costumes or tights that were wearable. Orlando was usually up his ladder sucking sweets and stuffing away bundles of musty plum-coloured velvet gowns. His voice was high-pitched and squeaky; he had a Yorkshire accent.

'Yes?' he would say, twinkling down through his round, rimless glasses. 'What have you come for?'

He knew damn well what I had come for. But this was part of the little wardrobe game. It was a ritual; it had to be played out.

'The parti-coloured tights, Orlando – the black and grey ones. Can I have them? It's for *Romeo and Juliet*. You know the ones I mean.'

'What are you playing?'

'I'm playing Paris.'

'Oh no, you can't have those for Paris.' He spoke with condescension – almost with scorn. 'They're for Romeo. Marius Goring has spoken for those already. And if they don't fit him, then Bill Fox is next in line. He's playing Tybalt. Did y'know that?' His chubby face widened in a smile, but little shafts of malice shot from his eyes. He was well aware that Tybalt was the part for which I had been hoping.

'Yes, Orlando. I do know that Bill is playing Tybalt. And I'm playing Paris. But I've still got to have some tights. So tell me – which ones can I have?'

He fished at the back of a cavernous pigeonhole and threw down a much darned, depressingly brown pair. 'Try those.'

'Don't be absurd, Orlando. Look, the waist is up under my arms.'

'Then what about these?' Another pair rained down on me. 'Don't just hold them up to you. Try them on.'

'No, I bloody won't try them on. See for yourself. The crotch is below my knees.'

He would start to giggle then – an hysterical, high-pitched giggle that came out between tongue and teeth like the buzzing of bees. 'Zzzz – zzzz – zzzz . . . Well, if the tights don't fit – we'll have to get another actor . . . Zzzz – zzzz – zzzz.'

'Orlando.'

'Oh, go away. Don't bother me. I've got to get *Cosi fan Tutti* on by Thursday. Zzzz – zzzz – zzz . . . ' With that he would turn his back and pretend to be busy with his shelves.

'Orlando, please – ' It was my last desperate attempt. 'What am I to do?'

This was his moment of victory; this was checkmate. He would turn to look down on me, his face shining and his stomach shaking with glee, while a high triumphant buzzing issued from his lips, 'Zzzz – zzzz – zzzz – zzzz . . . I'll tell you what you can do . . . zzzz – zzzz – zzzz – zzzz . . . You can go and fuck spiders.'

We all knew we were doing lacklustre work – just thumping it out as honestly as we could – but no one spoke of that; actors owe loyalty to the theatre and to the work in hand. Besides, we were all very fond of Billy Williams. But amongst the dross, there was one production that stood out shining like a jewel – John Gielgud's *The Merchant of Venice*. John was still playing *Richard of Bordeaux*; but he came to direct *The Merchant*, using Peter Warlock's 'Capriole Suite' for the music, and bringing in the Motleys as his designers. It was, I think, the best concept of the play I have ever seen – inventive, amusing, and gossamer light. Lord knows where the money came from to pay for the production: not that the scenery was expensive – it consisted almost entirely of fishnet and good lighting – but every costume had been designed and actually made to fit each individual actor. Such luxury had never been heard of at the Old Vic; we actors could not believe what had befallen us; the whole company took wing and soared. At least, Peggy Ashcroft soared as Portia, and Malcolm Keen gave his best performance of the year as Shylock.

I doubt if I rose very high in the air as Morocco*, but I do know I got off the ground; and that I did so was entirely due to John. For the whole of my first scene he made me stand stock-still – not a movement, not a gesture. The entire scene had to rest on the architectural strength of Morocco's long speech, and on my dubious power as an actor to sustain it with no other weapon than my voice. There could not have been a better exercise than Morocco, or a better teacher than John, to bring me face to face with the lifelong vocal problems of our trade – breathing, resonance, diction, phrasing – all the technicalities that have to be brought to the service of passion. During those rehearsals I could learn no more than I was capable of absorbing, but I did see that the learning would go on and on for the rest of my life.

* Peggy Ascroft recalls how Walter Sickert, who was a constant observer at the Vic, sent her a sketch around the margin of which he wrote, 'Quayle excellent as Morocco, one day he will play Othello'.

I was learning too about the theatre in general. I had been in enough productions – good and bad – to see what a subtle balance is needful for a production to succeed. Author, actors, director, and manager, I was beginning to realize, were all links in a circular chain: author and actors would appear dull if they were wrapped in the dustsheet of an uninspired production; the most imaginative director in the world was helpless without a good text and the right actors. None of them could afford to be arrogant.

Every few weeks we alternated with the Opera and Ballet Companies up at Sadler's Wells. The singers seemed as earthbound as ourselves, but the dancers whom we met in the corridors – Bobby Helpmann, Margot Fontaine, Billy Ashton – belonged almost to another element; and the *corps de ballet* were so adorable in their woolly tights and little coloured aprons. But there was no time, no place, for flirtation; we were always working, always rehearsing, and the girls lived under the stern eye of Ninette de Valois. Occasionally we would contrive a party after the night's performance – lashings of beer, mountains of sausages, pounds of cheese. We sat around on the floor like the young of all periods, eating and drinking and talking with profound seriousness about things like Art, and Truth, and Free Will. 'Fate – ' I used to say, ' – there's no such thing. Everything that comes to us is of our own doing.'

The Old Vic season was the start of a long and fond friendship with Peggy Ashcroft. I did not get to know Peg well until a good deal later, but that autumn she did me a kindness for which I have always been grateful. Grandpa, eighty years old by now, came to London and declared he wanted to see me act.

'What is this play you're in, my boy?'

'*Caesar and Cleopatra*, Grandpa.'

He sniffed. '*Antony and Cleopatra* I've heard of, but what is this *Caesar and Cleopatra*? Some new-fangled rubbish?'

I explained that it was by Bernard Shaw, but he was not impressed.

'I've got you a ticket for tomorrow's matinee, Grandpa. Then afterwards, if you feel like it, you could come backstage and meet Peggy Ashcroft.'

He was delighted. 'Oh, I would account that a great privilege, but she will not have time to see me, surely?'

'Yes, Grandpa. I've told her you're coming, and she said she would love to meet you.'

Dear, dear old man – I do not think he took in the play at all, and I am sure he would not have known a good production from a bad. But he certainly knew that there before him on the stage was a beautiful young woman, one of the foremost actresses in London, and that his grandson had the rare honour of acting with her. After the matinee he climbed the stairs to her dressing room, and there was a touching exchange of tea and courtesies. By the time he took his old-fashioned leave of Peg I knew he had finally laid to rest all doubts over my becoming an actor: if this was the kind of world his grandson had entered – if this lovely, intelligent young woman was the sort of actress he would be working with – then the 'boy' had chosen the right profession. He was satisfied.

I formed another close friendship that winter – with George Devine. He was three or four years older than me and with far more experience of the world, but we had much in common and I knew almost from our first meeting that this man would always have a significance for me. It was as though, unbidden, a door of 'Acceptance' had sprung open, and in walked paradoxical old George – assured and self-doubting, talented and frustrated, with his gritty voice, his bow tie and his black homburg, his sense of fun and absurdity, his chewed and sucked-at pipe and his thick clouds of Edgeworth tobacco.

George and I shared a dressing room with three others, one of them being Bill Fox. All actors are complicated to some extent, but Bill did appear to be less burdened with complications than most of us. He was assured, forthright, open, full of charm and with a certain air of privilege hanging about him. George, in contrast, had some undisclosed, half-hidden chip on his shoulder; and he was a man of so many and differing elements that every one of them was at war with the rest. He was well aware that he had a creative power locked up in him, but he had not yet found out how to release it. He was a good administrator, and had become business manager for his friends, the Motleys; but administration was only a sideline in this period of his life; his ambition was all directed towards acting.

George had only just come down from Oxford where he had been President of OUDS – an influential though slightly inflated office while it lasts; when over, one that leaves the high-flying balloon to make its own painful descent to earth. George had been a very big balloon indeed at Oxford; the previous year he had persuaded John Gielgud to go there and direct Peggy Ashcroft in *Romeo and Juliet*; the Motleys had designed the production, and George himself had played Mercutio. But now at the Vic he had been given a part for which he was deeply miscast – Posthumus Leonatus in *Cymbeline*.

George was portly, his voice was harsh, and his face was verging on the sallow; his eyes, without his glasses, had an unfocused look; for all his virtues both as a man and as an actor he was not an heroic figure; in no way could he be described as a 'Lion's Whelp'; yet this was the role that Billy Williams had offered him and which he, poor fellow, had been deluded enough to accept. He was like a boxer, entered for the wrong fight, on the wrong day, and at very much the wrong weight. The result was that the critics rent him savagely, while the Old Vic gallery, usually the most loyal of claques, booed him when he appeared on the stage. These were harsh blows; they hacked at the deepest roots of his confidence; they made questionable his whole purpose in life. It was not a pleasant situation to be in, and George bore it with great courage.

There was little he could do at short notice either about his voice or his bulk, but he got the idea that he might make himself more acceptable in the part by changing his make-up. Someone had told him that a strong foundation of yellow-ochre paint would make his face glow, give it – as it were – a radiance. George bought himself a stick of the required greasepaint and set about acquiring this luminosity. When the rest of us came in one night for the performance we found him in the dressing room, fully made up, waiting to try out on us the new face of Posthumus Leonatus.

'There,' he said, pushing back his chair and turning to face us. 'What do you make of it? I've been looking at it so long I can't judge any more.'

We all studied his face with the consideration one gives at a Private Viewing to an horrendous painting by a dear friend – a friend, moreover, who is standing close at hand.

It was hard to know what to say. George's face, caked in thick yellow paint, resembled nothing except a plump Chinaman in the terminal stages of jaundice. But this was no time for flippancy; it was a moment of very real psychological crisis; somehow we had to get George through it.

'I think it's an improvement,' I said, with cowardly neutrality; but at least it broke the ice.

'Oh – it's good. It's very good.' Charles Hickman was a kind man and a skilful diplomat.

George laughed nervously. 'Can you see a bit more, kind of – life – in my face?'

'Indeed, I can.' Again it was Charlie Hickman who stepped into the breach. 'Come and stand here under the light, George. It'll be easier to judge then.'

George came into the middle of the room turning up his saffron face towards the light bulb. He stood like a martyr at the stake – ready to face the fire, but praying for a reprieve. Charles gave him a long critical examination.

'Yes,' he said at last. 'It's a whole lot better. But in my opinion – and, mind you, it's only an opinion – I think the yellow is possibly just the tiniest bit too strong.' Then, as he saw George's agonized look, he hurried on, 'No – really and truly – I think you've solved it. Now it's just a matter of balance. Take the yellow down just the least little bit.' He turned to Bill Fox. 'What do you think, Bill?'

Bill was always direct, always enthusiastic. He spoke as if George had scored a try at Twickenham. 'First class, George. Bloody good. Well done.'

Between us, we pulled George through his ordeal. But, when he died, I think they would have found the words *Posthumus Leonatus* on his heart.

George was playing better parts than me, and he was being paid ten shillings a week less. It was unjust, but that was the way the deal had been struck and there was no going back on it. I was sitting pretty because I was living at home – in fact, I managed to save a bit – but it was hard for George who was renting a tiny flat in Great Newport Street. After the play at night he would often come back with me to Linden Gardens. E was very fond of him; she enjoyed cooking supper for us, and when he left to catch the last tube back to Leicester Square, she always gave him a jar of home-made jam or marmalade.

Sometimes, on a Friday night after we had been paid, George and I would take ourselves off to the Café Royal. The old Café Royal had a rich, bohemian atmosphere: downstairs it was almost a club, full of musicians, actors, journalists, painters – artists of all sorts; there were cafe tables with marble tops, red plush banquettes and vast, ornate mirrors with golden Cupids round them. Downstairs was too expensive for George and me; but we would take ourselves up into the balcony where it was a lot cheaper. For four shillings and sixpence you got a glass of lager and a Canapé Royal – which was a Welsh Rarebit sitting on a slice of ham. From below rose the chatter and clatter of people eating well and in good company; tobacco smoke drifted up mixed with the rich odours of food and drink. We would make our half-pints of lager last for as long as we could, looking down on the heads – not perhaps of the Great and the Good, but certainly of the Notorious and the Lively. Noel Coward was often there, and you could always pick out a few well-known journalists. James Agate might be right beneath us, robust and tweedy; no one would think he could be a dramatic critic. Over there, at another table, was Hannen Swaffer wrapped in gloom and a black cravat: no one could think that he could be anything but a dramatic critic. And down over there to the right was Augustus John – no mistaking that wild, fierce head. Round his table, the coming and going of friends, the drawing of corks and the serving of dishes, all combined to form a continual magnetic storm.

I found it reassuring to look down on all these famous characters. I had always thought they must exist on some remote, and unattainable level – but not so at all. Any moment that I felt like it I could drop a bread roll on Mr Agate's bald head; and after his recent notice of our work in *The Sunday Times* I certainly did feel like it. But I refrained; journalists always have the last word.

By the time you are seventy you have long ago realized that opinions on art merely go round in circles; and being old you try to keep silent – though this is often difficult. But when you are young, the vaster the subject the readier you are to tackle it – and God knows there is no end to the subject of acting. George and I discussed it endlessly; and one evening up in the balcony of the Café Royal we had a falling out. I had been arguing that an actor's final statement was himself; that, beside and beyond all the required skills, his own innate character was of huge importance.

George said, 'For God's sake, there is a thing called acting, isn't there? You can be a way-out homosexual in life, but totally believable as a lover of women on the stage. You don't have to be virtuous to play Desdemona. The best Desdemona I ever saw was a nymphomaniac – and a liar. But she could act. Look – look at old Augustus John down there. Are you telling me that he is a great painter because he's a great man? Rot. An artist's life has nothing to do with his work.'

'Damn it, George – don't generalize. Acting and painting are different arts. A painter doesn't exhibit his own self. When a canvas is finished, he hangs it up – or stacks it against the wall. If he doesn't like it, he destroys it and no one but he ever sees it. It is separate from him. He doesn't use his own blood for paint. We do. We exhibit our very selves – even our failings. What we contribute is what we bloody well are – what we become through living.'

The argument was heated but unresolved, and it has continued in my mind ever since. Possibly we were both right – but I think I was more right than George.

By March 1933 the end of the Old Vic season was in sight. I had no job waiting for me, but I had enough money saved – around seventy pounds – to give myself a holiday. I decided to go abroad.

I was nineteen now – a man – and across the Channel was a continent about which I knew nothing. Should I go to France? No – not adventurous enough. Germany? Well – that might be interesting. There had been a lot in the papers lately about this Hitler and his National Socialist Party – Nazis they called themselves. Of course, he was absurd with that stupid moustache and his hair flopping over his face – but he had managed to become Chancellor, and did seem to be giving the Germans back their self-respect. Yes, that's what I'd do – go to Germany. I could stay in these youth hostels they had all over the country and were very cheap. I might go canoeing down the Rhine; if I could afford it, I might even go have a look at the Alps.

I bought myself a tent and went for help and information to the German Travel Agency in Lower Regent Street.

Nothing was too much trouble for Hans Beckhoff, the fair-haired, blue-eyed young man who attended to me. Canoeing? '*Jawohl*' – I had come to the right man: he was an expert. In fact, he and a friend only last summer had accomplished the first canoe crossing of the English Channel. '*Ja, bestimmt*.' He had to warn me though that April was a bit early for canoeing down the Rhine; I might find it rather cold and wet. Why not make for Cologne – he gave me a list of youth hostels in the surrounding countryside – and see what the weather was like? And before I set out for Germany, he would be so happy if I would visit his flat in Notting Hill Gate – just round the corner from Linden Gardens, because he would like to show me his canoeing trophies: one of them – he said this with an odd, intense look – was most precious to him.

I went. He was the first German I had ever met, and I liked him. His flat was neat and circumspect. One wall was entirely covered with photos of Hans and his friend carrying, launching, or paddling their double kayak. Pinned up in the centre was the pennant they had flown at the bow of their craft when they crossed the Channel – a swastika. Above this unaesthetic (but as yet not monstrous) emblem, mounted and framed, was a personal telegram of congratulation from Adolf Hitler. I could feel Beckhoff's eyes fixed on me as I read it.

'Well – look at that!' I said. I knew more was expected of me, but it was the best I could do off the cuff. The hero worship that shone from Herr Beckhoff's eyes was, to say the least, unbalanced. In embarrassment I added, 'That's very nice.'

'Nice?' His voice was cold. 'Do you realize who that telegram is from?'

'Yes, indeed. It's from Adolf Hitler.'

'And you understand who he is?' He spoke deliberately, like a man tightening a screw. 'Adolf Hitler . . . is now . . . the Chancellor . . . of the Third Reich.' As he spoke he nodded to emphasize the significance of his words.

'Well, good luck to him,' I said. 'And to you. And thank you for all your help.' I was glad to get out of his flat.

Outside Cologne the country was sodden and the youth hostel empty.

Beside myself there were only two people in the place: a lumpish, inoffensive Brownshirt and a young, out-of-work waiter who was peddling packets of needles from village to village, from door to door.

'You can't earn much doing that?' I asked.

'Earn?' He laughed. 'No – I'm begging. But begging is illegal – so I offer a packet of needles. They are light to carry.'

I slept well on a straw palliasse, and early in the morning my waiter friend led me off to have breakfast. 'The first house to try is the blacksmith's. He is always the most generous man in the village.'

The blacksmith and his wife gave us a rollicking breakfast of coffee and delicious dry cake. We thanked them gratefully and walked out into the street.

'You see?' said my friend. 'You can go all over Germany like that and never put your hand in your pocket. Now, are you ready for a second breakfast? We'll go to the priest.'

But I had already had enough of begging for breakfast, enough of the slanting rain and the dull country round Cologne. Canoeing was out of the question. I went into the town, bought a railway ticket, and headed south for Bavaria where I fetched up at an inn outside Mittenwald. The cattle had not yet been turned out to pasture, and I was given a room above their stalls. At night I could hear them stirring beneath me, and the heat from their bodies kept me warm. All day I walked and climbed – the Zugspitze was outside my window – and in the evening I ate in the Bauernhaus where the farmers came to drink, and eat and smoke their pipes, and laugh.

A week later I was hungering for the great snowcaps that I had never seen. I went south into Austria – first to Innsbruck, then up into the Oetzthal to the tiny village of Obergurgl. There was still plenty of snow up there, snow whose surface melted by day and froze by night till all the glacier was a glistening field of ice: difficult for a novice like me. The season was over; all the skiers had left; only one strange girl lingered on, like the heroine of Leni Riefenstahl film. She was mountain-struck and could not tear herself away from the high peaks. I survived three days' tuition at her hands, and each morning it took all my courage to launch myself down the headlong slopes at which she set me. On the fourth day I came to a series of conclusions: if I broke a leg, I could not act; if I could not act, I could not earn a living; finally, that acting was a far greater adventure than skiing. I shook the impacted ice out from where it was lodged inside my shirt, and moved on south again. Having come this far, it seemed absurd not to have a look at the Riviera.

The bus ran over a cat on the way to Innsbruck, and all the peasants on board crowded to one side to see what had become of it; if we had been in a boat instead of a bus we would have capsized. The cat, though disembowelled, was far from dead. A labourer wearing a fez came out of the nearby field and stood looking down at the writhing animal. He had something of the appearance of Fernandel, with a long bony face and a mouthful of yellow teeth. I expected him to stamp on the cat and put it out of its agony; instead, he leered up at the faces pressed against the windows of the bus, then picked up the mutilated body by its tail and shouted, 'Anyone want a cat sandwich?'

At this witticism the occupants of the bus broke into great gales of laughter; they dropped their baskets; they clutched their sides; they fell back onto their seats gasping and choking with mirth.

I looked back as we drove on. The man was still standing in the middle of the road, still holding the cat by the tail, but now swinging it in bloody arcs round his head.

In one of the back streets of Genoa I bought an ancient bicycle – seventy pounds went a long way in those days – and set off to pedal along the Italian Riviera. It was a dull ride till I came to the French frontier at Ventimiglia; there, on a steep downhill slope, my brakes failed. I hurtled through the *douane*, scattering *gendarmes* right and left. The bike gathered speed; the wind whistled passed my ears; I was helpless. But there was no mistaking the infuriated shouts from behind; the *gendarmerie* meant business; the idiots were about to open fire. If they did I could not absolutely count on them to miss. I swung my wheel and crashed into the rocks.

It was a definitive pile up; it could not have been better done in the circus. To my relief I was relatively unhurt, but the bike was in a sorry state. The *gendarmes*, sympathetic and helpful now, suggested I stayed at the adjacent *trattoria* while the repairs were being carried out: I had no alternative.

Below the inn, an unkempt carnation farm staggered down in arid terraces to the sea. Each morning I walked down the steep path and spent the day swimming from the pebbled beach. It had no great beauty, this beach, and it was deserted except for myself and an old fat woman, dressed in the eternal black of widowhood, who appeared there every day. She would settle herself down by a rock pool, a respectable distance from me, then she would lift up her skirts and splash the warm sea water up between her legs.

One morning she and I were both busy with our own different pursuits when I became aware of an unusual noise, deep and disconcerting; the air vibrated with it; but I could not make out what it was or where it came from. Then into view moving slowly through the sky from west to east came a vast silvery hull – the *Hindenburg* – no more than 1,000 feet up and perhaps a half a mile out of sea. It was an astonishing sight, made doubly moving by the absence of spectators; there was no one to see the phenomenon but myself and the old woman – and she did not look very interested. Unhurried, majestic, the zeppelin moved on out of sight behind the headland, and the throb of its engines faded on the air. The old woman returned to her private ablutions, and I stayed ankle deep in the shallow waves, lost and abstracted. The zeppelin had taken perhaps half a minute to cross the narrow bay; during that time my mind had formed a vivid surreal picture of the whole scene – like a painting with myself a part of it. In the foreground was an expanse of pebbles shimmering in the heat; in the middle distance, two small and unrelated human figures – a young man naked at the water's edge, and the huddled, black blob of a woman. Above this composition was the limitless blue of the sky in which hung – like the embodiment of human dreams and fantasies – this grotesquely beautiful shape.

At last the bicycle was mended and I pushed on through Monaco and Juan-les Pins – only a small place then – till I came to Cannes. The whole coast was intriguing, luscious: the girls, the yachts, the cars, the shops. Good food, good wine, bougainvillea and mimosa all the way – I could understand its fascination. Only the smell of money choked me; it hung in the air like an extravagant perfume, a reminder that everything and everyone had a price.

When my money was gone, except for the exact amount I needed for my fare back to England, I first went to the station and made sure of my ticket; next, I sold what was left of the bike, and with those few francs I bought some fruit, a loaf, and a memorable piece of Roquefort cheese; then I boarded the train and headed for home.

It was a long, hard journey, and it brought me back to reality with a jolt. The third-class carriages were crammed with Senegalese troops – big genial fellows with tribal scars on their faces; they laughed uproariously, and they urinated up and down the corridors with joyous, lighthearted abandon.

CHAPTER 11

THAT SUMMER, THE HANNENS CAME BACK from their long Australian tour. I rushed for my prisoner's chains and festooned myself anew. Far from being over, my obsession was only increased; it grew into a long, drawn out disaster, spreading a blight over the next six years. They were painful years to live, and they are painful now to recall, but to ignore or deny them would be to pour a large part of myself into a Black Hole. Six years is too large a lump of life to be sucked up and spat into oblivion.

I was almost twenty, happy every day to be alive; in every way but one I was reasonably sane – as sane, anyhow, as other twenty-year-olds. I had hopes of success in the theatre, but no exaggerated expectations; I knew that I had some sort of gift and I hoped that one day it would find expression and be fulfilled. But success was not an expectation. What I did expect – and in this I was deranged, lunatic, moonstruck – was love. Instinct told me that love – such engulfing love as I felt for Hermione – could not possibly go unreturned; but it could: it did.

My friends did not quote Keats to me; they did not ask, *Oh, what can ail thee, Knight at Arms/Alone and palely loitering . . .?* But they did give me some trenchant advice.

'You need your head examined,' they said.

'There are other fish in the sea,' they said.

No doubt there were, but I had no eyes to see them. I was bewitched by a dream – an idealized vision of living and loving. And because I had spun the dream out of my own imagination, I was fast bound to it; Captain Ahab was not more inescapably lashed to Moby Dick.

There were others too contributing to this farrago – E for one. She too had a dream – to share a few years with this son of hers and help him in his work by giving him a background. She did not realize that her son, quite aside from the infatuation that bedevilled him, was beginning to feel uncomfortable sharing a nest with his mother. I loved her dearly, but I needed freedom. I could not tell her this; my words would have only destroyed her. So I kept silent; and she, instead of booting me out into the world as she should have done, got rid of the flat in Linden Gardens and moved, full of plans and optimism, to a small house in Chelsea: 7 Paulton's Square. Hers was a gentler, more understandable form of madness than mine, but it was madness nonetheless.

In the Hannen household, which was only round the corner from E's new home, there was no visible lunacy but plenty of tensions and undercurrents. The house was claustrophobic; stepmother and stepdaughter exchanged pleasantries, but there was no real trust or affection between them. Hermione longed to be out of the house; Athene could not wait for her to be gone.

That was the background against which I went on trying to be an actor – which in the first place meant getting a job. You can write on your own, paint on your own, but you cannot act on your own. Acting, like living, depends on others. I knocked at the door of every agent, waited patiently in the outer office of every management in London. I tried for the part of a pirate in *Peter Pan*, for a stoker in *The Hairy Ape*; for both I was turned down flat. At the time I put these rejections down to my youthful appearance – and I did look young for my age – but I suspect it had more to do with my clothes. No young actor going up for a job today would feel properly dressed unless in jeans and a sweater; that is the mandatory uniform; it shows your freedom of mind, your lack of class-consciousness, your innate seriousness as an artist and worker. But the fashion in 1933 was the reverse; then you were not taken seriously unless you wore a suit, a hat, and preferably carried a rolled umbrella. I already had the suit and now I had invested in an 'Anthony Eden' hat. It may have earned me consideration at some of my Shaftesbury Avenue interviews, but it was not the gear for either a pirate or a stoker.

One job I did land was a Shakespeare season at the Chiswick Empire with Anew McMaster, a famous Irish actor manager. At his peak, I suspect that Anew may have been a great actor. By now he was past that peak, but he remained a great professional.

Before the last scene of *Othello*, the lights came up slowly to reveal Desdemona asleep in her sacrificial bed. In the pause before he himself came on, scimitar in hand and naked to the waist, Anew was anxious that the sound of the wind should be heard, moaning and sighing round the tower. He said that he wanted to underline the loneliness of Desdemona, but in fact he was building up his own entrance. Unfortunately he had no wind machine; he could not afford one. Ever resourceful, always ready to improvise after years of touring round Ireland, Anew provided the wind himself. He would stand in the wings, sipping and gargling a glass of port, while his tiny wife, who functioned also as his dresser, dabbed at his slightly plump and patchily pink torso with a sponge of black paint. Between gargles and gulps he would purse his lips and give vent to a series of long, mournful whistles, each one rising in pitch. He was never to be hurried over this double ritual; only when he had drunk all the port and the wind had reached its melancholy climax, would he step out from the wings. Arrived centre-stage, he would slowly lift his head as though to address the 'chaste stars' overhead – at the same time making sure that he was standing in the centre of his spotlight. Then he would take a deep breath, and at last begin to speak.

'It is the cause, it is the cause, my soul . . .'

We, his supporting company, were a ragtag collection of actors and no great good came of the Shakespeare season at the Chiswick Empire. The best was that I met Mary Casson, whose photo I had pinned to the study wall under the fishy stare of Backhouse. Mary and I became fond friends, and she often took me back with her to her parents' home in Chelsea; the Casson family opened their arms and took me in as if I had always been one of them. Generous, wonderful people: I have rich memories of meals round their kitchen table.

My ascent of the beanstalk was slow; I had spurts of confidence that helped me up a few feet, then doubts and self-examination that brought me slithering down.

A young actor is a poor sort of rabbit; he believes he has something to contribute – indeed he had better believe it, or he is throwing his life away – but it is a flickering belief, a candle in a draft of wind. A small discouragement and the flame is almost blown out, a word of praise and it burns up again. All young people go through the same turmoil no matter what trade or profession they follow, but for the actor the process is particularly painful since what he has to offer, what he hopes will be found acceptable, is his very self.

I had known the path I wished to follow from the time I first saw Gielgud and Richardson acting in Shakespeare. I had hoped with all my heart that Tony Guthrie would ask me to join the new company he was forming at the Old Vic – but he did not. He had engaged a striking young actor called James Mason; there appeared to be no place for me.

It was discouraging. I had been drawn to the theatre because it had to do with words and people – with understanding and reality; because it sprang from imagination – and therefore from God, as I understood God. I was hungry for life – one life was not enough – I wanted to live six lives abreast, every one of them an adventure; the disciplines of the theatre seemed to be just that.

But now, having seen the kind of plays that were put on and the kind of actors who succeeded, I could not think where I was going to fit in unless it were in Shakespeare. I might have made a cowboy actor if I had been born in the USA, but I was too large, too odd-looking, to get a job handing round the cucumber sandwiches in the West End of London.

Athene was of great help to me during this period. She did nothing to prevent the catastrophe of my marriage to Hermione, but she gave me much wise counsel about acting.

'Which do you want to be?' she asked one day. 'A good actor? Or a successful actor?'

'Both.' The question made me smile.

'Of course. We all want both. But, for the purposes of my question, you must put one before the other.'

I thought it over; there was no serving up a glib answer to this shrewd woman.

'A good actor,' I answered.

'I'm glad you said that – because now I can tell you. If you try all your life, with all that that implies, to be a good actor, you will probably – and I can only say probably – end up a successful actor. If you try to be a successful actor, you will probably – and again I can only say probably – end up a bad actor.'

I have found her to be unerringly right.

I need not have been so anxious; time quietly took me by the hand and led me from one small, ill-paid job to another. It led me to *Magnolia Street*, a vast production of Charles B. Cochran's which we rehearsed for six weeks and which folded in as many nights. It led me to the Embassy Theatre at Swiss Cottage, where a mild, gentle old actor called Brember Wills uttered words of encouragement that I have never forgotten.

I was sharing a dressing room with him and Abraham Sofaer, an actor of considerable thrust and power. One night I mentioned that I had been asked to play Brutus in some remote production of *Julius Caesar*. Sofaer was indignant, almost outraged: 'Brutus? You couldn't possibly play Brutus. For a start, you are fifteen years too young.'

Brember Wills turned on him like a little old fox terrier. 'Don't talk like that to the boy. Of course, he's too young to give a definitive performance, but he can certainly play the part. There is no other way to learn except by playing the great parts.'

Dear Brember, there is probably not a soul alive today who remembers you; at last I have the chance to pay a debt of gratitude.

While I grappled with my pitiful disease of infatuation and with the birth pains of being an actor, matters of greater significance were shaping themselves on the Continent.

On the night of 30 June 1934, while I was playing Matt Burke in a fringe theatre production of *Anna Christie*, Adolf Hitler murdered no less than a hundred of his old Nazi colleagues – Roehm, Schleicher, Strasser, and all whom he considered his enemies. Clearly the Chancellor of the Third Reich was not a man to believe in half measures; but we in England went our placid way. Downing Street, we thanked God, was not the Wilhelmstrasse; you would never catch nice Mr Baldwin behaving in such an outlandish way. If that was how the Germans liked to be ruled, so be it; they were a very odd people. On the Fuehrer went. Step by step in the years that followed he blew apart all the military clauses of the Versailles Treaty: he reclaimed the Saar, brought in conscription for the German Army, marched into the Demilitarized Rhineland Zone – and no one said 'Boo' to him. Only Winston Churchill again and again uttered his dire warnings to both Government and Nation – and no one heeded him.

As for me, I was as heedless as the rest; I was passionately involved in my craft and in my personal life. Italy's attack on Abyssinia seemed brutal and ugly but remote; I did not feel threatened by the foundation of the Rome–Berlin Axis; the Spanish Civil War brought bombing and death closer to home – but that too was none of my business: I was an actor.

Later that summer John Gielgud offered me Guildenstern in his production of *Hamlet* and asked Hermione if she would 'walk on' and understudy Jessica Tandy as Ophelia. We accepted with gratitude.

For a long time, my spirit had been a battleground. Pulling me one way was E, disliking Hermione, full of forebodings, and telling me plainly of my folly: I was only twenty-one, Hermione was cold, introverted, not in love with me – and so on. Pulling the other way was Hermione, continually urging me to leave home and become independent: was I a mouse to be so dominated? If I stayed under E's roof, I would soon turn into a 'mother's boy'. With the contract for *Hamlet* in my hand and with the help of a friendly bank manager, I took the plunge – financial and emotional – and rented a small basement flat on Chelsea Embankment.

E never came near it. She had nailed her colours to the mast and the breach between us was irrevocable and hideous. When Hermione and I were married, she did not come to the wedding; she sent no message. And all along I knew in my heart that E was right. But I was committed; I had made a Declaration of Faith; I would have gone to the block rather than recant.

The Motleys, who had designed the *Hamlet* production, had become very sought after; their designs sprang from their own bright talent, but part of their success was also due to George Devine, who had become their business manager. They now occupied a large building that had once been Chippendale's workshop; it was opposite the New – now Albery – Theatre in St Martin's Lane. Hideous iron gates now seal off the entrance to the cobbled yard, and the workshops of the great cabinet-maker have been replaced by a building of typical ugliness belonging to the London Electricity Board. The 'Motleys' became an unofficial and unique club – a sort of eighteenth-century 'Coffee House'. It was the most haphazard coffee house in London; the people who dropped in from time to time – Peggy Ashcroft, Edith Evans, Gwen Ffrangcon-Davies, Jack Hawkins and Jessica Tandy, Robert Donat, the Redgraves, the Byam Shaws, Michel St Denis; younger actors like Alec and Merula Guinness, Steven Haggard – were all friends who enjoyed each other's company, shared each other's aims, and were to a greater or lesser extent under John Gielgud's patronage. At its centre was John himself, lord of the London stage – but never lording over it, always generous to young actors, and always blithely tactless.

1935 was a thin year, but in the autumn I got a job in a revival of *The Soldier's Fortune*. Balliol Holloway directed and played the leading part. He was a fine – indeed magnificent – actor and taught me a lot about Restoration plays; that sincerity (which was about all I had to offer) was not enough; that posture was dictated by the cut of the clothes and the upright style of the furniture; that hands could not be left dangling at the sides; that swords were not toys but were carried in order to be used – and that they stuck out through the vent at the back of the tailored coat like the spurs of a fighting cock.

Athene, who was playing Lady Dunce, became progressively annoyed by the behaviour of the young company at the Ambassadors Theatre. She addressed us after one performance – still in her costume and ringleted wig.

'Children, there are certain things you must learn. When you're in church, you don't rush up and down the aisles squeaking and smoking

181

cigarettes, do you? Then why do it in the corridors of a theatre? A theatre in its way is as sacred as a church. It is a church of the Imagination – so respect it. Make as much noise as you like when the performance is over, but in the half-hour before the curtain goes up do not interfere with the concentration of others, and be wise enough not to destroy your own.'

The beanstalk grew sharp prickles, but I was inclining my way up it. In February 1936 I was offered the part of Mr Wickham in *Pride and Prejudice* at the St James's Theatre; it was a comparatively small part, but it had two good scenes, and I was in a great production with a first-class company.

The designs were by Rex Whistler; Celia Johnson and Hugh Williams were Elizabeth and Darcy; Dorothy Hyson played Jane. I saw Dot every day for months on end – only Sundays omitted. I thought she was the most beautiful creature I had ever seen, but emotionally I was untouched. My commitment to Hermione was like a suit of armour.

That winter Gilbert Miller took me out of *Pride and Prejudice* and put me into his New York production of *The Country Wife* starring Ruth Gordon. No part for Hermione, but my contract provided me with a first-class passage, and if we turned that into two tourist passages, there would be no extra to pay. We sailed in the *Queen Mary* – not her Maiden Voyage, but the very year she came into service.

Poor Hermione was a bad sailor and lay seasick in her bunk for the whole crossing, but one day I poked my nose into the first class and was staggered by its opulence – the Oliver Messel decor, the huge mirrors engraved with designs by Doris Zinkeisen. The ship reeked of money – but of money spent with good taste.

New York was like every American movie I had seen: the Statue of Liberty, the tugs nosing the great ship into her berth at the Battery, the tang of different tobacco, the mingling of all the peoples of the world in a city lying somewhere between Babylon and Main Street: the poor so shiveringly poor, the rich so be-furred and be-rugged in their Packards; a prodigious, prodigal city, thrusting up into the sky to escape its own pulsing confusion; a city of such drive that it bewildered itself.

The very night after landing, I was taken by some chance acquaintance to a drinks party. I asked who was giving it; the man did not know, but it was bound to be a good party – a penthouse on Park Avenue. He thought it might have something to do with a Chinese writer who had brought out a successful book.

'I'm not invited,' I protested.

'Neither am I. What the hell.'

The penthouse was packed, awash with champagne. True enough, it was in honour of Lin Yutang – author of *My Country and My People*; there he was – mandarin-robed, encircled and squashed almost flat, but beaming delight. I asked another guest, a total stranger to me, if he would point out our host.

'I've no idea,' he said.

'You don't know either?'

'No, sir. I can't tell you who he is. But I can tell you what he is. He is the Ex-Lax King.'

The extremes of New York made me feel alien until, one crackling-cold night, I walked along Fifth Avenue and found myself standing in front of the Rockefeller Center. White cliffs rose into the black sky, framing a statue of Atlas carrying the world on his gigantic shoulders; I had never seen the like. That night I understood at least a part of that wonderful, terrible city; I shared something of the vision of its architects, and I felt no more an alien.

Hermione and I threw economy out of the window and stayed at the Algonquin; we could save on food and drink, but not on the room we lived in. Frank Case still presided over the hotel, and the famous circle – Alexander Woolcott, Dorothy Parker, and the rest – still met there. It was a pleasant place to live, and it did something to pull our shaky relationship together. We ate in Auto-Mats and at the cheapest places we could find. When we had saved some money, we would spend it going to the Cotton Club – not in Harlem, but in a nightspot in Times Square to which it had moved. I was told it was not what it had been, but nevertheless we saw the great Bill Robinson – and we bought some terrapins with the name of the nightclub painted on their shells. They were dear little things, hardly bigger than the face of a wristwatch. Hermione took off the paint with nail polish remover in case it killed them; and we bought an enamelled tank to keep them in, and some sand and rocks and water so they could swim and climb about.

Christmas came, and the snow fell; the sidewalks were barricaded behind mountains of snow. For a short while on New Year's Eve, we joined the swaying, chanting crowd in Times Square, then ran for the warmth of our room. We switched on the radio one night to hear King Edward VIII announce his abdication, but apart from that melancholy voice there was little news of England; we were cut off, as though on another planet.

The Country Wife was not a great success; Ruth Gordon was remarkable, but the play was too English, too mannered for New York to care about; Restoration, however well done, was not for the ladies of Bronx, so it was no shock when the play suddenly closed and we had to leave for home – and quickly while we could still meet our hotel bills.

The only passages we could get in a hurry were on board the *American Banker*, a cargo ship of 8,000 tons. There were two other passengers besides ourselves, but I never saw them from the day we sailed till we finally berthed, for we ran into one of the Great Storms. It was a wild crossing; we were hove-to in mid-Atlantic for a week, fighting to keep our head up into the enormous waves and not be rolled over on our side. In the small, all-purpose saloon, chairs and tables were lashed against the walls with ringbolts; all movement was hazardous.

I enjoyed the storm; I had never seen such power unleashed; but Hermione lay clutching the side of her bunk to save herself from being tipped out, and the terrapins slithered up and down, and from side to side, as the *American Banker* rolled and stood on her head. Sometimes a few of the little green creatures got washed clean out of their tank, and I had to scrabble about for them on the heaving floor of the cabin.

We had sold our flat in London, gambling that *The Country Wife* would run longer than it did; now we had nowhere to live. I bought a sixth-hand old Austin 12, and we pushed off into Buckinghamshire, terrapins and all, buying on the way a six-week-old bull mastiff puppy that took Hermione's fancy. It was an enchanting dog – and why not? I thought: it might take her mind off her miseries.

We came to rest with our menagerie at The Plough Inn at Speen, outside High Wycombe. The Plough was then a quiet country pub where there was little trade except for the local farm hands. The terrapins, still in their tank, kept warm on the hearthstone before the open fire in the bar while the farm hands gazed at them with silent civility. One night I heard one of them ask, 'What are they?'

For several moments there was no reply from the corduroys and leather gaiters. Then an elder amongst them said, 'I know what they are.'

'What?'

The man was in no hurry to divulge his knowledge. He took off his cap, scratched his grizzled head, then spoke with great deliberation. 'Those,' he said, 'are oysters.'

The peace of woods and fields was a rebirth after the fierce canyons of New York; the beauty of spring in England was breathtaking – but you cannot eat the spring, and lack of money was pinching hard when, in the early summer, Tony Guthrie asked me to take over from Michael Redgrave the part of Chorus in *Henry V* at the Old Vic; further, when the season there ended and Olivier's *Hamlet* moved to Elsinore, he hoped I would step into Laertes. I jumped at the chance – to be with Tony again, to play those parts, and to work with Olivier, by now the most talked-of young actor in the country. I rehearsed alone and, on my opening night, sat alone in a small dressing room, keyed-up and highly nervous, when there was a knock on the door – it was Larry, come to wish me luck. It was Larry – and it was not Larry. His hair was shaved high at the sides – the pudding basin cut of the period. He wore a long scarlet gown, a heavy gold chain around his neck, and a circlet on his head. This was no actor; this was Henry Plantagenet himself – Harry the King – on his way into history.

Alec Guinness – by now almost an old friend – was in the company that went to Elsinore; Vivien Leigh played Ophelia, a great deal more than adequately. She was enchanting – as lovely and delicate as a violet – and the obscenity of her language would have caused the hair to curl on a rocking horse.

On the opening night the rain fell in cataracts. Tony made one of his Immediate Decisions: rather than abandon the performance, we would present *Hamlet* in the centre of the great Marienlyst Hotel where we were staying. It was a brave move, for there was no time to rehearse; entrances, exits, positions, all would have to be improvised as we went along. Younger members of the audience were provided with cushions and instructed by Tony in his most governess-like manner to sit on the floor – and like it; members of the Diplomatic Corps and elderly, distinguished guests were perched on slender ballroom chairs; everyone else had to stand, climb on benches and tables, or otherwise fend for themselves.

Actors and audience alike rose to the occasion. Challenge drove the actors through. I do not know what pulled the audience along – they must have been damnably uncomfortable – but by the end they had caught fire in their Danish way.

It was the performance that night that planted in Tony's mind the idea that Shakespeare could not be properly acted in a proscenium-arch theatre, but demanded presentation almost in the round. The idea turned into resolve, and the theatres that he built with Tanya Moiseiwitsch are the result.

The remaining performances were given in the Castle courtyard, and were subject to the usual hazards of outdoor theatricals. The King, after a heavy shower of rain, slipped and sprained his ankle – whereupon it was found that the understudy did not know his lines. The Queen – though this could just as easily have happened indoors as out – so took to the Danish Aquavit that she came on one night to describe Ophelia's death, drew a deep breath, and inhaled half of her gauze veil.

Back in London, John Gielgud invited me to join the company he was forming for a season at the Queen's. John had shed his influence over the

London stage and transformed it; he had gathered the greatest company to be seen for years: as well as Michael Redgrave, who played Bolingbroke (the part for which I had secretly hoped), there were Peg Ashcroft, Gwen Ffrangcon-Davies, Alec, George Devine, Glen Byam Shaw and Angela Baddeley – all my old friends. It was an honour to be included in such a company, but I was bitterly disappointed that all he had to offer were the two small parts of the Earl Marshal and a Welsh Captain in *Richard II*. I knew I could make something of the Welsh Captain, but there was nothing to be done with the Earl Marshal. It was a comedown after Guildenstern, but I could not argue. It was take-it-or-leave-it – and I took it; I could not afford not to, and I did not want to be grand with John who had been so generous and helpful to me.

The company that met to rehearse at the Queen's was not only distinguished but very well-dressed. John's clothes were always exquisite, and the others followed his example; but I, who had no clothes except the roughest, reacted against the bow ties, the suits, and the suede shoes. Perverseness generally entered into me, and I was glad to escape when Gilbert Miller offered me an excellent part at the St James's. John – always generous – released me from my contract, saying he was sorry my parts had not turned out better: indeed, after the Earl Marshal, they only went farther downhill.

Gilbert Miller loved to put on plays that he had seen and enjoyed on the continent, often directing them himself by the simple method of copying the original production. He had seen *The Silent Knight* in Budapest; the English adaptation was by Humbert Wolfe.

Humbert Wolfe was a dying man, and the rhyming couplets into which he had turned the play did not always fully make sense. Being a well brought up young actor, I found it hard to speak the lines without understanding their meaning. On the first day's rehearsal, I was driven to asked Mr Miller – sitting out in the stalls – to explain one of these baffling pieces of text.

'Well – it means . . . it means . . .' He looked up to the dress circle and called, 'Humbert. Humbert. Are you up there?'

Humbert was not up there, nor apparently anywhere in the house.

'All right, Tony. Go ahead.' And to his secretary, 'Betty, make a note to ask Mr Wolfe.'

A few minutes later, and I stumbled at another hurdle.

'Yes? What is it now?' His querulous voice came to me out of the semi-darkness.

'I'm sorry, Mr Miller, but I don't understand this either.'

'It's clear enough, isn't it? It means . . . it means . . . Humbert. Humbert. Where is the man? . . . Go ahead, Tony. Betty, make another note for Mr Wolfe.'

The same scene was repeated several times throughout the day. It was painful to provoke it, but I was impelled by conscience.

The next morning I was standing in the wings when Gilbert came through the pass door. He was a short, gross man with bushy eyebrows that hung down like ivy. He came and stood so close to me that I breathed in a mingled odour of shaving lotion and mortality.

He gave me a pleasant smile. 'Tony,' he asked, 'you know Shakespeare, don't you?'

I was flattered. It even flashed through my mind that he might be thinking of involving me in some future project. 'A little,' I answered, with proper diffidence.

'Then I'm gonna quote some Shakespeare to you.' He stabbed his finger into my chest, and his words were driven at me with unmistakable meaning.

> *'Yon Cassius hath a lean and hungry look. He thinks*
> *too much.'*

From then on, I asked no more awkward questions, but found my way as best I could round the obstacles. I even invented a few lines of my own: Gilbert never noticed.

The Silent Knight was when I first came to act with Diana Wynyard. It also laid the foundations of a friendship with Ralph Richardson that lasted fifty years. I had always enjoyed and admired Ralph's work – more, almost, than any other actor; now, I found him to be every bit as original, as quirky, as magnanimous, as I had imagined him to be. One evening, as our run drew to its close, he told me he was going to the Vic to play Bottom and Othello. 'Good parts for you there,' he said. 'The Lovers in *The Dream* are no great shakes, but Cassio's a damn good part.'

A couple of days later, Tony asked me to play them. It mattered not which of the two men had first thought of the idea; I was happily grateful. Instead of having to fight every upward inch of the way, I was now beginning to feel an occasional tug from above.

The Dream, designed by Oliver Messel, was a wondrous affair: a display of exquisite Victoriana that had escaped from beneath a glass case and – literally – taken wing. We had fairies on wires, a full orchestra, Mendelssohn's music, and the Sadler's Wells Ballet and Opera Companies. Tony directed; Ninette de Valois was the choreographer. As well as Ralph, there was Vivien Leigh as Titania, and Robert Helpmann as Oberon. Ralph gave the greatest performance of Bottom that I shall ever see, absurd and sensitive, moonstruck but ever-hopeful.

Othello was less successful. Larry rejoined the company and gave a magnetic performance of Iago, full of the animalism with which he abounded. But Othello was not Ralph's part; every quaintness, every vocal mannerism that had led him to success as Bottom only contributed to his failure in the tragedy. It was not Tony's play either. Tony's strength was in acerbity, wit, satire – but he had no feeling for the simple grandeur of *Othello*. He was embarrassed by the violent directness of sexual passion.

There was a further fly in the ointment – a positive bluebottle: Tony and Larry had been persuaded by Dr Ernest Jones, the eminent psychologist, that the real reason for Iago's hatred of the Moor was a homosexual love for him – a love that Iago himself scarcely understood. Neither Tony nor Larry dared reveal this interpretation to Ralph, knowing it would be rejected and possibly cause the whole production to founder.

On the morning of the opening night, we did a light run-through of the play; all went well till the last scene when Iago is led away to be tortured. As Olivier passed the recumbent Richardson, lying on a makeshift divan and beginning to fill his pipe, Larry paused and bent down over him. It was the first time he had done this; I suppose he and Guthrie had agreed that the revelation must be made now or never.

Ralph was surprised. 'What are you doing, cocky?'

Olivier looked out into the stalls, hoping for support from Tony – but none came; it was the only time I ever knew Guthrie turn tail.

'We thought,' said Larry, 'that is, Tony and I thought that as I am being taken away, it might be a good idea if I were to bend over and give you a kiss.'

'Indeed?' said Ralph. 'Then let me give you due warning that if you do so, I will get straight up and walk off the stage.' He meant it too.

Larry was for me something of a demi-god; success shone round him in an aura; but there was no way that much of a relationship could develop. So I was very touched when one night he came up to me in the wings, put his arm affectionately round my shoulders, and whispered, 'Got anything lined up when this ends?'

'Afraid not. I'm rather worried.'

'You don't have to worry,' he whispered, and gave me a reassuring hug. 'You'll never be out of work for long. Believe me.' His warmth and generosity were reassuring. 'And I'll tell you why,' he went on. 'Because you are a bloody good actor – bloody good.' There was the smallest pause; then he said, 'And you haven't enough personality to worry a leading man.'

If you are ever foolish enough, or unlucky enough, to stop a full strength blow to the heart — one of real pile-drivers — from Joe Louis, Mohammed Ali, or whoever is the reigning heavyweight champion of the world, I do not think you would ever forget it. Not for the whole of your life. Forgive — certainly: forget — never.

CHAPTER 12

G RANDMOTHER'S FOOTSTEPS IS A GOOD GAME to play when you're small. You stand with your back turned, and you know for certain that your attackers are creeping up on you. You swing round – but there's not a movement to be seen; your little friends are motionless, a half circle of mocking innocence, but you know they are all much closer to you. Next time you turn, they'll be closer still; soon they'll be able to touch you. It's rather tingly.

The thirties were like Grandmother's Footsteps on a deadly scale. You heard what sounded like a gunshot; you swung round just in time to see Chancellor Dollfuss collapse in a heap. (Nothing to be done, though. Austria is a long way off, and they do play rough politics nowadays over there. So unlike our dear Whitehall and those charming, well-bred men in the Foreign Office.)

What was that crunching noise? You turn: only Mussolini gobbling up the last of Ethiopia. What revolting table manners the man has got; there are two chicken bones sticking out of his mouth. Oh dear, those are not chicken bones. They are the Emperor Haile Selassie's legs – and they are still waving about. (Really, I think we ought to do something. But what? Oh – send Sam Hoare to make a pact with Laval; Sam Hoare is bland enough to paper anything over.)

Nothing too extreme for a year or two – no gunshots to speak of, no crunching – but then terrible sobbing, cries of distress. You look round to find thousands of Jews on their hands and knees, sweeping up the glass of their own smashed windows; Jews being turned out of the honourable positions they have held for generations – in the Arts, Law, Medicine, all the Learned Professions. And looking you straight in the eye is Adolf

190

Hitler – behind him the sea of Brownshirts and the waving flags of the Nuremberg Rally. The Fuehrer shrugs. 'Denationalization of the Jews? Certainly. I've written it all in *Mein Kampf*. I've written a lot of other things too. But you never took the trouble to read it. You should have done. You really should.'

It isn't only the dictators who look you so honestly in the eye; it's the smiling ring of the nation's own, favourite daddies – Ramsay MacDonald, Stanley Baldwin, Neville Chamberlain. So, for that matter, does Monsieur Daladier – though, being French, he doesn't really count. Oh well, if all those sensible Prime Ministers and Cabinet Members – all with access to tremendously secret information – if they are all content, who are we to worry? Come on – cheer up. This is 1935 – King George's Silver Jubilee, bless his old heart. Go to Buckingham Palace and give him a cheer. Patch up your marriage. Try to get a decent job. And don't listen to that Winston Churchill: over-brilliant, an alarmist. Not entirely dependable, y' know.

What was that? That was a very loud noise indeed. Turn quick: catch them. Strange – everything looks the same; nothing has changed. Yes, it has – the map of Europe has changed. Austria has been swallowed whole. And there again is that extraordinary Hitler creature, smiling blandly and wiping a trickle of blood from the corner of his lips.

Those were the thirties, a decade of Grandmother's Footsteps drawing ever closer. With political courage they could have been halted, but there was no such courage – no such leadership – in either France or Britain. While the *Sieg Heil*s thundered out at Nazi Rally after Nazi Rally and Hitler whipped his Hessenvolk to ever higher frenzies of militarism, we actors had to get on with learning our lines, rehearsing plays, and wondering if our make-up might be a shade on the dark side.

Larry was right: I was not long out of work. Tony had a job in prospect for me, though not until the summer. He planned to form two companies: one, in which I was to be involved, would open with three plays at the Buxton Festival in August, and at the Old Vic in September; we would add two more before going on a long tour of Mediterranean capitals. A second company would move in on our heels and take over at the Vic.

In the interval, I got a job playing Essex to Lilian Braithwaite's Queen Elizabeth at the Haymarket Theatre. I must have been at least sixth on her shopping list; all the Robert Donats and Jack Hawkinses must have been unavailable. Poor Lilian, she was very ashamed of me. She invited me to lunch one day at The Ivy – fashionable meeting place of the theatrically famous – but, lest 'Ivor' and 'Noel' should see her with such an obscure leading man, she arranged for us to be tucked away behind a curtain on an upper floor. I did not care; it had taken me seven years to go from RADA student to playing a lead in the West End. I knew I was not in a great play, and I could tell by the blown-up photographs outside the theatre that I looked more like an Eskimo than the Earl of Essex. Never mind – I had done it.

The centrepiece of the Buxton Festival and of the subsequent season at the Vic was Tony's modern-dress production of *Hamlet* with Alec playing the Prince and with Hermione as Ophelia. The other plays were *Trelawney of the Wells* and *The Rivals*. I would play Tanner in *Man and Superman* when we returned to London; and before we went abroad, Tony would redirect his *Henry V*, and I would try to follow in Larry's sunlit steps; Alec would be Chorus.

Buxton was round-the-clock work; but occasionally there was time to escape from rehearsal and go for a walk in the well-tended Municipal Gardens beside the theatre, where all was circumspect and serene. But even in that faraway spa where ducks upended themselves in the dainty rivulet, where the older citizens played bowls ('Good wood, sir') and the younger ones produced sub-standard tennis ('Terribly sorry, partner. My racket slipped.') more ominous sounds reached our ears: the rumble of German troops massing on the Czechoslovak border, the strident rhetoric of Hitler demanding 'deliverance' for the Sudetan Germans.

Actors are no fools despite popular belief; they are well aware of the tide of history that is sweeping them along with all the tinkers, tailors, chartered accountants, bookmakers, pimps, and politicians. But they seldom take an active part in affairs, national or international; their work is too absorbing, their livelihood too precarious. Those who work in great repertory theatres like the National, the Royal Shakespeare (or, in those days, the Old Vic) are at work by ten o'clock in the morning, and do not get out of their theatres till eleven at night; they live in an enclosed order. At the Old Vic none of us doubted that war was coming; our anxiety was to get *Hamlet* on before the bombs fell.

At the end of September, with a shriek torn from the throat of the Furies, the crisis was on us. Chamberlain flew to Berchtesgaden; the modern Atilla was propitiated with grovelling servility, and back came the British Prime Minister waving his scrap of paper and declaring 'Peace in our time'. The House of Commons rose to cheer him – and Alec's *Hamlet* opened. For a while the crisis had passed.

Alec made a great and deserved success; so did Tony. Without resorting to any gimmicks – no guns, no soda syphons, no golf clubs – they brought the play into the present century: a major achievement.

192

All this while my marriage to Hermione was growing more painful; she found my looks wrong, my work wrong – everything about me was wrong. She withdrew into long moody silences that I could not break through. I had known for years that our relationship was destructive to both of us, but I could not find it in my heart to break the chain that held us together; it had been forged by an idealistic boy of eighteen, and I could not betray him. Perhaps, too, I could not bring myself to admit that E had been right and I had been fatally wrong.

The weeks passed, and we were into 1939. On the stage, the 'second' company were already performing *A Midsummer Night's Dream*, while up in the dusty rehearsal room we were still working on *Henry V* and just about to take ship for Lisbon. The two companies scarcely met; we had different times, different rhythms of work. I knew that Dot Hyson had taken over as Titania, but though we were in the same building, our paths never crossed.

The very day before we sailed for Lisbon I came running down from the rehearsal room, turned the corner of the last flight of stone steps, and stopped transfixed. Dot stood at the stage door talking to someone, her head thrown back, and laughing – laughing with a gaiety, a merriment, that I had forgotten could exist. It was like coming into brilliant sunlight after the darkness of a dungeon. I was dazzled. God knows, she was beautiful, but it was not only her beauty that so possessed me. It was beauty combined with a radiant lightness of heart. It was almost three years since I had seen her, and I had not known her very well then; but there and then I fell totally in love. There was no time to ask her to come and have a drink with me, a cup of coffee; she was just going to work and I was off abroad the next day. In any case, she was married – for all I knew happily married – to a successful young actor, Robert Douglas; I did not know then that the marriage was as wretched as mine. I could do nothing, say nothing: only watch her climb the stairs to her dressing room, then walk on out onto the Waterloo Road.

I succumbed to 'flu in Lisbon and had to play the first night of *Henry V* with a high temperature; I got through the ordeal on the wings of a potent brandy. The 'extras' came from the Portuguese Opera Company, and were of an altogether different size and shape from the Guardsmen who had provided Henry's army back at the Old Vic. For the 'Honfleur' speech, I had to mount an unsteady scaling ladder and urge on a score of uncomprehending Portuguese whose chain mail hung down beyond their fingertips, and whose helmets rested on their shoulders like coal scuttles. Dizzy with fever and seeing double with brandy, I had to look them in the face (such as were visible) and cry,

'On, on, you noblest English – I'

The absurdity of my profession – of life itself – struck me with such force that I almost fell off my ladder.

From Lisbon, we sailed to Italy, and the lighter men dropped one of our heavy wooden rostrums in the Tagus. They fished it out, sodden and dripping, and it was duly hoisted on board the liner; it was an ancient thing and immersion had done it no good – as appeared a few weeks later.

All over Italy the production of *Hamlet* and Alec's performance were acclaimed. People stood up and clapped when he walked into a restaurant; everywhere we were feted and entertained. But the atmosphere was forced; the intelligentsia cooed at us like doves, but from the background came the ever-growing strains of *Giovinezza*.

The PEN Club in Milan gave us a reception; canapés and delicate glasses of vermouth were followed by speeches of welcome. Our Italian hosts expressed their horror at the very thought that the country of Michelangelo and the nation that had given birth to Shakespeare should ever confront one another in enmity. War between our two nations, they protested, was unthinkable.

I went back to the theatre, my ears stuffed with hot air. To reach my dressing room I had to cross the stage where Fred, the stage carpenter from the Old Vic, was hammering nails into a piece of our dilapidated scenery and talking, between blows, to the resident Italian carpenter.

FRED: Do you think there's going to be a war, Enrico?
ENRICO (with regret): Yes, I think so.
FRED: And if there is a war, do you think you'll be fighting against us?
ENRICO (after slight pause): Yes, I think so.
FRED: By Christ, you'd bloody well better not.

There was more truth in those two men than in all the declarations of eternal friendship from the PEN Club.

From Milan to Rome, where I stood at the back of a surging crowd in the Piazza d'Italia and heard Mussolini deliver a flamboyant speech. He was a small, black, distant figure, but his voice resounded through loudspeakers, and the crowd roared their approval: *'Duce! Duce! Duce!'* It would have been impossible that sunshine day to foretell the grotesque ending – hanging by his feet from a girder in Milan.

On to Florence, and finally to Genoa where we embarked for Alexandria. Lying close to us in harbour was a gleaming, white vessel, one of the German 'Strength Through Joy' ships on which deserving citizens were sent to have a holiday at the expense of the State. Shortly before we cast off the German ship started to let off fireworks, and from each sparkling rocket there came a parachute that floated away across the town of Genoa – each parachute embellished with a Swastika. Sixty – eighty – a hundred of them, all bobbing away across the town: butterflies that bore the emblem of barbarism.

I fell through the stage on the opening night in Cairo – at least I fell through the rostrum that had been dropped in the Tagus. I came running on, sword in hand, shouting, *'Where is this king? Sirs, stand you all without.'* There was a cracking noise, and I fell through the rotted planks and disappeared from sight.

I was not hurt, but I was entombed in a dusty wooden cave. First I threw out my sword which was greeted by the audience with applause and a storm of laughter; then I jumped up and scrambled out myself. All the time I had been shouting, *'Oh thou vile king – give me my father'* – to which the king (Andrew Cruikshank) had only one – inopportune – line in reply: *'Calmly, good Laertes.'* This only increased the hilarity of the audience. By the time I emerged, both Andrew and the Queen (Cathleen Nesbitt) had given up all attempt to act; they had turned their backs to the audience with tears of laughter running down their faces.

Order was eventually restored, but Alec's Graveyard Scene and the whole ending of the play were wrecked. Alec was not best pleased to have his opening night in Cairo so ruined, but he was generous and had forgiven me by the next day.

I was still standing in the wings after curtain fall one night when the doorman came to tell me that there was a German gentleman wanting to have a word with me. I had no wish to talk to any strange gentleman, least of all a German. But there was no avoiding the man; he was treading on the doorman's heels. It was Hans Beckhoff, the young Nazi enthusiast who had been so solicitous in planning my German trip several years ago.

He was a lot changed: no longer boyish but authoritative, cigar-smoking. He was the head, he told me, of the German *Reisebüro* in Cairo. And of what else, I wondered? I would have taken a bet that he knew the strength and weakness of every British Army Unit stationed in Egypt. He had *Abwehr* stamped all over him.

'And you?' he asked. 'What are you doing?'

'I'm acting.'

'Yes.' His glance took in the painted scenery, the property swords laid out on the table. 'Yes, so I see.'

His smile was condescending – with good reason. Hitler was ascendant; the Western Allies had meekly submitted to every demand in turn; Europe was his for the taking – perhaps more. And while the youth of Germany prepared themselves for war – for the test of 'blood and iron' – here was a soft young Englishman who could do nothing better than be a *Schauspieler*, a play-actor. The veiled, contemptuous smile made me doubly angry – angry to have my profession so patronized; angrier still because I knew in that moment of personal antagonism that we represented two countries, and that mine – however much in the right – was in a position of military weakness and inferiority. How, how, how had we allowed ourselves to be so unprepared?

We stood in the wings of the Opera House saying nothing; there was nothing to be said. But though the formal hostilities might be delayed and delayed again there passed between us a mutual, unmistakable declaration of war. We shook hands coolly, and he left. I never saw him again and I do not know what became of him.

Just before we left Cairo, Hermione was taken ill with pneumonia and carried off to the American hospital. The company had to go on to Greece by ship, but I was given permission to stay behind for a few days, see Hermione safely through the worst, then fly on to Athens in time for the opening. She was not desperately ill, and with good nursing she recovered speedily; but she was frantic at the thought of my leaving her.

'There's going to be a war. I know it. I shall be taken prisoner and God knows what will become of me. You have got to stay here with me.'

I tried to calm her. 'I can't, my darling. You're through the worst now, and there's going to be no war for quite a while. I have simply got to go and take my place with the company. I cannot let them down.'

'I see,' she said. 'If that's how you feel – go. It's perfectly clear that you don't love me, and that's all there is to it.' With that she turned her face away from me and would not speak.

I took off in a flying boat from Alexandria in a dawn like a pink pearl. I could see the timeless line of the breakwater, a lighthouse flashing at its tip; it might have been the Mole and the Pharos of old. All tawdriness was wiped away in that glorious dawn; all that remained was the essence, the dream, of the great seaport – its founding by Alexander the Great, its rise under the Ptolemys, its glory under the Romans.

A few hours later we came down on the water; not in the Port of Piraeus – apparently there was a difficult crosswind – but in a quiet bay surrounded with hills where oaks and olive trees crowded down to the water's edge. I was met by a small motorboat and told that a car would come and take me into Athens. The beauty and silence of the bay had a strong effect on me; I felt that it was haunted, though not unhappily. There was no one around but myself and the man who had brought me ashore. I walked about under the trees for a while, then I went up to the man and said, 'Would you tell me where I am? What is this place?'

'This?' he replied. 'This is the Bay of Salamis.'

I had been lifted up and carried by my hair from one place of destiny to another.

A week in Athens, then on we flew to Malta. The grizzly game of Grandmother's Footsteps was about to take another step forward. In October Hitler had devoured Czechoslovakia, and the Allies had allowed it – abject and supine; now the *Duce* was tempted to try his hand. On 7 April Mussolini took a running jump into Albania – a small, defenceless country where he could hardly fail.

The Grand Harbour of Valletta was at that time sheltering an enormous concentration of British Naval Forces – greater than any assembly of ships I was to see in the war. The destroyers were packed so tight in their pens that you could walk from deck to deck; out in the harbour lay cruisers, carriers, battle cruisers, depot ships, while between them and the Customs House Quay sped Admirals' barges, pinnaces, and a fleet of humbler vessels.

Outside the Grand Harbour a ring of Italian submarines lay submerged; they had crept quickly into position and now awaited their chance to sink the British Fleet if war was declared. But Naval Intelligence was aware of their presence and arranged for there to be a few lapses in security – a few signals that somehow became known around the bars and narrow streets of Valletta: it became common knowledge that in the Anti-Submarine Exercises to be held next day live depth charges would be used throughout the Fleet.

Britain did not declare war, and the Fleet did go to sea. 'You never saw anything like those submarines,' a destroyer captain told me afterwards. 'The buggers came bobbing up to the surface like corks.'

Hermione arrived from Alexandria, recovered but implacable; I had committed the final, unpardonable sin in leaving her defenceless in Cairo. All genuine relationship had gone, and even conversation between us was strained when the company headed for home, each of us wondering if we should ever meet and work together again.

Hermione and I took ourselves off to Speen – to a tiny cottage we had bought cheap a year or two previously. There we holed up, spending as little money as possible and making what we could of our life together.

Money might have eased the situation, but we had none. I sawed logs through the whole of that beautiful summer and tried to prepare a vegetable garden so that at least we would be able to grow something when the war came; it was no longer 'if' but 'when'. Hermione spoke little save of practical matters – would I please clear the drainpipe where a bird had made its nest? Which of us should go up to the village and fetch the groceries?

We had no social life at all, but one day we did go over to see Cathleen Nesbitt who lived not far away. Around tea time a few of her friends dropped in – amongst them Dot Hyson and her husband, Robert Douglas. I had not seen her since that momentary encounter at the Old Vic, and again I felt as if a lance had been driven through me. We played silly games and Dot made everyone laugh. Hermione sat in frozen silence.

As we drove back her only remark was, 'You're a fool. You married the wrong girl. You should have married somebody like Dorothy Hyson. She would suit you down to the ground.'

She meant it as disparagement, but she was absolutely right – except that it was not 'somebody like Dorothy Hyson' that I should have married: it was Dot herself. But now it was too late. We were both married, both involved. She lived in London, I deep in the country – and penniless. I had no means of getting in touch with her.

During those summer months E came back into my life. The division from her had been a long agony, but now she changed her tactics: she put herself out to be charming and friendly to Hermione; she gave us advice on the garden and brought us little dishes of food she had cooked – very welcome since Hermione could cook no better than I could. She and I could even go for a walk down the lane without incurring Hermione's anger.

E would come quickly to the subject that was foremost in her mind. 'You know darling – you do know, don't you? – that the war is coming, and coming very soon?'

'Yes,' I said. 'I know.'

'Well – what are you going to do about it? You can't sit here pretending to be a turnip. You've got to get into it.'

'I know,' I said. 'But it's a question of timing.'

It was indeed a question of timing, because Hermione had a number of close friends who were pacifists, Conscientious Objectors. Some, like Clifford Evans, were militant in their pacifism. Others, like Richard Ainley, merely declared that they were artists and that the war was none of their business; let others go and fight the ridiculous thing – not they. These young men often came to stay in the cottage, and I knew that their friendship and presence kept Hermione from falling into some black pit of mental instability. So the moment for me to go and join the Forces had not yet arrived.

All through the summer of 1939 Hitler was massing his divisions on the Polish Frontier; the screw was tightening. With brutal cynicism he and Stalin had concluded their Non-Aggression Pact; now the Fuehrer was ready to make another great gamble, with every hope of winning. On 29 August he announced an impossible ultimatum to the Polish Government, and on 1 September, three days later, the German war machine drove into Poland – fifty-four front-line divisions against Poland's twenty-two infantry divisions and seven cavalry brigades, most of them not even mobilized. On 3 September, no longer able to escape our obligations, Mr Chamberlain announced to the country that we were at war with Germany. We stood under the apple trees in our ragged garden, his voice coming over a portable radio.

Hermione did not move: her hands were stuck deep in the pockets of her old jodhpurs, her shoulders hunched up round her ears. By her silence, her frozen inaccessibility, she cried aloud to me that this catastrophe of war – like everything else – was my personal fault.

I admitted many failings: yes – our marriage was my fault; I had loved her too idealistically and besieged her too hard; yes – I had been too young, too immature; yes – I should have stayed beside her in Cairo; yes – I was an inadequate human being and it was my fault that we were now so far apart that we could not even hear each other across the room. But damn it, no – the war was not my fault.

Later in the day she voiced the thoughts that must have been going round in her head for hours. 'What will you do? I suppose you'll go and join up? Something idiotic like that?'

'Yes,' I said. 'I will. Tommorow.'

PART 3

A TIME
OF WAR

CHAPTER 13

JOURNALISTS, THOUGH PERHAPS NOT THE MOST STYLISH among them, are apt to write passages that begin, 'The invasion of Poland removed all ambiguities from the mind of the nation,' or, 'Britain was united in its unflinching resolve to go to the help of the gallant Poles.' (Poles are always either 'gallant' or 'beleaguered' — sometimes both.) They talk as though Britain had one mind, one heart, one entity. Not altogether so. Some were over-fearful, others over-confident; a cinema newsreel showed a brief interview with an optimistic youth outside a London Underground Station.

'And you, sir — what do you think of the situation?' he was asked.

The fellow gave a broad grin and replied, 'I reckon we got 'itler taped.'

The nation was forged into one by bombardment, hardship, defeats, by the leadership of Winston Churchill. At the beginning of 1939, as citizens consulted their old school atlases and saw there was no possible way of reaching Poland or giving any help at all, Britain was made up of 50,000,000 individuals, most of them in mild shock. They consulted with their consciences or with their wives (it usually amounted to the same thing), nailed blackout material over their windows, nerved themselves to endure the coming air bombardment, and tried not to bump into lampposts in the dark.

There were some, however, who had anticipated the opening of Pandora's Box of Horrors; Reservists, Territorials, those who had already joined the Forces knew exactly where to go and what to do. My Uncle Reg, E's younger brother, was one of these. Several weeks before the declaration of war he had walked out of his successful medical practice in London,

203

leaving his partner to cope as best he could, and gone off to be Medical Officer to an anti-aircraft regiment somewhere in North London. I went in search of him and found him under canvas in the region of Barnet. As I entered the battery lines I walked into a different and orderly world; after months of despair and icy hysteria in a country cottage, it was a blessed relief. Here there was great activity – guns being moved into position, emplacements sandbagged, communications tested – but everything calm, everyone purposeful.

E loved her younger brother with the same passion that she detested her older brother. Reg was not good-looking, but he had an amused, quirky face and a wry outlook on life – a most unusual man. He was welcoming and helpful; he took me into the mess tent, gave me a cup of tea, and talked to me for half an hour.

Reg seemed the same in himself – relaxed and quizzical – but outwardly at least he had become a different man. The successful doctor dressed in black jacket and striped trousers had become a major in the RAMC, wearing his decorations from the First World War and quietly settling down to play his part in the Second. Only the familiar smell of his pipe tobacco linked the two versions of the man.

Yes – he fully understood why I had delayed in joining up, but now he suggested that now I do so pretty damn quick. The easiest place, he thought, for me to find would be the Depot of the Royal Horse Artillery near Regent's Park. 'Nip along there and enlist as soon as you can,' he advised.

I went the next day. It was easy enough: in a single moment I stepped out of the theatre and into the Army. I walked out of a female world devoted to ideas, to the realization of dreams, to the clothing of fantasies with words; I walked into a male world whose finite and brutal purpose was to deliver high-explosive shells where they would do most damage to the enemy.

Boots reverberated on the wooden floor of the Drill Hall; dust floated in shafts of sunlight; there was the smell of rifle oil.

'Next.' The Officer sat at a trestle table between two NCOs at the end of the Hall. He was very courteous to the steady trickle of volunteers.

'Any particular branch of the Regiment you wish to join?'

'Yes, indeed. The Field Artillery.'

'Why?'

'My uncle was a Field Gunner in the last war.'

'Was he? Good. Have you got your Certificate "A"?'

Certificate 'A' was a military exam of no great difficulty taken at school while in the OTC; only plain fools managed to fail it. I told him that I had passed the exam and gave him the details.

'Good.' he said. 'That'll help a lot. Well, I can promise you nothing, but I've no doubt that it can be arranged. I'm sure the Field Artillery will be glad to have you. Are you married? Aha. And how would you like your marriage allowance to be paid? Directly to your wife – well, that is the simplest way. That's all then, Mr Quayle. Be good enough to sign here. And your home address please.'

'I suppose you can't give me any idea of when – ?'

'Of when you'll be called up? Afraid not. Several weeks, I should think. Maybe months.' He smiled. 'There's a lot to organize. You can imagine.'

When I got back to Speen, Hermione looked at me as though I were some incomprehensible animal. At last she said, 'You must do what you feel you have to do.' That was all.

I did not have to wait months – barely one month. Early in October the buff envelope arrived – OHMS. I had the rank and pay of a gunner and I was posted straight off to an Officer Cadet Training Unit (OCTU for short). I was to report by 14:30 hours on 3 October to The Citadel, Plymouth – Training Depot of The Royal Regiment of Artillery (CD).

'What does the CD mean?' Hermione asked.

'I have no idea,' I said.

I had never been in Plymouth and I made straight for the Hoe, carrying my bag. I wanted to stand where Drake had stood and waited for the tide to turn and let him out to sea. Had he really filled that time of tension with a game of bowls or was that all a legend? If so it was a good one, and this was a time when we would be in need of legends to live by.

The cliff top was covered with searchlight units and A-A artillery of every kind. The guns were all manned, and the gunners on stand-by were kicking a football about. Like Drake and his captains, they had to wait – and theirs was the harder vigil. Drake knew that soon the tide would come sluicing out into Plymouth Sound and set him free to carry the fight to the enemy, but these men had to stick where they were, alert but defensive, for weeks or months, never knowing when the enemy would strike – only knowing for sure that one day, one moonless night, the *Luftwaffe* would come against them to flatten Plymouth.

The Citadel was near the Hoe – barracks built probably in the reign of Queen Victoria; Kipling's Soldiers Three would have recognized it. I looked in through the gateway, conscious that these were my last moments of civilian freedom. The barrack square was swept and neat; a white line painted on the ground made vigorous drill turns at the foot of the red-brick walls; identical doors each painted War-Department green stared symmetrically across at one another; red fire buckets were

205

suspended at regular intervals. I picked up my case and walked through the gates.

The guard sergeant ran his eye down a typed list that he had on a clipboard. 'What did you say your name was?' He was obviously a regular soldier. He had a narrow moustache, hard shiny toecaps and hard shiny eyes.

'How d'you spell it? Like the bird?'

The spelling of my name seemed to be an unending problem.

'No, not quite. It's got a "y" in it, and an "e" on the end.' I started to spell it out, but the sergeant was not listening; he was searching up and down his list. Abstractedly he said, 'Nice things to eat, quail's eggs. Very nice indeed. Ever had a quail's egg?'

'Yes, as a matter of fact, I have.'

Again, he paid no attention to my reply; he was intent only on finding my elusive name.

'Q' he muttered. 'Right – here we go . . . L . . . M . . . N . . . O . . . Ogden, Ormerod, Pringle – now we're getting warm.'

I glanced up at a neglected-looking painting that hung on the wall behind him; blackened by dirt and time, it depicted the insignia of the Regiment: the profile of the gun with the motto underneath *Ubique Quo Fas et Gloria Ducunt*. Above the gun, in a gentle curve, were the words 'Royal Artillery CD'.

'Ah, here we are.' The sergeant had stalked his prey at last. He spelt my name out letter by letter then looked at me accusingly, as though he had caught me in some act of deceit.

'All right. Your Troop Commander is Captain Rawlins. You will report to him as soon as you have drawn your kit. Quartermaster's Stores are in the southeast corner of the square. Your barrack room is C4. Draw bedding from the QM.'

I thanked him and was just about to leave the guardroom when I paused and pointed up at the painting.

'What does the CD stand for?' I asked.

He looked at me with observant, noncommittal eyes – eyes that had weighed men up from Kowloon to the Isle of Wight, and for the most part found them wanting.

'CD? Coastal Defence, of course.'

'I'm sorry, but what does that mean?'

'Mean? What do you think it means? What it says. It means defending the coast.'

An hour later I stood before Captain Rawlins. I knew a trap when I was caught in one, and this trap was the Army. What was it I had argued all those years ago at the parties with the ballet girls? That Fate did not exist? I had been wrong. Fate existed all right. Fate had just pushed me into 'CD'; somehow I had to get out of it.

'But I applied to go into Field Artillery,' I protested. 'When I joined up they assured me that I would be posted to Field Artillery.'

Captain Rawlins looked at me with guarded sympathy. He was not a young man; his fingers were tobacco-stained and his eyes smiled wanly through a mild distillation of gin. 'Bad luck, dear boy.' Cigarette ash fell on his tunic; he brushed at it vaguely, but some still lodged on his faded medal ribbons.

'Could you tell me, sir, what it actually is – this Coastal Defence?'

'Defending the coast – the ports. Here – Plymouth for example. Southampton. Portsmouth. Very important job. And then abroad – Hong Kong, Singapore – so on. Mainly six-inch guns. That's what you'll train on here.'

I could not take it in. 'You mean, sir, that the guns don't move?' Where was the dashing into battle under fire, the uncoupling of the limber, the frantic loading and firing of the first round?

'Of course they move.' He sounded impatient. 'They traverse, depress, elevate.'

I must have looked moronic, for he went on, 'They go up and down, y'understand? They go from side to side.'

'Yes, but they don't actually move from place to place?'

'Hardly.' He was patient, pitying. 'They're embedded in concrete.'

There was a pause. 'Can I transfer?' I asked.

Captain Rawlins gave a great sigh. 'Quayle, I'm an old Reservist. Let me give you some advice. This is going to be a damn big war. A damn long war. You and I are so small, we're not even pawns in it – more like crumbs.' He flicked the last of the ash from his tunic. 'All sorts of things will happen to you – some good, some bad. Be a sensible fellow. Just take what comes your way. It'll save you a lot of time and energy.' He rubbed a hand across his watery eyes and said wearily, 'Yes, you can apply to be transferred. But no one will thank you. No one will care. You'll only add to the bloody paperwork.'

I gave in without more of a struggle and accepted the card I had been dealt. Looking back now, I see that it affected my entire life.

There is nothing inspirational about a training course in Coastal Artillery. I ground my way through Elevation, Muzzle Velocity, Trajectory, and so on – all matters of complicated mathematics at which I was as hopeless as I had been at Abberley. But all the time, through all the drilling, all the lectures in Military Law, I was happy: I might be hopelessly cut off from the girl with whom I had fallen in love, but the long bondage to Hermione was over. Adolf Hitler had brought ruin to the world, but he had done for me what I could never have done for myself: he had smashed the padlock that held me chained to Hermione – the padlock of my own boyish commitment.

I scraped through the exams at Plymouth and was posted on to the School of Gunnery at Shoeburyness.

To reach Shoeburyness meant passing through London; in the few hours that I had there I would try to see Dot Hyson and tell her something of what I felt. I was appalled at myself; in seven years I had never wavered in my loyalty to Hermione, and to deviate even to this tiny extent made me feel like an adulterer. But I was resolved; I took the step. It was the most momentous since I decided to get born.

Dot was acting in a revue at the Chanticleer, a tiny theatre near South Kensington. She was astonished to see me; in fact, it took her several moments to recognize the soldier waiting for her at the stage door. I took her to have a meal at an Indian restaurant near South Kensington Station, and over the curry and chapattis tried to tell her of my feelings. She was very gentle, very kind, but reminded me that we hardly knew each other; we were both married, and we were at the start of a seemingly endless war. She clearly did not take me very seriously – and though it grieved me, I could not blame her. When I delivered her back to the stage door, she gave me a little kiss, then hopped inside out of the cold. I caught the last train to Shoeburyness in considerable turmoil.

The Gunnery Instructors at Shoeburyness wore white trousers, blue reefer jackets, and red bands round their caps; they were very Important Men. The course too was impressive, with simulated attacks by ships of every conceivable kind, from fast torpedo boats to pocket battleships: I remember not a word of it. There was not much room in my thoughts except for this golden girl I had found just as the world was crumbling; but I did think too, as I walked along beside the muddy flats of the Thames Estuary and watched puffs of A-A fire bursting round some reconnoitring intruder – the whole picture unreal, surrealist – I did think of what an appalling bloody mess we were in: Russia had signed a pact with Germany; our only ally was France – and against the solidity of France there was a big question mark.

In February 1940 I was gazetted Second Lieutenant and posted to the Hampshire Heavy Regiment. There are three forts stuck out in the middle of Spithead – Horse Sands, Spitsands, and No-Man's-Land – huge, squat, round towers with black and white checkerboard markings. These three forts, pleasant enough to sail past on a summer's day but desolate in winter, were the responsibility of the Hampshire Heavy Regiment, a Territorial Unit of good standing.

Through the sodden winter months we were as isolated out there as the lighthouse keepers on the Eddystone Rocks. The forts could be reached only by open tender, and that when the weather permitted; heavy seas often prevented the boat bringing our mail and rations from coming alongside. We were undermanned, and shore leave could hardly be obtained: that did not bother me; I had nothing to go ashore for. My marriage was in ruins, and Dot was inaccessible. It was savagely cold out in the middle of Spithead, and so wet that the walls of the dungeon in which I slept trickled perpetually with moisture. I had not been incarcerated for more than a few weeks when I swung my legs off my camp bed one morning and fell straight to the ground; my knees had seized up with rheumatism.

One small occurrence did break the monotony. All the military defences of Britain were in a high state of alert against a surprise German landing; one of the prime duties for anyone on watch at night was to keep a sharp eye out for the first sign of a German attack – be it a small raid or a massive invasion. Our six-inch guns would not have been the ideal weapons to repel a raiding party – they would have been a little indiscriminate – but we were well positioned to give the alarm. The observation post on Horse Sands Fort had a commanding view of the approaches to Portsmouth and was manned day and night.

Our Commanding Officer had been a respected local bank manager in civilian life; a keen Territorial, he had risen to be a lieutenant colonel. He was an amiable man and no doubt an admirable bank manager, but as a military commander he was less than inspiring. One cold March night he was himself on duty in the Observation Post, a trusty sergeant at his side. On the trestle table before them was a hand-driven generator in a wooden box – a simple mechanism connecting the OP with the entire Portsmouth defences. The handle only had to be given a twirl and the alarm would sound in every gun site in the area, on board every warship; it would even bring the C in C Portsmouth tumbling out of his bed.

Now, whether our respected Colonel had dozed off through natural fatigue or whether his drowsiness was brought on by a drop of rum in his cocoa is irrelevant; the fact is that he slumbered – momentarily. Suddenly he sat bolt upright in his canvas chair and gazed southwards in horror; then he grabbed the handle of the generator and spun it madly, shouting, 'Alarm! Take post!'

The trusty Sergeant was taken by surprise.

'What's the matter?' he demanded.

'There – look there!' The Colonel pointed southwards over the inky waters towards where the honest folk of Bembridge lay sleeping in their darkened homes.

'One hell of a fire. Don't you see? Low on the horizon.'

The Sergeant turned his field glasses towards the spot indicated. 'Just a moment, sir,' he ventured.

'Don't dither, man.' The Colonel cranked away with redoubled energy. 'It's the invasion! They're coming!'

Inaudible, invisible to the watchers on the fort, the mighty defences of Portsmouth rumbled into position. Gunners stood to their weapons and prepared to hurl a curtain of steel against the invader – be he on land, on sea, in the air, or a combination of all three. Searchlights began to sweep the sky and stab the dark waters of Spithead.

Still the Sergeant persisted. 'Don't, sir. Stop it, sir. Please stop. It isn't Gerry – really it isn't. Take a look through these, sir.'

The Colonel took the binoculars and stared through them. 'Good God!' he exclaimed in the awed tones of a man whose doom has been revealed to him. 'It's not possible.'

'Afraid it is, sir. Care for a fag, sir?'

By now, there was no doubt. Moment by moment higher in the sky, bathing the horizon in its soft orange glow, the moon was rising.

The searchlights closed down; the gunners went back to their bunks; and that might have been the end of it had it not been for the Admiral who did not take kindly to being startled from his warm bed in the middle of the night by some idiot soldier – some godforsaken 'Pongo' who could not tell the difference between the rising moon and a German attack.

Two days later, abruptly but without public humiliation, our Colonel was removed. He went bobbing away in the rations tender, his kit bundled up in the bottom of the boat. His place was taken by a full Colonel, a Regular, an efficient but taciturn man who took no pains to conceal his contempt for all of us hostilities-only soldiers or his equal rage and frustration at finding himself at the bottom of such a very dead end.

I felt for the man; I was at the bottom of a very dead end myself. I might with difficulty get a transfer to Field Artillery, but that would involve a long period of retraining, and England was painful to me. I could not help Hermione, who wrote surprisingly affectionate letters, but was clearly in great unhappiness. I had no way of seeing Dot. I did not want to go near the theatre; there was no looking back over my shoulder. I longed to put as great a distance as I could between myself and these several miseries. I was, as Captain Rawlins had told me, a mere crumb in the machine of war, but the crumb had intense personal feelings.

The war remained dormant, static; nothing much happened. Sometimes there were photos in the Press of French Generals visiting London to hold talks with our own top brass. The photos did little to give me confidence in the alliance; perhaps it was only the discrepancy between General Ironside – so very big, and General Gamelin – so very small. There were photos in the press of our 'lads' in the Expeditionary Force reading mail from home or playing football. There were photos of French soldiers riding on railways inside the Maginot Line, and there were articles about the impregnability of the great fortification. The articles were meant to reassure, but they were not very reassuring; anyone could see there was a nasty gap up towards Belgium and Holland where the Maginot Line did not extend. Anyway, what was to stop the Germans from finding a weak spot and crashing through – or even jumping over it?

Around 9 April, just when Hitler was gobbling up Denmark and Norway with the usual humiliating results for us British, an order was pinned on the notice board in Horse Sands Fort calling for volunteers to go to Hong Kong. I put my name down at once. God knows what would happen there, but it could hardly be worse than sitting behind some Coast Defence guns in the middle of Spithead; watching Dot struggle out of an unhappy marriage only to get involved with some other bloody man.

My posting to Hong Kong came through quickly; I must report to the Depot at Woolwich and prepare to embark for Hong Kong almost at once. On the day I was to go ashore there was a high sea running, the waves thundering into spray against the base of our prison fort. The duty boat came out, and I stood watching its efforts to come alongside, but the manoeuvre was impossible. It turned away and went rolling and plunging back to land leaving me marooned. The draft sailed for Hong Kong without me; so I missed the cheerful alternative of a Japanese bayonet through the guts or four long years as a prisoner of war.

A few more weeks went by, and there was another call for volunteers – this time for Gibraltar; again I put my name down.

On 10 May 1940 Chamberlain resigned and Churchill became Prime Minister, telling the nation he could promise nothing but 'blood, sweat and tears'. That same day, Hitler struck at Holland and Belgium. Twenty-four hours later my posting to Gibraltar came through; I was to embark at once at Southampton. God know this was no time to be leaving England, but my months of training in Coastal Defence would be of no immediate help. It was too late now to stop the wheels from grinding on. I could do nothing but carry out my orders and see what Fate had in store for me in Gibraltar.

CHAPTER 14

ABOUT 12 OR 13 MAY we crossed the Channel in darkness and put into Cherbourg to disembark an infantry battalion – the Manchesters, I think. They went ashore in silence and were lost in the night. I stood on the deck and looked towards the northeast wondering if I could see or hear anything of the distant gunfire; but of course the battle was much too far off. The ship did not move; it waited; none of us passengers knew why. After an hour the reason became clear; the infantry battalion returned and were re-embarked. Perhaps the situation was too bad to add further sacrifice; standing on the dark decks of the liner we could only conjecture. Then the gangways were pulled clear, the warps and hawsers cast off, and we stood out into the Channel.

Throughout the fast, unescorted passage I was full of bitter disquiet: at this moment of battle I was leaving behind everything and everyone that I loved. I had tried to join the Field Artillery only to find myself in Coastal Defence. I had tried to go to Hong Kong, but had been turned back by wind and tide. I had volunteered for Gibraltar – only desiring to distance myself from a painful situation with Dot – and now the storm had broken. They were not comfortable thoughts.

But when we slipped through the Straits in the dark and came to anchor off Gibraltar in the middle of a balmy spring night, it was impossible not to feel a lifting of the spirits. The outline of the great Rock showed clear against the soft Mediterranean sky; at its foot, where the town lay huddled, there shone a million lights dancing and twinkling across the water. For the last eight months the British had lived like parrots in a cage with a thick cloth thrown over us; here in Gibraltar there was no blackout at all. The lights shone out over the harbour as cheerfully as they

212

had shone out across the Thames in London in the easy-going world that Hitler had smashed and spattered with blood. I felt like a child seeing its first Christmas tree.

I came ashore the next morning in warm sunshine and was driven by truck up to the RA Headquarters at Europa Point. The narrow street, thronged with civilians, had the look of an Indian bazaar: there were children everywhere; women in summer dresses; no sign of concern or panic. They looked to me like people still dancing to a band that had long since changed its tune.

At Europa Point things were different. I got out of the truck to find the place abandoned. I wandered about until I found my destination – the office of 26 Battery-23 Regiment; it was empty. A white-jacketed orderly explained to me, 'Well, there's a bit of a flap, y'see. They've all gone off round the guns. Checkin' up, y'might say.'

I wandered into the Officers' Mess – leather chairs, out-of-date newspapers, even more out-of-date magazines, a resident smell of tobacco smoke. I looked at the pictures. Over the mantelpiece hung a huge painting of some past Gunner exploit – a battery going into action at full gallop, the horses wild-eyed, their drivers lashing them on under fire. Stuck in the bottom right-hand corner of the frame was a small piece of paper torn from a pad; on it was drawn the cartoon of a balloon with the simple caption: 'Going up?'

Around noon a gaggle of officers, all of them Regulars, returned from their tour of inspection. They were eager for news from home and pressed me with questions. How was the battle going in France? Would the French hold? Were things as bad as they looked? I could tell them no more than they already knew from the radio. Within an hour I was bundled off to take command of a half-section of Twin Six-Pounders – but not before I had stood a round of drinks to the entire Mess. 'Come on, Quayle. It's a tradition. Expected of every newcomer.' I fell for it; I was still very green.

My 'command' consisted of the Detached Mole, lying between the North and South Moles and supposedly protecting the entrance to the Inner Harbour. In fact, we could have offered no opposition at all to a land attack from Spain; the Six-Pounders could not be made to point that way; they were popguns, designed only to tackle fast torpedo boats trying to break into the harbour. Apart from that one unlikely function, they were useless.

The Detached Mole was – as its name implies – detached; it could be reached only by boat. It suited me well; I had my own small outfit to run without interference from above; no senior officers came near me and I certainly did not seek them out; I had not found them particularly congenial. I had a good bunch of men, a young Scottish sergeant major, and a small concrete box where I lived in primitive fashion. The only drawback to my sleeping quarters were the bugs that infested the porous concrete and dropped on me from above. They were not as powerful as the Yorkshire variety that had molested me in Leeds, but there were far more of them.

Regular Army discipline took me by surprise. One of the first rules drummed into us in Plymouth had been that under no circumstances, however great the provocation, must an officer or NCO strike a man of inferior rank. But on the Detached Mole it appeared to be commonplace and accepted as normal. Every afternoon a few men were given shore leave; the duty boat collected them in the late afternoon and brought them back at night, more often than not blind drunk. As a rule, they were tipped out some distance from where I slept. Once or twice, half-asleep, I heard them cursing and swearing as they stumbled up the stone steps from the water; then I would hear Sergeant Major Birse's voice, followed by what sounded like a blow – then silence. One night the rabble were landed almost outside my hut; they were fighting drunk. A moment later I heard the Sergeant Major's voice. 'Walton – Monk – you're drunk.' There followed the sound of two crunching blows.

Next morning at gun drill Walton could not see out of one of his eyes, and Monk was lacking two front teeth. I sent for Birse after gun drill; he was an oak tree of a man, only in his twenties but with several years of service behind him. He cut short my hesitant approach to this delicate matter. 'Excuse me, sir, but I know what you're going to say. Believe me, sir, the men don't mind at all. They'd far sooner take justice from my fist than be put on a charge. If they're on a charge, then their pay is docked. They would rather be hit in the mouth than in the pocket.'

A few days later I went on one of my rare expeditions into the town to change a book at the Garrison Library and ran into my OC. 'Getting on all right, Quayle?' he asked.

'Yes, thank you sir.'

'I must congratulate you. First-class discipline you're keeping. I never have any of your men before me on a charge.'

There was an Italian cargo ship lying in the Inner Harbour. Early one morning I saw a motorboat speeding towards her, and a moment later she was being boarded by Marines. At the same time a second Italian vessel – not in the harbour but lying out in the roads – made a desperate run for the shore and managed to beach herself on Spanish soil. It was 10 June; Italy had declared war. The Germans were across the Seine at Rouen; France was staggering; Mussolini had joined in the scramble for evisceration. So much for the PEN Club of Milan; so much for the bonds that would forever unite our cultured and civilized nations.

Sitting out on my Mole, glued to every news bulletin from the UK, I wondered what would now befall us in Gibraltar. The evacuation from Dunkirk had been accomplished, but France was clearly about to collapse. It was inconceivable that Franco would not join in the fray and attack Gib; there was nothing to prevent him; Gibraltar was as impregnable as a poached egg. The big 9.2 guns pointed the wrong way; they had been mounted and sunk in concrete so that they controlled the Straits, but they could not deal with an attack by land from the north; in the whole fortress we had only six anti-aircraft guns and two 4.5 Howitzers to cope with the heavy Spanish artillery with which Gibraltar was ringed. There were no pillboxes, no bomb-proof hospital accommodation for troops or stores, and only two battalions of infantry. The Spanish could have walked in with a troop of Boy Scouts. Daily, nightly, I expected that they would. But there was not a damn thing I could do; only swim in the sea when the jellyfish and stingrays left a clear space, wait, and pray that E and Dot were safe from German bombs.

In those wretched days of suspense, the only thing to lift the spirits was to see the Fleet come in. The ships would appear from southwards and circle round Algeciras Bay, the destroyers racing round the capital ships to protect them from submarine attack. Then, one by one, the great vessels entered the harbour in majesty, *Renown*, *Valiant*, *Ark Royal*, *Sheffield* – the battle cruiser and battleships leading, then the cruisers, then the carriers. Finally the destroyers themselves, with the satisfied look of sheepdogs when they have the flock safely penned. Always last came an old destroyer – HMS *Wrestler*, her engines labouring aloud. The gunners watching from the Detached Mole had been silenced by the might and power of the other ships, but they always cheered *Wrestler* into harbour. And from his bridge the Captain – my friend Neville Currey – would wave cheerfully back.

France surrendered; the armistice was signed in the fateful railway carriage at Compiègne. At the other end of the military scale, I and my half section of gunners were moved to the North Mole where we were smothered in coal dust but no longer 'detached'. The beer drinkers were delighted: now they could walk to the bars instead of having to wait for the duty boat. But their hopes were frustrated when a Fortress Order came out forbidding all troops to enter the town except on strictly military duty: Fortress HQ had a number of massive and simultaneous problems to deal with – both military and civilian. The military problem was that

Hitler had now moved twenty divisions to the Spanish Frontier and looked poised to strike through Spain in order to close the Straits of Gibraltar; the Fortress had to give an appearance of being unassailable even though the door was wide open. The civilian problem was at least twofold; foremost there were the Gibraltarians themselves.

When Italy had come into the war on 10 June, all the women and children – 16,000 of Gibraltar's population of 22,500 – had been sent off to French Morocco. 22,000 civilians could not be taken into the Rock and fed during a siege. They would be slaughtered by the thousands during the first bombardment of the town, defence would turn into a nightmare. But no sooner had they arrived in Morocco than France herself fell; the poor women were kicked straight out of Casablanca and had now returned to Gibraltar insisting hysterically that never again would they leave their homes and menfolk. 'Bayonet us!' they screamed outside Government House, 'but here we shall remain.'

The Italian Air Force did us a good turn; they sent a few planes to deliver some half-hearted and ineffectual attacks on the Rock. At once the ladies changed their minds; off they went once again with weeping and lamentation to take over large sections of London and hang their washing from the balconies in true Mediterranean style.

In the middle of these chaotic scenes some 12,000 refugees came pouring into Gibraltar from the south of France; these were British subjects normally living along the Côte d'Azur in various degrees of affluence but now scuttling for safety like cockroaches – outscampered only by the British consuls and vice consuls who had already made good their own escape. They came pouring into Gibraltar in every conceivable kind of vessel. I came across Somerset Maugham one night in a small tramp steamer moored beside the Coal Mole, and spent half the night talking to him. He was surrounded by a small retinue of female supporters, all of them behaving with calm and dignity, accepting the hard conditions and making no impossible demands. They were almost unique: most of the refugees were shameless. They protested against being sent to England; they demanded to be sent to Madeira, to the Bahamas, to South Africa – anywhere except to their own country where they might have made themselves useful. They were Riviera characters who only a few weeks ago were accepted as a normal part of the South of France landscape; in the stark light of the present situation, they were obscene.

One of those blazing days there crept into harbour a small collier, flying the French flag. She announced her presence not so much by her French flag as by the stench that surrounded her and the slime that ran down her sides; she carried an entire Czech artillery regiment. When their country had been overrun in 1938, these men had escaped one by one into Poland; they had fought there – and once again had managed to escape. They had made their way singly through the Middle East to France where they had fought once again, with old 75mm guns that were museum pieces from the 1914–18 War. With the French falling back on either side of them and finding themselves in danger of isolation, they had commandeered a train and made for Sète in the South of France. There the Colonel had boarded the coal boat, stuck his revolver in the captain's ribs, and ordered him to steam to Gibraltar. They had arrived in safety, but they had neither food, water, nor sanitary arrangements of any kind; they were sleeping down in the hold, lying on top of coal dust.

Permission to come ashore was denied by Fortress Headquarters – an unavoidable decision. Attack was expected any moment; 1,000 or so Czech soldiers wandering about the place would only have added to the turmoil; most likely they would have been mistaken for Germans and shot. Water in Gibraltar was running dangerously low, but enough for them to drink was sent out together with food to keep them going; and there, in their floating insanitary oven, they were forced to stay.

The ship lay not 400 yards from the North Mole; when the wind blew from the south our gun position was enveloped in the nauseating smell. The plight of these Czechs made me feel responsible and ashamed; so one day I rode out and went on board hoping I could do something – however small – to alleviate their misery.

I invited the Colonel and his Second in Command to come ashore and have a wash in freshwater in my concrete hut. There was no such thing as a shower – water was too precious; we all had to wash in saltwater. The Colonel declined my offer with great courtesy; if his men were not allowed to leave the ship, then neither would he.

The Czechs endured another week in their floating oven, then a liner arrived to take all our refugees to England; I went out in the tender that carried the regiment out to the ship. To my amazement, they looked as if they were coming off a parade ground; every one of them wore a clean uniform, a clean shirt, and all of them were shaved. They must have hoarded water for this occasion. I went aboard to shake hands with them and wish them good luck. As I turned away to run down the companionway steps, I came face to face with a young playwright whom I had known well a few years back in the South of France. He had been sitting in Antibes ever since war broke out, growing sleeker and plumper. He wore rust-coloured linen slacks, and his manicured toenails peeped daintily through his sandals.

'Why, hello Tony.' he called out. I could hardly bring myself to give him a civil reply.

The submarine pens were within a stone's throw of my popguns; the submarines never spent more than a few days in port, then they were off again harrying the Axis supply route between the South of Italy and North Africa. Malta would have been a much closer base, but as Malta was under heavy bombardment it was safer to make the long journey back to Gib.

It was striking to see how the bearing of each crew was markedly different – and in every case it reflected the character of the captain. If there was tension in the captain, there was tension in the crew; if the captain was relaxed, then so were the men serving under him. The most carefree bunch were the crew of *Turbulent*; their captain was Commander Linton.

Tubby was a bearded giant among men; he had played rugby for the Navy before the war which, at its outbreak, had found him on the China Station. The Navy considered him too old for submarine service, but he had insisted that he continue in that branch of the Service. He was a man of such size, such commanding presence, that I think not even the Lords of Admiralty could have withstood him. He was in every way larger than life – not only physically but larger in the invisible dimensions of courage and confidence. He looked as though he had planted his feet on the ground and declared, 'This is where I stand. Now build the ship around me.'

Tubby always spoke of the enemy as 'the beasts'. It made no difference if he was talking of individual men or a ship he had torpedoed; all of them, quite dispassionately, were 'the beasts'. 'I got a couple of the beasts off Taranto,' he told me once. 'Transports. Big ones. The second was spectacular. I put two torpedoes into her and she burst into flames and heeled over. Must have been carrying cased petrol. A terrible sight. Terrible. There were scores – hundreds – of the beasts on deck. I could see them clearly. She listed over towards me, and I could see the beasts all running down the decks and throwing themselves into the sea. But I think a lot of the beasts perished. The sea was on fire.'

If Tubby had any fears and doubts – and who does not? – he showed none of them. He imparted to his crew nothing but confidence. If I had asked one of them what he felt about going to sea under Tubby's command, I know what the man would have answered. 'Our skipper is indestructible. They'll never get him. Never. So I'm perfectly safe . . . But, if some awful bloody accident did happen – and I guess in wartime we've all got to go sooner or later – then there is no man I would sooner go with.'

Tubby did not return from his last mission. HMS *Turbulent* was lost with all hands off Corsica in 1943. He had sunk a cruiser, a destroyer, a U-Boat, and twenty-eight transport ships that would otherwise have brought vital supplies to Field Marshal Rommel. He was awarded a posthumous VC.

One hot day in July when the refugees had gone and Spain still hovered in the balance, a small open car pulled up near our gun position, and a big man climbed out and walked towards me: a Major General – the first I had ever seen. I was impressed: not so much by his rank as by the face of the man, by his whole demeanour. Since boyhood I had worked in the theatre – a performing dog, as it were, among other performing dogs. I had known and admired several outstanding dogs – dogs of intellect, dogs of resource, dogs of sensitivity and understanding, dogs that could do astonishing feats, feats that I wished I could emulate. The point is that we were all the same species: rough, smooth, shaggy or silky, we were all dogs. Even the Majors and Colonels I had met since war broke out were no more than a sort of poodle. But here was a different species of animal; here unmistakably was a tiger. Experience of life had engrained the face; the tawny eyes held a threat of danger.

'Are you in charge of this outfit?' he asked.

'Yes, sir.'

'Do you mind if I take a squint at things from here?'

Did I mind? What sort of a General was this?

'Of course, sir. Please. Here's the gun position.'

He sat on the concrete emplacement busy with binoculars, maps, and chinagraph pencils. I wondered who he might be. I knew there was a Governor whose name was General Sir Clive Liddell; but what the order of command was I had not the slightest idea. We lived an isolated life on our Moles, ignorant of what went on even in Gibraltar itself. But I did remember hearing that some Major General had been flown out in a hurry immediately after Dunkirk to take over the Military Command of Gib and put its defences in some sort of order. This must be he.

As he was leaving, he asked, 'You're not a Regular, are you?'

'No, sir.'

'What did you do in civilian life?'

'I was an actor.'

'An actor!' The tawny eyes lit up. 'Well – that's wonderful. I love the theatre – and theatre people. D'you know Noel Coward? He's a great friend of mine.'

I told him that I did know Noel slightly.

'I'm very glad to know that we have an actor on the Rock. You'll have to get busy and organize some entertainment for the troops. God knows

they need it. Could you put something together? A revue? Something of
that sort?'

'Yes, sir. I'm sure I could.'

'Good. I'll tell you what. I'll send my ADC down and arrange a time
when you can come and have lunch. See you soon.' And he drove off.

In such a simple, unforced way, there came into my life a man who was
to influence me profoundly and for whom I grew to have a great love and
respect, General Sir Noel Mason-MacFarlane, KCB, DSO, MC – but to
all who knew him, Mason-Mac.

A generation has grown up that has no inkling of the brutal decisions
that must be taken in war. When France fell and Marshal Petain made his
separate peace, the powerful French Mediterranean Fleet was in harbour
at Oran and Dakar. Should these ships fall into enemy hands, not only
would our position in the Mediterranean be jeopardized but we might be
unable to control the Atlantic. Admiral Somerville, commanding Force
H – the Battle Squadron based on Gibraltar – was accordingly despatched
to offer the following terms to the French. They could either (a) come
out and join the British Fleet and continue the war against Germany and
Italy or (b) they could sail to the West Indies or a port in Britain and be
incarcerated. If they accepted neither of those choices, then they had six
hours in which to scuttle themselves before they were fired on and sunk.
The chief emmissary was 'Hooky' Holland, Captain of the *Ark Royal*, a
passionate Francophile to the end of his long, intelligent nose and until
recently Naval Attaché in Paris. God knows how he had the strength to
deliver this appalling ultimatum, but he did. The French turned it down.
On 3 July at around six o'clock in the evening, the British Fleet opened
fire. It was all over in minutes; only a few ships escaped back to Toulon.

A few days later, in reprisal, the French sent some bombers over to
attack Gibraltar. I was having lunch with Mason-Mac that day; there
were only the two of us in the house when the bombs started to fall, some
of them quite close.

'Come on, Tony. We'd better get under the stairs,' he said.

We stood in the cupboard under the stairs while the explosions went off
all round. Mason-Mac was just taking a cigarette out of his case when a
bomb fell very near to us; he gave such a jump that the case fell out of
his hand spilling cigarettes all over the floor. For the eighteen months
immediately preceding the war Mason-Mac had been Military Attaché in
Berlin where his ambassador was Sir Neville Henderson. Henderson was
an 'appeaser'; he had been hand-picked by another 'appeaser', Sir Moran
Wilson; behind them stood further 'appeasers' – 'all, all honourable men'
– Lord Halifax, the Foreign Secretary, and the Prime Minister himself.

As Military Attaché Mason-Mac had seen Germany's preparations for all-out war in the near future; he had done his utmost to warn the British Government, but his reports had been negated by his own ambassador. Now he had developed for all politicians except Churchill a contemptuous loathing. His Ninth Circle of Hell was full of those who had been too cowardly, too self-seeking, to alert the nation – those who had known the truth but averted their eyes. The frozen Lake of Cocytus was full of them.

The war came – exactly as Mason-Mac had predicted – and he was posted to France to become Director of Military Intelligence. When the *blitzkrieg* struck – again as he had predicted – he was put in command of a small force, called Macforce, that fought its way back to Dunkirk. On his return to England he had walked straight into the attack of the politicians against whom he felt a savage indignation. Our predicament, he told the nation in an outspoken broadcast on the BBC, was the result of political ineptitude. These were not words to endear him to his civilian masters. He was given a few days' leave and then sent flying out to Gibraltar. His posting there served a double purpose; it put a dynamic man where he was desperately needed and it muzzled a General who refused to keep silent.

I should not have been surprised that the cigarette case jumped out of his hand.

Encouraged by Mason-Mac, I cooked up a few entertainments for the troops – a couple of revues and a pantomime. I was not proud of my military contribution, but I could see that I was being more productive than mouldering away behind some absurd little guns, covered in coal dust. I knew too that the shows helped the morale of the Garrison; the men – particularly those manning the guns high on the Upper Rock – had a lonely time of it; they saw more of the Rock apes than of their own species. These shows brought them back into the family and made them laugh. They made them realize too that they were part of a great and ever-growing body of men who, if attacked, would give a formidable account of themselves.

There was a mass of talent to draw on: the Black Watch produced a gloriously vulgar Scots comedian; the King's found a dazzling virtuoso of 'the spoons'; the Devons provided an entire orchestra and the best pantomime 'Dame' I have ever seen. Sir Robert Ricketts was a young graduate of the Cambridge Footlights; droll, dry, witty, he wrote his own songs and dialogue. He discarded his handbag and lorgnettes when he moved on with his battalion to take part in the invasion of Sicily.

After so much light entertainment, I was tempted to indulge myself a little. I also thought it might be no bad thing to give the Garrison something more substantial just for once, something to think about. What about *Noah* by André Obey? Michel St Denis had done a memorable production several years back, designed by the Motleys and with Gielgud playing Noah. It was a fine play, full of humour, and it carried a simple message – relevant to all of us serving on the Rock: God is not always around to reveal His purpose to us; sometimes He falls silent. Then we have to do His will as best we can – even though we cannot understand His purpose. Yes, *Noah* would be the very play – not too heavy, but moving; plenty of animals – a bear, a tiger, a monkey, a cow – and three good parts for girls. There were WRNS signal officers in Gibraltar by now, and the prettiest of these must be recruited.

I tracked down the animals' costumes from the original production in London, and a visiting destroyer brought them out.

We built our own scenery; it was simple, but good. We rehearsed fervently, and our performances were like the scenery – simple but good. We started our one week's run – and we were a success. We were not 'sold out', because there was no selling or buying – the seats were free to all members of the Garrison, allotted on the simple basis of 'first come, first served' – but the theatre was packed out with soldiers every night and they were great audiences to play to. I knew – we all knew – that our work had been worthwhile.

Before the last show Mason-Mac sent for me. 'Would it be possible,' he asked, 'to give one more performance? There are still gunners in isolated positions who haven't had a chance to see the play. They ought to. I want them to. Can you do it?'

I was delighted to climb once more into Noah's enormous padding, proud to be asked. Of course it could be done. Next day, then, would be the genuine Final Performance.

Next day, however, there were two unexpected arrivals in Gibraltar; the first was Michel St Denis who was on his way through in his capacity as 'Jacques Duchesne' – broadcasting to the French people both in France and in North Africa. I was daunted by the thought of this most eminent of directors seeing our modest efforts, but I could not prevent it.

The second arrival was Force H, returned from running the gauntlet of a Malta Convoy; several ships had been badly holed, and they had suffered heavy casualties. Shore leave was granted at once, and in no time the bars of Gibraltar were packed with sailors. Two hours later the Naval Pickets were rounding up the drunks, and the streets were awash with blood and 'red biddy'. Nelson's sailors would have approved of their descendants.

By evening, the square in front of the theatre was solid with sailors, gloriously drunk but so tightly packed that they could not fall down. They swayed, they sang, they ranted and roared, and all with the best of good nature. When the theatre doors opened, the tide of white – fairly white – uniforms surged forward and filled every seat in the house. A few khaki uniforms managed to squeeze in at the back, but only a handful.

We acted the first half of *Noah* to a wild chorus of catcalls, whistles, and barracking; they only served to make me more resolved. I felt that the whole honour of my profession rested on my shoulders; I urged my fellow actors on, and we fought the audience till at last I knew I had them subjugated. As I started on the long speech that brings down the final curtain, I was soaked with sweat but triumphant. The audience were gripped, silent, listening.

The last scene of the play is set on the desolate summit of Mount Ararat. Noah is calling to a God who no longer seems to hear him. His wife has gone mad; his children are fighting each other for possession of the earth; even his friend The Bear has tried to kill him; he is in despair.

Forgive me, Lord, he says, *I know I should not complain. But if I could only hear Your voice, have some sign – just to know You are satisfied. Are You satisfied?*

With those words comes God's answer – a rainbow that forms a great arch across the sky. Then the curtain falls.

I had reached these last words when my actor's mind, always busy on at least three levels at once, shrieked a warning. 'Don't say the line. Stop. You're asking for disaster.' But I was forced to say the fatal words. Without hearing them, the electrician would not project the rainbow; the stage manager would not know when to bring down the curtain. I nerved myself and called to Heaven,

'Lord, I am satisfied. Are You satisfied?'

There was absolute silence for a moment as the rainbow appeared. Then, before the curtain could fall, a stentorian voice from the gallery – a voice that could only have come from a leading stoker – shouted out, 'Am I fuck!'

The laugh that followed shook the theatre and went on, and on, and on.

Michel St Denis came round to see me afterwards. I had the impression that the whole evening had caused him considerable pain.

CHAPTER 15

I N MARCH (1941) THE GOVERNOR GENERAL, Sir Clive Liddell, asked me if I would like the job of ADC. Sir Clive was a dear, kind man, but without the drive or magnetism to turn Gibraltar around. In a few months, Mason-Mac had become the leader to whom every soldier in the place looked; he was the talisman of success. Morale, that had been low, was now high. The result was considerable bad feeling between the two men. I was faced with a problem of loyalties. Mason-Mac had no such feelings. 'Go ahead,' he said. 'Don't be an idiot. Take the job. You'll learn a lot.'

A few weeks later, Mason-Mac left Gibraltar to return to England and take command of the 44th Division with Headquarters at Canterbury – one of the key positions should invasion come.

General Liddell was a dear master, and easy to serve. If my job had been nothing but a social one, it would have been unbearable; but, as Mason-Mac had told me, there was a lot to learn. In mid-April Anthony Eden (then Foreign Secretary) and General Sir John Dill (Chief of the Imperial General Staff) arrived from Cairo. Bad weather or a fault with their plane – I cannot remember which – prevented them from flying on to London, and they were forced to stay as guests for a few days in Government House.

For several months the Italians had been bungling their invasion of Greece. Now Germany had come to their assistance; thirty-two German Divisions were thrown in to help the twenty-six Italian Divisions already operating in Albania. Britain was forced to take a political decision: we had few enough friends and allies; the Greeks could not be left in the lurch. General Wavell, fighting a brilliant war in North Africa, was stripped of 60,000 men who were sent to the immediate aid of Greece. On 6 April the Germans smashed through the Greek mountain frontier. By early April the British and Greek forces were withdrawing to a position South of Mount Olympus in a rapidly deteriorating position.

This was the situation when Dill and Eden appeared in Gibraltar. Both men were desperately anxious. They had taken a political decision and the responsibility for the lives of the whole Expeditionary Force, as well as its success or failure rested on them.

They expected Gibraltar to have a War Room with maps showing the changing front in Greece; there was no such War Room, but a big geography map was found in some school and spread out across the billiard room in Government House. They expected us to be in easy contact with London and were amazed to find that this was not so; telephone communication did not exist. All official messages had to be ciphered and deciphered. Our earliest information came from the ordinary BBC World Service. So, whenever the *News* came on the air the two men met together in the billiard room and listened to the little wooden box. Usually I was with them.

One day the one o'clock news was unrelievably gloomy; the British Expeditionary Force in Greece was in dire trouble. Dill sat in silence at one end of the room not even glancing at the map, his face white and drawn. Eden stood leaning over the billiard table, ash from his cigarette dropping on the map – Turkish or Egyptian cigarettes they were; I do not know which. There was no doubt of his deep concern, but he showed it in restlessness, continually changing his position and appealing to Dill.

'But what else could we have done, Johnny?' he asked almost plaintively. 'What the devil else could we have done?'

From Dill there was no answer at all. He sat at the end of the room in grey, frozen misery.

Politicians seem unable to avoid the pitfall of self-awareness; they display themselves with a theatricality that would make a professional actor cringe. They should be made to serve an apprenticeship in the theatre; four years of that turbulent and humbling experience would do much to make them lose their vanity. Eden, God knows, had served a hard apprenticeship, but of a different kind – the trenches of the First World War. There was no doubting his courage, his courtesy and his sincerity. I was critical of him only because I so wanted to admire without reserve one of our foremost leaders. Surely, I thought in my innocence, there was no way a man could rise to be Foreign Secretary unless he were a truly great man. It was dismaying to find that the Foreign Secretary could be stamped with one of the more obvious faults of my own profession.

I took Mr Eden on a long tour of the Rock before he left Gibraltar; he was anxious to speak to as many of the troops as he could. He was generous with his time in doing so, and it gave the men great encouragement to see him; but for all that his tour of the gun sites had a selfless, admirable purpose, I could not avoid thinking that here was a politician to whom every vote would count in the next election – whenever that might be.

A sergeant in the Black Watch said to him, 'You must be very tired, sir.'

Eden touched the man's arm, and with a slight smile replied, 'Not so much tired as terribly, terribly, worried.' There was nothing whatever wrong with the remark except that the timing, the rhythm, even the smile, were theatrical. The line had been written by Noel Coward.

I concluded, sadly, that it took an actor to know an actor.

So the great wheels of history turned while I sat on one of the world's prime targets, sleeping between clean sheets and thinking of the girl with whom I had fallen in love. I longed to see her with the same fervour that, a year back, I had fought to get far away from her. And once again, in the middle of a world convulsion in which individuals were mere specks of dust in a sandstorm, I was given the chance to make a personal choice. Early in June General Liddell was ordered home to England and suggested I might like to accompany him as his ADC. I took no persuading.

I sailed for home in HMS *Argus*, a small aircraft carrier crammed with soldiers of every rank and nationality. There were no cabins, no bunks; I slept out on the deck in blissful happiness. It was only later that I began to realize what a strong part Fate was playing in my war. Falling asleep, listening to the throb of the engines, I accepted this return to England as being a natural part of the wonderful adventure of being alive.

I did not know where or when we should dock, and there was no point writing to Hermione since I would surely arrive before any letter.

During the few days' passage, I often talked to a couple of escaped prisoners of war – Yorkshire soldiers who had been spirited out of the Spanish prison camp at Miranda, and smuggled into Gibraltar. (Both the Special Operations Executive and the Embassy in Madrid played a part in this underground traffic.) They were very simple men. I asked them where they had been taken prisoner. 'It was in Belgium,' they thought, 'during the first Gerry attack.'

'Then what?'

'Oh, they shut us up – first in Germany, then in Poland.'

'How did you escape?'

'We jumped off the roof.' They explained that they were both carpenters and had been put to work by the Germans mending the roof of their hut.

Seeing that the road was clear one day, they had simply jumped off and run for it.

'But how did you get away? Could you speak Polish – or German – or French?'

'No – but folk were very kind. They hid us and they passed us on till we got to Spain – and then we were put in this prison camp.'

They had crossed the whole of Europe – God knows how – guided and protected all the way by the 'underground'. They knew nothing of the risks run on their behalf, and they thought nothing at all of their extraordinary achievement. Innocence had been their shield.

We berthed at Gourock. I was given a railway pass to take me to High Wycombe; Speen was the nearest thing I had to a home, and the nearest station to home was High Wycombe; night had fallen by the time I arrived there. There was no transport to be had, so I started to walk carrying my bag; I had walked more than half the five miles before a driver stopped and gave me a lift. It was full moonlight as I stumbled down the familiar, flinty lane; the cottage was just as I had left it, folded in by its apple trees. It was dead quiet.

'Hermione,' I called.

No answer. Silence. Perhaps she was away?

Again, 'Hermione.'

The upstairs window opened and Hermione put her head out. 'What is it? What's the matter?' She was half-asleep.

A man put his head out beside hers: Clifford Evans.

'Good heavens!' he said. 'It's Tony!'

It was an odd homecoming. I was happy that she had found the love and companionship she needed – it was the very situation I had hoped for – and yet my idiotic dignity was affronted. The soldier's wife should be waiting for him with open arms, not asking her lover to open a bottle of cooking sherry to mark the occasion – and he a Conscientious Objector.

In the morning it was soon decided what must be done: I would go straight up to London and start divorce proceedings. Hermione and Clifford were concerned about where I would find to live, but I told them not to worry; I would fend very well for myself. I did; for one night I took a room at the Savoy. I had never stayed there before and I have never stayed there since, but for that one night the ordered luxury of the Savoy did me a lot of good; it restored my self-esteem.

E was living in Chelsea Cloisters, a block of flats inhabited almost entirely by Poles. E loved the Poles and I found her cheerfully mothering and befriending a whole contingent of them. She bribed and cajoled the management into renting me a tiny one-room flat in the building, and there I settled in, happy to be sharing life with her again after so many years of separation.

Dot, the essential reason for my return to England, was not even in London; she had gone to work as a cryptographer (low-level, but none the less a cryptographer) at Bletchley Park, home of the most secret operation of the war – ULTRA. I went to see her there and found her ill and exhausted with the long night shifts. Naturally, there were men in her life – with Dot how could it have been otherwise? – but nothing was resolved, no relationship looked permanent. I drew comfort from that, though her frailty worried me.

The Old Vic had been damaged by bombs – one of them had killed poor Orlando Whitehead – and Tony Guthrie had moved the Old Vic to Burnley. He came to London from time to time and we met one day in Berkeley Square – of all unlikely places. We sat on a bench under the plane trees and I told him that my marriage had broken up and that I had set in motion the wheels of divorce. He considered the news in silence; then he lifted his head and drew in a long breath through his dominant nose.

'I'm very glad. It will be a relief to all your friends. We thought you might be utterly destroyed.'

General Liddell's new job was a sinecure. He had the title 'Inspector General of Training', but the dear man was as ignorant as a teddy bear of modern warfare or the training it required. He was not perturbed; he turned up every day at his office near Buckingham Palace, smoked his cigars and dutifully read through training papers. He made lists of areas he would like to visit, and took me along with him.

He was keen to meet Dot, and I managed to arrange it once when she was on leave. The Liddells took us to the Savoy Grill and we danced to Carroll Gibbons' band: a bitter-sweet evening for me, with Paradise at hand yet infinitely removed. The General, like all male creatures, fell in love with Dot; from that night on, he used to send her dear, gentle love letters – even poems.

I felt calmer now I had seen Dot; there was nothing I could do to help the situation, but I could hold on and wait with a grain more optimism. A more immediate problem was what to do with myself. The position I was in was despicable. I could return to the Regiment, but they would only have sent me back to be totally retrained, and after life in Gibraltar I found that a hard prospect to face. I was in a quandary when Fate stepped in and dealt me another card – a Joker, as it turned out.

Auxiliary Units was a cloak-and-dagger organization designed to harass the Germans for as long as possible after they had made a landing in Britain. Since the enemy could launch an assault from anywhere on the

North European coast, from Belgium and Holland as well as from France, Auxiliary Units had been developed all along the south coast and up the eastern seaboard as far north as Northumberland. The men, all volunteers, were recruited mainly from the Home Guard; farmers, gamekeepers, coal miners, they had to know their own countryside backwards since they would be fighting by stealth and by night. By day, they had specially prepared hide-outs where it was hoped they might get some sleep.

I would never have known of Auxiliary Units had it not been for the job I so despised, and I might not have been accepted by them had it not been for a word of commendation from General Liddell; as it was, I was given the whole of Northumberland to organize. Hide-outs had to be dug and camouflaged, the right men recruited in secret, then trained in night patrolling and the handling of explosives – and all without the local inhabitants getting wind of what was afoot. We were a small organization but with sharp teeth; we did not expect to last many days after a German landing; but for at least forty-eight hours it would be, in Mason-Mac's words, 'one hell of a party'.

Yes – there are *tongues in trees, books in the running brooks,/Sermons in stones* – but there is not *good in everything*. There is no good whatsoever in war. Yet had it not been for the war I would never have known what force and unity lay hidden beneath the offhanded nonchalance of the British character; I would never have lived so close to the majestic country of Northumbria; I would never have been brought as a friend into the cottages and kitchens of its farmers and coal miners. It was part of my education; I would be the poorer without it.

Through the snowy winter of 1941 and into the spring of 1942 I recruited my patrols till we were some 200 strong. They mastered a variety of skills – to be deadly shots with a .22 Winchester fitted with silencer and telescopic sights; to handle plastic explosive on bridges, railway lines or simple telegraph poles; above all how to make a friend of the darkness and move about at night without breaking a twig or disturbing a sleeping bird.

The 51st Highland Division were in training in Northumberland and every few weeks we carried out a night attack on one of their Battalion or Brigade headquarters. Only the Divisional Commander knew of our intentions, and he welcomed them; it kept his Division on their toes.

We carried one attack a bit too far; it almost cost two of us our lives. We left a detonator in the wash house timed to go off at one in the morning, and half a dozen others in places where they would do no harm but were timed to explode at ten-minute intervals. That done, most of the patrol legged it for home – they were farmers and had to be up milking in a few hours; but two of us stayed hidden in a rhododendron bush to watch the fun.

The 'time pencils' worked accurately; just before one o'clock in the morning, the first exploded, then another, then another. The Jocks came pouring out of their quarters like a swarm of furious bees; it was working out just as we had hoped.

A few moments later however as we lay hidden in the rhododendron, it became clear that the joke was not such a funny one: the men had been issued with live ammunition. They raged through the grounds of the big house searching the bushes and firing whenever they thought they saw a movement. Thank God, the one place they never thought to search was the clump where we lay hidden. We intruders pressed ourselves flat on the ground and held our breath; one move, one sound, and a volley would have ploughed through us. It took two hours for the commotion to die down; then we wormed our way on our stomachs till we reached the perimeter wall, hoisted ourselves over it, and made off as fast as we could.

In the spring, with the threat of German invasion almost past, we were given a new Commanding Officer – Colonel The Lord Glanusk. He arrived in a Rolls Royce accompanied by two Welsh Guardsmen – one of them his driver, the other his batman. I did not take to him. He had none of the manners of true aristocracy, only an air of condescension. He disturbed the delicate relationship that had been established between myself and the Divisional Commander; worse, he undermined the family feeling that ran through all of my patrols, from Newcastle to the Border; he patronized them.

Before leaving Northumberland, he called me to his presence and informed me that he took 'a dim view' of me. I replied that I could only reciprocate his feelings. It was not the most tactful thing for a mere captain to say to his full colonel; perhaps some of Mason-Mac's refusal to kow-tow to his superiors had got into me.

The Lord Glanusk went driving off with his two extremely able-bodied Guardsmen, and I sat on the Kyloe Hills, staring out at Holy Island and waiting to be court-martialled. I might, I thought, get off with a Reprimand, but court martial was the more likely; either way, the prospect was gloomy. I decided to cheer myself up.

It was June and it had been a long time since I had seen London. I was my own master; I needed to ask no one for permission; I gave myself leave and took the train up to town. Dot predictably was either away or unavailable, so I made contact with one or two other girls – all attractive, but of minor importance. I made a date with one of them to collect her from her hairdresser's in Albemarle Street around lunchtime.

At the appointed time, I was outside the place, but she was still trussed up under the hair dryer.

Slightly put out by the dilatory ways of pretty girls, I started to walk up and down Albemarle Street past the entrance to Brown's Hotel. Brown's Hotel? Wasn't that where Mason-Mac had told me that he always made his London headquarters? I knew he was in Russia – had been there for a year now – but partly to fill in time, partly to put myself – however remotely – in touch with his powerful presence, I walked into the hotel and asked at the desk if General Mason-MacFarlane happened to be there.

The porter gave me a searching look, then turned away from me and spoke quietly into the telephone. He looked back, 'What name shall I say?'

'Captain Quayle.'

He repeated my unspellable name. Then, 'Please go up, sir. Suite number twelve, second floor.'

And there was Mason-Mac, the snow scarcely melted from his boots. He had come from Moscow via Stalingrad, Tehran, Basra, Cairo, and Gib itself. He had checked in only the previous night and had spent all morning at the War Office.

'And now – guess what, Tony.' His tiger eyes shone with pleasure. 'They're sending me back to Gib as Governor and C in C. There's going to be one hell of a good party there – and soon. Do you want to come with me?'

'Of course I do, sir. But I can't.'

'What do you mean – can't?'

'I'm in a bit of trouble. I've had a quarrel with my Colonel and I think I'm awaiting court martial.'

'Don't talk balls,' he said. 'Come and be my Military Assistant. You'll get your majority and we'll have a hell of a good time.'

'But what about my Colonel?'

'Damn your Colonel. Leave him to me. Be back here ready to leave in forty-eight hours. That's all.'

'You mean just walk out?'

'Yes. Walk out. Now, we'll have some lunch – then off you go to your crazy outfit wherever it is, and pack a few things. But don't be late back here, or I'll go without you.'

We had such a merry lunch that I forgot the poor girl under the hair dryer. As Lilian Baylis would have said, 'Well dear, you had your chance and you missed it.'

We took off from Plymouth in a Sunderland flying boat making ourselves as comfortable as we might on top of the mail bags; it was damnably cold, but I was far too happy to care. I knew that something extraordinary had happened, and without my initiative. Fate – perhaps God Himself – had intervened most positively in my life – not with a fanfare but in the most unobvious and trivial of ways: a pretty girl had been late for lunch. God had spoken, not from any Burning Bush or from the top of Mount Horeb, but from under a hair dryer and from Brown's Hotel, Albemarle Street, London W1.

The last year from June 1941 to June 1942, had been one of calamity for Britain – but also one of hope. The Dominions had poured out unstinted aid – they had given their blood and their lives: apart from them, a mutilated Britain had stood alone, ever more tightly encircled by Germany whose power now stretched unbroken from Norway to Ushant, from the Urals to the Atlantic. Air bombardment, though diminished, was a numbing, sapping strain. On 22 June Hitler had launched *Operation Barbarossa* against Russia, and the staggering speed of his sinkings of *Barham* and *Ark Royal* – dear old *Ark*, the most famous and best-loved ship in the Royal Navy. There was no sense of despair in the nation, no feeling of defeat; but every man and woman in the island had been driven to dig deep into their fortitude, to summon up all their awareness of tradition. 'What sort of people do they think we are?' Churchill had demanded. He was voicing the pride of a stubborn, undivided, but weary nation.

Hope had come from the West. On 7 December the Japanese had struck at Pearl Harbor – a terrible blow, but one that brought the US immediately into the war. The sympathy for America was intense, but so was the overwhelming feeling of gratitude and relief. Now we were no longer quite alone; a brother, young but with immense power, was at last fully with us in the fight.

Nevertheless, the reverses continued. On 10 December the battleships *Prince of Wales* and *Repulse* were sunk off Malaya. On Christmas Day the Japanese captured Hong Kong where they would have interrupted me eating my Chinese plum pudding if wind and waves had not combined against my going. On 15 February Singapore fell.

But the alignment of the planets was changing. In May and June of 1942, the battles of Coral Sea and Midway had halted the Japanese advance, and now at last – at last – the tide was about to turn. Mason-Mac's reappearance in Gibraltar was one of the signals that heralded that great turning.

CHAPTER 16

MASON-MAC WAS A POWERFUL MAN – six-foot, even stooping as he did. The stoop was the result of a series of violent accidents throughout his life – playing football at school, pigsticking in India, skiing in the Alps. The accident that finally damaged his spine beyond proper repair was a motoring accident in Hungary in 1933 when he was pinned for hours beneath his upturned car. By the time he returned to Gibraltar as Governor and C in C, a gradual paralysis was attacking his spine and he was beginning to lose feeling in his feet and hands. Sometimes he would stumble over a boulder, often he let his cigarette burn down to his fingers before he dropped it, hissing, into the bowl of water he used as an ashtray.

He sat now in his office, the sun falling across his desk, and quietly explained to us, the half dozen of his personal staff, the reason for his return and the task that lay ahead.

'Torch' was the code name for a vast amphibious operation – the greatest yet undertaken – that would soon be mounted by a joint Anglo-American Force. Landings would be made in Algeria and Morocco, while at the same time Montgomery's 8th Army would attack in the East. The Afrika Korps would be squeezed between two Allied Forces attacking from either end of the Mediterranean.

The Combined Fleet would be under British command – Admiral Cunningham – and the Supreme Allied Commander would be an American General – one General Eisenhower – who would make his Headquarters in Gibraltar during the early stages of the landings.

Gibraltar would be the springboard for Torch, the nerve centre of the whole operation for several weeks and possibly months. Military

Intelligence considered it probable that Hitler would make every effort to strangle this Allied initiative by attacking Gibraltar and trying to seal the Straits – only sixteen miles wide – either with or without Spanish cooperation. Such a leverage must be denied them. Gibraltar must be ready to launch Torch, and also be prepared to resist heavy and prolonged attack. To this end, the defences of the Rock had to be further strengthened; a whole new headquarters for the operation had to be tunnelled out; strengthened; additional vast cisterns of water provided; hospitals and food stores had to be constructed in the underground caves. The debris from all this fresh excavation would be used to extend the runway so that Flying Fortresses and heavy transport planes could land and take off.

'No,' he said in answer to a question. 'I don't know the exact date of the landings. And I wouldn't tell you if I did. One small leak of security, and the whole operation is jeopardized. That's all. Thank you.'

We rose and started to leave the room.

'Except for one last thing,' he added. 'A personal word. We don't yet know each other, though we soon will. I need from you – demand of you – your total effort and support, your total loyalty. I say "demand" not because I am so powerful and mighty but because I am so puny. I depend on your eyes, your ears, your brains to help me carry out my job.'

He had collected a good team to serve him: Commander Brown (DSC) had come from captaining a destroyer; David Woodford from politics; Bobby Capurro – a bear of little brain, but great loyalty – from the Gibraltar Defence Regiment; and finally the ADC, Flight Lieutenant Gatward (DFC). I liked them all, but Ken Gatward was unique: I loved the man. He was not what is termed 'cultured' – I doubt if he had ever read a play by Skakespeare or would have recognized a Mozart sonata – but he looked on the world with endless humour and compassion; his sensitivity was hidden behind laughter, and there was a seriousness lurking beneath all his jokes.

Ken had been flying on operations since the first day of the war. His most recent exploit – an epic – had been to take his Beaufighter across France on the anniversary of the German occupation of Paris. He was to time his arrival over the city at exactly twelve noon when it was the practice of a German detachment to march out of the side street, goose-step up the Champs Elysées and present arms before the tomb of the Unknown Soldier. Arrived over his target, he was first to throw out an enormous tricolour so that it fell over the Arc de Triomphe, then give the ceremonial parade a squirt of machine-gun fire – just to remind them of the retribution to come. Should he miss the goose-steppers, he was to fly on down the great Avenue and put a few bursts of cannon fire into the headquarters of the German *Kriegsmarine*, now established in the Place de la Concorde.

There was no cloud cover, so Ken and his navigator were forced to hedgehop all the way there and back. Everything went to plan except that the German parade (possibly tipped off, possibly alerted by the sound of the Beaufighter's engines) never emerged from the side street, and so escaped a nasty shock; but the citizens of Paris were cheered, and the occupants of the *Kriegsmarine* had to jump for their lives. Ken was awarded the DFC, and sent out to Gibraltar to join Mason-Mac's staff for a period of comparative rest.

If Gib had been busy a year before, it now became frenzied. Yard by yard the runway was pushed out into the Bay of Algeciras. It was impossible to conceal from the enemy that a major operation was afoot: the Spanish pillboxes squatted like toads a mere 400 yards from the Frontier fence; a spider could not have crossed the runway or a lizard scuttled up the North Face of the Rock without the *Abwehr* knowing about it; wherever I went in Andalusia – and occasionally I was lucky enough in the way of duty to escape from imprisonment – there were so many German officers in the hotels and restaurants that I felt a great desire to walk up to one of their tables and ask them how they felt now about their damned war?

Since it was impossible to fly over Europe, Gibraltar had become a vital staging point in all flights entering or leaving the Mediterranean basin. Government House became a hotel where Mason-Mac dispensed hospitality – largely at his own expense – to every 'visiting fireman' from Averell Harriman to the King of Greece.

I saw all these visitors at their most relaxed, when they were guests in another man's house not hidden by the masks they wore in public. The great generals fascinated me; they were so akin to star actors: not in their skills, but in their qualities of leadership, their capacity to find in their own personalities the quality that can inspire an army or an audience. Not all of the great generals were conscious actors, not all gave 'performances'; from some of them – Eisenhower, Slim, Wavell, Alexander – authority flowed as naturally as water from a spring; with others, as with some greatly admired actors, the process of leadership came from some inner source of self-awareness, then seemed to have hardened into egotism, vanity. Montgomery was one such; the American General Mark Clark another – though being a lesser man, his was on a lesser scale.

General Montgomery came through Gibraltar in August. He stayed one night, then flew on to take command of the 8th Army. It was the only time I met him personally, and he made a considerable impression on me – as he did on everyone. It was the very reverse of the miserable, hangdog demeanour that General Percival had presented on his way to take command of Singapore. Percival had lost Singapore before he arrived there; Montgomery had won the desert campaign without getting sand in his boots. He was a fighting cock – confident to the point of arrogance. At meals he dropped his voice so low that the entire table had to fall silent in order to catch his words of wisdom. A very impressive man: not a very attractive one.

Monty was not born to be a saviour, to redeem the world from its folly; he was born to lead men to face death in battle, to win victories. He did both supremely well.

One of our visitors around the beginning of October was the Chief of the Imperial General Staff, General Sir Alan Brooke. Mason-Mac was away – he had flown to London to take part in a planning conference – so it devolved on me to play the part of host. When dinner was over the CIGS said, 'In a few days the Prime Minister will be passing through Gibraltar. He may stay a while. His arrival here, and of course his presence, must be kept absolutely secret. You understand?'

'Indeed, sir.'

'If his arrival were to be spotted by the enemy, it would be highly dangerous. I gather the airstrip is within easy mortar range from the Spanish positions?'

He looked at me, so again I replied, 'Yes, sir. Catapult range, more like.'

The flippancy did not amuse him. 'Mr Churchill,' he went on, 'will be arriving in disguise.'

'Disguised as what?' I ventured.

The grey hawk's eyes turned on me again, and the terseness of his voice discouraged any more questions. 'I don't know what he'll be disguised as. He will be disguised.'

That was all the information he would divulge before going to bed that night and flying on east in the morning. We were left to speculate what form the disguise would take. Would the Prime Minister be dressed as a bearded professor? Or as Father Christmas? For sure he would be hidden behind whiskers – but what sort of whiskers could they possibly be? We decided that they would be the old-fashioned, hook-over-the-ears, moustache-and-beard-combined type and, most probably, ginger.

Mason-Mac returned from London, and a few days later came the signal we had been waiting for. Flight such-and-such would land at 06:00 on such-and-such a date.

It was the hour in the morning when 10,000 dockyard workers streamed into Gibraltar from Spain. The road from the airfield to Government House, interrupted many times by tank traps, would be clogged with Spaniards: ideal conditions for an assassin.

Ken Gatward and David Woodford had made their preparations; a fleet of staff cars were drawn up at a distance, and the airfield had been cleared to eliminate any suggestion of a reception committee. When the plane touched down, I would go forward with a filthy little pick-up truck that was used for collecting stores, bundle the Prime Minister into it and drive him back to Government House.

The plane was an hour late and the tide of dockyard workers at its height when at last it appeared – a black Liberator with an escort of Beaufighters. It circled the Rock, landed, then taxied to its appointed place in the middle of the runway. I went forward with my truck, undecided whether to switch the engine off – in which case it might never start again – or leave it running – in which case it would probably overheat and stall. I decided to switch it off.

For several minutes there was no movement from within, and I stood looking foolishly at the plane. Then, framed in one of the side windows, there appeared the familiar, shrewdly innocent face of Mr Churchill, peering out at the world like some gentle captive animal. But – no whiskers. I was shocked. Another long pause. Then a trap in the belly of the plane opened and out came a young American pilot; this too took me by surprise. I had not expected the Prime Minister to be flying with an American crew. The young officer made fast the ladder down which he had descended, and then whispered – though there was no one remotely within earshot – 'The first passenger to alight will be Air Commodore Frankland.' He spoke so quietly that I could barely hear him.

'I beg your pardon?' I said.

Again he hissed at me, 'The first passenger to alight will be Air Commodore Frankland.' With that he shot back into the plane.

A few moments later, walking backwards down the steep steps, there came the small, neatly-booted feet of the Prime Minister. He wore the uniform of an Air Commodore and carried a cane. Removing his cigar from his mouth, he looked round the nonexistent reception committee and made his famous 'V' sign. I held open the ramshackle door of the truck and invited him to climb into the passenger's seat.

'Oh, yes indeed,' he said. 'Is this part of the cover plan?'

I told him that it was.

'Good – good. But you know that I do have to take my detective with me. Do you mind if he comes too?'

'Not a bit, sir. He'll have to sit in the back though, and it's rather dirty.'

'Oh, that won't hurt Thompson. He can sit on those chains. He'll be all right.'

Off the three of us went, Mr Churchill peering up at the sheer North Face of the Rock and asking a few conventional questions. How many men were now stationed in Gibraltar? 10,000? He was surprised to learn that there were over 30,000. Did we get sufficient entertainment? Was mail arriving regularly from home? – and so on. There came a pause, and he said suddenly, 'Young man – are you prepared to sell your life dearly?'

It was a wholly surprising question – not one to answer pat. 'No,' would have been out of the question. 'Yes,' would have had too heroic a ring.

'I hope so, sir,' I replied.

'Because,' he went on, 'this old Fortress is soon to be the centre of historic events. I expect you know that.'

I told him that I did – though at the same time I thought it strange that he should confide in me, a total stranger.

By now we had come out on the road and were slowly grinding, in bottom gear, over the tank traps. Spanish workmen flowed past us on either side; some peered in – but there was no sign of an attack. I had not thought there would be – though that was only youthful belief that life is eternal: the Prime Minister might get blown up, but not me; while he sat beside me he was perfectly safe. All the same, I was glad to pull clear of the crowd and put on speed.

There followed a long silence, so long that I felt I had to break it. I was squashed up beside one of the greatest Englishmen who had ever lived; our shoulders were bumping together, and I had to push his leg out of the way to change gear: I could not sit mumchance.

I said, 'We were told, sir, that you'd be arriving in disguise. But I hadn't expected to see you disguised as an Air Commodore.'

The words angered him. He pulled himself round in his bucket seat and turned to look at me.

'Disguised as an Air Commodore?' he demanded. 'What do you mean? I am an Air Commodore.'

'Oh indeed, sir. I know that,' I stammered. (I lied: I did not know it at all.) 'I meant that I hadn't expected to see you wearing the uniform.'

He was mollified at once. 'Oh, yes,' he said. 'And what is more . . . ' With an effort he twisted the top half of his body even further round towards me and tugged at his tunic so that I could see the left breast. 'What is more, you see, I have my wings!'

I glanced to see what he was doing. With his left hand he was pulling at his tunic and with his right hand he was stroking the proud insignia. His eyes were full of tears. Then I recalled hearing on the news only recently that he and the King had both been given their honorary wings by the RAF.

I was overwhelmed by his childlike simplicity as much as by his emotion. Few are able – or have the courage – so to reveal themselves. His feeling sprang from the heart of a man who had seen too many young pilots take off from fighter stations and go to their deaths. They sprang from the heart of a man who knew that they – and they alone – had bought the breathing space that gave Britain and the free world the chance to survive; and they had bought it at the cost of their lives.

The Prime Minister became a frequent visitor; he never passed through without spending a night – occasionally two or three. He took a rest after lunch every day, and sometimes I would bring him his despatches when he woke up. Leslie Rowan, his PPS had arranged the signals and despatches from the various theatres of war in orderly piles round the floor of his bedroom. When I came in, I would find the Prime Minister wearing nothing but a cellular vest, crawling about on all fours like a child playing Bears: he was not in the least self-conscious.

Once, after some conference, he was in a hurry to get back to England, and his plane was due to take off around ten o'clock in the evening. He was seated in the big drawing room at Government House, surrounded by the usual imposing retinue, when a young RAF pilot appeared at the far end of the room.

'Ah!' Winston rose to his feet. 'Here's our pilot at last. Well – are you ready? Can we come now?'

'I'm afraid not, sir.' The young pilot looked apprehensive. 'We can't fly tonight.'

'Oh, why is that?'

'The weather report is bad, sir. A big front extending all the way up the Atlantic. It wouldn't be safe.'

'A front, eh? Then we must fly over it.'

The pilot shook his head. 'We'd have to go very high and we don't have oxygen.'

'Then we must fly round it.'

'We can't do that either, sir. We don't carry enough fuel.'

Winston was beginning to look like a furious child. 'Young man, I have a very important Cabinet meeting in London in the morning. I have to be there. We have got to go.'

White-faced, the pilot dug his toes in. 'I'm sorry, sir, but I'm responsible for your safety, and I will not take you.'

By now, Churchill had worked himself up into a rage. 'You don't understand. I'm telling you – I *want* to go.' On the word 'want', he clenched his fists and – like a small boy in a tantrum – jumped clean into the air. It was a wonderful sight – spontaneous, uninhibited, utterly natural.

The pilot stood his ground, and the Prime Minister stayed another night.

Next morning his Naval Aide, Commander Thompson – an ex-Naval officer with a hard-bitten look and the authentic voice of Plymouth gin – sought me out and asked if I could arrange some place where the Prime Minister could swim in the sea undisturbed and unrecognized.

'I'm afraid not,' I said. 'There's only one beach that isn't mined, and the different units take it in turns to go down and have a swim there.'

'Oh, do try. His heart is absolutely set on it.'

'I'm sorry. I can't change it now. Anyway, does Mr Churchill swim?'

He gave the question some thought, then replied, 'No, not actually. But he's very good at floating.'

Indeed he was. He floated like a duck on the rough waters of his destiny.

The build-up to Torch continued furiously. More troops arrived – telegraphists, teleprinter operators, more and more Special Units, a 'Y Intercept Unit' was installed at the bottom of the garden at Government House – a Top Secret branch supplying ULTRA at Bletchley in England with intercepted enemy messages.

The runway was almost complete when the first of the Flying Fortresses arrived – a moving sight to one like myself who had never before seen one of the great American planes. The Fortress had had a brush with enemy fighters on the way out. General Spaak, its distinguished passenger, was rushed up by Ken Gatward to Government House, where it took several hours for him to recover his composure.

Ken was quietly amused. 'Poor old boy,' he said when I asked after the General. 'Had a very nasty experience. Holes right through the fuselage.' Ken might have been more sympathetic if he had not himself been under fire for three years.

With so vast an operation as Torch, something was bound to go wrong. On one of the last mornings in October, we were expecting the arrival of a courier from London, bearing a personal message for Mason-Mac. The plane did not arrive. Around ten o'clock our consul in Jerez phoned to say that there had been a violent electric storm in the night and that he had heard rumours of a plane coming down off Cadiz; it could only be a British plane since no others flew that route. Ken Gatward was despatched immediately to see what he could find out.

Ken spent the next twenty-four hours walking up and down the beach at Cadiz throwing sticks for the Williams' dog and searching for any debris from the plane that might be washed up. He found some – enough to confirm that it was indeed the wreckage of a London flying boat with signs of burning about it. It appeared not to have been shot down, but to have been struck by the electric storm. And now came a further rumour – that the body of a man, a British Naval Officer wearing blue overalls, had been washed up on the beach and recovered by the Spanish coastguards.

Bobby Capurro was sent off at once with an ambulance to reclaim the body. There was some hope of succeeding in this since the coastguards, being a branch of the Spanish Navy, were known to be favourable to the Allies, while the Spanish Army was most definitely not. However, by the time he arrived the body had been handed over to the Army. This meant that it had almost certainly been searched, not only by the Spanish Intelligence but also by the *Abwehr*.

Later that afternoon the body was handed over, and Bobby Capurro brought it back. It was indeed the body of a British Naval Officer; he was wearing blue overalls, and in the breast pocket of his uniform jacket was a letter, in 'clear', addressed to the C in C Gibraltar. It read,

> Dear Mason-Mac,
>   Just to tell you that the date for 'Torch' is finally set. It will be 8 November.
>   Look forward to seeing you very soon.
>   All the best – Ike.

It was a monumental breach of security. Within days, almost hours, the American part of the attacking force would be putting to sea. Perhaps the entire Operation was compromised.

The Intelligence pundits of Gibraltar weighed the matter up and finally decided that the letter had, in fact, not been opened. Their conclusion was based on the sand that was packed evenly in the fly of the overalls. The smoothness with which each interstice was filled could only have been achieved by a body rolling face downwards in shallow water on a sandy beach. If the overalls had been unbuttoned and the letter extracted, the sand would inevitably have been dislodged. Short of putting the body back in the sea and repeating the process, it would have been impossible to reproduce the natural packing of the sand. It was therefore decided to reassure General Eisenhower and the War Cabinet that it was safe to proceed with Operation Torch.

The forerunner of the American team was General Mark Clark who arrived in great secrecy, was smuggled on board a British submarine, then put ashore at night on the beach where his men would soon be landing. It was an admirable piece of reconnaissance even if it smacked of a *Boy's Own* adventure story. But that was General Clark; he stood tall and impressive, but his nature veered to the flamboyant. There was a slight reverberation to him, as though somewhere inside he might be hollow.

There was nothing hollow about General Eisenhower who arrived on 4 November; he filled up all the space that he occupied – with integrity. He had been no more than a Lieutenant Colonel at the outbreak of war and he had never commanded troops in the field, so that it was impossible not to wonder if such an apparently simple man could have the authority needed for so great a task. The question was soon answered. He had some turbulent generals serving under him – powerful, vital men of all nationalities – but I never once heard of him showing bias to any of them; he was fair and impartial between Americans and British, between Free French and Poles; and he won the wholehearted respect of all of them. He listened to advice till the very last – then he took his decisions alone and stood by them.

Al Grunther, who came with him, was something else – small, shrewd, an international bridge player, a razor-sharp elf, as captivating and clever as they come. Eisenhower was lucky to have him at his side.

General Eisenhower cared little for the headquarters that had been dug out for him at the base of the Rock; it was a dripping wet, ill-ventilated dungeon, but it was the best that could be done in the time, and at least it was proof against bomb or shellfire. Admiral Cunningham too had his office along the same narrow tunnel. From this incongruous and troglodite post he controlled the movement of the Combined Fleets at sea. The din of teleprinters was deafening, and the heat like that of a Turkish bath. Air conditioning had not yet reached the Fortress of Gibraltar.

Tragedies need their scenes of comedy to heighten the intensity; *Hamlet* would fall short of its peak without the grave diggers. Great events are the same; they call for absurdity to set them off. Our absurdity was the episode of General Giraud, one of the heroes of the First World War, deeply opposed to the Vichy Government of Petain and Laval, and now living in retirement in the South of France.

It had been decided to coax General Giraud out of his quiet retreat and produce him at the critical moment so that he could, as it were, raise his own standard in Algeria and Morocco and bring over to the Allied side all those French troops who would otherwise take their orders from Vichy and oppose the landings with force. His reward would be to command those French troops – under the overall supremacy of General Eisenhower. Unfortunately, Giraud gained the impression that he was to be the Commander of the entire operation. Some rumour of this misunderstanding came to our ears.

SOE did their work with skill. General Giraud and his aide were extracted from their homes at night, taken out by boat to a waiting submarine, transferred far from land to a seaplane, and finally put ashore in Gibraltar in the late afternoon of 7 November – the eve of Operation Torch.

Mason-Mac feared a diplomatic collision but was too late to prevent it. We hurried along the dark HQ tunnel only to find that Giraud was already closeted with the C in C.

An American staff officer pushed past us in the narrow corridor. 'Could you tell me,' Mason-Mac asked him, 'if a tall man in civilian clothes is in there with General Eisenhower?'

'Why yes – two guys did go in there a coupla minutes ago. French, I think.'

'And tell me – does General Eisenhower speak any French?'

'No, sir. Nothing like that. But he's got Colonel Johnson with him, and he docs a bit of parleyvoo ing.'

He had hardly spoken when the door burst open and out stalked Giraud. Colonel Johnson's French may not have been academic, but clearly it had been to the point. Without any of the niceties of the Quai d'Orsay, General Giraud had had his position made clear to him and he was trumpeting with fury. He was a tall old beanpole, and he wore a long raincoat buttoned straight down from collar to knee. He made an outlandish figure in the dark tunnel, mortally outraged, his face white under the overhead electric bulbs, refusing to have anything whatever to do with the landings.

Dinner that night was a fiasco. Giraud, like Eisenhower and Grunther, was a guest at Government House. To avoid another clash, and so that the seating plan should not imply some further ambiguity, the Americans stayed away, while we British did our best to make small talk with the French. Thank heavens they were tired – small wonder after such a journey by land, sea and air – and they retired early.

In the middle of the night, I was sent down to the HQ tunnel to give to Admiral Cunningham a signal for him that had come through Government House channels. It was around two a.m.; the first landings must already have taken place. I found the Admiral in his office, dressed in a submariner's thick sweater, an ancient uniform jacket, and with the sweat trickling down his face. I could not help asking him if he might not feel cooler if he shed some of his arctic gear.

'I dare say. But this is what I always wear when I go into battle. I know damn well I'm not at sea, but I'm going into battle just the same – and I'm commanding the Fleet from under all this rock. If I don't dress right, then I can't think right. So – ' He shrugged and gave a grin.

The Americans kept to their rooms for breakfast next morning, but at eight o'clock General Giraud and his aide joined the small British staff to listen to the BBC *News*. The General sat, his fingertips pressed together, an expression of remote disdain on his scholarly face. He understood not a word that came from the radio, but his aide understood very well.

Landings, said the announcer, had taken place on a large scale during the night in Algeria and Tunisia, and were meeting a certain amount of resistance from the French. 'But,' he continued – and this was when I learnt never, but never, to trust the veracity of the media – 'General Giraud, one of France's great heroes from World War One, is at this moment on French North African soil and has issued the following call to his countrymen: "Frenchmen – do not bear arms against your Allies, the Americans and the British. I am here to lead you to victory. Rally to me."'

The General had the announcement translated to him; after that, breakfast was eaten in silence.

The landings had gone well, but the auguries for cooperation with the French looked dismal. Mason-Mac now decided to intervene and try to break the deadlock. He had not been Military Attaché in Copenhagen, Vienna, Budapest, Berne and Berlin without learning diplomacy; and he spoke fluent French. By mid-morning, and with Al Grunther's help, he had arranged a meeting of reconciliation. Two hours later, after copious consumption of excellent sherry, Giraud had happily accepted his subordinate position and was in a hurry to be on his way.

I took him to the airfield and put him aboard a Hudson where he sat in the co-pilot's seat gazing down with impatience at the aircraftmen struggling to start the plane. At their third attempt, he put his head out through the window and called out in pedantic voice, '*Mais depêchons, depêchons. Chaque minute compte.*'

Two days later General George Patton flew in to report personally how things were going on the beaches. He was lucky to land alive for no notice had been received in Gibraltar of his intended arrival, and every gun on the Rock prepared to open fire; some did. At the last moment, the

General's plane managed to identify itself, and the firing ceased; otherwise one of the great commanders of the war would have finished his career almost before it had begun.

He arrived at Government House in time for lunch – tall, round-headed, round-faced, crop-haired, with staring baby-blue eyes and a curiously high voice. He was walking into the dining room still wearing his pearl-handled revolvers when I reminded him that he really did not need these personal weapons about him. He was quite docile about it, and left them on a chair outside.

Morale was one of Ike's concerns. How was the morale of Patton's men? 'Very high,' he was told. In fact there had been only one case calling for disciplinary action.

'What was that?'

'There was a young lieutenant,' replied the high squeaky voice, 'who left his foxhole against orders.'

'You mean he quit? Deserted?'

'Not exactly. He went to pull in his sergeant who had been wounded and was lying outside. Still, he had his orders and he had no damn business leaving his foxhole.'

'What have you done with the man?' Ike asked.

'I've shipped him off Stateside,' Patton replied. 'But I've not court-martialled him.' And he then delivered himself of an unforgettable line. 'I reckon you can crucify a man, but there's no need to rivet the nails.'

A few weeks previously, on the night of 23 October, the 8th Army had launched their massive attack on El Alamein and forced Rommel into retreat. Now the Afrika Korps and their Italian allies were being pressed from either end of the Mediterranean. The tide had not only turned; it was beginning to run fast. Final victory in North Africa came six months later: in May 1943 all Axis forces surrendered; 250,000 prisoners were taken, more than half of them being German. Rommel escaped back to Germany, but von Arnim, the Commander in Tunisia, was taken prisoner; also von Thoma, his Second in Command. Von Thoma and a staff colonel came through Gibraltar on their way to imprisonment in Britain; they were brought to Government House on Mason-Mac's orders and allowed to rest there for a few hours in a secluded wing before flying on. They were kept under close guard, but treated with correctness. After his experiences in Berlin, I think it afforded Mason-Mac a certain grim amusement to have the German General as prisoner under his roof.

Von Thoma, with his high-crowned cap and soft, blue leather coat looked ill and dispirited, but his staff colonel was jubilant; for him the war was over.

'Aha!' he said before boarding his plane that evening. 'Now for the roast beef of jolly old England!'

The sound of battle receded; Darlan was assassinated, and Ike moved his Headquarters to Algiers. In Gibraltar we felt deflated; we had prepared ourselves for battle, for siege, but neither had come. Yet the strengthening of the Fortress had to continue; Hitler was still capable of trying to close the Straits, either with or without Spanish help. (That he thought of doing so was revealed in German General Staff plans at the end of the war; 'Operation Gisela' was the code name for the siezure of Spain and Portugal to deny them as Atlantic ports to the Americans.)

The General's health was showing signs of deterioration. Every day he made long tours of the tunnels to keep up the spirits of the men working. Often he stumbled and fell; then he would come home with his knees cut and bleeding and the fuse of his temper an inch or two shorter. I did not enquire into the cause knowing that I would be struck down by his tiger's paw – no doubt to be picked up a moment later with affection and remorse.

Sir Hugh Cairns, the Australian neurologist, on one of his Middle East tours, talked to me earnestly about the General. 'He has dislocated or broken his spine too often. He must get it operated on – soon. If not, he'll become paralyzed. Can't you get him to chuck his hand in?'

I told Cairns it was impossible. Mason-Mac was a patriot and a professional soldier. Nothing would make him 'chuck his hand in'. He would continue to serve till he seized up and dropped dead.

For myself, it was a busy time – busier than ever; yet, just turned thirty, it was a time to take stock. I sensed that in an indefinable way I had come together, that the various fragments were coalescing. I knew who I was.

I came across a passage in Havelock Ellis' autobiography and was struck to the core.

I have been a dreamer and an artist, a great dreamer for that is easy, not a great artist for that is hard, but still always an artist, whether in the minor art of writing, or the greater art of comprehending, or the supreme art of living, wherein it is something to have tried even if one fails. So that if I am often sad – for the art of living is finally the art of loving, in which one becomes a master too late – I am always content.

The supreme art of living. That was what I had struggled but failed to say in my arguments with George Devine – and even if I could have formulated the idea, I would have shrunk from being so didactic. Of course 'living' was the supreme art; and, as with all arts, the way to it was hidden, obscure;

Above: Richard Burton as Prince Hal,
Alan Badel as Poins and AQ as Falstaff
in *Henry IV Pt. 1*, Stratford 1951.
(*Angus McBean*)

Right: As Bottom in *A Midsummer
Night's Dream*, Stratford 1954. (*Angus
McBean*)

Above: As Mosca in *Volpone*, with
Ralph Richardson, Stratford 1952.
(*Angus McBean*)

Left: As Tamburlaine in *Tamburlaine
the Great*, New York 1956. (*Herb Nott*)

Top right: With Gwen Ffrangcon-
Davies and Alan Bates in *Long Day's
Journey into Night*, London 1958. (*Angus
McBean*)

Right: As Orlovsky in the film, *Oh
Rosalinda!*, 1956.

Far right: As Eddie Carbone in Arthur
Miller's *A View from the Bridge*,
London 1956. (*Tony Armstrong Jones*)

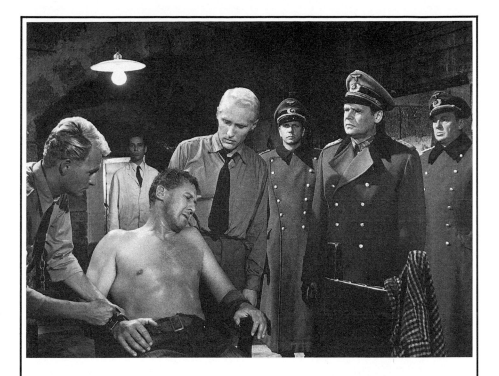

Above: As Major Franklin in *The Guns of Navarone*, 1961 (*Kobal Collection*)

Right: As Cardinal Wolsey in *Anne of the Thousand Days*, 1969. (*Universal Pictures*)

Left: As Captain van der Poel in *Ice Cold in Alex*, 1958.

Above: As Galileo in Brecht's *Galileo*,
New York 1967.

Right: As Oedipus in BBC Television's
Oedipus at Colonus, 1986. (*BBC*)

Top left: With Peggy Ashcroft in
Arbuzov's *Old World*, London 1976.
(*Zoë Dominic*)

Left: With Celia Johnson in *Chin-Chin*,
London 1960. (*David Sim*)

Above left: Dot, Jenny and Rosanna.

Above: With Christopher on the *Puss Cat*.

Left: At the helm.

Below: The end of an odyssey: *Jenny Rose* drops anchor at Ithaka, 12 August 1974.

it had to be sought in opposites; it had to be found through a mysterious and often harsh apprenticeship. I copied the passage out and learnt it by heart. Old Havelock Ellis had shed a great light on my path.

My daily life was busy and fascinating. My job often took me into Spain where Mason-Mac had been at pains to build good relations with the Army. When I was asked to spend a weekend in Seville with the staff of the Captain General of the 2nd Military Region, Mason-Mac insisted that I go – and was justly furious on my return when I could not remember the name of a Spanish General whom I had heard – and not just for my benefit – express doubt in Germany's final victory.

Dot had taken up her abode in my mind – or in my blood: I did not know which. Films had made her famous, and her photo was in every weekly magazine that reached us from England. I knew that I was not the only man in love with her, but I did not realize how far the infection had spread till, on board a destroyer one day, I saw her framed photograph screwed to the bulkhead facing that of the King across the wardroom.

I was very aware of the inglorious part I had so far played in the war. If the fighting had retreated from me once again, then I must go in search of it. I had no idea how – but every day that passed made me more specialized, less useful in any ordinary regimental capacity; but if Gibraltar was to turn into a military backwater, then I must get out of it.

More and more visitors came pouring through Gib; the entertaining must have cost Mason-Mac a fortune. Government House began to resemble the Quangle Wangle's Hat.

> . . .*And the Golden Grouse came there,*
> *And the Pobble who has no toes, –*
> *And the small Olympian bear, –*
> *And the Dong with a luminous nose.*
> *And the Blue Baboon, who played the flute, –*
> *And the Orient Calf from the Land of Tute, –*
> *And the Attery Squash, and the Bisky Bat, –*
> *All came and built on the lovely Hat*
> *Of the Quangle Wangle Quee.*

Hugh Beaumont came for the second time bringing with him a glittering troupe of stars: Beatrice Lillie, John Gielgud, Edith Evans, Liz Welsh, and Dorothy Dickson – Dot Hyson's mother. The troops adored them and I was happy to see them, but they disturbed me. Once again, as when I was a boy on the music halls, I had the feeling of standing on the other side of the Looking Glass. I was fond of them, proud of the contribution they made, but they reminded me of a world on which I had turned my back.

I felt the same when my dear friend Ralph Richardson turned up, making a film about the Fleet Air Arm. He came to have lunch at Government House, and later we sat on the beach and talked about the theatre – about acting.

He asked me, 'What do think, Tony, makes for success in an actor?'

It was so far from my mind that I could not readily answer.

'I'll tell you,' he went on. 'It's to be different from everyone else. Look at this beach.' He waved a hand at the expanse of grey pebbles. 'You see. They're all the same. Good, sound, grey pebbles – all the same. Therefore not very interesting. Which one catches your eye?' He pointed. 'It's that one, isn't it? Because it's green – bright green – different from all the others. That's how it is with acting.'

He was right, but it was all outside my compass.

There came no *Orient Calf from the Land of Tute*, but Noel Coward arrived from India and stayed for a week. He was a dear man of wit and courage, and by no means as trivial as he proclaimed himself to be. He invited me to dinner one night at the Rock Hotel and arranged for it to be served in a small private room. This surprised me a little, but I put it down to his lavish hospitality, till slowly it began to dawn on me that he intended this to be the setting for a good old-fashioned seduction scene. I became sure of it when he said, 'Tony, you really are a silly boy. I tell you – you are more in love with me than you are with Dorothy Hyson.' He meant it too; he must have been used to great sexual success.

I quickly disabused him of the notion, and he was sensitive enough to back off at once. After that, we had an excellent dinner together, and ever after remained the best of friends. I shall always be grateful for the encouragement he gave me when I started to write.

And besides, to the Crumpetty Tree came characters with a heavier tread, weightier responsibilities: the Adjutant General, Sir Ronald Adam – scholarly and sensitive; the Chief Planner, General Freddy Morgan – rugged and ever sanguine – Freddy, who on the day he was evacuated from Dunkirk, pulled a staff together round him and began to plan the re-invasion of Europe; General Marshall – creator of the modern American Army – grave and good; Lord Louis Mountbatten – dashing, but mightily elevated; General Ismay – dear 'Pug' – Churchill's Chief of Staff, whom of all men I would have chosen to be my father if I had had any choice in the matter; General De Gaulle – stiff and solemn through carrying the destiny of France on his shoulders. All of them settled for a night or two on the *Quangle Wangle's Hat*.

In May, Ken Gatward was recalled to Britain for flying duties. I missed him badly; he had been an endlessly light-hearted and close companion. In replacement, I suggested to Mason-Mac that he invite Flight Lieutenant John Perry to be his ADC. Perry had been serving for several months as an Intelligence Officer with the RAF. He was an amusing, efficient, civilized man – and wasted in his present job. I liked him, and was grateful to him; he was a close friend of Hugh Beaumont's and had been largely instrumental in bringing out the glittering concert parties to the Rock.

John gladly accepted the job, and took up his post as ADC just in time to become involved in a great tragedy.

CHAPTER 17

MASON-MAC'S YEAR IN RUSSIA had not been congenial. He and his mission had been 'tailed' everywhere they went by the Secret Police, he had achieved only two visits to the front, and he had had to endure from our Russian allies their contemptuous disparagement of our military efforts. His only constructive work, he felt – and that only after months of obstruction and delay – had been to extricate many thousands of Poles from their appalling prison camps in Uzbekistan and arrange for them to be sent on to the Middle East to join the growing Polish force being assembled by General Anders.

In the course of this difficult year in Russia, he and General Sikorski, President of the Polish Government in exile, had become warm personal friends, so it was with joy that at the end of June he received a signal saying that General Sikorski, accompanied by his daughter and several of his staff, would arrive from Cairo on 3 July and hoped to spend the night as his guest before leaving for London next day. Unfortunately this message coincided with a signal from Whitehall asking him to look after Mr Maisky, the Russian Ambassador, who would be passing through Gibraltar on the same day and at approximately the same time. The situation was highly embarrassing since the Soviet and Polish Governments had just broken off diplomatic relations over the revelation of the Katyn massacre. Mason-Mac's sympathies were entirely with his Polish guests, and he was not going to have Sikorski's short stay disturbed. I was deputed to stage-manage Mr Maisky's arrival and departure in such a way that Russians and Poles never met.

Early in the morning of 4 July, while the Poles slept or stayed in their rooms, I met Mr Maisky's plane, gave him a good breakfast in a remote wing of Government House, then took him off on a tour of the Rock, explaining that he only had a couple of hours before his plane must take off once more for Cairo. Maisky was an exasperating man; not knowing I had been an actor, he spent most of his time telling me how impoverished the London theatre was compared with that of Moscow.

On the top of the Rock, at Flagstaff Hill, we got out of the car and looked northwards towards Spain. 1,500 feet below us was the airfield; in the far distance the sun was touching the distant snowcaps of the Sierra Nevada. The Ambassador surveyed the scene and said to me, 'What do you think will be the future of Spain?'

His condescension had so antagonized me that I replied without hesitating. 'I think there is only one solution for this unhappy country – the restoration of the monarchy.'

There was a moment's silence, and then he said, 'I do not think this is the time for restorations of monarchies in Spain.'

We drove back in silence to Government House, collected his bags, and carried on down to the runway; within a few minutes he was on his way.

General Sikorski had a busy day; he talked at length to the Polish Liaison Officer, Lieutenant Lubienski; he invested Mason-Mac with a high Polish order, and he spoke to a parade of some hundred Polish refugees who were at the moment in Gibraltar. Gib was at the end of a long, underground escape route that led all the way from Poland. The refugees, some military, some civilian, always arrived emaciated and exhausted; we kept them until they had recovered their strength, then sped them on their way back to Britain where most of them joined the Polish Armed Forces.

Victor Cazalet, an MP and now Sikorski's Liaison Officer, was travelling with the party. He and I were old acquaintances, and that afternoon we played squash together. Victor gave me half a dozen points and wiped the floor with me – but then he was a champion squash player. At about ten o'clock that evening we loaded our guests into several cars and took them to the airfield to see them off. The takeoff was a protracted business – goodbyes to be said, checks to be made, and so on – but at last from the far (western) end of the runway we could hear the thunder of the Liberator as it began its run; it roared passed us and lifted off.

We had been standing in small groups on the tarmac: I was with the Station Commander, Group Captain Bolland; Mason-Mac and John Perry were a few yards off. With the plane safely airborne, the thunder of its engines less insistent, we turned and headed for our cars. Then something shocking happened – not an explosion, not a crash, but a sudden cessation of noise. Silence. Bolland, standing beside me, gave a shout, 'Christ! She's gone in the drink.'

We rushed to the eastern end of the runway and turned our headlights out to sea: nothing but darkness and black waves. Then the searchlights came on from high up on the Rock, sweeping backwards and forwards till they lit up a horrifying sight: half a mile out to sea, one wing of the plane was sticking up out of the water. That was all; the rest of the fuselage had disappeared.

There were no fast rescue launches on the unprotected, eastern coast of Gibraltar. They had to come all the way round from the harbour on the west. People were launching little rubber boats, rushing for telephones. In the confusion and darkness, I lost sight of Mason-Mac and John Perry. I helped somebody launch a rubber dinghy – for whatever use that was – and I remember a young Polish pilot stomping up and down the beach sobbing and beating his head with his fists. 'You don't understand,' he kept saying. 'You don't understand. This means the end of Poland. The end of Poland.'

Three bodies were recovered that night – Sikorski, Klimecki, and a British brigadier. Only one man was found breathing – the pilot, Prchal; he was unconscious and both his legs were broken, but he was alive.

Mason-Mac and John Perry eventually came back to Government House. They had waited in the harbour for the rescue boats to return with their grisly load. Mason-Mac was exhausted; he sent off a Most Immediate signal informing London of the tragedy, then took himself off to bed. Lubienski, the Polish Liaison Officer, was holding himself together with difficulty. I invited him to spend the night, and turned out of my bedroom so that he could get a decent night's sleep.

Early in the morning Mason-Mac was in his office, but handed over to me all the macabre details of what now had to be done – the identification of the bodies, the provision of coffins, and so on.

My first thought was to get one of the Services to provide a doctor who would take charge of all this; I did not know much about dead bodies, but I did know that in the heat of Gibraltar they were likely to deteriorate. I rang all three Services in turn, and all three refused to have anything to do with it. The Navy said that Sikorski was a soldier and had been in an RAF plane – so it was none of their business; the Army said that he had fallen into the sea and therefore it was none of theirs; the Air Force said that although he had certainly met with an air crash, and in one of their planes, the President of Poland was a soldier; they also declined to handle it.

The next problem was that there were no coffins in Gibraltar, since those who died were no longer buried. The burial ground on the North

Front had been bulldozed to enlarge the airfield and to improve the arc of fire; anyone unfortunate enough to die or be killed in Gibraltar at this time had a weight tied round his feet and was pushed down a chute into the sea.

I phoned our consul in Algeciras to see if he could rustle up coffins at short notice.

'How many do you want?'

'I've no idea. At the moment three or four. It may be as many as a dozen – even more.'

An hour later he called back to say that he had been able to locate some coffins, but only of the poorest kind. They were made of zinc and were covered with a thin veneer of wood. 'Put them on a truck,' I said. 'They'll have to do.' Within half an hour a big truck came through the Frontier gate and started to unload at the mortuary where Lubienski and I were waiting for them.

The mortuary was a small, whitewashed building with a low ceiling; it was very hot. Two bodies were laid out on the floor, each lying on an army blanket. Sikorski was recognizable not so much by his features – death had totally changed his face – but by the broad black stripe down his uniform trousers. He must have been preparing himself for rest, because his upper half was clad in pyjamas. He had various wounds about his face and what looked like a deep indentation in the corner of one eye. Klimecki I could not have identified, but Lubienski did.

There now arrived a Gibraltarian whom I had managed to track down; in jollier times he had been an undertaker.

'Do you wish to have the bodies embalmed?' he asked, removing his bicycle clips.

'Can you do that?'

He shrugged. 'No.'

'In that case,' I said, 'it's a silly question.'

'Do you want them wrapped in winding sheets?' he asked next.

'Do you have a winding sheet, or a couple of them?'

Again he shrugged. 'No.'

'Then that is another useless question.'

Lubienski and I folded the thin blankets over his two compatriots' bodies, lifted them up, and laid them as reverently as we could in their flimsy shells.

'Do you wish the coffins sealed?' asked the undertaker.

'Yes,' I said. 'Please get on with it.'

The fellow set to work with a soldering iron; first he soldered the flimsy zinc lid, then he screwed down the even more flimsy wood veneer that covered it. It occurred to me that there would be no way of knowing which corpse was in which coffin; so with the point of my penknife I scratched an 'S' in the varnish of General Sikorski's resting place, and a 'K' on the coffin lid of his companion.

The undertaker had barely finished his work when a bearer party arrived from the Somerset Light Infantry, the coffins were placed on gun carriages, and taken with great solemnity through the streets to the Roman Catholic Cathedral.

In reply to Mason-Mac's strong suggestion that the bodies should be flown back at once, the Polish Government in London signalled that they did not wish this to happen; they were sending a destroyer immediately – the *Orkan*; she would berth in Gibraltar at exactly 07:30 hours on the morning of 8 July. During this period of waiting, a Guard of Honour was mounted by the skeletal Poles whom Sikorski had reviewed the previous day. I protested to Lubienski that it was a physical ordeal that they could hardly bear. 'They're not strong enough. They will collapse.'

He replied, 'It is an honour. They must be allowed to do it.'

During the day of the 7th many high-ranking Poles arrived from London for the funeral procession – amongst them Dr Retinger, a small intelligent man with a sensitive face who had been one of Sikorski's chief political advisers; he stayed in Government House.

Every move of the ceremony was rehearsed and timed – the service in the cathedral, the slow procession to the quay, the troops lining the streets with arms reversed and heads bowed. I went to bed that night thinking that all arrangements were safely made.

I was awoken sometime after midnight by Brigadier Parminter, a jovial round man with a monocle, but now looking unusually grave.

'Are you awake?' he asked.

'Yes. This is me. I'm awake.'

'You're sure you're quite awake?'

'Of course. What is it?'

He told me: General Sikorski had burst his coffin. Through the heat and lack of any embalming fluids, the body had decomposed and the most appalling gases were now pervading the cathedral. The Guard of Honour had been driven, choking, out into the street.

'Now,' said Reggie. 'The alternatives before us are these – we can either re-solder the lid, or we can transfer the General's mortal remains into a different coffin. If we do the former, it may well burst again on its way down to the quayside. It will take a lot of jolting when the gun carriage goes over the cobblestones. If we transfer it to a new coffin – and remember it's only another of these flimsy things from Spain – then

254

there is the possibility that we may not get the cathedral fumigated in time for the service in the morning. Which are we to do?'

'Beyond me,' I said. 'We must go and wake up the General.'

Together we trotted off upstairs and knocked on his door. He shot up in bed, lit a cigarette, and said, 'Yes, yes? What is it?' He was anxious to show that he was in command of the situation even before he had heard what it was.

'My God,' he said at last. 'This is one for the Poles to decide.'

Now the three of us set off down the half-lit landings of Government House till we came to the door of Dr Retinger. He was sitting up in bed, working; papers were strewn all over the bedclothes and there was an ashtray full of cigarette stubs by his side. When we had finished our tale, he made an immediate decision. 'The body must be put in a fresh coffin.'

I spent the rest of the night trying to locate lead sheeting. A picture had come into my mind of the *Orkan* pushing her way through the North Atlantic, perhaps in heavy weather, and the coffin of their President and C in C splitting its seams once again. There was no time now for us in Gibraltar to seal the coffins in strong envelopes, but if I could find some lead and have it taken aboard the destroyer, there must surely be a Naval artificer who could do the job. I woke up one Royal Engineer unit after another to see if they had any lead in store. At around six in the morning, one OC said that he thought he could lay hands on some. He was surprised at the quantity I needed.

'Never mind,' I said. 'Load it on a truck and make absolutely sure that it's delivered to the quayside not later than seven thirty in the morning. I'll be waiting for it.'

I got up early in the morning and visited the cathedral. By now, everything was in order; the place was silent, fumigated, the Guard of Honour standing round the catafalque; no trace of the night's horrendous happenings.

I drove down to the quayside. No sign yet of the Royal Engineers, but there alongside was the *Orkan* with steam up, ready to cast off. I saluted, went on board, and spoke to the captain – or tried to speak to him as he had no English at all. An officer speaking very broken English was found, and I explained to him that at any moment the funeral procession would be arriving – indeed, I could already hear the faint sounds of the funeral march. The procession was leaving the cathedral.

As I spoke, a fifteen-hundredweight truck pulled up on the quay, out jumped half a dozen knobbly-kneed Engineers, and they began to struggle up the gangway with enormous rolls of lead sheeting. Tragedy was turning into farce. The captain, indignant, demanded who they were and what were they doing: it was easy enough to understand the gist of his words. I tried to explain to his junior officer exactly what had happened: I had arranged for the lead sheeting to be rushed on board so that when they were clear of the harbour and had not yet put to sea, the ship's engineers could cover the coffins in a strong sheath of lead. The captain was distraught; he seemed unable to take in what he was being told; and all the time the sound of the 'Dead March' was drawing nearer. Now the coffin was entering the dockyard gates.

'Where,' I asked, 'do you intend to put General Sikorski's coffin?'

'In the wardroom.'

'No . . . no . . . ' I insisted. 'Not in the wardroom. It is hot in the wardroom. You must lash the coffin on deck.'

The captain shook his head impatiently. But now there was no more time to discuss or argue; I bundled the bewildered Engineers off the ship, and ran ashore myself as quickly as I could before the gun carriage stopped in front of the gangway. The coffin was carried on board and laid reverently on the deck; the Polish dignitaries followed; the bosun's whistle shrilled; everyone stood to attention and saluted. The *Orkan* cast off and headed out towards the sea, while ashore the band played the Polish National Anthem, and a seventeen-gun salute thundered from the Rock.

I was becoming restless and self-accusatory. I had been in the Army for three and a half years and never been in action: E and Dot in London had been in far more danger. But where was I to go? What was I to do? How was I to use my limited skills?

A friend in SOE said, 'For heaven's sake – come and join us in SOE. It's an independent sort of life, and as a bonus there is the parachuting. You'd enjoy it.'

I laughed. 'Parachute? Not on your life. I'd be terrified.'

I had said the words in jest, but they stayed in my mind, and I realized there was truth in them. The thought of jumping out of a plane did scare me; I had to admit it. And once the admission had been made, there was only one way to exorcize the fear.

I went to Mason-Mac and told him that I hated to leave him after all the enormous kindness and friendship he had shown me, but I felt the time had come when I must do something more active.

'Such as?' he asked.

'SOE.' I replied. 'I don't know who else would take me, but they might.'

He growled, but with affection. 'You're a fool,' he said. 'But if that's how you feel, I'll try and help you. Sorry to lose you, but I understand.'

Mason-Mac had flown back to England for more reports and conferences, when a posting came through for me to report as soon as possible to SOE Headquarters in Cairo. If I was going to move, I was glad to move quickly. But I sorely felt the need for a bit of a fling before starting a new life. Home leave was out of the question; all I had time for was a couple of days in Seville. I knew Mason-Mac would have given me leave, but his deputy, Major General Hyland – a very strait-laced officer – would certainly refuse. I decided not to ask him. I would change into civilian clothes after lunch on Saturday, take one of the Government House cars and slip out through the Frontier into Spain. Early Monday morning, I would be back in Gib ready to give the Major General his signals and despatches.

The first part of the plan went well. The food was good, the wine was delicious, and so were the little gypsy girls. At three on the Monday morning I started off back to Gibraltar – an easy drive in the time. By dawn, I was nearing Cadiz.

There is a long stretch of straight road there between tall eucalyptus trees. To the right are salt marshes; to the left is dense woodland. It was already quite light as I started down this stretch, in no hurry but cruising along at about fifty miles per hour. In the far distance, I could see the tiny figure of a man walking on the crown of the road. I did not slow down since I had the right of way and expected him to step aside. As I drew nearer, I could see that he was walking with his head down, not budging from his course in the middle of the road. I pressed the horn; he did not even look up. I slammed on the brakes and swerved over to the right. At the very last moment, the man raised his head and I saw the startled look on his face. He scuttled away into safety; then, like a frightened rabbit, darted back again into the car. I hit him full. The body went up in the air; it thumped on the roof, then fell off behind. I stopped and walked back. The man – an elderly peasant – was lying with his head in a pool of blood and one leg doubled under him. He was unconscious, but muttering, 'Madre de Dios, madre de Dios'.

It was a bad situation to be in for both of us – worse for him, much worse, but none too good for me. I was absent without leave. I confess I had a momentary temptation to drive on – but it was only momentary. I picked him up – he was light but smelt like a polecat – and as gently as I could laid him in the back seat of the car. With every move he screamed in agony; his head fell back, and soon the leather seat was covered with blood. Then I turned the car and drove back into Cadiz.

Women with brooms were brushing their doorsteps and calling to each other across the streets; one of them directed me to the nearest hospital. The unshaven young doctor who came to investigate seemed to care little for his patient; he handled the poor man with a casual brutality that caused the unconscious man to yell again with pain. The doctor was far more interested in me. Who was I? Where had I come from? His hostility was extreme – not, I was sure, because I had knocked a man down, but because I was British. It was no surprise to me when two *Guardia Civil* arrived to take me to the local jail and lock me up with the other sweepings of the night.

Luckily I still had a few *pesetas* in my pocket, and I bribed the jailer to let me use the telephone. I got through to Gibraltar and spoke to John Perry who promised to think up some story to tell Major General Hyland and also alert our consul in Cadiz to do his best to extricate me. By noon, after a farcical legal process, I was set free and allowed to continue on my way.

By now, I had come to understand the cause of the accident. The poor old man was a charcoal burner who lived in the forest with his wife; during the night, she had died. Stunned, blind and deaf to everything except his grief, he had stumbled out of the woods and there met his end at my unwitting hands.

I had been driving with caution when the accident happened; now I drove like a madman. I raced through the Frontier controls, turned into the yard of Government House, tore off my blood-stained clothes, washed the red Andalusian dust from my face and hands, and all the while listened to John Perry describing what it was that I was supposed to have been doing: I had gone out with a friend on anti-submarine patrol in his Motor Torpedo Boat. While out in the Straits, there had been a submarine alert; silence was imposed; there was no way that I could inform HQ of my predicament. I had to wait until the MTB brought me back.

Major General Hyland was unimpressed. He listened, silent and frosty, while I spoke. Then he said, 'I'm disappointed in you, Quayle. You should be court-martialled. But since you are due to leave here the day after tomorrow, I have decided not to take that step. Consider yourself damn lucky.'

Yes – I did deserve to be court-martialled; but Mason-Mac would have only laughed. He would have cuffed me but not held it against me – not have the escapade inserted in my Confidential File at the War Office where years later I found it lodged. But Mason-Mac and Hyland belonged to different breeds. There are few Mason-Macs around today – or Pug Ismays, or Freddy Morgans; if there are, I do not meet them.

The men of the 8th Army had long moved on from Cairo, fighting their way across North Africa then north through Sicily and on into Italy, but Cairo still swarmed with soldiers. The pungent smell that hung over the city was the same as Alexander the Great's men must have had in their nostrils when they had come that way 2,000 years before – spices, dust, and dried camel dung. Petrol fumes were added now to the aroma, but otherwise it could have changed little. The kites soared and wheeled overhead as they had done for centuries; to their keen eyes victors and vanquished were as one; both were the providers of stinking, edible garbage.

I reported to SOE Headquarters and was interviewed by a young colonel with parachute wings and a broken leg; he looked like Charles Boyer.

'Any idea where you want to go?'

I told him I would like to be dropped into Greece, if that were possible; that I had a slight friendship with King George of the Hellenes, and wondered if it might not be a good idea to organize some right-wing resistance rather than leave all the fighting to the Communists. I was pathetically unaware of the situation in Greece.

The colonel did not chide me for schoolboy ignorance. He shrugged and told me to come back in a week; by then the picture would be clearer. Meanwhile – no, there was no harm at all in my talking to the King.

King George was enthusiastic for my idea and gave me two magnificent meals at the Mohammed Ali Club; I had never eaten in such splendour. But though the food was superb, I doubted if this royal approach would lead anywhere. The King's principal aide, Colonel Levidis, was a plump little man with well-manicured nails – not a soldier but an old-fashioned courtier. I would not have liked to entrust my life, or that of anyone else, to such smooth soft hands.

When I next saw Charles Boyer, he told me ruefully that the situation in Greece had grown so complicated that they were sending no more Liaison Officers. How would I like to go into some other Balkan country? Bulgaria, for example? – or Romania?

I explained that I was ready to go wherever I was sent, but had no particular affinity for either of those two countries.

He pondered. 'Then what about the Far East? Behind the Jap lines? They badly need fellows out there.'

I considered I was being reckless enough to be dropped behind German lines. The idea of being caught by the Japanese and having slivers of bamboo pushed up under my fingernails or into some other tender part of my anatomy was too frightening to contemplate. I declined – without, I hoped, sounding too cowardly.

The colonel had a bright idea. 'I know,' he said. 'What about Albania? Albania's the nearest thing to Greece. How does that idea take you?'

'Fine,' I said. 'Albania let it be.'

There followed several weeks of courses – in explosives, ciphering, deciphering, and in the rudiments of the Albanian language. We even had a few lessons from Jasper Maskelyne – one of the magicians from my music-hall days; he instructed us in various idiotic skills, like writing in invisible ink. The Albanian lessons – all too few of them – were conducted by an enchanting old lady called Fanny Hazluck, a great authority on the ancient laws and language of the Albanians. She was an enthusiast, but gave us little instruction in the kind of questions we were most likely to need – questions such as: How deep is the river? Can the mules get across? Where are the enemy? How many of them are there? A company? A brigade?

One unforgettable day she made us learn by heart the opening lines of a fairy story: *Kotzamitzi rana vorbet. Plaku shkuli komett.* This meant that the mousiekin fell in the pot, and the old woman wrung her hands. At the time it seemed as useless a piece of literature as any I had come across; in a few months it was to save my life.

No one at HQ could tell us much about the situation in Albania – chiefly because no one at HQ knew much about the situation themselves. To have dropped a mission 'blind' into a wild, mountainous country like Albania would have been folly; so in April two British officers, Billy MacLean and David Smiley, had been parachuted into Greece close enough to the northern border to make their way on foot into Albania and find out what was going on. They came out while I was in Cairo, and I saw them briefly before they flew back to London for interviews with everybody up to Anthony Eden.

To abbreviate their complicated story: Albania was moving towards civil war, but war had not yet broken out. There were at least three political groups in charge of their own guerrilla bands – *cetas* as they were called; by far the strongest was the LNC (National Movement of Liberation) which the Communist Partisans dominated but did not yet control; there was the Zogist Party whose strength lay mainly in the north of the country; and there was the *Balli Kombettar* (Ballists, for short) who were accused by the Partisans of collaborating with the Italians, but who in reality were only men who hated Communism with the same passion that they hated their Italian invaders. These different *cetas* all claimed to be harassing and killing Italians; in truth they were far more intent on destroying each other.

A small number of BLOs (British Liaison Officers) had recently been dropped in; but they were few and scattered, separated by 6,000 and 7,000 feet mountains deep in snow, out of touch with each other, and depending on a tenuous radio link with HQ at Bari. With proper organization men, stores and ammunition could be dropped in by plane, but it was almost impossible to get anyone — or any documentary evidence — out. This was true not only of Albania, but of Greece as well where ever since the Germans had occupied the country in place of the Italians, all ways of getting out by sea had been blocked.

There were three of us about to be dropped into Albania; the other two were Brian Ensor from the Irish Fusiliers, and Gordon Lazell, a gunner like myself. Brian and I took ourselves off most nights to have a look at the belly dancers, but Gordon would never go out; he stayed at home, read the Bible and wrote letters to his fiancée. He was experimenting with smoking a pipe, and one day asked me to show him how to pack it; it seemed rather hot, he said. He showed me how he rammed the tobacco in, and I wondered how he had any lining left inside his mouth.

'But why do you want to smoke a pipe?' I asked.

'Because,' he explained, 'I'm sure we shall see quite a bit of action in Albania, but there are bound to be periods of boredom. I thought that if I learned to enjoy smoking a pipe, it might get me through times of frustration. Even loneliness.'

He still packed the tobacco far too tight. When Brian and I came back at night, we could still smell the acrid fumes hanging in the air of the 'safe house' where we lived in Zamalek. (Not such a 'safe house' either; one night my wristwatch was stolen from the chair by my bedside as I slept.)

Gordon was the first to fly off; he parachuted safely to his allotted zone, and next day was taken on a long reconnaissance. He slipped on a rock, the sub-machine-gun he was carrying went off, and his head was blown apart.

Poor Gordon, if only he would have known what awaited him, he could have spared himself weeks of misery, sucking away at a red-hot cinder.

Hitherto the airfield at Derna on the North African coast had been used for flying sorties into Albania — a long flight. But now the Allied advance had gone so well that all the toe and heel of Italy was in our hands, and it was possible to establish an SOE base at Bari on the Adriatic coast. From there the flight across the Adriatic and back was much shorter — a great lightening of the burden on the RAF. Brian Ensor and I were put on a transport bound for Taranto; from there we were to make our way to the new headquarters of Force 266 in Bari – Force 266 being the code name for the Albanian Section of SOE. The days at sea were idyllic; the sun shone; the war might not exist; I spent hours watching a battalion of Gurkhas wrestling each other on the canvas-covered hatches aft. They threw each other about like puppies, but always laughing, always with a sensibility for one another.

The first thing that took my eye as our truck drove through the streets of Taranto was a huge cinema poster: *Greer Garson e Laurence Olivier* it proclaimed *nel Orgoglio y Pregiudizio*. It took me a moment to recognize *Pride and Prejudice*. Movies it seemed could overleap all frontiers, all obstacles – even war. Millions could die but the Gross Takings were what counted.

Arrived in Bari, I was packed off to do a week's parachute course. I thoroughly enjoyed the first drop – less so as we did one jump after another. By the time we had completed the night drops, I found I could not put a toothbrush in my mouth; the nerves in my teeth and gums had become hypersensitive.

We were a mixed lot: some were men from the Parachute Regiment doing a refresher course; others, like myself, belonged to SOE and were being dropped in different parts of the Balkans; others again wore civilian clothes, and were clearly agents. No one enquired into anyone else's business.

We jumped from a Dakota – the old DC3 – going out through a side door in sticks of five or six. Before every jump, the sergeant despatcher walked along between the lines of waiting men showing each in turn that the strop of his parachute was securely hooked to the static line that ran the length of the plane. Once assured of this, you were supposed not to fiddle any more with your harness – just line up and *GO* when the time came.

We had a couple of Poles amongst us; they were to be dropped back into their own country and were wildly excited at the prospect. They were the greatest friends, but always making a pretence of fighting one another. On one of our drops the Poles were numbers One and Two in the stick; I was lined up close behind them at number Three. The pilot lowered his flaps; the warning light came on; Pole Number One clasped either side of the door ready to pull himself out into the roaring slipstream. At that moment, his friend at Number Two banged him on the arm and shouted something in his ear. I saw the man's face turn in utter horror; the despatcher shouted '*GO*' – and he went.

I hit the ground not far from the Poles and found them, as always, fighting. They were howling with laughter, but slapping each other around even harder than usual. I asked what the hell had happened.

'You know what this bastard did?' said Pole Number One, convulsed with laughter but giving his friend a murderous punch. 'He told me I was not hooked on.'

It was decided in Bari that I should be dropped inland near Pogradec to look into the possibility of seaplanes landing on Lake Ohrid and taking off again during the night – not so much to bring people in as to get them out. Then, in mid-November I was told that the plan to drop me by parachute had been abandoned owing to the serious fighting that had broken out between the Partisans and Ballists. I was still to carry out the Lake Ohrid mission, but instead of being dropped I was to cross the Adriatic by boat, then make my way by foot across the country to Pogradec. I must be ready to leave within the next couple of days.

I felt nothing but joy and relief to be going at last. I was sick to death of waiting in Bari, sick to death of the Officers' Club where every day and all day the Italian orchestra played 'Lili Marlene' in waltz time, march time, as a tango, and as a foxtrot. I had all the optimism and confidence of youth: others might be captured or killed, but not me – I was immortal. I wiped from my mind Hitler's recent edict that Allied officers found behind German lines, even though wearing uniform, should be treated as *agents provocateurs* and shot.

I knew that I was no hero, but I did want to prove to myself that I was not a coward. And I wanted to make some sort of offering to Dot: I was like a penguin that lays a hopeful pebble at the feet of his penguin love. If she scorns it, he pushes it again and again towards her enchanting webbed feet before finally giving up. But if she accepts his offering, if his pebble finds favour in her sight – ah, then they start to build a penguin nest and raise a penguin family. I wanted to achieve something in the nature of a pebble that I could lay before Dot. It did not have to be as spectacular as the blowing of the Gorogopotamos Bridge in Greece – one of SOE's most resounding successes – no, it could be something far less dramatic; but it had to be convincing. And here was the opportunity: I was to have a mission of my own; I was going into enemy-occupied country where I had no one to rely on but myself – and a wireless transmitter that might or might not work.

The *Sea Maid* was a sixty-foot diesel engine fishing boat, a noisy, dirty little tub under the command of Lieutenant Washington, a Naval Reservist. He was a grey-haired man with a depth of quiet courage; during the desert campaigns he had been part of the 'Coast-Watching Flotilla' – small boats that had nosed along the African coast at night on secret missions. He and his volunteer crew of four were dressed to look like Italian fishermen. We were armed with two light machine guns.

The boat was already loaded with food and ammunition; we cast off in the afternoon. Washington's plan – and he had made this run many times – was to be at least halfway across the Adriatic when night fell; he could then make the final run-in under cover of darkness with less chance of being spotted by a German E-Boat or aircraft.

We arrived half a mile off the coast, and hove to. Ahead of us loomed the black outline of the mountains rising straight up out of the water, but no signal of any kind. We waited rolling about for the best part of an hour, Washington occasionally glancing at his watch. He needed to be well clear of E-Boat patrols before the dawn came. At last, reluctantly, he headed back to Italy. My first attempt to land had failed.

Bari had no explanation; 'Sea View'* had simply gone off the air. Either Major Field, the officer sent to Albania by SOE to try to sabotage communications in the Valona area, had not managed to get to the rendezvous in time or he was being hunted and had to lie low.

I hung about for another couple of weeks, ready to leave at once, but again forced to endure the strains of 'Lili Marlene'. One day HQ became alive: Sea View had come back on the air; their signals were strong and regular.

Again we crossed the Adriatic without incident; again we arrived at the pinpoint at the base of the towering mountains – only to meet with blackness.

'Are you sure?' I asked Washington. 'Are you absolutely certain that we've got the right place?'

His navigational skill was being challenged. 'Yes,' he said. 'I'm damn sure.'

Once again we had to turn back. By now the wind was freshening and there was the likelihood of a heavy blow from the north. Washington decided to run and shelter round the heel of Italy in the little harbour of Otranto. We sheltered there for several days, moored immediately behind a hospitable RN Minelayer who invited all of us from the *Sea Maid* to share their Christmas dinner. It would have been a bleak Christmas indeed without their company and good spirits. When the storm was over, we headed north again to Brindisi and awaited orders.

They came abruptly. Washington must get me over to Sea View as fast as he could; Field had had an accident with some gelignite and was badly wounded; he had to be evacuated at once. I was to forget about Lake Ohrid; I was to take over Field's job.

*'Sea View' was the name given to a narrow inlet on the rocky Albanian coast south of Cape Linquetta. It was one of the few places where we were able to land, and a base had already been established here.

Exactly what the job was there was no time to explain. I would have to find that out when I got there. 'Do the best you can,' I was told. 'Send out all the Intelligence you can, and make yourself a bloody nuisance to the Germans. But whatever you do, keep open the base at Sea View. It is vital.' That was all the briefing I got.

On the last day of 1943 there was a heavy swell at sea, and the *Sea Maid* rolled and plunged like a pig. I was not sick but so wretched that if an E-Boat had come up out of the darkness and attacked, I would have been glad to die. But we closed the shore, the water calmed, and I felt better.

Suddenly, stabbing out of the darkness, came the signal for which we had crossed the Adriatic three times. Washington answered with his hooded Aldis lamp, then drove unerringly into a doglegged creek, steering his boat between the rocks with bare two fathoms to spare on either side.

Ahead was a narrow beach, hemmed in by precipitous cliffs and lit by an enormous fire against whose leaping flames the reception party stood silhouetted. I rowed ashore. Field lay beneath a pile of blankets; the top part of his head was swathed in bloody bandages, but his jaw was free.

'You'll soon be back in hospital,' I said. 'I'm taking over from you. Don't talk unless you have something special to say.'

For a moment, I thought he had not heard me; then his lips moved and he said slowly, and very clearly, 'I wish you joy of the damned place.'

ADRIATIC SEA

VUNO

GJORMI

GUMENICA

DHERMI

MONASTERY

GERVANI GARRISON

CLISSORA PASS

TRAJAS

DOKATI
VILLAGE

THREE HOUSE BASE

CELA'S HOUSE

SCOTTY BASE

BIVOUACS

GRAMA
BAY

VALONA

PROPOSED BEACH
FOR SUPPLYING PARTISANS

THE CAVES

SEA VIEW

N

FROM ITALY

COUNTRY UNDER PARTISANS

266

CHAPTER 18

FIELD HAD ESTABLISHED HIS WORKING BASE in a ravine a few hundred feet above the sea; it consisted of half a dozen small caves whose low roofs were full of scorpions. Goatherds had kept their animals in the caves until recently, so they were full of lice as well.

Already occupying one of the caves, I found Sandy Glen, a Naval Commander in MI6, plotting the harbour defences of Valona, and Dale McAdoo, an American Major of the OSS, also involved solely in Intelligence. We were all pursuing different ends, but difficulty of supply had driven the three organizations (MI6, SOE and OSS) to club together in the same infested cave.

Early in the morning of New Year's Day, Bombardier Crane, the radio operator I had inherited from Field, came to report and give me such background as he knew. Crane was a first-class radio operator, and something much more besides; he was the embodiment of the British soldier at his best. Dauntless, sturdy, snub-nosed, cheerful in the worst conditions, he had stood firm at Agincourt, at Waterloo, and at Ypres. I was lucky indeed to have inherited him.

I asked Crane how he and Field had moved about the country taking with them the transmitter and the cumbersome charging motor.

'By mule,' he told me. 'We've still got half a dozen quite decent mules. Our best was killed a couple of nights ago.'

'By Germans?'

'No, sir. Wolves.'

Wolves. I had not expected wolves.

'Who are all those?' I asked. There were a dozen or so scarecrows in the remains of Italian uniforms sitting around by the cave mouths.

'Them? Oh, the poor buggers took to the mountains when Italy made peace. The Albs have treated them worse than animals. Can't blame them after what the Ities did here. Now they're beginning to drift in here. We send 'em back to Italy in the *Sea Maid*, but she doesn't come very often.'

'How do we feed them?'

'It's getting to be a problem,' he replied. 'And it looks like getting worse.'

It took me days of talking, miles of walking, before I began to understand the situation in my area; then I realized how fatuous, how hopelessly contradictory my orders had been. 'Make yourself a bloody nuisance to the Germans,' I had been told, and, 'Send out all the Intelligence you can.' The two functions were dangerously incompatible.

On the inland side of the mountain that rose straight up behind Sea View lay the large village of Dukati, and through Dukati ran a supply road for the German Divisions in Greece. The whole area was Ballist country, fervently anti-Communist. It was clear that the very existence of Sea View depended on the cooperation of Dukati. And to keep Sea View open, I had been told, was vital.

Inland of Dukati however was a wild tract of mountains where the Partisans held sway. They were not sufficiently trained, not well enough armed, to take strong offensive action against the Germans; but their presence was a threat, and the enemy were obliged continually to mount small, hard-hitting drives against them.

Within forty-eight hours of my arrival, a shepherd furtively slipped a letter into my hand. It read:

MESEPLIK

1st January, 1944

Dear Captain Cuayle

We are informed of your arrival on our area of Valona.

The partizan forces of the 1st and 5th Brigade are new on the area of MESAPLIK after having wiped out all reactionary forces of 'BALLI KOMBTAR' and the German forces that were here some days ago.

In the name of the partizan Headquarter for the area of Argirocastro and Valona, of the 1st and 5th Brigade, we invite you to come personally here at MESAPLIK for discussing matters that interest our struggle against the Germans and the enemies of the

Allies. Being that the area where you are now is under the controll of the reactionary forces of 'Balli Kombtar', we cannot come there to meet you; for this reason we please you to come and meet us here as soon as possible. You may find us at LEPENITZA or BRATAY.

We hope you will come –
V.F.L.B.

For the Headquarters of Argiro-Valona Area, Comisar of the 5th Brigade,

(Signed) Hysni Kapo
Comander of 1st Brigade
(Signed) Shehu

Considering I had only landed on New Year's Eve, the 1st and 5th Brigades had remarkably good Intelligence.

Before anything else, I had to talk to the headman and elders of Dukati and find out exactly where we stood.

As well as Sergeant Crane, I had inherited from Field a most unusual Albanian. Xhelil Cela was around thirty and had been taught English at the American School in Tirana. He regarded himself as a rich man, and so he was by Dukati standards; by ours he was a very modest farmer indeed. He and his family grew a bit of maize, owned several hundred goats, and lived in a ramshackle, sprawling farmhouse with wooden floors. He was tall, thin to gauntness, with the flat back to his head common to many Albanians, and a mouthful of gleaming metal teeth. I liked and trusted him from the start. He arranged my first meeting with the elders of Dukati, inviting me to stay the night in his home.

'Only, Major Queel,' he said, 'You must not come near my house if you see a black Mercedes. That is the car of the German Colonel. He commands the garrison down the road. He will be staying with me tonight. But tomorrow he will drive away. Then you are safe to come down the mountain. Don't be afraid of the dogs. I will keep them shut up.' White and gold teeth glinted in a smile.

'Why do you have anything to do with the Germans?' I asked.

His reply was simple and believable. 'The Germans will leave Albania one day. But we in Dukati promised Major Field – and now we promise you – that we will never betray your base.'

I crossed the mountain (it took me three hours to climb up, but only one to come down on the far side) and needed no binoculars to see the

German car parked outside the stone farmhouse. There were goats all over the place; women were gathering firewood; they wore baggy trousers and embroidered waistcoats – like the advertisements for Balkan Sobranie cigarettes, but considerably less attractive. I waited half an hour, an hour, then the German Colonel came out, got in his car and drove away. I slept in the bed that he had just vacated. I was grateful to him for airing it; the farmhouse was dripping wet.

When darkness fell, the elders began to arrive. Most were small farmers; one was a teacher, another a lawyer in Valona. All were Moslems; all carried rifles. They had beaten off a partisan attack, they said, a few weeks earlier and were expecting another. Their dress was a mixture of East and West; some wore traditional Albanian hats; some wore tweed caps; all wore breeches. They realized this was a meeting of importance, and they weighed their words. Every one of them spoke Italian, two or three spoke French, and Cela acted as Albanian interpreter.

Their position was clear. Major Field had wanted them to attack trucks and convoys passing through towards Greece, but this they had refused to do; in reprisal the Germans would have destroyed the entire village. What would be the good of that? The English Major had been angry with them for not killing Germans, but he could not understand that his war and their war were different. The Allies would certainly defeat the Germans, and the Germans would withdraw; but that was when the Albanian war would begin. Dukati would have to defend itself against the Communists. Yes, they would attack the Germans, but not while the Germans were in full command of the country – only when they started to withdraw from Albania, and from Greece too. Meanwhile, they asked for arms to carry out this task when the day came. They appreciated they were not helping the Allies with sabotage and ambushes, but they felt they were making a very real contribution by protecting Sea View, and concealing our presence from the Germans.

'What,' I asked, 'if attacks were carried out by myself and my own men?'

They pulled down their mouths. No, they could not agree to that; Dukati would be accused of duplicity. Its destruction would be equally assured.

I tried my last approach. I understood their predicament, I told them, but my hope was to prevent the two political parties – Ballists and Partisans – from tearing Albania apart. It was important that Sea View continued undisturbed; it was also important to give support to those who were fighting the Germans. What would be their attitude to the passage of arms to the Partisans across their territory? It was a naive question, but I was a newcomer.

They shook their heads. 'If the Ballist leaders in Valona came to hear of it, Dukati would be attacked by Ballists and Germans together.'

The meeting broke up with courtesy but little hope.

Next day I went in search of the 5th Partisan Brigade, two mountain ranges inland. Cela escorted me as far as he dared, but turned back as we entered Partisan country. I walked on alone till I came to a village called Trajas.

Half a dozen enormous dogs came at me as I approached; three feet high they must have stood, as big as lions and seemingly as fierce. They were mastiffs, descended from the hunting dogs of ancient Assyria and Greece; I had to put a couple of revolver shots near them before they would sheer off.

They were distrustful of me in Trajas — distrust ran like the plague through every mountain village in Albania — but they were cautiously hospitable; they gave me a place by the fire where I could dry my sweat-sodden clothes, they fed me, and in the morning they produced a man who said he would be glad to bring me to the Partisans.

Pavlo was a merry old Communist with a lean face and big moustaches; he carried a leather pouch of rank Albanian tobacco, and smoked endlessly. He had fought for the Republicans in Spain and was wholehearted for his cause, but at the same time he had a detachment from life, as though instinct told him he might not long be for it. I liked him greatly. No, he did not think the Partisans were at Lepenitza or Bratay. They were always on the move, he explained, but we might find them in Gjormi — a village only two days' march over the mountains.

Gjormi had been shelled and mortared flat by the Italians; it was little but a pile of stones. News of my arrival seemed to have gone ahead of me; the place swarmed with men — young for the most part — wearing a red star in their caps. Because of my high cheekbones and because my hair was cut down to a stubble (the less to harbour lice), they took me for a Russian. 'Death to Fascism' they shouted, giving the clenched-fist salute: 'The Freedom of the People'. They pressed round me full of excitement. I was led to one of the few hovels left standing, stepping over the blood of a large goat that was being done to death — for consumption later, I assumed. The room was cleaner than I had expected: whitewashed walls, a fire, bright red rugs and cushions on the floor.

Shefqet Peci, Komandant of the 5th Brigade, was a formidable man; curly black hair topped an animal face with deeply seamed cheeks. Hysni Kapo, the Komisar (*nom de guerre*, Besnik), was a young man of my own age with a subtle, pointed face. Both were hung about with all the *accoutrements* of war; hand grenades dangled from their belts. The grenades were not altogether weapons of offence. Prisoners on both sides were frequently tortured to death, and rather than be captured, Partisan leaders preferred to pull the pin of a grenade, bend double and blow themselves to pieces.

We settled down on the floor to several hours of heated talks, interrupted only by the arrival of the goat – dismembered, boiled, and now served up in a large iron pot. Other Partisans joined us for the meal; we sat in a circle facing clockwise round the pot and fished out gobbets of meat with our left hands. As guest of honour, I was presented with the head.

The position of the Partisans was as uncompromising as that of the Ballists. Major Field, they said, had dropped in to them by parachute; they had protected him, and he had promised them support. None had come. In the end, he had betrayed them by moving his base into the territory of their enemies and giving to the men of Dukati the arms and supplies he had promised to the Partisans. (It was untrue; Field had given nothing to Dukati.) If the only way they could get supplies and arms was through Dukati, then they would prefer to do without. They would give no assurance not to attack the village. But why, they asked, could arms not be dropped to them by plane?

I knew this might in the end be the only solution to 'making myself a bloody nuisance to the Germans', but it would mean abandoning the base at Sea View, moving secretly out of the area of Dukati (and how was that to be done?) and joining forces wholeheartedly with the Partisans. It would mean taking an active part with one side against the other. The only hope of patching up a truce between them would be gone.

'We have not enough planes to supply the whole of the Balkans,' I told them. 'Besides, in one sea sortie we can bring in more stores and ammunition than in six air sorties.'

'Then make a sea base in Partisan territory.'

'Where?'

'At Vuno – down the coast from where you are now. We control that area. That way you can supply us and leave your present base undisturbed.'

It sounded dubious, but I promised to look into it at once.

When the Brigade moved off in the morning, a sorry looking band, Besnik hung back to say a last word.

'I know you will not fail us,' he said quietly. 'The young do not fail one another.'

I got back to Sea View to find there had been no sortie while I was away, but two dozen more Italians had arrived – one of them a senior General who had commanded a division in Greece, General Infante; another a young army doctor who had been fired at by Partisans and hit in the arm. He was desperate to get back to Italy and have his arm amputated. I assured him we would try to send him quickly; meanwhile we had no medicine to offer him stronger than a tablet of aspirin.

The plight of thousands of Italian soldiers in Albania was extreme. At the beginning of September when Italy had signed the Separate Peace with the Allies, many Italians had made a dash for the mountains hoping to join the Partisans; they had taken with them as peace offerings whatever arms and ammunition they could carry. Others had simply run off, having no stomach to continue the fight on either side. A third group had stayed with their units, and to them the Germans had offered the alternative of fighting on beside them, or going to work in munition factories in the north.

The worst off were those who had hoped to join the Partisans; they had been relieved of their coats, uniforms, boots, weapons and ammunition; then they had been turned out into the mountains with a farewell burst of machine-gun fire. The Italians had been their oppressors for years, and the Partisans were not slow to take revenge. Even those who had merely run away were soon in great distress; they were treated by the peasants with contempt. Some were harnessed together like mules and for a daily handful of maize bread forced to drag the clumsy wooden ploughs. While they could stand, they were fed; when they were too feeble to work, they were turned loose to fend for themselves. Many of them died where they fell, beside the mountain tracks. How the survivors found their way to Sea View I do not know, but they did – some wounded, almost all with malaria. I was as though there were a dotted line leading them across the mountains to Dukati, then from Dukati straight to Sea View.

Crane was right; the problem was growing. The Alpini were fine men, uncomplaining and self-reliant; they made themselves useful in a dozen different ways. But we could barely support ourselves with the sporadic supplies that arrived from Italy; it was quite beyond us to feed a growing number of sick Italians. We could only share with them what food we had, pray for a speedy return of the *Sea Maid*, and hope that there would be room on board for our unwelcome guests.

I sent off a signal to Bari requesting an urgent sortie, then pushed off down the coast to Vuno as I had promised the Partisans. I took with me Gunner Gray, who was another of my lucky inheritances; he was an ex-Commando, and before the war had been a slaughterer in Liverpool. It was a scrambling march of several days with not even a mule track to follow, but we arrived there in the end and made contact with the local Komisar. To my delight, there too was old Pavlo waiting for us – always joking, always smoking his vile tobacco.

The proposed beach was suitable enough, its only drawback being that it lay within half a mile of the road that was in constant use by the Germans. But the cover was good; with care and secrecy the unloading could be done at night. There was a ruined monastery a short way inland from Vuno, hidden in a fold of the hills; here I left Gray to establish a base for the proposed operation and to act as courier across Ballist country. For guard and companion he would have Pavlo. I wrote to Besnik telling him I would signal for a boatload of stores and arms to be sent to Vuno as soon as possible, but that future shipments would depend on his own plan of action. The local Komisar undertook to deliver the letter. Then I set off back to Sea View.

I passed one night in a village called Dhermi – Ballist country. I was given food for which I was very thankful, and offered a bed for the night. I was dog-tired, but for some reason decided to lie down fully dressed, not even taking my boots off. In the middle of the night I woke to hear trucks pulling up in the village, then shouts in German. I dived out through the window at the back as German soldiers burst in through the front; if they had been less clumsy they would have caught me. As I stumbled up the hillside in the dark, I wondered who had betrayed me; it could only have been a Ballist.

At Sea View I found that there had been no sortie; General Infante was still there; the Italian doctor's arm was turning septic; Dukati had withdrawn its 'guards' and more Italians were arriving daily. One of McAdoo's agents, Ismail Carapizzi, had been murdered. A crop of problems. I tried to deal with them one by one.

I sent ever more urgent signals to Bari requesting a sortie.

I listened to Infante sagely pointing out the danger we were in. I was well aware of it, but felt I could not move out of the area without a directive from Bari.

I visited the wounded Italian every day. As a doctor he knew the wound in his left arm would soon turn septic and that he must have the arm amputated before gangrene reached his heart and killed him. I could give him no assurance as to when a boat would come, and found it unbearable to face his accusing eyes.

The withdrawal of our so-called 'guards' counted for little, since at best they were only a few undependable goatherds. But it was a sign of dissension in Dukati, and I sent for the elders to come and speak to me.

I was helpless to stem the flood of wretched malarial Italians but decided they must be left on their own at Sea View while I established a second base further south, halfway between Sea View and Vuno. If the Germans were to follow the trail now being beaten across Dukati mountain, they would drop down on the triple base of SOE, MI6, and OSS: a tidy haul.

The murder of Carapizzi carried different implications. Ismail Carapizzi was an old-time Albanian Communist who had spent his last five years imprisoned by Mussolini. Released by the advancing Americans, he had volunteered to go into Albania and work as an agent for the OSS. He had already carried out several successful missions. On this occasion one of the local goatherds, a tousled-headed youth called Mysli, had offered to guide and escort him across the mountain to Dukati. What followed was told to us by Cela.

When Mysli arrived in Dukati without his charge, he was asked what had happened. He explained that there had been a gunfight with brigands in which Carapizzi had been killed; he himself had become scared and run away. A search was made, and after two days Carapizzi's body was discovered. Three shots had been fired into his back, one through the palm of his hand, and he had been stabbed a number of times. The eight gold sovereigns he was carrying to finance his mission were not to be found.

Mysli was locked up by the headmen of the village and sentenced to be shot at dawn.

The mountains of Albania have their own customs, fiercer and more strictly observed than any laws. If two men bind themselves to cross a mountain and are attacked, then both must survive or both must die; one of them cannot come down alone, and live. His word can never be trusted again. It is possible that he did not commit a murder, but with no evidence except his own the truth cannot be known. The equilibrium of trust in the community is disturbed. Such a man is better dead than be left alive and become the cause of a blood feud that could last a hundred years. In those mountains a man is accounted guilty unless he can prove himself innocent.

The war had destroyed an ancient concept of life, death, and honour. The balance had become a great deal more complicated. During the night before the execution, all the male members of Mysli's family – his father, uncles, brothers and cousins – some thirty men, all armed, had assembled in the village and declared that if the execution were carried out they would go straight to Valona and reveal to the Germans the full story of Dukati's complicity with the Allied mission. The village had been faced with a civil war of their own. Mysli had been released.

The elders – armed, bandoliered and sombre – appeared in Sea View. The Mysli affair, they hoped, would help me to understand the pressures they were under. They themselves believed that their only hope of survival in the coming civil war was to obtain the friendship – and weapons – of the British. In the village, however, there were hotter and more frightened heads ready to sell us to the Germans. I took the withdrawal of our 'guards' to have been a compromise between the two extremes.

Cela's embarrassment as he translated was acute. When the elders had left to cross back over the mountain, he sat on the rocks outside the cave, smoking cigarette after cigarette.

'Where do you stand in all this?' I asked him.

'Major Queel,' he answered after a pause. 'Once I was very strong Ballist. Then one day I see men of my party shoulder to shoulder with Germans, fighting against other Albanians – against Partisans. I took the Ballist emblem from my hat and threw it on the ground. Since that day, I am nothing. Not Ballist. Not Communist. Only against Germans. And now I am in great troubles.'

I glanced at the man's fierce profile as he gazed out to sea. He had spoken from his heart.

There was no reply from Besnik to my letter. Perhaps it had never reached him. Even if it had, it would have been almost impossible for him to get a message to me in the heart of Ballist country. Sooner rather than later I would have to go in search of him again.

Bari passed on a directive from Middle East HQ:

British Missions in the Balkans should prepare to support a major Allied attack across the Adriatic – 'Operation Underdone'. A strong force is planned to strike north eastwards across Yugoslavia towards the Danube. The first objective: to reach the Danube before the Russians, and establish the Danube as the east-west frontier. The second objective: the annihilation of the German divisions withdrawing from the southern Balkans. Liaison Officers to keep in touch with and encourage all parties prepared to attack and destroy the enemy when roads and mountain passes are choked with men and vehicles. Local Resistance groups should be ready to rise up and create havoc.

It was exhilarating stuff – possibly the way in which Dukati could be armed and play its part – but I still lacked any decision from Bari on my own immediate problem of Partisan versus Balli. Nor was there any reaction to my suggestion of trying to land stores at Vuno. A signal did inform me that the Navy had been hunting a submarine and had closed

276

the Adriatic to all small craft moving at night. A sortie would be sent to Sea View as soon as possible.

More Italians arrived; we now had well over a hundred. The establishment of a second base had become an urgent necessity.

A day's march south, towards Vuno but well inside Ballist country, I found the perfect bay – well-protected but much bigger than Sea View. The entrance was three times wider and there was a good depth of water almost to the beach.

The place was called Grama Bay. I recalled that *gramos* was Greek for 'a letter', and there was some Ancient Greek lettering carved in a rock face near the sea – probably chiselled out centuries ago by sailors heading north into the Adriatic, hoping to propitiate the gods of sea and wind.

Cela collected the local goatherds together. Half a dozen of them assembled under the trees on the headland – small, lithe men with thick black coats, each carrying his rifle. Cela translated their speech of welcome.

'They say that you are their guest. That they must die before you die. They will think no more for their wives, or for their children, or even for their goats. Only to serve you.'

One of them, little more than a boy with a face made thin by sickness or hunger, saluted me; he touched his heart, lips and forehead, then seized my hand and kissed it. His name was Bil-Bil.

I left Cela in charge of putting up some bivouacs in a grove of oak trees above the bay, and hurried back to Sea View – to find that I had missed the *Sea Maid* by twelve hours. Brian Ensor, my cheery young Irish friend, had landed, hoping to push his way through to a mission inland. The *Sea Maid* had taken off General Infante and fifty of the Italians. One of them would have been the Italian doctor; through all the long days of waiting he had managed to survive, but for not quite long enough. He had died as they lifted him aboard.

Bad – the worst – news arrived. The monastery where I had left Gray had been surrounded one morning at dawn by a German detachment. There had been a short, violent gun battle. Pavlo was dead – shot through the chest. Gray had been taken prisoner. Poor old Pavlo. Poor bloody Gray. He was in for some ugly treatment. And I was responsible.

That then was the end of supplying the Partisans through Vuno. It was impossible to believe Gray would not talk; I certainly knew I would under torture. I rushed off a signal cancelling the proposed Vuno operation, but informing Bari I had moved to Grama where future sorties should be sent. I included rough soundings that Crane and I made from our canvas boat one night using a stone and a length of parachute cord.

It started to rain, and turned very cold.

With the rain came more news; it did not immediately affect my own plight, but it was bad. A few weeks earlier a large HQ mission had been dropped into Albania under the command of a Brigadier. The mission had been attacked by the Germans; the Brigadier was wounded and taken prisoner; his mission was scattered and on the run. The second-in-command had managed to escape; but after appalling hardships, including the amputation of his frost-bitten toes, he had died.

The rain turned to sleet and snow; the rocks were covered in ice, making arduous the move of the whole base to Grama. We left sixty Italians at Sea View. They had food enough, but looked as forlorn as abandoned children.

On 10 February (the dates are accurate, for it was the only period of my life that I kept a diary of events – never of thoughts) expecting a sortie at Grama, I sent for a party of Italians to come south from Sea View. No sortie came, though we flashed all through the night.

During the morning of the 11th, our new 'guards' – the herdsmen who had greeted me with such serious courtesy – came running into camp beside themselves with fear.

'*Tedeschi! Tedeschi!*' They pointed to the south, towards Vuno.

Even Cela could not find out from them how many Germans were approaching or how far off they were.

'*Molti! Molti!*' they cried. '*Diece minuti fa!*'

Well – ten minutes were ten minutes. We hid the heavy charging motor and took to the hills.

The approaching enemy turned out to be no more than a patrol of three men, one of them carrying a large walkie-talkie. They came up from the south, walked through our camp, then started to climb up the mountain, passing within a couple of hundred yards of where we were hidden. Brian Ensor and several of the others were for wiping them out – it would have been easy enough – but I stopped them. The patrol must have been in touch with their parent unit through the walkie-talkie; their position would be known; Dukati would be implicated and every kind of fat would be in the fire. Three Germans had a narrow escape from death that day.

It was inevitable that the Germans would now send a sizable formation through the mountain in search of us – but possibly not at once. I felt we could return to Grama, prepare to evacuate at the shortest notice, but not be panicked into flight. We found the camp intact except for some minor looting by the goatherds.

Two nights later a sortie did arrive at Grama – but not the *Sea Maid*. It was a big trawler, a hundred feet long at least; she dropped anchor far outside the entrance to the bay and lay rising and falling in the swell. I paddled out in one of our small canvas boats to urge the captain to bring his vessel into the bay where the water was calmer and where the labour of unloading would not be so great.

'Your captain? Where is your captain?' I shouted up to the dark hull to which I was clinging.

The reply was drunken laughter and a torrent of words that I took to be Serbian. Next moment a heavy ammunition box was dropped on my head, followed by another, then another till the flimsy boat was in danger of sinking.

We plied to and fro for hours. The bottoms of the canvas boats would have been ripped out if we had run them up on the pebbled beach; we had to wade into the icy water up to our waists to steady them, then form a chain to pass the heavy boxes ashore. Every time we paddled back to the trawler we took two of the Italians.

We were all becoming very tired. I scribbled a furious note to whoever might be in command of the ship. 'For God's sake, come ashore and speak to me. It is safe to bring your boat in. There is plenty of water.'

Half an hour later I made out a heavy wooden tender heading for the shore – one man rowing, another sitting in the stern. She ran easily up on the beach, and out of the stern rose the figure of an enormous man, a man built on the scale of the Trojan War.

An American voice called, 'Well – what's all the trouble?'

I explained through chattering teeth that it was perfectly safe for him to bring his boat into the bay. That I had taken soundings. If he stayed outside, we should never get the job done.

'I am the captain of this ship,' he replied, 'and I do not think it is safe. Therefore, I shall remain outside. What's more, in another twenty minutes, I shall up-anchor and sail.'

'But there are still a dozen Italians waiting to get aboard.'

'That's your business. If they get aboard in time, I'll take them. If not – not.'

He turned, climbed back into the tender, and was rowed away.

We struggled on till we heard the trawler's engines come alive, then the rattle of her anchor chain being winched aboard. Most of the Italians collapsed on the beach in despair; some tried to swim out to the ship. Three were drowned.

The strange American commander had at least brought some mail. There were several letters for me from E. Beloved E – she wrote to me as regularly as she had done when I was a boy at school. There was no word from Dot. I hunted through the pile again – but no, I had made no mistake. Instead, there was a typewritten envelope with a London postmark. I was not used to getting typewritten letters.

I tore it open and read:

Dear Major Quayle,
   I have the pleasure to inform you that, at the last committee meeting, you were elected a member of the Garrick Club.

CHAPTER 19

THAT NIGHT OF 13 FEBRUARY GIUSEPPE MANZITTI came into my life – with such typical quietness that I did not know till the next day that he had arrived. He came shyly in the morning, smiling
through thick glasses and speaking careful English.

'Manzitti,' he said, introducing himself.

I had heard of him – a great deal. On New Year's Eve we had passed one another on the beach at Sea View but without meeting; he was being repatriated, wrapped in an Army blanket, his teeth rattling with malaria. I was astonished to see him, though I was getting used to the gaps in HQ's information.

'Why on earth have you come back?'

'My malaria is cured,' he said simply.

Manzitti had been Intelligence Officer at Italian Headquarters in Valona. When Italy signed the separate peace in September, he had made straight for the mountains where he had a shrewd idea he might find the British mission and offered his services to Major Field. For three months he had been of invaluable help to both Field and Sandy Glen. He had gone many times into Valona wearing civilian clothes to gather information on the newly-arrived German units. They were dangerous missions, for he could have been recognized on any corner; the town still held numbers of Italians – even men of his own staff – who had opted to join the Germans.

As well as doing Intelligence work, he had gone far inland, trying to get word to his helpless, hopeless compatriots that they must try to reach Dukati, then climb the mountain westwards to the sea; there they might find salvation. It was Manzitti who had started the trickle that was now turning into a torrent.

'But why did you not stay in Italy? Why come back to Albania?'

He shrugged. 'I cannot be of help in Italy. All my family are in Genova, and the Germans control Genova. Besides –' and he smiled almost apologetically, '– I wanted to come. The Albanians are poor people. They are in such troubles that I think I love them.'

It was the first time since I landed that anyone had spoken a word of love, let alone shown it. I had heard and seen nothing but suspicion, cruelty and hatred.

Munzi, as we British had distorted and abbreviated his name, was a deceptive man; he bore no resemblance to a Greek or Trojan hero, yet he had been an athlete and skied for Italy. He was so unassuming that it was possible to mistake his lack of assertion for lack of positivity. It was only when I got to know him that I realized fate had sent to me a brother – a braver, gentler, wiser brother to share the extreme unpleasantness of the next two months.

As well as Munzi, there was another important arrival; Captain Peter Rous came in that night to be my second-in-command. He was a first-class professional soldier but, poor man, one who had little idea of the tangle he was getting into.

Dale McAdoo departed, understandably recalled by OSS. He and his masters must have become highly alarmed at the German interest in our stretch of sea coast and the changed climate of Dukati. We left behind his radio operator, Sergeant Kukich, a fine man but over-temperamental for these conditions.

We got busy concealing the newly-landed stores, hiding them in a dry cave near the beach and covering the entrance with branches and bushes. We had to work fast since any day, any hour, we might be driven out of both Grama and Sea View.

For days I had been expecting a visit from Skender Muco, the Ballist leader in this southern part of the country, and on 15 February he arrived escorted by a bodyguard. He wore a motorcyclist's black leather jerkin, and a black leather cap with earflaps. To my surprise he was barely older than myself, slight and frail-looking, with a smile of considerable charm. Politically he and Besnik were implacable opposites, but in appearance, in fervour, they were not dissimilar. He had studied at the Sorbonne and spoke excellent French; when French failed us, he spoke Italian and Munzi translated. Our talks lasted all of 16 February.

Our camp at Grama was hidden under the clump of oak trees that overlooked the bay. It was a place of pagan beauty, the grass nibbled short by sheep and goats, and the stones of a Christian shrine sprawled across the turf. The place had an air of sacredness about it, but to no aspect of a Christian God, not to any Holy Trinity. The ancient gods held it in their strong grip; it was their living presence that filled the grove.

Under these oaks, a few leaves clinging to their boughs, we held our talks. They were not – they could not be – productive. Muco argued powerfully against our supplying the Partisans with arms. When the war ended in another year or eighteen months, did we British want to see the whole of the Balkans fall into the hands of the Communists? If we pursued our present policy, this was bound to happen – from Bulgaria, through Yugoslavia and Albania, down to Greece. As an Albanian who cared only for his country, he was committed to preventing a tyranny of the Right from being superseded by an equally appalling tyranny of the Left.

I explained to him that policy was shaped in London and Washington, not in a bivouac awaiting German attack. Our Prime Minister had said that we would give arms to whoever fought the Germans. The Partisans in Albania were fighting – however ineffectually. I sympathized with his position, but I could not help the Balli Kombettar until they managed to turn themselves round and fight against the Germans with whom they were now entangled.

'That is exactly what we will do,' he asserted. 'We will attack them the moment they start to retreat. We will destroy them. Only first give us the arms.'

The talk was like a blindfold mule staggering round and round the same circle. 'But before that day comes,' I said, 'you will use the arms against the Partisans. I cannot give you weapons with which to kill men who are your enemies but who are fighting alongside us. And how do you think you will ever escape from this entanglement? Every time you Ballists join with the Germans in an attack on the Partisans, you become further enmeshed.'

On the 17th he took leave of us, and I watched him and his bodyguard begin their climb, two diminishing shapes on the vastness of the mountainside. Very small figures they looked, on a very large canvas.

A signal came from Bari: we must not expect a sortie till the beginning of March – at least another two weeks.

The signal decided me; we must move, and now. It was painful to leave our sixty Italians, but we could not take them along with us. In Sea View they were provided with shelter and food; they must take their chance till we returned. I had no justification for any more delay; Dukati could not be trusted; our position was known to the enemy; I had already delayed dangerously long.

As though confirming the decision, Cela arrived from Dukati where he had been for the past week; he was in a state bordering on panic. The

German garrison, he said, had been increased to brigade strength. Their plan – and he was well placed to know it since the Colonel slept in his house – was to post one line of patrols along the ridge of the mountain and another along the Dukati road while the Brigade combed the forests and ravines. The drive could be expected any day; it might already have started.

Dukati, he told us, insisted on providing us with 'guards'. He could not prevent this but he trusted no one except his own two men, Morat and Zechir. We must keep hidden, come down into the valley only when he says so, cross the road at night, then establish ourselves afresh in the mountains inland of the village.

We put our remaining mules in the care of the goatherds, saying we would return for them. Without the mules we could carry neither batteries nor charging motor, but the animals would be a dangerous encumbrance. We took the radio transmitter and headphones, but before hiding the heavy equipment sent a final signal to Bari warning them we would be off the air for an indefinite period. We took with us the four best *Alpini*, then we left Grama carrying nothing but our packs and the dead weight of 1,000 gold sovereigns.

It took over a week to cross the mountain and drop down into the valley, a week of delays caused by the terror of the Albanians guiding us and our awareness that if we did not follow their instructions they would not hesitate to betray us. Cela flitted between us and Dukati; sometimes he brought us food himself; sometimes he sent Morat or Zechir.

We became increasingly certain that we were trapped more by Dukati than by the Germans; of them there was no sign – only alarms and rumours. The worst nuisance – worse than cold, wet, fleas and lice – was to be pestered daily by the herdsmen who came offering us food, even water, at exorbitant prices. And, being dependent on them, we had to pay.

German traffic on the Dukati road had increased. Cela told us that a big attack had been mounted against the 5th Brigade and would last several weeks. He admitted, shamefaced, that Dukati had sent a *ceta* of fifty men to join the Germans in this all-out drive.

Not all the shepherds' tales were invented. Although we saw no Germans in our part of the mountain, they had clearly beaten their way along the coast we had just left. Herdsmen had been killed, amongst them Bil-Bil, the boy who had saluted me with such Moslem courtesy; his finger had been hacked off to remove a silver ring.

On 29 February my field glasses picked up a sight I had dreaded – our sixty Italians being marched along the road towards Valona under guard. I saw one of them drop behind to fasten his bootlace, then he ran to catch up with the others.

It was damnably cold, and rained without pause. We could not light a fire and dry our clothes. At night we slept in holes and caves under the ground, huddling together for warmth like puppies. Crane was embarrassed by such proximity, but I told him this was not the time or the temperature in which to be standoffish.

He laughed. 'All right, sir, I'll cuddle up. But watch out. My wife says I nearly shove her out of bed in the night.'

By morning I had every sympathy with Jim's wife.

On the night of 1 March, we crossed the road. There was a certain amount of German traffic, but we had only to wait for one convoy to pass, then nip across before the next came. We forded a torrent, waist-deep in icy water, then climbed up 500 or 600 feet into the mountain of Trajas on the inland, eastern, side of the road. By first light, we were on a plateau where there was a scattering of empty goat pens; in these we collapsed. They were alive with fleas, but so were we; and though their roofs let in the rain they also let out the smoke from the fires we now felt safe to light. Every one of us was exhausted, even the *Alpini* were done in. I had a fever and was grateful to Jim Crane for some aspirin. He alone had provided himself with a bottle when he left Italy; not one of the rest of us had thought of it, and medicine had not been spoken or thought of at HQ.

We awoke to a jolting shock.

Throughout the long walk, Peter Rous and I had taken it in turns to carry the 1,000 gold sovereigns. They were a heavy burden, but there had been a further reason for alternating the load; if our 'guards' did not know who carried the mission's funds, there would be less chance of them trying a speculative murder. Now, when Peter woke up among the goat droppings, he discovered that his pack was missing. So was one of our 'guards' – Old Ali. At one of our stops in the darkness Peter had taken off his pack together with all the other gear he was carrying, and had been too weary to realize its loss when we moved on.

Our predicament, if it were possible, had worsened. Out of radio contact and with the bulk of our money gone, we were completely exposed.

'But we're not up the creek yet,' I told everyone. 'Somehow we'll get back the gold, and I've still got three hundred sovereigns in my belt. A reserve. So try to look unconcerned. Meantime we must make a pretence of sending and receiving signals. These men' – the village had sent a fresh lot of villains to guard us – 'must be given no idea that we are out of touch with Italy. If they cotton on to that, then we are really done for.'

We named the place Three House Base. They were not houses, but there were three of them.

Zechir was sent back to Grama with a mule to find the batteries and charging motor. During the days he was gone we kept up a pantomime – ciphering, deciphering, tapping out meaningless messages from a transmitter that could not transmit. One of the new 'guards' eyed the process with great interest and made some enquiry of Cela. The man had apparently served in the Albanian Army and was not altogether a fool.

Cela looked frightened. Fear always made him smile; now the gold and the silver were dazzling. 'He wants to know how you can transmit and receive without batteries?'

Peter Rous stepped in. 'Emergency pack,' he stated, tapping a small panel in the transmitter. 'Modern invention. Very useful.' The guard seemed satisfied.

After four days little Zechir returned triumphant with batteries and charging motor. Now we had no petrol. But Zechir was not put out. 'I will get some,' he said.

We watched through our field glasses while he stepped out on the road, stopped a German truck, and held out a few eggs. The driver climbed down, filled Zechir's can from his fuel tank, took the eggs and drove on. An hour later, we were back on the air.

Our first signal was an urgent request for medicine. Peter Rous had been taken seriously ill; he had a temperature of 103 and was drifting in and out of delirium. I asked that a Spitfire should be sent to make a free drop on our plateau by daylight – it was a large expanse of grassland with no peaks in the immediate neighbourhood – and I gave our exact map reference point. I thought of Ken Gatward, and wished he were around to do the job; it would have been done accurately and without fuss.

The answer came back: yes, a Spitfire would be sent, but we must spread out a large white cross on the ground to mark the exact place for the drop.

I suppose it was natural for the staff in Bari to think that to make a white cross we only had to pull the sheets off our beds. Large enough for a pilot to spot; they had not imagined our condition; not considered that we had nothing white about us, and nothing we could lay our hands on. Peter lay sweating and muttering under a thick white blanket, but it would have been too small to cut up into a cross. The upshot was no plane, no drop, and no medicine. Peter had to make do with Crane's aspirin tablets. His temperature, which had risen to 104.5, began slowly to fall.

HQ seemed to be possessed with a madness of insensitivity. No sooner had we been told that a plane could not find us without a white cross, than a Spitfire flew the length of Dukati valley, only a few hundred yards from our plateau, shooting up whoever and whatever it saw. It killed a couple of peasants who were standing by the roadside, and it hit and left in flames one of the Dukati farm trucks. The driver of this too was killed. It did not improve our relations with the village.

A further lunacy was the slow procedure of the Bari radio operator. The man should have known that we were on the run, that our batteries were probably failing; but instead of rattling out his important messages he wasted precious minutes over procedure, telling Crane to change frequencies. The result was that we received only one message – that we should stand by for a sortie at Sea View on 14 March. Then our batteries were exhausted and we could hear Bari no more. What arms they were sending, or for whom they were intended, I had no idea.

I was clear in my own mind, however, that they could only be given to Dukati. Arms could not be delivered to the 5th Brigade except by air, and if Dukati were to play their part in 'Operation Underdone' they must be provided with the means to do so. Which came first, the withdrawal of the Germans or the outbreak of civil war, was a gamble that had to be taken.

The elders were delighted and promised to have mule teams standing by at Sea View on the 14th so that all material could be carried away immediately and hidden in the mountain. They would also send mules to Three House Base to carry our heavy radio equipment back once again to Sea View. I was reluctant to leave Peter Rous, but he was getting stronger every day, and he had Corporal Davies, his own radio operator, to look after him; I felt I had to be at Sea View to make sure nothing went wrong. On the 12th, four RAF fighters strafed the Dukati road. They only succeeded in wounding one Albanian who was too slow to throw himself on the ground. It did not make us any more popular with the locals.

Before dawn on the morning of the 13th, just as the mules were loaded up and we were about to leave, Morat gave me a letter he had been handed during the night. When I asked who had given it to him, he shrugged and turned away. The letter read:

12 Mars 1944

Sear Major

We had wished and wish also to meet as soon as possible. You jour selve proposed befor some time ago to have a meeting with the presentative of the Shtob of this area.

287

We called you for this meeting but you did not come, because of the reason You replyd in the letter.

We don't believe that the meeting is only in our interest but in the interest of both parts because we are fighting the same anamy; therefore we ask that the meeting showld be as soon as possible. It is necessary to sea each other and not by writting.

We propposse that You come at gumenica with date 20/III/944.

Yours sincerely,

Komisari Brigades V-te   Komandanti Brigades V-te
(Hysni Kapo)   (Shefqet Peci)

Dated the 12th and delivered into our base the same night, it showed that Partisan communications were indeed remarkable. I had no means of sending a letter back to them, but I resolved that I would be in Gumenica on the 20th.

It had been raining for days and the river was in spate, but we struggled across and were far up Dukati mountain when light broke.

The remaining days of my mission are best told by my pocket diary, supplemented with extracts from a long report that I wrote later.

March 13: Arrived at a shepherd's hut 17:00 hours and taken in. They thrashed their small daughter. I could not interfere. I was their guest.

March 14: On to Sea View. Advance party of Young and Bowkett living in difficult conditions. All blankets and coverings stolen by the shepherds. Large Italian party arrives – almost all from Infante's staff in Greece.
Flashed but no sortie.

March 15: Discover cached petrol also stolen. Now we must buy back our own petrol to charge batteries.

(Later Comment from HQ Report: The Italian officers made a lamentable impression on me. Many were young and fit, but took it for granted that the soldiers should carry their packs. They refused to work – would not even walk to a cache a few hours away and collect some tins. They took everything we did for them as a matter of course. The soldiers, in contrast, were willing, cheerful and hard-working. They clearly hated their officers. If this is how the Italian Army was officered in North Africa, no wonder they suffered such defeats.)

March 15 (cont.): Conditions perfect.
   Flashed — but no sortie.

March 16: Received signal saying boat did come last night. It must have stood far out, for we were all looking for it. Rain and high wind.

March 17: Sergeant Kukich can get no contact with his own OSS base in Bari. Bowkett at last makes contact at 12:30 hours. No messages for us. Fleas and lice do not improve morale.

March 18: Bowkett makes radio contact at 12:00, but unable finish schedule owing to flat batteries and pompous procedure of Bari operator. Kukich makes contact with American HQ at 2:30 — No signal for us.
   Flashed — but no sortie.
   I can wait no longer. I must be at Gumenica on the 20th to meet the Partisans.

March 19: Left Sea View early and crossed mountain. Snow crisp and firm. Crossed road and forded river after dark. Back at Three House Base on Trajas plateau. Peter greatly recovered — but v. bad news. All the gold has once again been stolen, and all our guards have disappeared. Gold was taken from under his head as he slept. Lucky for him and Davies that they did not wake up. They would have been murdered. We are now left with only what is in our pockets — not much.

March 20: To Gumenica — a long day's march. Peter strong enough to come with me and anxious not be left behind. Arrived nightfall to face savage recriminations.

(Later Comment from HQ Report: The 5th Brigade had taken a hammering, and the talks were bitterly acrimonious. I had promised help, but none had come etc. etc. I explained how the Vuno operation had been prepared, but prevented by the German action. Since then, the whole Vuno area was devoid of Partisans, the 5th Brigade was being hunted through the mountains, perpetually moving, and I myself had been on the run. Peci and Besnik were scornful. 'We are wounded. Our feet are frostbitten. If you provide us with arms, we will go on fighting. Without arms we shall soon cease to exist.'

We had been talking a mixture of French and Italian. As tempers rose I saw Peci start to loosen his revolver from its holster. Something had to be done, and quickly. I stood up and said, *'Jusqu'a ce moment nous avons parlé en français et italien. Adesso voglio parlare albanesi — shqiptar.'*

They were incredulous. Had I been able to speak their language all along? Had I understood all their private conversations?

I delivered myself of the only Albanian I knew.

'Kotzamitzi rana vorbet. Plaku shkuli komett.'

There was a moment of astonishment, then they broke into roars of laughter. The crisis had passed — thanks to Fanny Hazluck.)

> *March 21: Left Peter with the Partisans. They were reassured, he was delighted. All he needed now was a radio operator. I promised to send Davies to him at once.*

(Later Comment from HQ Report: Peter was a strong man. He had been delirious ten days before. Now he marched off through the rain with the bedraggled remnants of the 5th Brigade, a head and shoulders taller than any of them, and speaking not a word of any tongue but his mother English.)

> *March 21 (cont.): Was escorted through Partisan country, but completed the last few hours of march alone. Nearing the plateau of Trajas, came under fire.*

(Later Comment from HQ Report: A dozen or more rifle shots came from above, deliberately aimed, kicking up the stones at my feet. I ducked behind a big rock and lay low for half an hour. The firing stopped, but the message was clear: Do not go visiting the Partisans.)

> *March 22: Sent off Corporal Davies to join Peter. Could find only three litres of petrol for him. Hope to God he catches up with the Brigade and manages to make radio contact, or both he and Peter will be in ugly position.*

No fun being shot at by supposed friends so decide leave Three Houses and cross back into Dukati mountain – to bivouac high above Cela's house. A good position, but cramped for six men. Named it Bothy Base. News that not one, but TWO, sorties have arrived at Sea View.

March 23: Left Bothy and climbed over to Sea View.

(Later Comment from HQ Report: There had indeed been two sorties – ten tons of food and ammunition that we had requested weeks ago, and five tons of clothing we had not asked for and could not dispose of. The uniforms could not be conveyed to the Partisans through Ballist territory, and no one in Dukati could walk about in a British greatcoat. Who in God's name had sent them? And why?)

March 24: Back over mountain to Bothy. Mule tracks hidden in deep snow. Blizzard. Arrived Bothy very tired. Told Skender Muco had arrived in Cela's house and wished to see me. Go down, but on arrival too weary to talk.

March 25: Usual inconclusive argument with Muco. Climbed back up to Bothy. Dead tired. Munzi talks of home in Genova and of girl he loves. Could not sleep.

(Later Comment from HQ Report: I never saw Muco again. Soon afterwards he was ambushed and killed, though I never learned if it was by Partisans or Germans. I hope he met a quick death.)

March 26: Signal from Bari agreeing I come out and make personal report (this in reply to mine saying position had become untenable). Told to stand by for sortie. No date given, and radio contact all to hell through lack of petrol. Further signal, promoting Crane to Lance Sergeant. Trust Jim – he had chevrons ready waiting in his pack.

March 27: No reply to my urgent signals, so decide to cross over to Sea View and await sortie. Snow worse. Four feet everywhere, and deeper in drifts. Ice on summit.
On the seaward side meet long train of women struggling uphill with heavy ammunition boxes on their backs. (Dukati trying to hide stores before next German drive.) Cela begs me

not to interfere with immemorial customs. Mules could not get through deep snow – women could.

Flashed but no sortie.

March 28: Sorting out boxes of ammunition and uniforms. Fifteen tons of confusion in a dark cave.

Flashed – but no sortie.

March 29: Continued sorting stores and ammo. Several machine guns – but too heavy even for women to carry through snow.

Flashed, but no sortie.

March 30: Learnt that boat HAD come previous night, but to wrong beach. HQ confused to the last.

That is the last entry in the diary.

Conditions were perfect that night. I lay out on the cliff above the creek signalling out to sea – but no boat came. I did not have the strength to climb back to the cave, so I slept out on the headland in the rain.

In the dawn I woke up vomiting. The beach, thirty or forty feet below me, looked sheltered and inviting. I crawled down to it. The sand was soft as a bed. The rain did not bother me. I lay down in the sand and covered myself with a groundsheet.

Through my sleep I could hear Crane's voice. 'Are you all right down there, sir?' He was standing on the low cliff looking down on me.

I wished he would not disturb me. I wished he would go away. 'Yes, I'm perfectly all right.'

'Don't you want to move back to the cave?'

I was very content where I was, so I told him, 'No. Leave me alone. I want to sleep.'

We must all of us have been a bit off our heads, even Jim Crane, because that is what he did for a long time. Then he came back with two of the others and they half dragged, half carried me into a little grotto near the beach. I lay half-conscious in the grotto for three days while Jim nursed me like a mother.

A boat did come at last on the night of the 3rd; HQ even sent it to the right place. I remember nothing of that night – what boat it was, how I got on board, or where we landed: Bari, I guess. What I do remember clearly is next morning sitting alone in the back of an Army truck (perhaps it was an ambulance) being driven to hospital.

I could not believe what I saw going on round me; the world was full of cheerful ordinary people. The driver was joking with his mate; when I looked out through the flap at the back of the truck, the streets were full of men in Allied uniforms; all cheerful, all confident, all going the same way. Not one of them was tainted with fear; not one of them would undergo a nightmare transformation before my eyes and turn into the enemy. They were my friends, every one of them.

The joy to be back amongst my own was so great that it was almost pain. I jolted along in the back of the truck sobbing with happiness.

CHAPTER 20

I HAD JAUNDICE AND MALARIA; nothing serious, but sufficient to lay me flat for several weeks; time enough to lie and contemplate the total failure of my mission.

I remember a welcome visit from Billy MacLean and David Smiley – just leaving for their second Albanian mission – and some less welcome visits from our HQ staff.

'"Operation Underdone"?' enquired the young staff major. 'Oh, "Underdone" was dropped weeks ago. Didn't you know?'

If I had had the strength to get out of bed, I would have killed him with my bare hands.

HQ brought other news that put me into great anxiety; there had been no radio contact with any of my team since I had returned to Italy. There were only two possible reasons for their silence, both of them agonizing to contemplate: either they were once again being hunted – or they had been caught.

The hospital was a modern Italian building, well designed as a civilian hospital but altogether too small for the needs of the 8th Army. The staff had no time to keep strict ward discipline, and when I grew stronger I was allowed to paddle around. I wandered downstairs one day and followed the signs 'To the Operating Theatre'.

There had been a stream of ambulances arriving through the night, and the corridors on the ground floor were lined with stretcher cases awaiting attention. Most of the men that day were Ghurkas – possibly the same men who had landed with me from the transport a few months back. Their faces were olive green with shock and pain, but they made no sound of complaint.

I walked along till I came to the 'turn-around' outside two operating theatres. The circular space was now taken up with ordinary bed cases; some men were asleep, some reading, some smoking, some sitting on each other's beds playing draughts or chess. The doors of the operating theatres stood wide open and I could see the surgeons working with frantic concentration. The twin theatres were like slaughter houses, the floors awash with blood; one of the surgeons was operating in his bare feet. And a few feet away the soldiers wrote letters, chatted and smoked, as though it were the most normal scene in the world, as though they were in their own homes and Aunt Mary was in the kitchen next door trimming a rabbit for the Sunday stew.

News came to me that Mason-Mac had left Gibraltar and was now in Italy, in charge of Allied Military Government. I got a message off to him, and his reply was immediate: as soon as I was well enough to move, he would have me flown over to Naples for convalescence. The change in my fortunes was so violent that it made me feel giddy.

My old master had brought John Perry with him from Gibraltar; they were established, together with his senior staff, in a handsome villa on the outskirts of Naples. From my bedroom window I looked southwards across the great sweep of the bay to Vesuvius; I had missed the eruption by a week or so, but there was still a dense plume of vapour rising into the air from the summit of the volcano.

I was glad indeed to see Mason-Mac, and I could tell that the pleasure was mutual. I had never thought male tigers to be fatherly or affectionate, but Mason-Mac did show me great affection, though often it was only to growl and walk away twitching his tail. For me, to be with him again was an assurance that life was built on sound foundations, that a world of sanity did exist, that it was not a perpetually dissolving nightmare of betrayal and brutality, of dependence on a fragile radio link with a Headquarters that was far from dependable.

Mason-Mac's new parish was extensive and complex. He had no military command, but he was responsible for the administration of the whole of Italy behind the fighting lines – for everything from the price of bread to the abdication of the King. Italian politics were a potential minefield. As soon as Rome was liberated, the Italian people had to be allowed to choose the government they wanted; at the same time the country could not be allowed to slide into uncontrollable confusion while General Alexander and his armies fought their way slowly north. There were plenty of Italians – Marshal Badoglio, Count Sforza, Benedetto Croce, and Ivanoe Bonomi – already stirring the political pot, not out of mischief or malice but out of genuine differences. For all their sincerity I suspect there might have been a dash of malice, like a spoonful of paprika, in the cauldron.

In all these manoeuvrings, Mason-Mac had a vital part to play, but was always hampered by an ill-conceived chain of command. He had on his staff two Political Advisers – Harold Caccia from the Foreign Office and Sam Reber from the State Department. He could seek advice from the British High Commissioner in Italy, Sir Noel Charles – an immensely charming, immensely handsome, all-too-typical product of the Foreign Office. The only advice that it would have been wise to take from Sir Noel was the name of the best shirtmaker in Jermyn Street. Harold Macmillan was also in Italy with his American opposite number, Bob Murphy. But Mason-Mac had no direct access to either of these two; he had to report to the Supreme Commander who was still in North Africa, and it was from Eisenhower that he received his indirect directives.

I am driven to describe this political cat's cradle because it had a bearing in a few weeks' time on what happened to me – and an even greater bearing on what happened to Mason-Mac.

For a few weeks I led a divided life. Part of me was in Naples, eating, sleeping, swimming, watching the landing craft as they plied to and from the desperate beachhead at Anzio; part of me had never left Albania. I was haunted by the thought of the companions I had left there and from whom there was no sound.

I had the chance of a talk with Harold Macmillan who came to lunch one day. I told him of the dilemma of Liaison Officers like myself whose task was to urge ignorant Balkan peasants into attacking the enemy, but knowing perfectly well the price those peasants would pay in death and the destruction of their villages.

He listened to me, then his moustache twitched in a pussycat smile. 'Yes, very painful. But it has to be done. You and your like are at present holding down between forty and fifty German divisions. Better those divisions are in the Balkans than on the Western Front.'

Field Marshal Alexander came too. He had a striking air of courtesy and calm – a deliberately self-imposed calm, I thought. He was fighting several battles at the same time, but refused to let anything rattle him. I remember the neat deliberation with which he straightened the vent of his uniform whenever he got out of his car or stood up from a chair.

Suddenly, two thirds of the way through May, there came a signal for me telling me to return at once to Bari: Sea View had come back on the air. I flew straight back to Bari and made preparations to get the mission out. I sent a Top Priority signal: 'Personal from Quayle. Definitely repeat definitely coming for you tonight. Stand by 20:00 hours.' They ought to get that during the afternoon radio schedule. It would cheer them.

The old *Sea Maid* had taken seven hours to cross the Adriatic; the young Italian captain of the MAS expected to be across in an hour and a half. I made sure that we had two Carley Floats on board, and around six in the evening we thundered off into the darkness. Two hours later, we were rolling in the darkness off the Albanian coast, the familiar black mountains towering overhead.

'You're sure this is the place?' I asked.

The Italian skipper was quite sure.

'Can't you come a bit closer?'

'No,' he replied. 'It's impossible. I cannot risk my ship.'

He did creep in a little closer under urging, but there was no signal from the coast. Then, out of the thick darkness, I saw a feeble flicker – their torch battery must be flat, I thought – but it was the right signal. We replied, and back came the feeble response. We started to crawl towards the land. It took for ever. 'Ahead'. 'Stop'. And every time the tinkle from the engine room, 'Ahead' – tinkle tinkle. 'Stop' – tinkle tinkle.

Half a mile off the coast, the captain said, 'I will go no closer.'

'There are no rocks,' I assured him.

'I cannot be certain. We will wait for you here.'

There was nothing for it. I deflated one of the Carley Floats, threw it into the other, and climbed down.

'I shall be gone two hours,' I called. 'So make sure you don't move your position.'

I was still well off the land when I smelt the wood smoke from the fire they must have made – acrid, nostalgic. Then I was in the dogleg creek; I turned the corner, and there were the flames leaping up in the same way as they had the night I landed, the dark figures silhouetted against them.

My friends were in bad shape. All but one had grown long beards; only Jim Crane was clean-shaven. Through all their ordeals he had kept a soldier's pride in his appearance.

Kukich, the American radio operator, was off his head; he stalked about the beach with a loaded revolver in his hand threatening to shoot anyone who tried to steal his boots. I promised him that he would soon be back in Italy and would have as many new boots as he could wear or string round his neck. He half believed me, but went on muttering to himself, threatening with his revolver anyone who came near him.

Munzi, dear Munzi, looked like Ben Gunn from *Treasure Island*. His clothes were torn and muddy and his beard was a tangled mat, but the same wise, gentle eyes twinkled through his thick-lensed glasses; they were full of tears.

In a huddle, slightly apart from the main group, stood half a dozen scarecrow Italian soldiers. Munzi asked if it would be possible to take them.

'Of course,' I said. 'Of course we'll take them.'

It was urgent to get Munzi out to the MAS to assure his compatriots that it was safe to bring the boat into the bay. It was urgent too to get Kukich off the beach before he killed someone.

By a miracle our old collapsible boat had not been found by the Germans. It was easier to handle than the Carleys, so I sent Munzi off in it with Kukich and four of the Italians. I warned him that the MAS might have drifted northwards in the freshening wind, but I was sure they would find it easily. Those of us left on the beach – Crane, Cela, Morat, Zechir and the other remaining Italians stayed by the fire and waited for the arrival of the MAS.

They had had a rough time, they told me. The Germans had placed posts all along the valley of Dukati, and a second line on the summit of the mountain. When all escape routes were blocked, a battalion had driven along the coast combing the ground as they went. Shepherds had been killed, their flocks driven off. The mission had lived in holes, eating little, moving every night to a different hiding place. Once they had lain in a swamp and watched a German patrol beating the bushes all around them. Dukati, said Cela, was no longer safe for any Allied mission. We would be betrayed immediately.

I looked at my watch; Munzi had been gone an hour. And now I discovered that in the confusion Kukich had taken with him the only working radio transmitter. If we were left behind, we should be not only without clothes, food or money, but without any communication whatever. The wind was rising, beginning to blow strong from the south. We must at all costs find the MAS.

Around midnight we launched the two Carleys, half a dozen of us in each – uncomfortable, but perhaps not too dangerous. We kept the floats fastened together with a long warp so that we formed a giant cuff link; it saved us from becoming separated, but made the floats uncontrollable. Crane kept up a constant flashing; if a German patrol spotted us – too bad.

From the darkness there was no reply.

I told Jim to try signalling to the north. 'They've drifted. They must have drifted a long way.'

Again he flashed.

At last, very faint and distant, there seemed to be a reply. Crane signalled, 'Come and fetch us'. But since the floats were spinning round, he was signalling to every point of the compass. We gave up flashing and settled down to bail and paddle for our lives. Half an hour had gone by and our strength was ebbing when there was the ship right ahead of us in the murk, rolling almost on her beam ends in the waves. A line was heaved, and a moment later we were hauled aboard gasping and panting.

Munzi was sobbing and incoherent. 'I told them it was safe. They wouldn't believe me . . . Italians . . . my own people.' His head rolled from side to side in agony, grief. 'We waited two hours. Two hours. They said you must be drowned. They were going without you . . . And I knew you had no radio . . . I begged them . . . I went down on my knees to them . . .'

The engine room telegraph rang, and we began to move. Forty knots the thing went, skimming and bouncing over the waves. An hour and a half later we landed in Brindisi.

I left my friends in hospital to be deloused and debriefed, and flew back to Naples where Mason-Mac was waiting for my return. I told him that Number 1 Special Force had asked me to go into northern Italy to work with a large group of Partisans, and that my own HQ wanted me to go back into Albania. What was I to do?

He thought over his reply for quite a while. 'I don't know what more you're trying to prove,' he said at last. 'Stop running about in the mountains. There are others who can do that. Stay here on my staff and help me with this impossible job. You'll be a damn sight more use doing that, I promise you.'

I took little persuading. I had recovered my health, but I doubted if I had the will and mental energy to start all over again in the north of Italy. I knew for sure that I would never again put myself at the mercy of the Albanian Section in Bari.

I did a lot of flying in the next few weeks. I was in Rome the night the 5th Army broke through the last German defences and came pouring in. I think I must have gone with Harold Caccia and Sam Reber, who had the task of organizing a representative gathering to choose an Italian government. They drove round the dark streets of Rome, knocking on the front doors of politicians who had prudently gone to ground through the long night of Fascism.

Next morning General Mark Clark himself entered Rome. He raced round the city in his jeep, stopping at all the vantage points where the press photographers, alerted and ready, were awaiting him. General Clark was not a man to be modest about his victories. He chose the most famous steps, the most beautiful fountains in the city as the background for his photographs.

On 8 June I flew to Rome again, this time escorting Ivanoe Bonomi and Benedetto Croce. A handful of their colleagues came to see them off at Naples airport, and their voices sounded in my ears like so many London pigeons. *'Auguri,'* they cooed. *'Auguri . . . auguri.'*

The political meeting was held in the ballroom of the Grand Hotel; representatives of five political parties had been gathered together with instructions to try and form a government, and to decide under whom they would serve. It was Winston Churchill's wish, emphatically stated and passed through the laborious chain of command, that he would be satisfied with no one else as Prime Minister of Italy but Marshal Badoglio, who had signed the armistice and had carried out his word honestly and honourably.

All day long the politicians conferred, while a growing crowd of journalists gathered outside the Grand Hotel. It was late afternoon when the politicians came out at last and announced to the world that they could form a government – but not under Badoglio: only under the premiership of Bonomi.

Mason-Mac was waiting in his suite at the Grand Hotel. Beside my useless self he had with him Harold Caccia and Sam Reber. At once he was besieged; journalists were pushing into the foyer of the hotel and down the corridor clamouring for him to make an announcement before the last editions of the evening papers went to press.

Mason-Mac was trapped. If he announced that the Allies refused to accept Bonomi, it would appear to the Italian people that although we had liberated them we were nothing but another totalitarian régime, imposing our will on the country. If he did not insist on Badoglio, then he incurred the wrath of Winston Churchill.

Harold Caccia begged him to stall, to try and communicate with London. There was no time; there were no fast communications with either London or Washington, and an answer could not be delayed. Mason-Mac took the decision; he accepted the wishes of the day-long meeting and announced that the first Prime Minister of Italy would be Ivanoe Bonomi.

Mason-Mac was not in good health; his spinal paralysis had advanced and he was often in pain. In the days of his full mental agility I do not think the old tiger would have let himself be trapped in such a cage. He was well aware of the thunderbolt that would be hurled at him from Downing Street. He could only laugh wryly.

I told him I had to leave him and go back to Bari for a few days; I had business there to finish.

'How long will you be gone?'

'A week. Not more.'

'You may find me gone when you come back. Winston doesn't waste time. If he demands my head on a platter – and I'm sure he will – there'll be no hanging about.' He saw me starting to protest, and went on, 'So, as I say, if you find me gone when you come back from Bari, remember this. You are to stay and to hold the hand of my Number Two – Ellery Stone. He's an American and a good one, but he's going to need help – especially from the British. There's a tendency among Americans to think that we are all conniving bastards, so it's important that he has a British officer close to him who can prove that there are exceptions. Understood?'

'Yes, sir.'

'All right. Off you go.'

My first day back in Bari I walked into the HQ mess and saw, lunching there, a man I was unlikely to forget – a tall, handsome man with the head of an ancient hero. It was the American captain who would not bring his trawler into Grama Bay.

I turned to the mess sergeant. 'That big man over there, at the long table. Who is he?'

The sergeant was surprised at my ignorance. 'Don't you know, sir? That's Sterling Hayden, the movie star.'

I turned and left the room. I had no desire for further acquaintance with Mr Hayden.

I was kept busy in Bari for longer than I had expected: a commando was preparing a raid on the big guns protecting Valona harbour and needed all the local information they could get; more important to me was the future of my friends that had to be resolved.

Morat and Zechir could not cope with life in Italy and begged to be sent home. They were duly landed back at Sea View, but I doubt if they could have lived long; within weeks civil war was raging and the Partisans saw to it that few men were left alive in Dukati.

Cela, who had supported us with such courage through every adversity, was in despair for his family but knew that he could never return to Albania. Work had to be found for him in Italy.

Jim Crane went back to the Royal Regiment of Artillery proudly wearing his three stripes.

That left Munzi, for whom I had a particular responsibility and affection. I recommended him for an immediate Italian decoration, and he received it. But outward symbols meant little to Munzi; he thought only of trying to reach his beloved girl in Genova, now under heavy Allied bombardment. It struck me that he could be of great use on Mason-Mac's staff, and that this would be the best way that he could now serve his country. He was a lawyer, able, wise, dependable; he could be trusted by both sides in any friction between the Allies and his own countrymen. I took him with me when I flew back to Naples.

I was too late; Mason-Mac was already gone, recalled to London. There was no likelihood of his return.

Munzi went his way and was absorbed, wasted, in the Italian Army. I joined Admiral Stone's staff as Mason-Mac had wished. Before taking up my duties I asked for, and was granted, two weeks' leave in England.

The two short weeks taught me a lot about my country. Spread out before me was the devastation of London, the unimaginable tons of masonry that had come blazing and crashing to the ground. Less obvious, but almost tangible, was the stubborn courage of the people in every city of the land who had endured the storm, and held fast. Until America was drawn into the battle, they had had no hope of winning the war; but they had held on, and held on, and never for a moment contemplated the possibility of defeat. Now they were shabby, ill-fed and tired, but bonded together in the crucible.

The leave taught me a lot about myself as well. During the ten years between leaving school and joining the Army, I had been little more than a young colt, not always happy but happy even in unhappiness, galloping round the meadow in exuberance. Yet underneath the coltishness there had always been a strong purpose, or a hope, or a dream, that I would one day find my place in the great Art that had beckoned to me. With the outbreak of war I had simply closed my mind to any such purpose; I had refused to contemplate that there could be a future when the war was over. It had not been hard to do, and it had nothing to do with being virtuous; if the world had to go through the greatest, most dreadful convulsion that had ever overtaken the human race, then I was glad I was alive to experience it. I had wanted to be part of the flood, not a spectator standing on the bank.

But now indeed the war was coming to an end; there would be a future. With that realization all my hopes came leaping out of their underground confinement. The war, catastrophic as it had been — as it continued to be — was only a long incident in my own journey through life. Like Odysseus I had banished Ithaca from my mind only because I thought I could never arrive there; now I could glimpse Ithaca through the ragged tail of the storm, and to reach it became a hunger.

I spent a lot of time with E. She had done me the greatest of many loving services; she had kept in touch with Dot through the years, and a genuine friendship had sprung up between them. Without it, the story could have had a different ending.

I saw Dot, but the situation was unchanged: she liked me, she was fond of me – but that was all. Never mind. I had waited a long time and I could wait a while longer.

I went down to the country to see Mason-Mac. He was frail and walked with difficulty, but he was full of the old tigerish spirit. He had had a painful meeting with the Prime Minister in which neither had yielded an inch. It was obvious that his active military career was at an end. Now he was waiting for an exploratory operation by Hugh Cairns to determine the cause of the paralysis that threatened the whole of his spine; meantime he was full of plans to enter politics and take his revenge on Churchill by standing against him in the first postwar election. He laughed as he said it, but I knew he was only half joking.

One day I ran into Harry Butcher, Ike's Naval Aide, on the pavement in Piccadilly Circus. 'Hi, Tony,' he greeted me. 'Great to see you. What luck. You're the very man I'm looking for.'

'Me? Why?'

To my horror, standing on the pavement outside the London Pavilion, he then and there told me of a vast airborne operation that was afoot. 'It could shorten the war by a year,' he declared to anyone within earshot. 'It'll be an Anglo-American-Polish operation. One hell of a big one. And it will be in the Low Countries.'

I was flabbergasted by his lack of security – though I suppose Piccadilly Circus is as secure a place as many others for the revelation of vital military secrets.

'But how can I be of use?' I asked.

'You're a parachutist,' he said, 'and you have your head screwed on. A lot of journalists are going to be jumping with this expedition, and we need someone to nurse them through the battle and see that the press and the fighting forces don't get in each other's way. You'd do it wonderfully. What d'you say?'

He did not wait for an answer, but pulled a notebook out of his pocket and wrote down an address at the War Office where I should report that afternoon. Then he waved me a cheery goodbye, and plunged into Scotts for what was no doubt going to be a very good and expensive lunch.

I did not go to the War Office, and I did not drop with the forces at Arnhem. I went quietly back to Rome and saw the rest of the war out there. Ithaca had become my goal.

Before flying off, I bought Dot a Georgian pendant and had it sent round to the theatre where she was playing. It was a pretty thing, but it fell far short of the penguin pebble I had hoped to nudge towards her feet.

PART 4

A Time
of Peace

3 October, 1989

On 3 August 1989, in the middle of rehearsing a play, I was told by an eminent Harley Street specialist that I had an inoperable cancer of the liver, that I might live another six months, but probably no more than two. I must certainly resign from the play as I would soon be feeling too ill to give much of a performance. I did so reluctantly, knowing I had left the producers in the lurch. I faced leaving life itself with even greater reluctance. Most grievous of all was that I must leave Dot to fend for herself; we were neither of us so childish as to think we could avoid death and separation, but I had always hoped that it might be she who went first while I was still active and able to take care of her.

Of less concern – though urgent enough – was how to complete this book. I had not yet done with the war years – not started on the last forty years of my life. I had no revelations to make, no scandals to lay bear, but with all my heart I wanted to give thanks for my family, for the love and friendship with which I have been surrounded, for the many chances I have had to reach out – like the figure in Leonardo's engraving – and touch the encircling ring of my own limitations.

I was fortunate enough to be led to another Harley Street doctor, in many ways as orthodox as the first, but a man of great humanity and of a positive outlook. His prognosis was not necessarily any different from the first, but his interest did not end with courtesy and commiseration at the door of the consulting room; instead, he has given me a strict régime that may delay the cancer – and he makes me believe that it will. He has also given me the conviction that the mind plays a crucial part in the fight, and that the mind can conquer.

If I had any inkling of the timetable, I would have given less space to the earlier part of my life and more to the remaining, wonderfully rich, forty years. But perhaps that too, like everything in my life, has happened for the best. Anyone's early stages are always the most interesting because that is when the character is being formed, when every day brings a new influence, a different awareness of the world. After thirty-four the character does not change: the plant has drawn its nurture from the soil and the changing climate; now it blossoms according to its kind, and it is difficult for me to write about my own flowering – such as it has been.

Feebleness of mind and body are the handicaps; it will be a battle between what to keep and what to cast away. But compression may be more readable than verbosity, and many autobiographies lose their way towards the end – the path overgrown with triviality. I hope that the timetable may prevent that from happening to me.

CHAPTER 21

WALK THROUGH THE LOOKING GLASS one way, and you are at war; walk the other way, and you are at peace. 'Ge-dink – ge-donk' went the green baize doors at Abberley, impervious to those who pushed through them: only a step between the 'private side' and the 'boys' side', between war and peace – both worlds engrossing while they existed, then both gone like a dream. My mind shuttered off the war years as if they had never happened. I was left with only a rage against the long line of bureaucrats and politicians – blinkered, smug, supine – who had contributed to the making of this unnecessary war. It is a rage that has grown with the years.

London for all its scars, its killed and wounded, was the same at heart. There were no bus conductors – they were all in the Forces – but they had been replaced by merry little Cockney 'Clippies'. Theatres were full; the Old Vic had moved back to London from Burnley and was installed at the New under the joint directorship of Ralph and Larry. There was a third member of the Triumvirate but, like Lepidus, he did not count for very much. Hugh (Binkie) Beaumont ruled his kingdom of make-believe from Shaftesbury Avenue; he had become very powerful, controlling a large part of the West End theatre. (Until now it has seemed an error of taste to call him 'Binkie' against the background of war, but that was his familiar and famous name, and from now on I shall call him nothing else.)

Tony and Judy Guthrie gave me a loving welcome home; what was more, Tony gave me a job – Jack Absolute in *The Rivals* with Edith Evans – and pressed me to come and live in their attic till I found somewhere more permanent. I accepted happily. Their home was unchanged – there was a new cat who even looked like Myrtle and followed Myrtle's kitten ritual – and they themselves were little altered – Tony a shade older and more acerbic, Judy a little more careworn and addicted to a nip of whisky.

I asked Tony why he had given up control of the Old Vic. He drew a loud breath in through his nose.

'Ten years was enough. I led the Vic out into the wilderness when the theatre was bombed. I'm not the right man to bring it back to London again. It should be in younger hands. Actors whom the public want to see. Besides – I'm tired.'

I found my friends not greatly changed, though both of them looked a bit older and more careworn. The first night that I had supper with them in the old familiar kitchen, I looked up and noticed that the clothes rack had been removed. 'Oh, look,' I said. 'It's gone.' Tony's reply was rather tart; 'Yes,' he said. 'We are not barbarians, you know. We also have a refrigerator.'

I felt that life was becoming almost too much of an effort for Judy to keep up with him. She had hitched her wagon to such an incandescent, restless star; she was becoming worn out in the effort to keep up. She was having a few more nips of the whisky than before the war, and she was still working like a slave in the house with little time to do any writing of her own. She had, as far as I could see, exactly the same clothes that she had worn before the war broke out six years ago.

She and I were alone in their living room on the afternoon of the opening night at the Criterion. Judy was wearing an old cotton shift and cleaning the floor with a long-handled mop and soapy water – the perpetual cigarette stuck in the corner of her mouth. I asked her if she was not going to begin to get ready for the evening's performance.

'Oh, yes,' she replied. 'But there's plenty of time for that.'

'What are you going to wear?' I asked.

'Wear?' She stopped and pushed a stray lock of her black hair. 'Probably the same dress that I've worn to every first night I've been to. You know the one. A black and gold affair.'

'Oh?' I said. 'I thought perhaps you might have bought a new dress by now.'

She looked at me with an almost bitter ruthfulness. 'A new dress?' She echoed. 'What sort of a life do you think any wife of Tony would have who bought herself a new dress?' She turned away and went on with her mopping.

She loved Tony dearly, and it was the only time in the years of our friendship that I ever heard her utter one single word that could be taken as criticism.

I could not decide what to do with my own life. I knew I belonged in the theatre and that I had a current of energy in me: but how to release it? Where to direct it? During six years of war I had not thought once of Larry's words. For heaven's sake, what did 'personality' matter to a soldier? Nothing had mattered but doing the job in hand. But now I was back in a profession where self-evaluation mattered greatly; an actor could spend years trying to struggle up the wrong mountain. It was the Himalayas that I wanted to climb – always had been: I might never scale the greatest peaks, but neither would I be content trundling up and down Snowdon. Yet perhaps Larry had been right? He could well have been.

A conversation with Lewis Casson only further confused me one night when I visited him in his dressing room.

'What are you going to do now you're out of the Army?' he asked.

'Start to be an actor again.'

He lifted his dripping face from the basin and gave a snort. 'Do you want my advice?'

'Of course.'

'Then don't.'

'Why not?'

'Because you've got the wrong face – the wrong mask. You have it in you to be a fine tragic actor – perhaps a great one. But your face will always be in your way. You will always have to play comedy and you're going to find that very frustrating.'

'What do you suggest then?'

He was towelling his face now, perhaps embarrassed at speaking so frankly. 'Stay in the theatre – but be a director, or go onto the administrative side. But don't break your heart being an actor. There. Sorry to have been so blunt.'

My novel *Eight Hours from England* (Heinemann 1945) was published and it was well enough received to make me wonder if I might not turn to writing instead of acting. But although I could write, I knew I did not have enough experience of life to be a writer: no, I was an actor. I could earn enough money as an actor to support Dot – always supposing that she would marry me: I could never do that as a writer.

I found almost the entire literary world strangely self-satisfied, as though writing a book were in itself a praiseworthy act. On the first night of J.B. Priestley's *An Inspector Calls*, I went round immediately after the curtain fell to see Ralph in his dressing room. He was still on stage, but waiting for him to come off was Jack Priestley. I congratulated him very warmly on the obvious success of the evening.

311

'Yes,' he said. 'It's a little masterpiece. I decided to do a very bold thing. I would take the principal character off the stage for the last ten minutes – and in those ten minutes I would write the most tense and dramatic scene of the entire play. Yes – a masterpiece.'

He invited me to come along that evening to a party he was giving in his apartment in the Albany. He was a very good host and as I left he came to see me to the door. 'Ralph tells me you've written a first novel,' he said. 'Well done. I hope you have a big success with it. I've just got out a novel myself.'

'Oh, really? Have you?'

'Yes. It's called *Bright Day*. You should read it. It's in quite a new style, very succinct. Very original. Get it and read it. Remember – *Bright Day*.'

My dithering and doubts began to be resolved for me.

Binkie, I'm sure at John Perry's instigation, asked me to direct a big production of *Crime and Punishment* starring John G, Edith Evans, and Peter Ustinov. It was my first step as a director – and a giant one. A huge cast and a very complicated set: as much to do with choreography and the pattern of sound as it was to do with the fundamentals of acting. And this had come about because of the little shows I got up for the troops in Gibraltar which John Perry had seen and liked, especially my production of *Noah* which had had such a surprising success. John and Edith could not agree on a director, so John Perry intervened and suggested that I do it, and they compromised on that. I had to draw on every scrap of knowledge I had ever gleaned – mostly from Tony G, but it succeeded wonderfully and ran for a long time.

One of the problems of rehearsing *Crime and Punishment* was that Edith had an excess of vitality. She was always bouncing up and down demanding this, questioning that, suggesting the other. At the same time she was always asking me how to fall – because as Madame Marmeladov she had to collapse on the floor in a dead faint. I did my best to show her how to give at the knees and let her body roll over sideways. 'Oh, that's wonderful,' she said. 'Do it again. And again. Oh, show me, show me.' I got tired of this and decided that it was she who must fall and not me. So I got the stage management to produce a couple of mattresses, and I found some expert who knew all about rolling and falling. We would spend half an hour every morning before the rest of the cast arrived in Edith practising falls. She was indefatigable; up and down she went, up and down again. But it did have the effect of knocking some of the ebullience out of her. She was a great deal quieter after her morning's work-out. *Crime and Punishment* was a big success. It led to my doing another, *The Relapse* starring Cyril Ritchard and Madge Elliott which ran for over a year.

I seemed to be turning into more of a director than an actor.

All the old friends were coming back from various theatres of war. One or two did not come back at all, but most of them did – amongst them Glen Byam Shaw limping very badly from a bayonet wound in the leg. I always thought of Glen, with his courtesies and bow ties, as one of the most tranquil and passive men I have ever met, and it was grotesque to think of him engaged in a hand-to-hand fight with some Japanese and having a bayonet pushed through his thigh. No matter – he was alive, though limping. He was about to do a production of *Antony and Cleopatra*, for Binkie – naturally – and asked me to play Enobarbus in a production with Edith Evans and Godfrey Tearle. Enobarbus may have been only a foothill, but it was a large foothill and it belonged to the right range of mountains.

Edith was an old friend by now, but I had never met Godfrey Tearle before. I found him a very agreeable companion. We had a long tour before coming into London and often I would drive with him, and he would reminisce about his days in the theatre before the war, and of when he had been the young leading man of Sir George Alexander's company at the St James's.

He told me of the punctiliousness that was demanded in those days – 1917 to be exact. Alexander sent for him one day.

'Tearle, I am told that you have been seen walking in Piccadilly in the forenoon incorrectly dressed. You wear a lounge suit and that is not the right attire for a young leading man in my company. The correct dress for a gentleman in the forenoon is a morning coat and top hat. You will have to rectify this error or I shall take it that you wish no longer to be a member of the St James's company.'

Times have indeed changed.

I think that poor Edith always hoped for a Great Romance to blossom out of this tour, but it did not; Godfrey spent his entire time running away from her. On Saturday night he would jump into his little open touring car and race away into the country where she could not find him. It must have been a sad disappointment for poor Edith.

E had returned from Dorset where she had been driving a rattling WVS tea truck round the gun sites, happy to have me, she thought, really home at last. She found a mews flat in Devonshire Close and set about building yet another nest for the two of us. I could not stop her, though I did not think it was a very good idea. It could never last for as long as she hoped. It was perfect for her, but it was only comfortable for me – and who in his early thirties wants comfort? Independence and privacy are the requisites.

I saw a certain amount of Dot. She was more friendly than she had ever been – in fact, she was enchanting – but she was still involved with some man or other. I could not tell to what extent, but I did feel that what I had thought for years to be my destiny was slipping away from me. Well – I would just have to make the best of it. As my friends had once told me, there were other fish in the sea. So there were – very pretty fish too. But after so long a time, I did not like to give up; I felt that if I did, I would be doing Dot a wrong as much as myself. For some deep-seated reason, I felt that her happiness as well as my own depended on the two of us coming together. Such an idea clearly did not possess her; she remained friendly, but distinctly distant.

Tony went off to direct a play in New York, taking Judy with him, and left the 'lodger' in charge of their home. Alec Guinness came back from driving his landing craft around the Mediterranean supporting the various landings. I had last seen him out in Italy. I asked him if he would like to come and be the lodger's lodger. He accepted it as readily as I had done, and for a month or two we led a very happy existence at the top of Old Buildings. Then Merula with her little son Matthew came back from the country, they found a house to live in, and he went off – though not before he had landed the wonderful part of Herbert Pocket in David Lean's *Great Expectations*. His film career was launched. But I did not stay roosting for long alone. Another friend came back from the war – John Kidd, the very gentlest of men who had been serving most of the time with an independent brigade out in Burma. John, who had a horror of the most harmless insects and reptiles – John, who had shuddered to see a gecko on the wall of his room in Malta – had survived the whole ordeal except that one side of his face had broken out into a violent nervous rash. He was an amusing companion with a dry, ready wit.

I had spent most of my gratuity on buying a good table, chair, and a desk light so that I could finish my book – there being not a single table in the Guthries' flat that did not wobble. John came back one night to find me with all the chapters in piles and laid out in front of me. There was fresh foolscap at my side, the desk light shining downwards, and me sitting triumphant behind it all. 'There – ' I cried out as he came in. 'What do you think of that?'

He took in the picture for a moment and said, 'Very handsome. Very handsome indeed. And there's that nice Mr Keats with only a candle.'

Antony and Cleopatra had barely completed its short run when in the early spring of 1947 Binkie asked me to take over at very short notice the part of Iago in a production of *Othello* he was putting on in London with Jack Hawkins as Othello and Fay Compton as Emilia. The play had already been on tour for several weeks on the continent going round the various campsites, and Iago had been played by Alec Clunes; but Alec had suddenly been taken ill and a new Iago had to be found at a week's notice. Could I do it? I told them that I thought a week was too short for me. If he could stretch it to two weeks, I could manage. The part was too enormous to do with just a bare twelve days' rehearsal, especially when the others were already established. He agreed, and the opening night was postponed.

I found in myself – it did not take much finding – a demon of energy. Iago, whatever else he was, and whatever his motives were (and jealousy in itself is motive for almost anything) seemed to me to be possessed of such an energy. The joy of playing this great part was slowly to reveal this manic condition from behind the mask of honesty; then to replace the mask of honesty; then to replace the mask as though it had never slipped. As we went on rehearsing, a further thought came to me: what extraordinary courage Iago had in deliberately provoking such passion in Othello who could have snapped his neck in one instant.

It was the first time in my life that I had tackled one of Shakespeare's greatest peaks, and it was a heady experience. I had bad 'flu on the opening night which might have given a further edge to my performance; anyway, I remember Dot coming down when the curtain fell, very concerned about my health and with a different look in her eyes – a look I could not read.

A few days later, we went for a walk together in some woods just outside town. She stopped after a while, turned to me and said, 'I have been such a fool. The other night I knew you were struggling against 'flu, and it came to me suddenly that I cared for you more than anyone in the world. You have stopped asking me to marry you. So I am asking you. Will you marry me?'

I knew the answer at once, but after so many years I did not feel that the walls of Jericho should fall flat at the first sound of the trumpets and the rams' horns. 'Oh, Dot,' I said and put my arms around her. 'What words to hear. But I must think about it. I'll let you know by this evening.'

Long before evening I phoned her to say, 'Yes – with all my heart.'

The wanderings of Odysseus had lasted ten long years – mine only eight; but I had come to my Penelope at last. Without her I could have been nothing, done nothing; with her love and help, our two lives joined together, I could lift the world up and carry it aloft.

The only person who came really badly out of my happiness was poor E. After six years of almost continuous absence abroad I was home with her again, and she was looking forward to a few years before I should get married. Poor darling, she was disappointed; I was married within months. The blessing was that she dearly loved Dot, and it gave her great happiness to see her son married to a girl whom she looked on almost as a daughter.

We were married on 3 June 1947, a day of blazing sunshine when sixty guests managed to drink exactly sixty bottles of champagne – and one of them was arrested afterwards.

Then off we drove in my highly unreliable old car to the South of France, where Max Reinhardt somehow arranged for us to rent a little villa that had belonged to Henri Barbusse, the French writer. It was in a small village called Miramar and lay halfway between St Raphael and Cannes. The place was idyllic; it was a very simple house indeed with no proper kitchen, but bedroom windows that opened right onto the sea on the top of a cliff. You looked through pine trees down to the Mediterranean, and it had its own private beach – it was the most perfect of places to spend a honeymoon.

By that time I had an old fifth-hand YSS (the forerunner of the Jaguar). It got us there safely, though at a very low speed, but it kept catching fire as we drove back. Fortunately the French garages were all helpful; in fact, one of them came out in the middle of the night to help extinguish flames. We arrived back in England.

A large job awaited me there – Stratford: not as director of the whole place, but as co-director with Michael Benthall of half the plays for the coming season: it made casting far easier if there were two minds in concert rather than he doing half and then bringing in other directors who had other ideas on the season's casting. Sir Barry Jackson was then the head of the Shakespeare Memorial Theatre, as it was called. He was an enormously esteemed old bird with a rather academic turn of mind, but immensely distinguished; he had run the Birmingham Repertory for years and made it famous; he had also run the annual Malvern Festival where many of Bernard Shaw's plays were launched. He had a problem though: once he had agreed to Michael and myself putting the season's plays together, he could hardly overrule either of us, and we had things very much our own way. Michael, for example, brought Robert Helpmann, who was his great friend, Claire Bloom, and Noel Willman. I brought Diana Wynyard, Godfrey Tearle, and Esmond Knight who by then was three parts blind but a wonderful, strong addition to the company. Nobody brought Paul Scofield – he brought himself: he stayed on from the previous year at Stratford.

There was no way that Michael and I could let it be known that it was we who put this season together. Naturally all the press thought that the Shakespeare Memorial Theatre had taken a giant leap forward, and they all applauded Sir Barry. That was fair enough. It was a little galling, but we had no complaints. We had wonderful notices, and the whole season took off as no previous season had done.

It was an ecstatically happy time of my life. Dot was on her way to her first baby and stayed in London during all the cold weather. She had very cleverly bought at a low mortgage a somewhat bomb-damaged house in Pelham Street – such a quiet street then – and was busy getting together whatever pregnant mothers have to get together. I took off on a frosty January morning to drive to Stratford with my friend Esmond Knight.

Es had an uncle, a famous falconer called Captain Knight, who had a still more famous golden eagle called Mr Ramshaw. During the cold hard winter he came down with his eagle to give some falconry lessons to those interested. He was a Falstaffian figure with big pockets in his jacket, all full with stinking squirrel's meat which he would fling to the bird as it swooped to the lure. One night as I was strolling back to the Arden Hotel where I was staying and where Sir Barry Jackson and his close friend Scott Sunderland were also staying, I became aware of a lot of unruly noise. The loudest seemed to come from the gardener's shed – a great screaming and a banging. I realized that it must be Mr Ramshaw. For whatever reason – crying out for a mate, screaming to break down his wooden walls – Mr Ramshaw was raising hell. The lights were shining from the front room of the Arden and through the window I could see the Captain finishing off his second bottle of whisky with the aid of two disreputable looking friends. The songs they were bawling would have put Toby Belch to shame and must have reduced the two maiden ladies who ran the little hotel to a paroxysm of terror. I was amused to think that they must have alarmed Sir Barry and his friend along the corridor. Their shoes had been put neatly outside the bedroom door to be polished in the morning, but I could picture them clutching each other's bony frame, not daring to come out and confront the roaring monster.

Out in the tool shed in the garden Mr Ramshaw could be heard beating his giant wings and screeching loud. And 400 yards up the road lying quietly in Holy Trinity Church were the remains of the prodigiously great man – William Shakespeare, a man whose brain you cannot enter without loving him; a man who has helped to shape our English destiny.

Dot stayed warm in London till she had given birth to this first baby, Rosanna – a little girl as full of sunshine as our honeymoon had been. A few weeks later, I went up to London and brought them both down to

Stratford and in the spring entered Hall's Croft, the old house that had once belonged to Shakespeare's daughter Susanna, who was married to Dr Hall. The house was still in private hands; it had not been acquired for the National Trust – and it was in a somewhat derelict condition; you could almost hear the woodworm squiggling about in the beams. But for us, it was like a dream come true. Into this very hallway, over these very flagstones, up that wide oak staircase, Shakespeare himself had walked to visit his daughter and his grandchildren. Outside in the garden was a mulberry tree that, as legend had it, was planted by Shakespeare. I had come to a place where I felt I truly belonged.

One day in the early autumn of 1948 I had two crucial meetings in London. In the morning I was asked by a powerful lady in Metro-Goldwyn-Mayer if I would join that august body at a large salary to become a writer/producer. She made clear that she was making similar enquiries in various directions, but I was certainly one of the half-dozen final choices. If I worked out well (and I would have to learn the whole of the business of MGM from top to bottom), then I would become a kind of Darryl Zanuck; if after a few years it did not work out, then they would pay me to retire in great comfort for the rest of my life. It was a tempting enough offer, both from the point of view of money (we were very hard up – I think I got paid something like thirty pounds a week for all the work I was doing at Stratford), but more than that I felt that I could have some influence on this mighty motion picture industry. It was a naïve thought and Dot quickly disabused me.

'Oh, by all means,' she said. 'If that's what you want to do, I'll come along and help you. Of course, life won't be quite as you imagine. You won't have the influence that you think you will have. You'll have to fly about all over the place to rooms filled with cigar smoke being nice to people to whom you don't wish to speak. But don't worry. I'll be fine. I'll live in a nice climate with a swimming pool surrounded by lots of handsome young men.'

So my mind was half made up when I went to the second meeting. This was with Lt.Col. Fordham Flower, eldest son of the late Sir Archibald Flower, the head of the brewing family, who had been responsible for the building and endowment of the Memorial Theatre.

Fordie quite simply and straightforwardly asked me if I would take up the directorship of the Shakespeare Memorial Theatre from the next season. I had never expected, or even imagined, to be made such an offer; but as he spoke, I sensed that this was the adventure for which I had been preparing all my life. With one big effort, the SMT – a well-thought of, well-respected, but always slightly provincial theatre – could be turned into the foremost English theatre. And if it became such a centre, then it would become the theatrical centre for all English-speaking peoples. It would be an artistic achievement, and a political one – it would help bond the nations together.

Dr David Lewis, the great navigator and single-handed sailor, writes,

> *I do not understand the power that drives me, but I will try to analyze it as best I can. There seems to be a restless spirit inherent in the very nature of mankind that impels us across new frontiers . . . The basic character of this exploring urge would appear to be always the same regardless of the way it is manifested. Thus it may equally be expressed in searching for truer forms of artistic expression; in seeking into the workings of the mind and soul of man; in the search for scientific truth; or in coming to grips with untamed nature. Thus each of us has his own deeming, possesses the potential for his own personal kind of adventure.*

I was lucky to have known by the time I was only sixteen that my adventure had to be in the theatre; that it would be an exploration of *the workings of the mind and soul of man*. It would also have to be an exploration of myself, for without understanding yourself you cannot get far in the interpretation of others.

And now, held out to me, was this wonderful possibility. I could see only one snag, and that a large one: in accepting responsibility for running the entire theatre, I would necessarily have to subordinate all ambitions as an actor to the good of the theatre as a whole. There were many leading parts, for which I was now arriving at the proper age, that I would have to forgo. This was a serious matter, and I had to ask Fordie to give me a day or two before I gave him a firm answer.

I asked Tony Guthrie's opinion. We met in Leicester Square and walked round and round it (why did we always seem to have these important meetings in the most unlikely squares of London?).

'Do you set such great store by your acting?' he asked.

'Yes I do. I don't think that I am necessarily the greatest actor in the world, but I know I have a talent and I know that it would be death to let it waste away inside me while I sat at a desk behind several telephones.'

We walked in silence for a time. And then at last he said, 'I think you ought to do it. I'm sure you ought to do it. A chance like this comes only once in a lifetime. You may never have wanted to run a theatre or even to be a director, but you might regret it. I think you would regret it always if you were to turn it down. You must just see to it that you keep enough acting going that you don't lose touch with it. But do it. Accept the job.' He reflected a moment and added, 'But whatever you do, don't do it for more than five years. If you have given everything you can to that theatre, you'll be a burnt-out cinder by the end of five years. You won't have an original thought left in you. Nor should you have. You should be spent. That's the time when you move aside and let in a fresh man with a fresh slant on things. Do not go on after five years.'

I made only a few stipulations: (1) I was to be in control of the entire theatre, everything from the restaurants to the workshops. Naturally I would deputize, but all must be answerable to me. I wanted no business manager intervening and frustrating my artistic aims. (2) I wanted no contract of any kind. I wanted the support of the Governors all the way. If the time arrived when they could not give it to me, then they must cut my head off. If I lost confidence in them, then I could walk out. Both sides were to be free. (3) The Governors must realize that you cannot run a great theatre from the middle of Warwickshire. I had to have some sort of base in London; therefore, I would keep my own small home in South Kensington and, naturally, pay for it myself. They must provide me with accommodation in Stratford. Up to now, they had not done this; I had had to pay for my roof at both ends of the line. My salary would be increased from thirty to sixty pounds a week.

Fordie and I never signed a letter of agreement between us. He agreed entirely with what I said, and we both stood by it. There was never the slightest argument from then on.

It was a harder task than I had imagined; I was up against a whole variety of oppositions. First, there was the perfectly understandable opposition of Barry Jackson himself who, from the moment the announcement was made in the press that he was leaving and I was going to take over, only spoke to me once, and that was to advise me to look after the academic side of life which he was so carefully fostering at Stratford. However, he never officially moved out of his office, so I had no room with a telephone from which to work. The assembling of the next season's plays – the designers, directors, composers, actors – all had to be done from my own home. I had no official secretary, and manifestly I had Jackson's curse and not his blessing.

Then there was the vociferous opposition of the newspapers, particularly the Birmingham press. Again it was understandable enough, but it did not help matters. They were all outraged that their favourite son, Sir Barry Jackson, who had contributed so much to the English Theatre as a whole, should be ousted by this upstart Quayle. Who was he? Where did he come from? What had he done to prove himself? Even *The Times* devoted a second leader to the question, wagging its aunt-like finger in reproval at me for being so presumptuous.

Finally, there was opposition from the Executive Council itself, the very people from whom I had expected the warmest support. Only Fordie stayed firmly beside me – or rather we stood back to back. We had to protect each other not only at the start, but throughout my term of office.

Fordie had spent most of his adult life in the Army; he had come home after the war to take on the Chairmanship of his family brewery and the heavy burden of being Chairman of the Board of Governors at Stratford. The family, apart from his own wife and children, were often divided against each other, frequently arguing over the way in which the brewery was being run. And if they could not get at Fordie that way, then they chose to attack him through his Chairmanship of the theatre. There was hardly a member of the Executive Council who knew the first thing about the theatre; several of them were local professional men, or chartered accountants, who did not understand in the least what I was trying to do or the possibilities that were open before them; all they knew was that it was hazardous and might bring disaster on their good old chug-along theatre. There was hardly a season, and hardly a board meeting, where Fordie and I were not protecting each other from criticism, and even after a very good financial season, they would shrink back in horror at what was being put forward as the next season's offering. There was one meeting where I put before them the proposal that we invite Glen Byam Shaw to join me as co-director; they would have none of it. How could the Stratford Theatre afford another director? With two directors, I argued, we could form two companies. I would take one of them away for a year and try and earn some much needed money. In the end, I had to threaten resignation and walk out of the meeting. I meant it too. They debated amongst themselves for another hour, and finally agreed to my plan.

The final argument I remember came over the Cycle of the Histories that we mounted for the Festival of Britain in 1951. I wanted to do something original for that particular year, and I had worked out very careful plans to produce the Histories from *Richard II* to *Henry V* in strict sequence, if possible rehearsing them all together and opening them at consecutive performances. Again they would have none of it. How could they afford to rehearse a company for so long? Where was the money to come from? I could not tell them the answer. We had precious little. Then they considered that to do a whole Cycle of Histories in one season was far too hazardous a project. So halfway through the Cycle we had to break off from presenting the Histories and put on one of Shakespeare's popular plays as a kind of safety net; they decided it ought to be *The Tempest*. Accordingly, we opened one play, then rehearsed the next, opened that, then rehearsed the next, and so on. And in the middle of it all, breaking the back of the entire plan, came a very pretty production by Michael Benthall of *The Tempest*. Naturally, the impact fell flat. It took months of the season before the critics began to wake up to the fact that it was indeed a consecutive cycle of plays, that the mounting, the design, the whole progression had been most carefully planned; by then it was too late to change opinions one way or the other. The notices had been written on each play, not on a concept of the whole.

Through all the years, Fordie remained staunch and absolutely dependable, a true friend. He did not look like a businessman in the least, nor like anyone who has to do with the theatre. He looked like someone who had prospered on the land: tall, with grey hair, and very expressive wide set, grey-blue eyes. I shall always revere him and be grateful to him. Indeed I am grateful to the whole Flower family because from the very first it was they who worked and generously gave their time and energy – and often their own private money – to help build the theatre at Stratford.

There were the usual problems of putting together the next year's season, but there was also a silent opposition from the very theatre itself. The building was of a hideousness that nobody who had not sat in it at that time could possibly appreciate. It was built like a cinema, a long shoe box of a place. The walls were lined with big panels of French-polished wood, the gift of the Commonwealth nations, each country contributing its own panel. The panels were not only garish to look at, but light bounced off them during the action of the play. The dress circle was set so far back that you were almost sitting outside the theatre. It was a monstrosity, and I remain amazed at whatever building committee it was that could have selected the young woman who won the competition. One of the first major jobs that I was obliged to do was to pull the dress circle nearer to the stage, thrust two wings out on either side so that the dress circle audience was linked visually and physically with the action, and tear down the dreadful strips of shiny veneer. But I had to wait to earn some money before I could start.

Compared with these obstacles, the mere putting together of a season of five plays with their directors and designers and a company of thirty actors seemed childishly easy, although it did take an enormous amount of thought and work. All I could do was to lash myself to the mast and call to my friends in London to come and help me. And they did; they responded most generously.

The first stake to be driven into the ground in the coming season was to have enough big names in the company to interest and excite the press. The public followed the press, and the press was only excited by Great Big Names. In a way it did not matter whether they were good actors and actresses as long as they were famous, sensational. The press did not really care which they were, because they could either 'make them or break them'. It was good copy for them either way. If the trapeze artist succeeded in completing five double somersaults, that would be headline news; if the famous actress made a hash of Cleopatra, that was equally good news. We were emerging from the days of great critics and moving into the dubious sunshine of the Beaverbrook press.

Fortunately I had a lot of suitably sensational and very good friends who rallied to my aid. Diana Wynyard and Godfrey Tearle both came back for a season, and John Gielgud and Peggy Ashcroft were already showing signs of great interest. From the very beginning John was always enormously helpful and full of suggestions. It was through him that I discovered Alan Badel playing Richard III in Birmingham; Alan also joined the company. It was John, too, who sent me chasing off to Spain and Paris in search of the designer Mariano Andreu, whom he wanted for *Much Ado About Nothing*, a production that turned out to be one of his very best. Michael Benthall generously came back several times; Tony Guthrie came and did a brilliant *Henry VIII*. The Motleys did a lot of work for us; so did Tanya Moiseiwitsch whom I had first known at the paint frame at the Old Vic; she had been working very closely with Tony Guthrie and had just completed the first production of *Peter Grimes* at Covent Garden.

When those sensational top liners had been duly contracted, then the next range of actors had also to be found: really sound supporting actors who were almost stars but not quite. And finally, to add piquancy to the dish, there must be two or three youngsters whom you can introduce not for the sake of the critics, but for the sake of the theatre, so that they have a chance early on to learn their job. We made several discoveries in this way: Robert Shaw and Robert Hardy, in the '49–'51 seasons, were two of the most conspicuous. I could hardly claim that Richard Burton was my discovery; he was already quite successful. He had attracted attention in *The Lady's not for Burning*; he had made a film of a play by Emlyn

Williams; and when I first saw him he was playing the lead in *The Boy with the Cart*. All the same, when I asked him to play Hal in *Henry IV* and *Henry V*, it was his first major break – and he seized it with both hands.

Despite all this hard work – without a telephone or secretary, acting every night, and directing half the productions – that winter of 1948 was one of the happiest of my whole life. I got up to London to see Dot almost every weekend. Meanwhile, there I was in Stratford-on-Avon working on the plays of this genius of the English language and the English spirit.

CHAPTER 22

THE THEATRE ITSELF is the quickest to recognize and understand the truth of things theatrical. The theatre knows immediately whether there is hope or only loss in any particular theatrical venture. Years – literally years – before the critics have seen through some actor or actress, the theatre has given him or her a smiling but silent thumbs up: or it just might as easily be a thumbs down. In spite of the lamentations and cries over Barry Jackson's departure, confidence quickly grew in the profession; there was a strong feeling that something of great interest was happening down in Warwickshire. All my old friends rallied generously to my aid, not only for personal reasons, but because they thought they were truly helping to lift the Shakespeare Memorial Theatre – that old monstrous great building – into the premier theatre of the world.

John Gielgud came and played and directed for two seasons, which at the salaries we were paid was enough to ruin any man. With him came Peggy Ashcroft, then Gwen Ffrangcon-Davies. And following on their heels a long list of the most illustrious names in the English theatre: Michael Redgrave, Ralph Richardson, Margaret Leighton, Harry Andrews. The cast lists began to look like theatrical *Who's Who*.

None of this could have been achieved without the help of Binkie who quietly used all his influence to help me in the battle. I asked him to join the Board of Governors which he did at once, then to move immediately to the Executive Committee. I asked him out of friendship, but I asked also because he would more than counter-balance the baleful influence of Emile Littler, who was flagrantly ambitious to become Chairman himself and was therefore attacking Fordie on every possible occasion.

Littler once said to me, 'I'm very proud of our workshops in Birmingham. We make all our own clothes for the pantomimes. And do you know, Tony – there is not an elephant in the whole of this country that walks into the ring that is not wearing a caparison that is not made by us.'

'Really?' I replied. It seemed an inadequate retort to such a proud statement, but I could think of nothing else.

'Oh yes,' he said. 'You know those brightly-coloured things they wear over their heads and down their backs with baubles sewn on them? Well, every one of them is made by us in our Birmingham workshops.'

I soon began to pay the price for subordinating myself as an actor. I cannot say that playing Antony is exactly subordination, but that is what it became. Michael Langham was engaged to direct the production of *Julius Caesar*, but after a few days John G said that he really could not cope with Michael who would have to go. Michael duly went, and John asked me to take on the production, which I felt obliged to do although I was already playing the part of Antony. It is always difficult both to direct and act since the director's first concern must be for the entire production and not exclusively for himself.

I know I helped John with his performance as Cassius; he was playing it in a heavily romantic way and although he was so much my senior, it took a certain amount of resolution to make him see this and then appear on the stage with him at night. But at last, after about a week's rehearsal, I told him that he was giving the performance of Brutus, not Cassius. He shot one of his sideways smiles at me and shook his head. 'My dear Tony, you can't teach an old dog new tricks. I'm far too set in my ways for you to alter me.'

I was not trying to alter him, I was just trying to persuade him to give a different and unexpected performance. 'Have you ever stood in Whitehall,' I asked, 'as the hard men in bowler hats are coming out of the Ministry for War with their rolled umbrellas and their Guards' ties strolling up towards their clubs in Pall Mall and St James's? No? Then go and look at them. There you will see wind, weather and bitter disappointment stamped on almost every one of them, because there simply is not room at the top. And Cassius feels cheated of his right to be at the top. He's a hard, long-serving soldier.' John changed his performance almost overnight with enormous success and went on to repeat it on film in California.

Each season the main battle at Stratford was of course the artistic one. What happened on stage was paramount: the quality of the performance, the direction and the decor. The quality was dependent on the financial foundation, and the financial foundation of the Memorial Theatre was extremely thin. We had to play to over 90% capacity for the entire season to break even. And since I had lengthened the season by four weeks, this took some doing. There seemed to be little chance of making a tiny profit to put by for further developments. Occasionally the Arts Council gave its great cough and asked if perhaps we would like a little money from them. I would go and consult Fordie, and we would both agree that it was wiser to decline their offer courteously. The moment we started to depend on outside help our bloodstream would become vitiated, and if ever the support were withdrawn we would collapse. While we could exist on our own box office, we must continue to do so. The only way that I could see that we could ever make money was to hire another director, as I had suggested to the Governors. We would have two companies, and while one stayed in Stratford, I would take the other off on a tour of Australia and New Zealand. I was endlessly on the lookout for this co-director but it took several years for the right circumstances and the right man to appear.

Tony Guthrie came down to a masterly production of *Henry VIII*. It was a beautiful summer; he and Judy lived on a covered punt which they paddled up and down the Avon. They were blissfully happy on it, jumping into the water stark naked. And when you came to eat a meal with them, they used the empty spaghetti tins to offer you a drop of gin. I asked Tony if he would consider coming to join me at Stratford. To my surprise, he answered that he would, but there was a condition attached.

'I have one great ambition. And that is to build what I call my "Tin Globe". It all sprang from that first night in Denmark which you will remember very well. I want to build a theatre with a permanent set surrounded on two sides by the audience in order to bring the people nearer to the actors and so communicate far more in the way that Shakespeare himself did. All this proscenium-arch acting is merely a version of opera. Rubbish.'

Of course it was rubbish. I knew it too. In order to reach the top of the upper circle we were all being forced into giving great operatic performances. But since this was the only theatre we had, we had got to make the best of it.

'What then is your condition?' I asked.

'That you build my "Tin Globe" right here beside the Avon, on the bank side, or on this garden behind the old theatre. It'll be an eye-opener for the people. They'll see how far, far better it is than that dreadful shoe box in which you're acting now.'

I said that I could see very well that it would be better, but what were we to do about the SMT itself? He slipped a hand through the air. 'Oh, never mind that. Just bulldoze it and push it into the river.' And he laughed like a naughty schoolboy.

'My dear Tony,' I said. 'There is nothing I would like more. But I don't see how the two things can exist side by side. And I can tell you right now, there would be a head-on collision with the Governors. They see themselves as the custodians of the place. They're never going to allow me to tear it down. There would be an outcry. I have enough problems on my hands without that.'

He shrugged. 'All right then. I'll build it somewhere else, and you must go on looking for a co-director. But this I assure you, build it I shall. It may not be in this country at all. So much the worse for this country.' And that was the end of it. He went and built it in Canada.

The Guthries were not the only people to find diversion on the Avon. For some time I had felt the need for an outdoor activity away from my office and the theatre, so I bought myself a two-seater, folding, canvas canoe. It was our first boat, only a small one, but it added another dimension to our lives. I plied up and down the Avon, with Dot, the children, or Paddy Donnell, our Stage Director, and many of our most important decisions were taken in that canoe.

There were few holidays during these years but Dot and I took the boat to Scotland, to the Lakes, to the Mediterranean even, and one mid winter, to Cornwall, where for a week we took it out each day around Falmouth Bay and the Helford River. One day we were quite far out when there was a great hiss, and then another: two porpoises were playing around us, criss-crossing and bumping underneath, then nudging the canoe from side to side. Dot seemed a little nervous, but I was exhilarated and missed them when they disappeared. The weather was rough and blustery and we seemed to have the wintry sea to ourselves. Later I discovered that the local fishermen had lined the walls of the quay and made bets each day on whether or not we should return. It was a wonderful little boat; it gave me a sense of freedom and a knowledge that I could always escape, even for a short time, from the pressures that would build up each season.

In the theatre, as on the water, there is always a new movement stirring just below the surface. The public is quite unaware of it, and so too are most of the critics, but the movement is continual. Now, in 1948, George Devine had come back from Burma where he had been serving in the Royal Artillery. He was, I think, more changed than most of us, but he was still his dear old self, but less genial, and far more determined to live his own adventure and to forge ahead with his own plans to promote new life and energy into the British theatre. He and Glen had worked closely before the war with Michel Saint-Denis, both at his pre-war theatre school, the London Theatre Studio, – and in various productions: with John Gielgud at the New and Queen's Theatre seasons and, immediately before the war, at Michel's season at the Phoenix Theatre. They came together again when the war ended and persuaded Ralph and Larry to embark on an imaginative plan that would expand the existing Old Vic with the addition of a new institution for the development of the theatre. It would be known as the Old Vic Theatre Centre, and as well as a children's theatre and an experimental stage project, there was to be a school that would be a successor to the pre-war London Theatre Studio. The purpose of the school would be to supply the Old Vic with its actors, stage managers and designers. It would not be like the general run of schools; not like RADA for example, where young people were turned out to earn their livings in the many different ways beginning to be available to actors. No, this was to be specifically intended for training students for work at the Old Vic, with both technical courses and acting classes which were devoted equally to improvisation and to interpretation. George, Glen and Michel – the Three Boys as they were called – were absolutely dedicated to the ideals of this school which eventually opened in January 1947. For two of its six years it prospered exceedingly. Not surprisingly with three such men at the top, the standard of training was magnificent, and the work they produced was a joy to behold. However, it was not long before the vision began to crumble. The Governors refused to renew Ralph's and Larry's contracts as directors of the Old Vic – their reasons were to do with the fact that they appeared to be spending more time abroad touring, or making films, instead of taking care of the fortunes of the theatre – and the School fell on perilous times. While the Old Vic company returned to its Waterloo Road premises, now restored and made safe after extensive war damage, the School moved to premises in Dulwich. The links between the theatre and the school soon became tenuous, the financial support the school needed was lacking, and as the Governors' policy towards it changed a deep division set in. The climax was reached when Michel, Glen and George offered their resignation unless the differences between themselves and the Governors could be resolved. No assurances were given and so the three resigned; the theatre community was stunned.

The Governors cast about for succour and support and turned to Tony Guthrie to rescue the situation. Tony, being nothing if not draconian, made one drastic clean cut and decided that the Vic School and the touring children's theatre known as the Young Vic, which was breaking new ground and was a forerunner of many youth theatres that have come after, must be closed.* It was a decision that was to leave behind a degree of bitterness among those involved for many years, and the outcry in theatre circles and in the more intelligent press was extreme.

Information about the situation reached me very quickly, and there were two things I thought we should try to do. The first alternative was to try to link Stratford with the Old Vic, jointly financing the School. I put this plan to Fordie who seemed very pleased with the idea, and eventually it went up to the Governors of both theatres. It was turned down flatly by each in turn. Neither Stratford nor the Old Vic wanted anything to do with the other. Such a high boundary wall surrounded them both that neither was willing to step up and clasp the other's hands at the top. Yet it was a very good idea: we could have continued producing Shakespeare in Stratford, and the Old Vic could have done the same in London with any other play apart from Shakespeare during that same period. Then, in the autumn, we would change around with our productions coming to London, and the Old Vic's productions going to Stratford. We would save on resources, overheads, workshops (and one great achievement Sir Barry left behind him were the most magnificent workshops on which the Stratford theatre had spent a small fortune). It would have meant a huge saving for both theatres at a time when economy was badly needed. Neither wanted anything to do with it.

At the same time, I also thought it would be a constructive act to incorporate RADA into this scheme of things. There was nothing particularly unique about RADA; no reason why it should be called Royal, and there was nothing different in its training from that of a lot of other first-class schools – in fact, the same teachers frequently taught at the same schools. If RADA were to merge with us, then there would be some justification for having the title Royal. It would be serving what was virtually the Royal Theatre – or the National Theatre. To become a student at RADA would be to have a very definite purpose in life, and for the two great theatres, instead of having to fish around in the hodgepodge of actors who might or might not have some training, they would be able to call on students specifically trained for these sort of classic and modern plays they put on. Again, I was met with absolute blank refusal. Perhaps I was considered an over-ambitious young man. I do not know. I only know that my plans were completely thwarted. I was beginning to see that I could not keep up this pace, and that another few years would bring the end to

*This complicated situation and the ensuing struggle are comprehensively covered in Irving Wardle's *The Theatres of George Devine*.

Tony Guthrie's suggested five-year time limit for remaining at Stratford. There was not personal gain in it for me.

The other alternative was to let things rip, let the Old Vic school close, and then hope to fish out of the smoking ruins one of my two great friends, either Glen Byam Shaw, or George Devine. This was exactly what happened. The Old Vic school closed and out staggered the two men. The most immediately and obviously suitable for the job was Glen. I asked him to come and join me as co-director. He said, 'Dear old boy, I think I would quite possibly like to, but I have been working very, very closely with George and Michel, and I don't want to jump from the frying pan into the fire. If I come and join you, we shall have to work together like brothers. There is no other way. You are the Hamlet of this place and I will come and be your Horatio – and gladly – but only if we see absolutely eye to eye on everything, and can act as one. So I will come for six months – on trial, if you like – or at any rate so that we can both test each other out. You can see if you like having me around, and I can see if I like being here.'

So under those conditions Glen came. It did not take him six months; it took him barely two weeks to decide that he wanted to come and so we started the most happy partnership that there can ever have been. Between the seasons of 1949 and 1950, I had already taken the company on a flying visit to Australia. I had a two-fold purpose: one was to show gratitude to a great country for their mighty contribution in the war; the other was to see if we could make money. I hope we succeeded in the first, and I know that we succeeded – however slightly – in the second. The expense of flying an entire company and two big productions with all their scenery and costumes out to Australia was vast. But after eight or ten weeks playing there, we came back showing a small financial profit. Glen and I now started to plan to do it on a much bigger and longer scale. 1952 would be the year that he consolidated his position in Stratford as co-director. At the end of that season, I would take one company off to New Zealand and Australia for a whole year's touring while he put together a completely different company and ran the theatre at Stratford.

I have many rich memories of Glen, but one which often springs to my mind is the day that he rode with us in the railway compartment bound for Tilbury. We now had two little girls; he said to them, 'Now – Jenny, Rosanna – I have got a song that I'm going to sing to you and which I want you to learn.' Aged five and three, they leaned forward in their little blue coats. 'It's very easy,' he went on. 'It's called "That's as far as I want to go." Have you got that?'

'Yes, Uncle Glen,' they said. '"That's as far as I want to go".'

'Very good. Now here's the song.' And he sang:

> *That's as far as I want to go,*
> *That's as far as I want to go;*
> *I found a button in the stew,*
> *Likewise a pair of braces too.*
> *When they said do you want any more,*
> *I simply answered. 'No – I don't want to find the trousers*
> *too.*
> *That's as far as I want to go.'*

I think he sang it largely to cover up his own unhappiness at our leaving him alone to run that great theatre. He felt a little over-burdened by the responsibility although he need not have done so for he put together an altogether remarkable season. His towering triumph was a great production of his own of *Antony and Cleopatra*, with Peggy Ashcroft and Michael Redgrave in which they gave two wonderful performances.

I enjoyed every minute of the Australian tour and I loved the country and its people. There were many times when I was tempted to stay there, but there were stronger calls coming from home. I had a very clear picture in my head of what the 1954 season at Stratford was going to be and how it could be the end of my term of office. As Tony Guthrie had told me, at the end of five years I ought to be exhausted – a cinder – and I was. I hardly had an original idea left in my head.

The last production we had mounted at Stratford, and now took with us to Australia, was my own production of *Othello*. I did not want it to be seen by the critics so I slipped it in for a couple of weeks when the season was over. Once again – and as always – the actor suffered from being a director. All my energy had gone into the production, and not nearly enough thought into the creation of the character of Othello. It was acceptable and occasionally good, but not great. However, John G did come and see it, and after the performance came round full of enthusiasm and with a proposal.

'I have an idea to put to you,' he said, 'and I think it's rather a good one. Supposing that I were to come in and play Iago when you return from Australia, and we'll get Peg to come and play Emilia. Then when your season is over, we will take this production of yours, and one of mine, the very successful *Much Ado About Nothing*, as well as Peter Brook's wonderful *Measure for Measure*, to America. You're always talking about taking the company to America. Well, this is the way you can do it.'

Naturally I was thrilled. I did not think he was the ideal Iago, nor did he, but in these circumstances, it would be a miracle to have both his strength and Peg's with us.

'There's only one problem,' he said. 'And that is that I shall not be free to join you till around halfway through the 1954 season, so it's rather tough luck on whoever plays Iago. But if you want this plan to go through, he'd have to move out when I move in.'

I accepted it as inevitable, as though it had been planned between us. Naturally Glen knew the full circumstances. The thought that the 1954 season would be my last at Stratford sustained me through the whole hard-working tour. I wanted to leave having fulfilled all the tasks I had set myself: to have raised the theatre into one that was internationally known and internationally recognized; to have found a co-director of the place and, finally, to have achieved a swan song by taking the company on a successful tour of the USA.

The Australian tour over, Dot and I flew back across the Pacific; our children and the company followed by ship. We arrived in New York only to find that some insuperable difficulties had arisen which to my dismay meant that the entire American tour had to be cancelled. Such setbacks are not unusual in the theatre, but they are always desperately disappointing, and this one was almost heartbreaking. I had hoped to be able to bow out after a successful American season, but now Glen and I had to rethink our plans for the future.

It was becoming more and more clear that the Old Vic looked destined to become the National Theatre. Nothing was concluded, but events were moving that way. If that were to become a reality, then Stratford would be fighting for a place in the sun. The Old Vic/National Theatre would be on the inside track. It would be well subsidized: actors could live at home in London; they were not confined to a diet of Shakespeare; they could range through the centuries; they could pick their plays from any foreign country they wanted while we were stuck in Warwickshire like rabbits growing fur all over us. We had to find a London theatre where we could present every sort of play, then change around and bring our own productions into London. It was too early as yet to know how this was to be financed, but it had got to be done or our premier position would very soon be lost. We called George Devine in on our discussions and plans, and he was enthusiastic about them. The idea was that Glen would continue to run the SMT and while George would be in charge of the London end of things, I would act as a link between the two theatres – sometimes working in one, sometimes in the other. George was asked to go and find a London theatre that might be available and suitable for these plans.

A month or so passed and we all met in a friend's flat in Sloane Square. We asked George if he had found himself a theatre as yet.

'I have indeed,' he said.

'Where? Which one?'

He said, 'Come here.' He led us to the window and pointed down to the far end of the square. 'That one.' It was the Royal Court.

'But it's surely not big enough for our needs.'

He shrugged. 'Perhaps not. But that's the theatre I want. And that's the theatre I'm going for. I know it's not any good to you at all, but I have to follow my own course.'

Now Glen and I had to set to work thinking again. If George were not to be a part of this triumvirate, then who was? The most obvious choice was Peter Hall, a brilliant young director who had already worked at Stratford and was well on his way to becoming a great man of the theatre. Peter was enthusiastic, but now I became the problem. I felt I had no more energy to give to the administrative side. My spirit rebelled at the thought of organization; more hours of sitting behind a desk with a row of telephones in front of me. I was tired of lording it over other actors, to quite an extent determining their lives. I had much to do to determine my own destiny. Except for my own precious family, I was very much a loner and I had come to the end of what I could do at Stratford. Already I had overshot Tony G's stipulation of only five years by a couple, including the year of 1948 when I had literally been the director of the place, but had had to keep it concealed. I had been there working wholly for Stratford for seven years. When I told Glen of this he was aghast. 'Oh no, I implore you – not for my sake, not for Stratford's sake, but for your own sake – don't throw all this away. You must not do it.'

'I've got to,' I said.

'No, really dear friend, I implore you. You are in a position here – a position you have earned yourself – of great power.' He repeated the word, 'Power. And Power is hard come by. The opportunity will never come to you again. You cannot – you must not – be allowed to throw it all away.'

'Dear Glennie,' I told him. 'I've got to. I don't want power. I don't like power. I never have liked it. I have done my job here, and now I will be happy to go back to being a perfectly ordinary worker in the theatre – back to being what I set out to be: an actor. I may not be all that good an actor, or all that successful. It doesn't matter. I've got to get out of this pompous position I'm in and find my own salvation inside myself. So it's no good trying to dissuade me. My mind is perfectly clear.'

He tried no more, but was desperately unhappy. The 1955 season at Stratford was remarkable for the presence of Larry and Vivien. I had been pursuing them for years, but they had always eluded me. It was Glen who had finally got them to agree to come and do a season; Glen who had called himself a Horatio. *Titus Andronicus* was one of Peter Brook's greatest productions, and it was a great experience to be part of it. To my mind, Larry gave one of his very greatest performances as Titus. He brought to it all his skill, all his presence, and a degree of emotion that did not always appear in his work. It was a very great performance indeed, made more poignant by the fact that his marriage to Vivien was in trouble. Poor Vivien, she was suffering badly from manic depression, and she had turned against the very man she loved most in the world – against Larry. Her behaviour was sometimes quite rational, but sometimes aggressive and desperately hurtful to him – both off stage and on. Standing there beside them while Titus was speaking words of love and comfort to poor mutilated Lavinia, she would be cursing him with the most extreme obscenities imaginable, with a piece of bloody gauze tied over her mouth. The audience could not hear what she was saying or realize that she was speaking at all, but it was perfectly audible to those of us who were there.

In spite of this Larry's Titus ranks with all the finest performances and I put it foremost among all the great tragic performances I ever saw him give. Throughout the season, he was dear and generous and wholly professional.

I had fought against playing Aaron; I did not think I had the right qualities for the part. But Peter Brook persuaded me that I could do it and bolstered by his belief in me, I found that I could, and I pushed it further and further until I was giving, I think, an unusual performance; certainly it was one that I would rate as one of the very best that I have ever done. It was almost entirely due to Peter Brook who, from the beginning, had an extraordinary concept of how the play sits on the stage – a concept that was at once original, strange, and macabre. He had had a firm hand in the designing of all the clothes and an equally strong influence on the sound effects – you could not call them music. They were strange and eerie noises with which he had been experimenting for months with his own tape recorder. Without doubt, *Titus* was one of the notable theatrical achievements for a decade or more in its stunning originality. It was the last play that I ever acted for Stratford.

Fordie, too, was loath to accept what I told him. But in the end he understood what I was trying to say. Between him and Glen, they came to me with a proposal that I should begin to taper off at least my close work with Stratford. 'Take some time off,' they said. 'Work at something else. Go to America and act there. Make some films. Anything you like. Only don't sever your connections with this place.'

I could not refuse, and in fact it is exactly what I did. Tony Guthrie asked me to come and play Tamburlaine the Great in a production that he was putting on with his own Stratford, Ontario company, and which Roger Stevens would then bring to New York. I accepted eagerly. I had seen his monumental production when it came to Stratford; Donald Wolfit was playing in the lead and he was magnificent – if a little overweight. We rehearsed in Toronto where Tony and Judy invited me to stay in their flat with them, and the two of us would walk to rehearsal every morning through air so cold that I thought my eyeballs would freeze in their sockets. The production was designed by Leslie Hurry at the very top of his form and it was magnificent. Tony later wrote that it was the best production that he had ever done, and I am sure it was. I have never seen anything to equal it. Unfortunately our conditions of work were very poor. We rehearsed, some forty or fifty of us, in a basement belonging to the University of Toronto. It was clean and dry enough, but of a rather modern, depressing nature – with parquet flooring and rumbling waterpipes that ran round the walls. It was here that Roger Stevens and Bob Whitehead, who were to present the play in New York, came to see it in the last few days of rehearsal. What they saw was an overcrowded room with a great confusion of people, mostly in jeans and t-shirts, pushing and pulling carts about the place, occasionally breaking into echoing song: it must have been very confusing and depressing. I felt that Roger left that rehearsal with a strong sense of having poured a lot of money away on a real loser. He did very little to presell the production before it came to New York, and we opened to very poor advance booking.

New York's Winter Garden was a magnificent theatre to play in, and I relished the experience. The company was augmented by twenty or more singers, and two men cracking great bull ships accompanied the entrance of the conquered King of Persia. We ran for three weeks, and then Roger took the play off. By now, I think he saw that it was uniquely good, but it was too late to whip up much trade. We did, however, collect a small devoted bank of devotees – several hundred of them. They came night after night and clapped themselves into a frenzy. On the last night after the final curtain fell, they all gathered round the front stalls and steadily kept up their applause. I had gone back to my dressing room and pulled off several layers of heavy costume before the stage manager came and said I had to go down and say something to these folk. So down I went and there were the faithful 400 – applauding and applauding. Not, I think, out of enthusiasm but out of grief to see something so strangely beautiful and barbaric disappear as though it had never been.

On coming back to England I was immediately offered the part of Eddie Carbone in Arthur Miller's *A View from the Bridge* which was to be directed by Peter Brook. It gave me the change of diet and direction that I badly needed at the time.

Through this production I saw a lot of Arthur Miller and Marilyn Monroe – a strangely incongruous pair, I thought. There have been so many books written about Marilyn that I do not want to add another word to them beyond saying that she was a most enchanting, lovable, self-destructive creature. She came to our house one day partly pleased and partly disturbed at having been mobbed on a shopping expedition. She asked to be left alone for a while to put herself to rights. When she had not appeared after an hour, we sent out a search party and found that she had hidden herself away in a little loo which happened to have a slippery floor and a rug on it. She had pushed the rug up so that the door would not open, thought she was trapped there by some alien force, and had just sat down and waited to be rescued. She never thought of straightening the rug.

On another occasion we were both in the line-up for a Royal Command Performance – it was *The Battle of the River Plate* in which I had a part. Marilyn never came to the very short rehearsal in the morning intended to show us where to stand behind the giant screen and how we should walk out one by one into the audience through a gap in the curtains. So when she arrived – late as always – she had no idea where to go or what to do. At a distance she looked very pretty, but close to it was not so good. White make-up was slipping off her face and her flame-red, strapless dress was falling off altogether. The designer, Bumble Dawson, had literally sewn her into it at the very last moment.

'Tony, Tony,' she whispered. 'Tell me what I do. I walk on the stage and I turn left and curtsey. Is that right?'

'No Marilyn, dear. You walk on, you curtsey to your front and go off to your right.'

'Oh, I see. Thank you. Tony, would you just shake me down into this dress a bit? I think it's coming off.'

So I grabbed a handful of the top of the bodice and shook her down into it. And again she would say, 'Tony, Tony. Tell me again. I'm sorry. Which did you say? Curtsey to the right, walk off to the left?'

'No, Marilyn, curtsey to the front and walk off to your right.' So we went on and on all the way along the line.

Just ahead of her in the alphabetical line was Victor Mature, enormous and broad-shouldered. He had not said a word to her as we slowly shuffled towards the opening in the curtain. Just as he was about to have his name called and walk out onto the stage, she turned to him and said, 'Oh,

Victor. Tell me, Victor. What do I do? I don't know what to do. Tell me.'

He turned his head very slightly towards her and said, 'Fall on your ass, baby,' and walked through the curtains to a big round of applause. Next moment she followed him, dithered to the right, to the left, and brought the house down.

Whether the dithering was to wind herself up to what she had already half decided to do or whether it was entirely natural, I have no idea. You could not tell. She was a young woman of such total contrasts and yet a seamless garment.

Shortly after that I went off with Larry and Vivien to play *Titus* on a very glittering tour that took us to Paris, Venice, Belgrade, Zagreb, Vienna and Warsaw; and when that was over I returned to New York to play Galileo at the Lincoln Center.

I was pursuing a livelihood to be sure. I had responsibilities for certain. We now had a third child, a son, Christopher. It was true that I was looking for success, but not material or financial success in the first place, only the success that would bring me a greater range of parts and a greater possibility of releasing more of myself as an actor. I had never meant to be a 'star'; I had never much liked the qualities that went with stardom. But I did want to play great parts, and in playing them I wanted to achieve a transparency so that the workings of the heart could be seen and communicated.

The notice that I have most cherished – indeed the only one that I have kept – is that written by Brooks Atkinson after seeing *Galileo*: 'But it was impossible for (Charles) Laughton to be simple, direct and unemotional about anything. He was a showman at heart. His pompous acting and his overbearing attitude towards the drama reduced epic theatre to the level of exhibitionism. Many years later, *Galileo* emerged as a sharp-witted play of high ethics when Anthony Quayle played it without egoism'.

Without egoism. If ever the actor is led to think of himself as the 'mighty me', he is bound to take his success or failure personally; he will either be overinflated or overcast, dejected, down. Both of these false positions are simply avoided. The actor realizes that his talent has nothing to do with himself personally; his attributes, his talents, are simply on loan for the period of his life. He is neither the better nor the worse for having them. They are there to be used. He himself is there to be used. He is a lightning conductor through which the current passes: no more and no less. Some cables are constructed to carry a very high charge, some only a small one, but so long as each carries its maximum load it is doing its proper function.

All of which means that I had learnt that the only way to live was to the glory of god – or rather, to the glory of God. I had long since been unable to say the Nicene Creed. I was unable to believe in it. But I certainly did believe in God – God as Energy, as Spirit, as Imagination, as the Force that informs the whole of life. Sometimes a blind and cruel force, but certainly one of great glory.

The ride was not always a smooth one; it had many disappointments. At the time they would distress me, but looking back now I think that they were intended. All through the war I had had a growing feeling that there was some guardian angel who would push me firmly in one direction or another. I have the same feeling now. Such firm directions were annoying at the time, but looking back I can see that they shaped my life. One such came soon after *Tamburlaine*.

Opportunities were opening for me in America, and I felt that I could not refuse offers with a family to look after. One of them was from Katharine Cornell to direct and act in Chrisopher Fry's *The Firstborn*. It was a good play, by no means Fry's best, but I accepted to do it. As soon as my plane touched down I was met by my agent in high excitement, who whisked me straight off to the pier in New York where he had arranged for me to meet William Wyler. Wyler was just finishing his breakfast. He came immediately to the point.

'I'm going to remake *Ben Hur*,' he said. 'With Chuck Heston in the lead. I saw you play Tamburlaine here a few months ago and I want to offer you the part of the second lead, Messala. What do you say to it?'

'I say yes to it,' I replied. It was quite an easy reply to make. I had seen the original film when I was a boy, and I remembered Francis X. Bushman playing the part. So yes, thank you very much.

He was slightly perplexed. 'You mean that's all there is to it? – Just yes?'

'Yes,' I answered once again. 'There's nothing to be said. Yes, I would love to do it.'

'Well,' he said. 'Then there's no point continuing the conversation. I'll get in touch with your agent here and we'll fix things up.' He held out his hand. 'See you in Rome in May.'

'May? Oh no, I can't do that.'

'Why not?'

'Because I have a play to do here in New York – then in Israel. I won't be through for several weeks after that. More like the end of June.'

There was a pause and then he asked, 'What play is it you're doing?'

'Oh, it's a play of Christopher Fry's.'

'Then don't do it.'

'I've got to.'

'Have you signed a contract?'

'No.'

'Then walk out on it. Don't hesitate. Just walk away. If there's a lawsuit or anything ugly like that, then we'll settle it.'

'No,' I persisted. 'It's nothing to do with a contract. It's simply that I've said that I will do it. And I've got to do it. I couldn't do otherwise.'

He went on for another ten or fifteen minutes trying to press me to change my mind. In the end, he gave up, dropped the whole subject and said, 'Well, that's that then. No point going on discussing it. I haven't time. Goodbye.' And saw me to the door.

So I never played Messala in *Ben Hur* – and Stephen Boyd did. Messala was a part in which nobody could have failed, and in which, I think, I would probably have made a big film success: the kind of success that rolls on and on carrying the actor for years. I would doubtless have moved to Hollywood, and I would doubtless have changed my entire life. And I would have been very lucky if my marriage had held together and our family had grown up as the united loving unit they are. At the time I was infuriated to have missed such an opportunity – they come very seldom – but now I see that it was nothing but that guardian angel who held out his hand and said, 'No, my boy. Thus far and no farther.'

There was a rather similar case over a film called *Ice Cold in Alex* – a very good film which turned into almost a classic and in which I had a wonderful part – the only really wonderful part I had in films. When it came out, the film had such a success and I had such splendid notices, that I did not see how I could fail to have a whole crop of offers all springing from this rough, tough, but subtle South African that I was playing. I did not get one single offer – not one. Again, the way to film success was firmly barred by the guardian angel.

And again I know that had film success come my way, my family would have been quite different and Compass, the touring company that I started six years ago, would never have existed. Success has indeed been meted out to me, but not in the ways in which I had expected or looked for. In the most obvious ways, it has been denied me only to preserve my outlook and energy for a far less obvious, but far more rewarding, course.

I do not know how Dot put up with me through all these years while I was flitting between London and New York acting here, acting there, making films, a lot of the time abroad. She had had eight years of Stratford to endure, but now with absolute love and loyalty she stood by me through the whole of these turbulent years.

ITHAKA

As you set out for Ithaka
hope your road is a long one,
full of adventure, full of discovery.
Laistrygonians, Cyclops,
angry Poseidon—don't be afraid of them:
you'll never find things like that on your way
as long as you keep your thoughts raised high,
as long as a rare sensation
touches your spirit and your body.
Laistrygonians, Cyclops,
wild Poseidon—you won't encounter them
unless you bring them along inside your soul,
unless your soul sets them up in front of you.

Hope your road is a long one.
May there be many summer mornings when,
with what pleasure, what joy,
you enter harbours you're seeing for the first time;
may you stop at Phoenician trading stations
to buy fine things,
mother of pearl and coral, amber and ebony,
sensual perfume of every kind—
as many sensual perfumes as you can;
and may you visit many Egyptian cities
to learn and go on learning from those who know.

Keep Ithaka always in your mind.
Arriving there is what you're destined for.
But don't hurry the journey at all.
Better if it lasts for years,
so you're old by the time you reach the island,
wealthy with all you've gained on the way,
not expecting Ithaka to make you rich.

Ithaka gave you the marvellous journey.
Without her you wouldn't have set out.
She has nothing left to give you now.
And if you find her poor, Ithaka won't have fooled you.
Wise as you will have become, so full of experience,
you'll have understood by then what these Ithakas mean.

C.P. CAVAFY

AFTERWORD

BOATS

WHEN I LEFT STRATFORD I found to my delight that a lot of work started to come in, not only plays, but movies; some good, some fair, but all reasonably well paid. I felt an increasing need for more outdoor activity and something I could involve my family in; so I became somewhat more adventurous in my idea of boating. At the Boat Show I fell in love with a 22-foot catamaran designed by Bill O'Brien, and I ordered one for us. It was a light, well-constructed boat, mainly glue and plywood, but put together very well, and there were enough bunks in the hulls and main cabin for the whole family to sleep on board. We were fortunate to find a mooring and anchorage in Hampshire's beautiful Christchurch harbour. The harbourmaster, Roy Stride, and his family became important helpers and friends; they were full of useful advice.

I knew nothing whatever about navigation, and hardly any more about sailing; I had only done a very small amount of dinghy sailing, but undaunted I set out with Dot on a whole series of short expeditions, first to the Isle of Wight, then further afield. I thought I would not venture out with the children until we had a little more experience, so we planned a longer expedition, and started off on a beautiful summer's day for Bridport.

We had a wonderful sail and arrived late in the afternoon. The mainsail had ripped and torn away from many of the plastic slides. We put into Bridport, found a sailmaker, and he soon repaired them.

Early in the morning we started for home. I had read in some sailing manual that there could be an ugly rip off Portland Bill, and if you had

343

conditions of wind over tide, you had better steer clear of the Bill by at least three miles. I knew nothing of tides, I had no tide tables – nothing. And what I counted as three miles was probably more like a mile and a half, if that. We were going along with a nice fresh westerly breeze behind us, only under the mainsail – the big Genoa would have been too much – towing our little plastic dinghy behind us, when the wind started to freshen and the tide turned against us.

Almost at once, the sea became sloppy, big waves foaming, coming to a head and jumping about on either side of us. The dinghy started to collect water. I pulled her painter in tight and hoped for the best: it was too late to try and get her aboard. I also completely misjudged the time when we should have hauled the mainsail down. As a result we went faster and faster. First we were planing down the sides of the waves – and that was exhilarating; but then she started to bury her two pointed bows in every wave that came in our direction. If this went any further, she was obviously going to turn over. The great question was how to get the mainsail down. It was blowing so hard now, and the boat was controlled with such difficulty that I knew Dot did not have the strength to take the wheel, nor was she acrobatic enough to climb up on the curved roof of the cat and pull down the mainsail without getting washed over. We were in a real predicament. I was standing at the wheel for something like twelve hours. Dot made a sandwich and handed it out to me from inside, but the wind blew it straight out of my hand. I looked into the cabin at one point and saw her crying and took it most terribly to heart. Oh dear Lord, I thought, I have ruined her life. She should never have married me. But later on she said she had felt so dreadfully inadequate that she had poured herself an enormous whisky and become maudlin about how very inadequate and unhappy she had been during all her childhood days. It was a great relief to me.

Somewhere off Dalston Head, the situation had really become too dangerous. Come what may, we had to bring this damn mainsail down. So I told Dot to get herself ready and summon all her strength to do it, and I put the boat's head up into the wind and tried to hold her there on the little outboard motor. She clambered to the top, attacked the mainsail with both hands, and in a moment she had it down. She was exhausted, but it was done and I could get lashings round it. We went on our way with a sense of having been saved from the ocean. We crept round, soaked to the skin, and dropped anchor close into shore in Studland Bay just north of Old Harry Rocks.

The morning was dead calm. We were only a few yards from the beach. This was the joy of the cat: you could creep in very close if there was a sandy bottom. And there, picking her way among the shells and debris on the beach, was a pretty little vixen sniffing the air, one paw raised. After the turmoil of the previous day, it was the prettiest sight imaginable. We had a great seafaring saga to tell the Strides when at last we got back into Christchurch harbour. They laughed a lot, but I made a resolution that I was never going to undertake a long trip again unless I had mastered coastal navigation. I had been an utter fool.

Two years later I had become quite efficient and experienced at navigation. I was dreaming of a bigger boat, but was uncertain what kind we would need. It was while I was in Greece on my way to join the filming of *The Guns of Navarone* in Rhodes, that the sort of sailing we might do, and the sort of boat we would need to do it, became very clear.

It was on a day of spring sunshine and snow showers that Dot and I drove from Athens to Delphi. There was not a tourist to be seen – incredibly, we had it all to ourselves. There it was, exactly as Leonard Greenwood had described it: the great temple, then a little higher up the hillside the theatre, and on the third tier the stadium. We could see the very stone starting blocks that the athletes had used.

At the entrance to the little museum was the Omphalos Stone – the Navel Stone of the world: a huge egg-shaped piece of rock with an indentation at the top and inscribed on it in Greek lettering 'Lysastros Lifted Me'. I recalled the Greek attitude to all wonderful, inanimate things – that they had a life in them of their own. The Omphalos Stone made me think of the story of Zeus, how when he wanted to determine the centre of the world he let go two eagles to fly east and west: where they met would be the very centre. They met over Delphi. I looked up and there – sure enough – were two great eagles soaring and wheeling above our heads. It seemed a day of little miracles.

Down below lay part of the Gulf of Corinth, the water glittering in the sunshine over the tops of the olive trees that sloped steeply downwards. I had an overpowering desire to build a boat that I could sail here, with my family on board, and follow in the wake of Odysseus as he returned home to Ithaca. Odysseus had always been for me the most heroic of all the Greeks, not for his wiliness or for his cunning, but for his determination and his endurance. Looking down on that small patch of blue, I knew that it might take years before I could return on such an adventure but I knew, too, that I would do my utmost to bring it about.

It was only a few months later, at the next Boat Show, that I found a prototype of the very boat that could turn the dream into a possible reality. It was a Scottish fishing boat that the Miller Brothers in Fife had redesigned as a motor-sailer family ketch. Wonderfully robust and comfortable, it had six berths, a large cockpit and ample storage space.

I asked them to build us one to our specifications, adding long cupboards for easier living on board, and two feet on the length, bringing it to forty foot overall. The colour would be blue and white, and the name would be the *Jenny Rose*.

I was due to do some shooting on *Lawrence of Arabia* in Almeria, on the coast of Spain, and I begged the yard at St Monance to try and finish our boat in time for me to sail her there via Gibraltar and live on her during my working weeks. The excitement of the launching was intense. The skipper and two crew arrived, and we set off down the east coast. There were problems, there were crises, but somehow we managed to iron them out. We were lucky.

After sailing one night through a particularly phosphorescent sea, the next morning brought us within sight of Gibraltar. I felt a great surge of emotion as we rounded Europe's point and the whole lion-headed Rock lay clear to port. I had a big order of groceries for the *Jenny Rose*, so I landed and walked up through the town until I came to Lipton's in Main Street.

It was here that something strange happened. I asked for the manager, and a very nice young man in a white coat appeared and took down the long list of all my needs. When I had finished I said to him, 'Well, you're obviously from South Wales – whereabouts do you come from?'

He smiled and said, 'Pontypridd, I was born in Pontypridd.'

'Goodness,' I said, 'I know this is a silly question, because you are much too young, but did you ever hear of a certain Dr Lewis who lived in Pontypridd?'

His face changed expression. Astonishment and wonder came into his eyes. 'Dr Kingsley Lewis, do you mean?'

'Yes,' I answered.

'Oh, Dr Kingsley Lewis brought me into this world. He delivered my mother too. Did you know him?'

'Yes, I did know him a little,' I said.

'Well, Mr Quayle, he was a wonderful man. Do you know that all through those terrible years of recession, when the coal mines were idle, and the men out of work, he would come around all the houses and look after the miners and their wives and their children absolutely free. Never took a penny, not a penny. Everyone loved him, they thought he was a saint.'

I picked up my groceries, and my eyes were full of tears. This young man had unwittingly spoken a blessing over two long dead and unhappy lovers.

When we arrived in Almeria – just Skip and I, the crew having gone home from Gibraltar – there was great satisfaction in living on board the

Jenny Rose. Sam Spiegel's great motor yacht was alongside in the harbour; his skipper and mine knew each other, but mine thought nothing of the Spiegel yacht and its large crew. At least we could sail, and our brown sails looked pleasant and workmanlike.

Dot came out to join me, and when I had finished in the film, Rosanna and Jenny arrived for the school holidays and we had our first memorable cruise. We sailed around Majorca, Minorca and Ibiza. We saw whales spouting, we saw two enormous turtles, and were never without our escort of dolphins and flying fish. It was magical weather and living on the boat and swimming off it seemed a dreamlike existence. As we made for home, and our new mooring on the Beaulieu River, we were sad that the first long cruise had come to an end.

In fact, it was only the beginning of a whole new way of life. Having a boat of this kind meant that the moment there was any free time we could take off on some adventure. I was ready as the navigator, Rosanna as a super bosun, Jenny and Dot as cook and crew, Christopher being then too young to join us. Every holiday was a challenge.

We had ten splendid years of crossing to France, of exploring the Normandy Coast, the Brittany rivers, and all of the Channel Isles.

Then I thought it was the moment to find a base nearer to Greece: I found friends who helped bring the *Jenny Rose* through the French canals and then on to Malta. It was still impossible to carve out sufficient time for the further journey to the Greek Islands, so I bought an old house, small but beautiful with its pool and walled garden, and we made the most of the waiting time enjoying Malta, its people, and the sailing.

I do have one outstanding memory from that period. In 1972 there was a spectacular eruption on Stromboli, the volcanic island off Sicily. I felt it warranted a closer inspection, so I set sail for the Lipari Islands with Christopher and Rosanna's husband, Richard. I do not think any of us will ever forget the vast plume of smoke, the rumblings, the pumice floating all around us, and the overwhelming smell of sulphur.

Eventually, there were three whole months free of commitments, and it was actually possible to plan a long cruise to the Ionian Islands.

It was thirteen years since I had looked down from Delphi and vowed to return and sail my own boat into the Gulf of Corinth below.

In the July of 1974 we set sail from Malta, and four weeks later we were actually standing on the deck of the *Jenny Rose* in that exact patch of blue, looking upwards to Delphi, as we opened a very special bottle of champagne.

In August we sailed into the harbour of Ithaca.

E

MY DARLING OLD E had had a lonely life. Since I was seven years old the only time I had been with her was during my school holidays. When school had finished, I left home and we were more or less estranged for years. Then there had been the absence of the war for six years; then my marriage to Dot. Always she had been alone. I had not lived up to her expectations either. I was not a distinguished member of the Bar. I was not tipped in any way to be the Lord Chief Justice. In fact, I was simply not cut out to be a public figure whatsoever. And the nearest thing I got to a DSO was an honourable mention in Despatches. But she did have one wish – and no doubt the greatest of them all – wholly fulfilled. I was married to one of the most dear and beautiful women in the whole of England. And she did have two marvellous little grandchildren (she was not to know it that a third, a boy, Christopher, would before long join the ranks). During the summer of 1950 she came and stayed at a small residential hotel just up the road from where we lived in Stratford. She was ill; she had cancer of the lungs – and knew it. She was incredibly brave. Even though she was my mother and I knew her well, I was astonished at how she could be startled by small things but rose above big troubles like a great ship. She doted on her first granddaughter, Rosanna, and had very little interest in the newborn baby, Jenny. It was the premonition of death. There was only time to give so much love to one small child, and in Rosanna she saw herself.

'I told you,' she said one day, 'that little girl is me. Not like me, she is me.'

In many ways it's uncanny how true her words are. Rosanna does not look in the least like E, but her spirit is the same. Her ability to cope with life, to breast difficulties, to make every day a challenging joy and create a whole circle of warmth round her – especially for children.

During the late autumn, E went into hospital and was operated on. They removed one lung, but it was not a success. Eventually, early in the New Year just as we started to rehearse the Histories, I moved her to a private nursing home. I helped her out of the car and she stood unsteadily on the pavement for a few minutes looking up at the building.

'What are you looking at, darling?' I asked her.

'Nothing particular,' was her reply. 'Just taking in the outside. I don't suppose I shall ever see it again.'

It was a simple statement of fact, in no way maudlin or self-pitying. She never did see the outside, not ever again. She kept up her spirits to the very last. She herself could not have a drink, but she kept a bottle of scotch in her cupboard and guests were welcome to help themselves. And she was good company right up to her death.

One of the last things she ever said to me – and she said this in great seriousness – was, 'Do you realize, my darling son, what a wife you have married?'

'I do,' I answered.

'Then mind you are very good to her, always. If you ever hurt her in any way, I swear I will come back and haunt you.' Those were the last words she ever said to me. I had to leave her and drive back to rehearsal in Stratford. Dot came to see her every day and was with her to the end.

CHRONOLOGY

ANTHONY QUAYLE'S CONTRIBUTIONS TO
THEATRE, FILM AND TELEVISION:

THE EARLY YEARS TO THE OUTBREAK OF WAR

1913   Born 7 September, Southport, Lancashire

1931   Henry in Arnold Ridley's *The Ghost Train*, directed by Jack De Leon at
the Q Theatre
Orsino in *Twelfth Night* with Gerald Cooper as Malvolio, directed by
Cooper at the Croydon Repertory Theatre
Richard Coeur-de-Lion/Will Scarlett in *Robin Hood* by Henry Hamilton
and William Devereux, with Roger Livesey, directed by Theodore
Komisarjevsky at the Q Theatre

1932   Toured the Music Halls as a feed to Naylor Grimson (*The Meanest Man
On Earth*)
Hector in *Troilus and Cressida*, directed by Frank Birch at the Festival
Theatre, Cambridge
Aumerle in Gordon Daviot's *Richard of Bordeaux* with John Gielgud and
Peggy Ashcroft, directed by Gielgud at the New Theatre
King of Navarre in *Love's Labour's Lost* with Abraham Sofaer and Robert
Eddison, directed by Tyrone Guthrie at the Westminster Theatre
Season with the Old Vic Company:
Cetawayo in Shaw's *The Admirable Bashville*
Mamillius/Old Shepherd in *The Winter's Tale*
Morocco in *The Merchant of Venice*
Paris in *Romeo and Juliet*
Belzanor in Shaw's *Caesar and Cleopatra*
All directed by Harcourt Williams (except for *The Merchant*,
directed by John Gielgud) with a company including Peggy
Ashcroft, Malcolm Keen, Roger Livesey, Marius Goring, Alastair
Sim, George Fox and George Devine.

1933   Brian Kinsella in Grenville Darling's *The Haunted Legacy* on tour with the Abbey Theatre

Shakespeare Season in Anew McMaster's Company at the Chiswick Empire:

    Cassio in *Othello*

    Hastings in *Richard III*

    Anew McMaster directed the plays and acted in the title roles

1934   Bennie Edelman in *Magnolia Street* by Louis Golding and A.R. Rawlinson, with George Devine, directed by Theodore Komisarjevsky at the Adelphi Theatre

Matt Burke in Eugene O'Neill's *Anna Christie*, directed by Judith Furse at the Imperial Institute and then at the Embassy Theatre

Guildenstern in *Hamlet* with John Gielgud and Jessica Tandy, designed by the Motleys, directed by Gielgud at the New Theatre

1935   Captain Courtine in Thomas Otway's *The Soldier's Fortune* with Balliol Holloway and Athene Seyler, directed by Holloway at the Ambassadors Theatre

1936   St Denis in *St Helena* by R.C. Sherriff and Jeanne de Casalis, with Raymond Huntley and Alec Clunes, directed by Henry Cass at the Old Vic

Mr Wickham in Jane Austen's *Pride and Prejudice* (adapted by Helen Jerome) with Celia Johnson and Dorothy Hyson, designed by Rex Whistler and directed by Gilbert Miller at the St James's Theatre

Mr Harcourt in William Wycherley's *The Country Wife* with Roger Livesey and Ruth Gordon, directed by Gilbert Miller at the Henry Miller Theater in New York

1937   Took over the part of Chorus from Michael Redgrave in *Henry V* with Laurence Olivier, directed by Tyrone Guthrie at the Old Vic

Lacrtes in *Hamlet* with Laurence Olivier and Vivien Leigh, directed by Tyrone Guthrie at Elsinore

Horatio in *Hamlet* with Christopher Oldham, directed by Michael Macowan at the Westminster Theatre

The Lord Marshal/Welsh Captain in *Richard II* with John Gielgud and Michael Redgrave, directed by Gielgud at the Queen's Theatre

Beppo in Eugene Heltai's *The Silent Knight* (adapted by Humbert Wolfe) with Ralph Richardson and Diana Wynyard, directed by Gilbert Miller at the St James's Theatre

Season with the Old Vic Company:

    Demetrius in *A Midsummer Night's Dream* with Vivien Leigh and

Ralph Richardson, the Sadler's Wells Ballet and Opera Companies, choreographed by Ninette de Valois, designed by Oliver Messel and directed by Tyrone Guthrie

1938   Season with the Old Vic Company (continued):

Cassio in *Othello* with Ralph Richardson as Othello and Laurence Olivier as Iago, directed by Tyrone Guthrie.

Earl of Essex in Andre Josset's *Elizabeth, La Femme Sans Homme* with Lilian Braithwaite, at The Gate Theatre and the Theatre Royal, Haymarket

Season with the Old Vic Company:

Ferdinand in Pinero's *Trelawney of the Wells*, directed by Tyrone Guthrie

Laertes in *Hamlet*, directed by Tyrone Guthrie.

John Tanner in Shaw's *Man and Superman*, directed by Lewis Casson

Captain Absolute in Sheridan's *The Rivals*, directed by Esmé Church

The Company also included Alec Guinness, Andrew Cruickshank and Hermione Hannen

1939   Old Vic Tour in Europe and Egypt:

Took over the title role from Laurence Olivier in *Henry V* with Alec Guinness as Chorus, directed by Tyrone Guthrie

Continued as Laertes in *Hamlet*

LONDON AFTER THE WAR

1945   Novel, *Eight Hours from England*, published by Heinemann

Jack Absolute in Sheridan's *The Rivals* with Edith Evans and Michael Gough, directed by Tyrone Guthrie at the Criterion Theatre

1946   Directed Dostoievsky's *Crime and Punishment* (adapted by Rodney Ackland) with John Gielgud and Edith Evans at the New Theatre

Enobarbus in *Antony and Cleopatra* with Edith Evans and Godfrey Tearle, directed by Glen Byam Shaw at the Piccadilly Theatre

1947   Novel, *On Such a Night*, published by Heinemann

Took over from Alec Clunes as Iago in *Othello* with Jack Hawkins and Fay Compton, directed by Peter Powell at the Piccadilly Theatre and the Lyric Theatre, Hammersmith

1948   Directed Sir John Vanbrugh's *The Relapse* with Cyril Ritchard and Madge Elliott at the Phoenix Theatre

Films: Marcellus in *Hamlet* with Laurence Olivier, directed by Olivier

Durer in *Saraband for Dead Lovers* with Stewart Granger and Joan Greenwood, directed by Basil Dearden. (*Saraband* in USA)

THE STRATFORD YEARS

1948 Joined the Shakespeare Memorial Theatre, Stratford-upon-Avon as a co-director with Michael Benthall.

Faulconbridge in *King John* with Robert Helpmann and Ena Burrill, directed by Michael Benthall

Claudius in *Hamlet* with Paul Scofield and Robert Helpmann alternating in the title role, directed by Michael Benthall

Iago in *Othello* with Godfrey Tearle and Diana Wynyard, directed by Tearle

Petruchio in *The Taming of the Shrew* with Diana Wynyard and Esmond Knight, directed by Michael Benthall

Directed *The Winter's Tale* with Esmond Knight and Diana Wynyard, designed by Motley

Directed *Troilus and Cressida* with Paul Scofield and Heather Stannard, designed by Motley

Became Director of the Shakespeare Memorial Theatre

1949 Directed *Macbeth* with Godfrey Tearle and Diana Wynyard

Benedick in *Much Ado About Nothing* with Diana Wynyard and Leon Quartermaine, directed by John Gielgud

The title role in *Henry VIII* with Harry Andrews and Diana Wynyard, designed by Tanya Moiseiwitsch and directed by Tyrone Guthrie

Australian Tour:
 Macbeth and *Much Ado About Nothing*

Directed Mary Chase's *Harvey* with Sid Field and Athene Seyler at the Prince of Wales Theatre

1950 Co-directed (with Michael Langham) and played Mark Antony in *Julius Caesar* with John Gielgud and Harry Andrews

Co-directed (with John Gielgud) *King Lear* with Gielgud and Peggy Ashcroft

Directed Terence Rattigan's *Who Is Sylvia?* with Athene Seyler at the Criterion Theatre

1951 Glen Byam Shaw joined the Stratford Memorial Theatre as Co-director

Directed *Richard II* with Michael Redgrave and Harry Andrews, designed by Tanya Moiseiwitsch

Co-directed (with John Kidd) and played Falstaff in *Henry IV, Part I* with Michael Redgrave and Richard Burton, designed by Tanya Moiseiwitsch

Falstaff, in *Henry IV, Part 2* with Richard Burton and Harry Andrews, designed by Tanya Moiseiwitsch and directed by Michael Redgrave

Directed *Henry V* with Richard Burton and Richard Wordsworth, designed by Tanya Moiseiwitsch

1952   Caius Martius (Coriolanus) in *Coriolanus* with Michael Hordern and Laurence Harvey, designed by Motley and directed by Glen Byam Shaw

Mosca in *Volpone* with Ralph Richardson and Raymond Westwell, directed by George Devine

1953   Australia and New Zealand Tour:

Jaques in *As You Like It* with Keith Michell and Barbara Jefford, designed by Motley and directed by Glen Byam Shaw

Directed and played Falstaff in *Henry IV, Part 1* with Keith Michell and Terence Longdon

Directed and played the title role in *Othello* with Leo McKern and Barbara Jefford, designed by Tanya Moiseiwitsch

1954   Directed (assisted by Patrick Donnell) and played the title role in *Othello* with Raymond Westwell and Barbara Jefford, designed by Tanya Moiseiwitsch

Bottom in *A Midsummer Night's Dream* with Keith Michell and Muriel Pavlow, designed by Motley and directed by George Devine

Pandarus in *Troilus and Cressida* with Laurence Harvey and Muriel Pavlow, directed by Glen Byam Shaw

1955   Falstaff in *The Merry Wives of Windsor* with Keith Michell and Joyce Redman, designed by Motley and directed by Glen Byam Shaw

Aaron in *Titus Andronicus* with Laurence Olivier and Vivien Leigh, directed by Peter Brook

1956   Directed *Measure for Measure* with Anthony Nicholls and Emlyn Williams

Resigned from the Directorship of the Stratford Memorial Theatre.

Tamburlaine in Marlowe's *Tamburlaine the Great*, directed by Tyrone Guthrie at the Winter Garden in New York.

AFTER STRATFORD: THEATRE, FILMS AND TELEVISION
AT HOME AND ABROAD

1956   Eddie Carbone in Arthur Miller's *A View from the Bridge* with Richard Harris and Ian Bannen, directed by Peter Brook at the Comedy Theatre

Films: Orlovsky in *Oh Rosalinda!* with Anton Walbrook and Michael Redgrave, directed and written by Michael Powell and Emeric Pressburger

    Commodore Harwood in *Battle of the River Plate* with John Gregson and Peter Finch, directed and written by Michael Powell and Emeric Pressburger (*Pursuit of the Graf Spee* in USA)

1957   Aaron in *Titus Andronicus* in European Tour

Films: Dr Seagrave in *No Time for Tears* with Anna Neagle and Sylvia Syms, directed by Cyril Frankel

Frank Smith in *The Man Who Wouln't Talk* with Anna Neagle and Zsa Zsa Gabor, directed by Herbert Wilcox

Jim Preston in *Woman in a Dressing Gown* with Yvonne Mitchell and Sylvia Syms, directed by J. Lee-Thompson

Frank O'Connor in *The Wrong Man* with Henry Fonda, directed by Alfred Hitchcock

1958   Directed and played Moses in Christopher Fry's *The Firstborn* with Katharine Cornell at the Coronet Theater in New York and the Habimah in Tel Aviv

James Tyrone in Eugene O'Neill's *Long Day's Journey into Night* with Gwen Ffrangcon-Davies and Alan Bates, directed by Jose Quintero at the Edinburgh Festival and the Globe Theatre

Films: Captain van der Poel in *Ice Cold in Alex* with John Mills and Harry Andrews, directed by J. Lee-Thompson (*Desert Attack* in USA)

1959   Marcel Blanchard in Noel Coward's *Look after Lulu!* (after Feydeau) with Vivien Leigh and Robert Stephens, directed by Tony Richardson at the New Theatre

Films: The Reverend Howard Phillips in *Serious Charge* with Cliff Richard, directed by Terence Young. (*Immoral Charge* in USA)

Slade in *Tarzan's Greatest Adventure* with Gordon Scott and Sean Connery, directed by John Guillermin

1960   Cesareo Grimaldi in Billetdoux's *Chin-Chin* (adapted by Willis Hall) with Celia Johnson, directed by Howard Sackler at Wyndham's Theatre

Film: Jim in *The Challenge* with Jayne Mansfield, written and directed by John Gilling. (*It Takes a Thief* in USA)

1961   *Film*: Major Franklin in *The Guns of Navarone* with Gregory Peck and David Niven, directed by J. Lee-Thompson

Television: Betumain in *The Rose Affair* (ABC)

The General in *A Reason for Staying* (BBC)

1962   *Films*: Colonel Brighton in *Lawrence of Arabia* with Peter O'Toole, directed by David Lean

Vizard in *HMS Defiant* with Alec Guinness and Dirk Bogarde, directed by Lewis Gilbert (*Damn the Defiant* in USA)

1963   Co-directed (with John Mills) and played Nachtigall in Gert Hofmann's *Power of Persuasion* (translated by Donald Watson) with John Mills and Joyce Redman at the Garrick

Film: Verulus in *The Fall of the Roman Empire* with Alec Guinness and Sophia Loren, directed by Anthony Mann

1964   Charles Dilke in *The Right Honourable Gentleman* (from *Sir Charles Dilke: a Victorian Tragedy* by Roy Jenkins), with Anna Massey and Coral Browne, directed by Glen Byam Shaw at Her Majesty's Theatre.
Films: Richard Baker in *East of Sudan* with Sylvia Syms and Jenny Agutter, directed by Nathan Juran.
Captain in *Danger Grows Wild* with Marcello Mastroianni and Yul Brynner, directed by Terence Young (*The Poppy is Also a Flower* in USA)

1965   *Films*: Duncombe in *Incompreso*, directed by Luigi Comencini (English title: *Misunderstood*)
Dr Murray in *A Study in Terror* with John Neville and Donald Houston, directed by James Hill
Bamford in *Operation Crossbow* with George Peppard and Sophia Loren, directed by Michael Anderson
Television: A Samurai Warrior in *Miss Hanago* with Yoko Tani (ATV)

1966   Leduc in Arthur Miller's *Incident at Vichy* with Alec Guinness, directed by Peter Wood at the Phoenix Theatre
Directed *Lady Windermere's Fan* with Coral Browne and Juliet Mills, at the Phoenix Theatre

1967   The title role in Brecht's *Galileo*, directed by Jules Irving at the Lincoln Center in New York
General Fitzbuttress in Peter Ustinov's *Halfway up the Tree* with Eileen Herlie, directed by Ustinov at the Brooks Atkinson Theater in New York
Television: Daniel Bloch in *Waste Places* (ATV)

1968   *Films*: Older Englishman in *Mackenna's Gold* with Gregory Peck and Omar Sharif, directed by J. Lee-Thompson
Brigadier Bewley in *Before Winter Comes* with David Niven and Topol, directed by J. Lee-Thompson

1968–69   *Television*: Adam Strange in *The Strange Report*, a series for ITC

1969   *Film*: Cardinal Wolsey in *Anne of the Thousand Days* with Richard Burton and Geneviève Bujold, directed by Charles Jarrott
Television: Mr Edwards in *Red Peppers* (BBC)

1970   Andrew Wyke in Anthony Shaffer's *Sleuth* with Keith Baxter, directed by Clifford Williams at St Martin's Theatre
Directed Dostoievsky's *The Idiot* (adapted by Simon Gray)

with Derek Jacobi, designed by Joseph Svoboda, for the
National Theatre at the Old Vic
Acted *Sleuth* at the Music Box, New York

1971–72   Toured the USA with *Sleuth*

1972   *Film*: The King in *Everything You Always Wanted to Know about Sex* with
Woody Allen, directed by Woody Allen

1973   *Films*: Admiral Minto in Terence Rattigan's *Bequest to the Nation* with
Peter Finch and Glenda Jackson, directed by James Cellan Jones (*The
Nelson Affair* in USA)
Jack Loder, Head of MI6, in *The Tamarind Seed* with Julie Andrews and
Omar Sharif, directed by Blake Edwards
Television: Aaron in *Moses, The Lawgiver* with Burt Lancaster, a series for
ATV
Read Robert O'Brien's *Mrs Frisby and the Rats of Nimh* on Jackanory (BBC)

1974   *Television*: Cosmo Bastrop in *Jarrett* with Glen Ford (TV movie, USA)

1975   Directed James Stewart in Mary Chase's *Harvey* at the Prince of Wales
Theatre

1976   Rodion Nikolayevich in Aleksei Arbuzov's *Old World* (translated by
Ariadne Nikolaeff) with Peggy Ashcroft, directed by Terry Hands
at the Aldwych Theatre
Films: Admiral Canaris in Jack Higgins' *The Eagle has Landed* with
Michael Caine and Donald Sutherland, directed by Lewis R. Foster
Television: General Amir in *21 Hours at Munich*

1977   *Film*: Professor Griffith in *Holocaust 2000* with Kirk Douglas and Simon
Ward, directed by Alberto de Martino

Television: Tom Bannister in *QB VII* (USA)

1977–78   Rodion Nikolayevich in USA Tour of *Old World* (renamed
Do You Turn Somersaults?) with Mary Martin, ending
up at the 46th Street Theater in New York

1978   Took over from Alec Guinness as Hilary in Alan Bennett's *The Old Country*
with Rachel Kempson, directed by Clifford Williams at the Queen's
Theatre
Tour with Prospect Theatre Company:
Directed and played Sir Anthony Absolute in Sheridan's *The Rivals*
The title role in *King Lear*, directed by Toby Robertson
Films: Jaggers in *Great Expectations* with Michael York and Sarah Miles,
directed by Robert Fryer
Sir Charles Warren in *Murder by Decree* with Christopher
Plummer and James Mason, directed by Bob Clark

Television: The Old Man in *Ice Age* with Michael Williams (BBC)

1979   *Television*: Falstaff in *Henry IV, Parts 1 and 2* (BBC)
        The Detective in *Dial M for Murder* with Angie Dickinson in
        New York

1980   Malvern Festival:
        The Dean of Paddington in Oscar Wilde's *Lord Arthur Savile's Crime*
            (adapted by Constance Cox)
        Captain Shotover in Shaw's *Heartbreak House*
        The Company included Honor Blackman, Margaret Rawlings and
            Patrick Cargill, and the plays were directed by Clifford Williams.
        Television: Kyros Kassoulas in *The Last Bottle in the
        World*, Tales of the Unexpected (Anglia)
        Rubrius Gallus in *Masada* with Peter O'Toole (mini
        series, USA).

1981   On tour and at the Malvern Festival with the Triumph Theatre Company:
        Hornblower in John Galsworthy's *The Skin Game* with Googie Withers
            and John McCallum, directed by Clifford Williams
        General Burgoyne in Shaw's *The Devil's Disciple* with Mel Martin and
            Denis Lill, directed by Richard Digby Day
        Directed and played the Reverend Augustin Jedd in Pinero's *Dandy
            Dick* with Googie Withers and John McCallum
        Television: Lord FitzMorris in *The Manions of America*
        (mini series, USA)

1982   Directed and played Dr Perryman in Ronald Millar's *A Coat of Varnish*
            (adapted from the novel by C.P. Snow) with Peter Barkworth at the
            Theatre Royal, Haymarket
        Hobson in Harold Brighouse's *Hobson's Choice* with Penelope Keith
            and Trevor Peacock, directed by Ronald Eyre at the Theatre Royal,
            Haymarket
        Directed Pirandello's *Rules of the Game* with Leonard Rossiter and Mel
            Martin, on tour and at the Theatre Royal, Haymarket

1983   Appeared as Elgar in the Elgar Commemorative Concert in Westminster
            Abbey

THE COMPASS YEARS

1984   Formed Compass Theatre Limited:
        The first Compass production:
            Directed and played Lord Ogleby in *The Clandestine Marriage* by
            David Garrick and George Colman, with Roy Kinnear and Joyce

Redman, designed by Tanya Moiseiwitsch, first on tour then at the Albery Theatre

Television: John Douglas in *The Testament of John* with Jane Lapotaire (BBC)

Doctor Geneste in *Lace* (mini series, USA)

1985   For Compass:

The Duke of Drayton in William Douglas-Home's *After the Ball is Over* with Patrick Cargill and Maxine Audley, directed by Maria Aitken, first on tour and then at the Old Vic

Co-directed (with Nigel Jamieson) and played Prospero in *The Tempest* with Tony Britton and Clive Francis, first on tour in England and Scotland, and then at the Hong Kong Arts Festival

Cauchon in Shaw's *St Joan* with Jane Lapotaire and Tony Britton, directed by Clifford Williams, on tour with *The Tempest*

Television: Abdullah in *The Key to Rebecca* (mini series, USA)

The Bishop in *The Miracle* with Richard Chamberlain and Keith Michell (Channel 4)

1986   For Compass:

The Reverend Augustin Jedd in Pinero's *Dandy Dick* with Margaret Courtenay, directed by David Gilmore, on tour in England, Scotland, Wales and the Isle of Man

Television: Oedipus in *Oedipus at Colonus* in a production of Sophocles' *The Theban Plays* (BBC)

1987   For Compass:

The title role in *King Lear* with Isla Blair and Kate O'Mara, directed by Don Taylor, on tour in England, Scotland and Northern Ireland

1988   For Compass:

The Mayor in Nikolai Gogol's *The Government Inspector* with Brian Murphy and Paul Rhys, directed by Don Taylor, on tour in England, Scotland and Northern Ireland

Films: Distinguished Gentleman in *The Legend of the Holy Drinker* with Rutger Hauer, directed by Ermanno Olmi

General Villiers in *The Bourne Identity* with Richard Chamberlain and Denholm Elliott, directed by Roger Young

Sir James McDowell in *Buster* with Phil Collins and Julie Walters, directed by David Green

1989   *Television*: The Pope in Jack Higgins' *Confessional* (Granada)

COMPASS LIVES ON

Tim Pigott-Smith joined Compass as an associate director in the spring of 1989, his first undertaking being to direct Peter Shaffer's *The Royal Hunt of the Sun*. After Anthony Quayle's death in the autumn of that year he succeeded him as Artistic Director, and is equally committed to Compass's ideals of bringing major plays to parts of the country and sections of the community that they might not otherwise reach. In the spring of 1990 the Company moved its offices to Dean Clough in Halifax. Plans for the future include a production of Shaw's *Caesar and Cleopatra* with Robert Hardy, scheduled for early in 1991.

RICHARD ASTLEY

INDEX